MW01048409

Planner

Know When and Where to Catch More Fish

Snook rank among the most popular inshore fish statewide.

FS Books:
Sportsman's Best: Inshore Fishing
Sportsman's Best: Offshore Fishing
Sportsman's Best: Snapper & Grouper
Sportsman's Best: Sailfish
Sportsman's Best: Trout
Sportsman's Best: Redfish
Sportsman's Best: Dolphin
Sportsman's Best: Snook

Sport Fish of Florida
Sport Fish of the Gulf of Mexico
Sport Fish of the Atlantic
Sport Fish of Fresh Water
Sport Fish of the Pacific

Baits, Rigs & Tackle
Annual Fishing Planner
The Angler's Cookbook
Florida Sportsman Magazine

Florida Sportsman Fishing Charts
Lawsticks
Law Boatstickers

FLORIDA SPORTSMAN

By the editors of
Florida Sportsman magazine

Month-by-month fishing reports by
Mike Conner and FS Staff

Special fishing tips and analysis by
Senior Editor Vic Dunaway

Other copy and editing by Sam Hudson,
Jeff Weakley, David Conway, Will Claunch

Graphic design by Jim Henderson

Find us on Facebook twitter

Welcome to Your
2011 Fishing Planner

You're holding the single most important source for catching fish during 2011 in Florida's richly abundant tidal waters.

Keep your *Fishing Planner* handy throughout the year. You'll find the easiest-ever way to pinpoint the best tides in your favorite spots. Whether it's Chokoloskee in the fall or Ponce Inlet in the spring, the *Fishing Planner* gives you the complete picture for a year of great angling.

In addition to exact tide heights for every rise and fall, special fish symbols tell you the maximum current flows. These often are the best fish feeding times.

Remember, the most important key to catching fish is not the choice of lure color or style, or the hook pattern or the rod and reel. The ultimate key is to locate fish and locate them at a time they're willing to take your offering.

Every month's tide table is accompanied by exclusive summaries of what species will be hot, with a fish-of-the-month spotlight feature. On top of that, you'll find big-picture rundowns for each tide station region, and complete articles about how the tides, barometer and other factors affect your angling.

Finally, you'll find a handy summary of fishing regulations, a special weight table to estimate how much your fish weighs, a list of record weights for popular species, a guide to the preferred water temperatures for various fish, and other content that will help you year-round.

All of us at *Florida Sportsman* magazine extend to you our best wishes for a great year on the water. And be sure to do your part to save and protect the marine resources for all the tomorrows that lie ahead.

—*Karl Wickstrom*, Editor-in-Chief
Florida Sportsman magazine

Contents

Tide Stations

PATHFINDER

TIDE-FINDER GUIDE MAPS

MAYPORT
Station
Page 8

Fernandina
Mayport
Jacksonville
St. Augustine
Daytona Beach

MIAMI
Station
Page 34

Cape Canaveral   Palm Beach
Sebastian   Hillsboro
Vero Beach   Ft. Lauderdale
Ft. Pierce   Miami
Stuart   Homestead
Jupiter   Key Largo

KEY WEST
Station
Page 60

Chatham River
Florida Bay
Marathon
Key West

ST. PETE
Station
Page 86

Apalachicola   Sarasota
St. George   Punta Gorda
Tampa   Ft. Myers
St. Petersburg

ST. MARKS
Station
Page 112

St. Marks   Tarpon Springs
Steinhatchee   Clearwater
Suwannee   Naples
Cedar Key   Upper 10,000
Homosassa   Islands

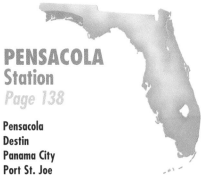

PENSACOLA
Station
Page 138

Pensacola
Destin
Panama City
Port St. Joe

How to Use Your Fishing Planner Tide Tables

Here's the easiest possible way for you to get a fix on today's tides, or the tides coming up next weekend, or during that vacation you're scheduling.

The *Fishing Planner's* new tide-table format eliminates the clutter and gets right to the important elements, giving you the times for highs and lows. Times are already adjusted for daylight-saving changes. Right above each time you'll find the expected height of the tide in feet in relation to mean low tide.

The fish symbols indicate the periods of maximum tidal flow, generally around the full and new moon days. These fast-moving, large volumes of water tend to set off feeding sprees because of the numerous forage fish moving through the buffet line.

The four moon phases show at the top of the date squares, the full moon being a white circle and the new moon all black. The first quarter is white on the right half, while the last quarter is black on the right.

A helpful way to know what's coming next is to remember that whatever

er shows on the right will increase each day. It's a right to left movement. Thus, when you see a first-quarter phase you know that brighter nights and the full moon are coming next. Conversely, black on the right means the new moon is on the way.

To the left of the tables is a list of all the corrections provided by the federal government for various locations other than the basic tide station. Unfortunately, two of the tide stations have corrections for small coastal areas not normally associated with the main zone. One is St. Marks, which includes corrections for Naples and the Upper 10,000 Islands. The other is St.

 First Quarter   **Full Moon**   **Last Quarter**   **New Moon**

Petersburg, which includes corrections for Apalachicola. But you'll get accustomed to these minor nuances as you use the tide data on the water.

At the bottom of each tide-table month, you'll see three or four dates with the sunrise and sunset times given. Mom may want you home by dark. And the law will frown if your lights aren't up to snuff.

Also accompanying each of the 72 tide-table pages are valuable summaries of what's biting that month and how to catch them.

...area

...t opens at the begin-
...ulations for 2011 season. Take
...to the winter's dent in the stocks.
...d on flats and inshore structure.
...eat **trout** bite over grassflats and
...**redfish** over grassflats and oys-
...calm surface, and tails early and
...n Northwest beaches and in bays.

...p on wrecks and reefs in southern
...**Spanish** shadow copious bait pods
...rs and lipped lures are tops for king-
...l spoons and jigs retrieved at warp
...n **tuna** and **wahoo** prowl offshore
...ia start heading south along Gulf
...rival.

...light: SNOOK

...a lock this month.
...are deadly around
...day and night, though
...ompare favorably. Still
...sand, but most are on
...h flies, plugs and jigs
...oridges.

Overall, the Fishing Planner for 2011 is an info package you'll want to use again and again.

Here's wishing you tight lines and strong tides.

MAYPORT STATION

Fernandina • Mayport
Jacksonville • St. Augustine
Daytona Beach

River to Reef

Update 2011: Short, but sweet. That sums up the shortened season on **red snapper** in Northeast waters. Anglers did report plenty of "genuines" last year over prime live bottom, subtle ledges and favorite wrecks.

In the bottom mix was **vermilion snapper, gag grouper, sea bass** and **cobia**. Of concern was the number of short gags for the most part. Big cobia were in good supply and bottom anglers routinely keep rigs ready to toss live baitfish for fish that show up.

Offshore trollers paid close attention to water temps, and the action was best at temperature breaks, rips, diverging currents, and as always, weedlines and flotsam. **Dolphin** were in good numbers where water temperature was in the high 70s, and **wahoo** and **tunas** hit the decks for

anglers who stuck to waters in the lower 70s. Trips to the far edge of the mighty Gulf Stream put anglers on **yellowfin tuna**, and **king mackerel** were plentiful for skippers who slow-trolled blue runners and ribbonfish along inlet tidelines.

Snook took a serious hit from the prolonged freeze in Northeast waters, and for now, catches will be rare unless mild winters again extend the linesider's range north. Anglers plying the St. Johns River did well on **redfish, crappie,** snook, **bass** slam. Redfish sight fishers reported good tailing activity in spartina marshes on big fall tides. **Seatrout** anglers consistently found fish just inside inlets farther up the St. Johns in winter months. Surf anglers

Flounder will take flies and other artificials.

depended on the pogy pods to point the way to bull reds, **tarpon**, **mackerel**, **blacktip sharks** *and* **jack crevalle**.

Seasonal variety, unspoiled marsh country, rich offshore waters and the storied St. Johns River make Northeast Florida an especially attractive region for angling.

The state's greatest tidal fluctuations occur here, up to six feet at times. During a full moon in October, a surf fisherman standing at the water's edge at low tide could find himself eye-to-eye with a bluefish six hours later.

The weather changes as dramatically as the tide. Summer is mild, barring tropical systems, but fall and winter bring cold fronts and nor'easters. Such windy weather modifies the effects of tides. When easterly winds and rising tides push water onto inshore marshlands, anglers find time to poke around new territory for redfish and sheepshead.

Migratory gamefish such as Spanish mackerel, cobia and kingfish begin to show along the beach in the spring, when the wind lets up and the water temperature climbs into the upper 60s. At about the same time, dolphin schools appear in warmer blue water when it hits the mid 70s. Jacksonville anglers wisely keep in touch with their Daytona Beach counterparts, who get the first wave of fish. As winter approaches, the fish return whence they came.

Lots of activity centers around tidelines outside inlets, where dark, nutrient-rich water flowing out of bays and rivers meets the clear Atlantic. Forage fish are abundant in this junction, and predators such as king mackerel and tarpon feed well here. A falling tide at the mouth of the St. Johns River, for example, produces a well-defined tideline.

Farther upriver, or along the Intracoastal, the same outgoing tide may find light-tackle anglers catching trout, redfish and flounder at the mouth of one of the many small, brackish creeks that weave their way through this region. The fishy inhabitants of these backwaters are year-round residents, and all feed best during periods of moving

Wahoo are targeted by fast-trollers and live baiters.

tides. Good places to fish are often near structures such as oyster bars, bridges, docks and dropoffs.

For the Atlantic Coast from near the Georgia border at Fernandina Beach southward to Daytona, the tides are semidiurnal, with two highs and two lows each day. The two highs are about the same height, and so are the lows, for any given day. The tides are measured just south of the mouth of the St. Johns River.

Average Tidal Range at Mayport: 4.5 feet

Average Range of Spring Tides: 5.3 feet

Jacksonville to Daytona Beach
Including the St. Johns River

Snap Happy

TIDE CORRECTIONS
For Mayport

	High	Low
Nassau Sound, Ft. George River		
St. Marys, St. Marys River	+1:19	+1:13
Crandall, St. Marys River	+2:08	+2:02
Fernandina Beach, outer coast	-0:30	-0:03
Fernandina Beach, Amelia River	+0:20	+0:14
Chester, Bells River	+0:37	+0:39
SCL RR bridge, Kingsley Creek	+0:47	+0:41
Nassau Sound	-0:15	+0:04
Amelia City, S. Amelia River	+0:42	+1:01
Nassauville, Nassau River	+0:52	+1:35
Mink Creek entrance, Nassau R.	+1:46	+2:30
Halfmoon Island, highway bridge	+2:48	+3:19
Sawpit Creek entrance	-0:14	+0:28
Ft. George Island, Ft.George R.	+0:17	+0:37
St. Johns River		
South Jetty	-0:35	-0:19
Pablo Creek bascule bridge	+1:27	+1:13
Fulton	+0:17	+0:40
Dame Point	+0:34	+0:53
Phoenix Park, (Cummers Mill)	+0:46	+1:23
Jacksonville, (Dredge Depot)	+1:12	+1:48
Jacksonville, (RR bridge)	+1:54	+2:11
Ortega River entrance	+2:15	+2:48
Orange Park	+3:37	+4:12
Green Cove Springs	+5:14	+6:11
East Tocoi	+6:35	+7:16
Bridgeport	+6:46	+7:30
Palatka	+7:14	+8:19
Welaka	+7:34	+8:23
Atlantic Beach	-0:37	-0:20
St. Augustine Inlet	-0:33	-0:03
St. Augustine	+0:02	+0:41
Daytona Beach, (ocean)	-0:45	-0:34

INSHORE

Trolling finds winter concentrations of **seatrout** along Intracoastal Waterway (ICW) edges and in the deeper adjacent creeks. Curly tail grubs or shrimp-tipped jigs are best. Warm mud flats and spoil island dropoffs hold **redfish** and **flounder**. Surf fishing turns up mainly **bluefish** and **whiting**. When whiting are in, inlets will have wall-to-wall boats. **Sheepshead** will take fiddler crabs and shrimp even on coldest days; soak baits on bottom near pilings of bridges and docks, and along jetty dropoffs and oyster-strewn creek holes.

OFFSHORE

When weather allows, run east to the famed Elton Bottom or deep wrecks for **gag**, **red**, and **black grouper**, and **red snapper**. Stay legal by checking latest, seeminly ever-changing regs on seasons and limits. **Sea bass**, **African pompano** and **cobia** will hang at the deeper wrecks. Sea bass relish squid or cutbait, African pompano and cobia rarely turn down a live baitfish over structure. In depths over 130, live or dead baits take delicious, white-fleshed **scamp grouper**.

January Spotlight: RED SNAPPER

The **red snapper** fishery was closed last year in South Atlantic federal waters and it remains to be seen what is in store for 2011. The fishery is a mainstay in Northeast Florida, and depending on sea conditions, anglers must decide between long runs to 21 fathoms or fishing nearshore wrecks. Those true, firetruck-red (a.k.a. genuines) snapper are suckers for live baits such as cigar minnows, finger mullet and menhaden and greenies, and even cut squid, over rocks and ledges in at least 120 feet. Shorter runs to shallow wrecks produce smaller reds, typically under 15 pounds. Christmas tree or chicken rigs are suitable for the smaller fish. Before gearing up for a trip, check the latest regulations governing the fishery.

SUNDAY	MONDAY	TUESDAY	WEDNESDAY	THURSDAY	FRIDAY	SATURDAY

'Hoo's your buddy?

1
6:08a 5.1' — 6:21p 4.2'

12:02p -0.1'

2
7:00a 5.1' — 7:13p 4.2'
12:02a -0.4' — 12:55p -0.3'

3 ●
7:48a 5.1' — 8:00p 4.2'
12:53a -0.5' — 1:42p -0.4'

4
8:33a 5.0' — 8:45p 4.2'
1:40a -0.6' — 2:26p -0.4'

5
9:14a 4.9' — 9:27p 4.2'
2:24a -0.5' — 3:08p -0.4'

6
9:52a 4.7' — 10:07p 4.1'
3:06a -0.4' — 3:47p -0.2'

7
10:29a 4.6' — 10:46p 4.1'
3:46a -0.2' — 4:26p -0.1'

8
11:04a 4.4' — 11:25p 4.1'
4:27a 0.1' — 5:04p 0.1'

9
11:40a 4.3'
5:11a 0.4' — 5:42p 0.3'

10
12:05a 4.1' — 12:17p 4.1'
5:58a 0.6' — 6:22p 0.4'

11 ◑
12:47a 4.1' — 12:59p 4.0'
6:51a 0.8' — 7:04p 0.5'

12
1:34a 4.1' — 1:46p 3.8'
7:46a 0.9' — 7:50p 0.5'

13
2:27a 4.2' — 2:41p 3.7'
8:42a 1.0' — 8:40p 0.5'

14
3:25a 4.2' — 3:41p 3.7'
9:38a 0.9' — 9:32p 0.3'

15
4:25a 4.4' — 4:41p 3.7'
10:32a 0.7' — 10:26p 0.1'

16
5:21a 4.5' — 5:37p 3.8'
11:25a 0.4' — 11:20p -0.2'

17
6:14a 4.8' — 6:30p 4.0'
12:15p 0.0'

18 ○
7:03a 5.0' — 7:21p 4.2'
12:12a -0.6' — 1:02p -0.3'

19
7:51a 5.1' — 8:11p 4.4'
1:03a -0.9' — 1:47p -0.7'

20
8:39a 5.2' — 9:02p 4.5'
1:52a -1.1' — 2:31p -0.9'

21
9:27a 5.2' — 9:52p 4.7'
2:41a -1.2' — 3:16p -1.0'

22
10:15a 5.1' — 10:44p 4.8'
3:32a -1.1' — 4:03p -1.0'

23
11:05a 4.9' — 11:37p 4.8'
4:26a -0.9' — 4:53p -0.9'

24
11:56a 4.7'
5:26a -0.6' — 5:47p -0.8'

25 ◑
12:34a 4.7' — 12:51p 4.4'
6:31a -0.3' — 6:47p -0.5'

26
1:35a 4.7' — 1:52p 4.1'
7:39a -0.1' — 7:49p -0.4'

27
2:43a 4.6' — 2:59p 3.9'
8:46a 0.1' — 8:51p -0.3'

28
3:53a 4.6' — 4:08p 3.8'
9:49a 0.1' — 9:53p -0.2'

29
4:57a 4.6' — 5:11p 3.9'
10:50a 0.0' — 10:53p -0.3'

30
5:55a 4.7' — 6:07p 3.9'
11:46a -0.1' — 11:49p -0.4'

31
6:45a 4.7' — 6:57p 4.0'
12:37p -0.2'

Redfish catch to end the day.

	January 1	January 15	January 30
SUNRISE	7:23 a.m.	7:24 a.m.	7:19 a.m.
SUNSET	5:37 p.m.	5:49 p.m.	6:02 p.m.

MAYPORT

Jacksonville to Daytona Beach Including the St. Johns River

Striped Missiles

TIDE CORRECTIONS
For Mayport

	High	Low
Nassau Sound, Ft. George River		
St. Marys, St. Marys River	+1:19	+1:13
Crandall, St. Marys River	+2:08	+2:02
Fernandina Beach, outer coast	-0:30	-0:03
Fernandina Beach, Amelia River	+0:20	+0:14
Chester, Bells River	+0:37	+0:39
SCL RR bridge, Kingsley Creek	+0:47	+0:41
Nassau Sound	-0:15	+0:04
Amelia City, S. Amelia River	+0:42	+1:01
Nassauville, Nassau River	+0:52	+1:35
Mink Creek entrance, Nassau R.	+1:46	+2:30
Halfmoon Island, highway bridge	+2:48	+3:19
Sawpit Creek entrance	+0:34	+0:28
Ft. George Island, Ft.George R.	+0:17	+0:37
St. Johns River		
South Jetty	-0:35	-0:19
Pablo Creek bascule bridge	+1:27	+1:13
Fulton	+0:17	+0:40
Dame Point	+0:34	+0:53
Phoenix Park, (Cummers Mill)	+0:46	+1:23
Jacksonville, (Dredge Depot)	+1:12	+1:48
Jacksonville, (RR bridge)	+1:54	+2:11
Ortega River entrance	+2:15	+2:48
Orange Park	+3:37	+4:12
Green Cove Springs	+5:14	+6:11
East Tocoi	+6:35	+7:16
Bridgeport	+6:46	+7:30
Palatka	+7:14	+8:19
Welaka	+7:34	+8:23
Atlantic Beach	-0:37	-0:20
St. Augustine Inlet	-0:33	-0:03
St. Augustine	+0:02	+0:41
Daytona Beach, (ocean)	-0:45	-0:34

INSHORE

Sheepshead pile up at the jetties so bundle up and soak live fiddlers, clams and shrimp along the rocky bottom. Bring plenty of terminal tackle—snags are common. Or soak a mud minnow in the same spots and chances are good you'll hook **flounder** and **black drum** and the occasional **redfish**. **Bluefish** seem to dominate the surf most days, and also pour into the Intracoastal Waterway.

Redfish take to mud flats at midday, when water is warmest. They can be slow to bite, so fish cut mullet, live shrimp or at least a scented bait strip. **Trout** season is closed, but catch-and-release fishing is best in ICW creeks. **Whiting** will feed in the surf, even if the water is roiled; fish peeled shrimp on a dropper loop rig.

OFFSHORE

February seas can be rough, but **tuna** and **wahoo** are possible for anglers picking their days and fast-trolling off Fernandina Beach, particularly near the Ledge and current rips in blue water. The fish are big, 60 to 90 pounds. Take high-speed lures dragged 20 feet down on a planer or downrigger. For tuna, drag a cedar plug on top. Deeper wrecks are holding **amberjack**, various **groupers** and **black sea bass**.

February Spotlight: WAHOO

This is big **wahoo** time. The late winter fishery from now until early spring is from Daytona Beach north. Sixty-pounders can be expected. Veteran anglers out of Jacksonville head to the Ledge in 140 to 240 feet of water and troll where water temperatures are close to 70 degrees. The drill is to zigzag from the deeper to shallower lengths of the well-known dropoff. Best trolling speed is 6 to 8 knots or a bit more. Standard issue equipment for this game includes wire lines, planers, skirted ballyhoo rigs, large fast-trolling plugs and heavy monofilament.

February 2011

SUNDAY	MONDAY	TUESDAY	WEDNESDAY	THURSDAY	FRIDAY	SATURDAY
		1	**2** ●	**3**	**4**	**5**
		7:31a 4.7' / 7:42p 4.1'	8:12a 4.7' / 8:24p 4.1'	8:49a 4.6' / 9:02p 4.1'	9:24a 4.5' / 9:39p 4.2'	9:57a 4.4' / 10:14p 4.2'
		12:40a -0.5' / 1:23p -0.4'	1:26a -0.5' / 2:04p -0.5'	2:08a -0.6' / 2:41p -0.5'	2:46a -0.5' / 3:16p -0.4'	3:23a -0.3' / 3:48p -0.3'
6	**7**	**8**	**9**	**10** ◗	**11**	**12**
10:30a 4.2' / 10:49p 4.2'	11:03a 4.1' / 11:25p 4.2'	11:39a 4.0' / 12:03a 4.2'	12:18p 3.8' / 12:46a 4.2'	1:02p 3.7' / 1:36a 4.1'	1:54p 3.6' / 2:35a 4.2'	2:56p 3.6'
3:59a -0.1' / 4:18p -0.1'	4:35a 0.1' / 4:49p 0.1'	5:14a 0.4' / 5:23p 0.2	5:58a 0.6' / 6:04p 0.3'	6:50a 0.8' / 6:52p 0.4'	7:48a 0.8' / 7:48p 0.4'	8:49a 0.8' / 8:49p 0.3'
13	**14**	**15**	**16**	**17** ○	**18**	**19**
3:42a 4.2' / 4:04p 3.7'	4:47a 4.4' / 5:07p 3.8'	5:45a 4.7' / 6:05p 4.1'	6:38a 4.9' / 6:59p 4.4'	7:28a 5.1' / 7:51p 4.7'	8:18a 5.2' / 8:42p 4.9'	9:07a 5.1' / 9:34p 5.1'
9:50a 0.6' / 9:51p 0.0'	10:48a 0.3' / 10:52p -0.3'	11:43a -0.1' / 11:51p -0.7'	12:34p -0.5' / 12:46a -1.0'	1:22p -0.9' / 1:38a -1.3'	2:07p -1.2' / 2:29a -1.4'	2:53p -1.4'
20	**21**	**22**	**23** ◖	**24**	**25**	**26**
9:56a 5.0' / 10:25p 5.1'	10:46a 4.8' / 11:18p 5.1'	11:38a 4.6' / 12:14a 4.9'	12:33p 4.3' / 1:14a 4.7'	1:33p 4.0' / 2:21a 4.5'	2:40p 3.9' / 3:31a 4.4'	3:49p 3.8'
3:21a -1.3' / 3:40p -1.3'	4:14a -1.1' / 4:29p -1.1'	5:12a -0.7' / 5:23p -0.8'	6:15a -0.4' / 1:02a -0.4'	7:21a -0.1' / 7:27p -0.2'	8:27a 0.1' / 8:33p 0.0'	9:30a 0.2' / 9:37p 0.1'
27	**28**					
4:37a 4.5' / 4:53p 3.9'	5:34a 4.5' / 5:48p 4.0'					
10:29a 0.2' / 10:37p 0.1'	11:24a 0.1' / 11:33p 0.0'					

Wahoo taken off St. Augustine.

	February 1	February 15	February 28
SUNRISE	7:17 a.m.	7:07 a.m.	6:54 a.m.
SUNSET	6:03 p.m.	6:15 p.m.	6:25 p.m.

Jacksonville to Daytona Beach Including the St. Johns River

Beat a Drum

INSHORE

Redfishing action rises with the water temps; fish shell bars, marsh-grass edges, mud flats and deep holes with jerkbaits, skimmer jigs, spoons, and crab and shrimp flies. Toss a topwater to entice **seatrout** along grassy shorelines and oyster edges for early in the day or late afternoon. If trout are slow to take a plug, try soft plastics.

The mud flat bag can include **flounder**, **sheepshead** and **black drum** this month. **Bluefish** still ravaging the surf zone, but also a decent number **whiting** and **pompano** for anglers with surf rods and sandfleas, fresh shrimp or cut clams.

OFFSHORE

Deeper wreck **cobia** are a possibility when seas allow safe transit. Same goes for anglers wanting to run to the Ledge for big **wahoo** and **tuna**. A varied lure spread should include diving plugs and skirt/ballyhoo combos to cover the water column. If you want a **red snapper**, live-bait or soak cutbaits near wrecks and reefs in 80-plus feet of water. Be sure to check the latest regulations on red snapper before heading offshore.

TIDE CORRECTIONS For Mayport	High	Low
Nassau Sound, Ft. George River		
St. Marys, St. Marys River	+1:19	+1:13
Crandall, St. Marys River	+2:08	+2:02
Fernandina Beach, outer coast	-0:30	-0:03
Fernandina Beach, Amelia River	+0:20	+0:14
Chester, Bells River	+0:37	+0:39
SCL RR bridge, Kingsley Creek	+0:47	+0:41
Nassau Sound	-0:15	+0:04
Amelia City, S. Amelia River	+0:42	+1:01
Nassauville, Nassau River	+0:52	+1:35
Mink Creek entrance, Nassau R.	+1:46	+2:30
Halfmoon Island, highway bridge	+2:48	+3:19
Sawpit Creek entrance	-0:14	+0:28
Ft. George Island, Ft.George R.	+0:17	+0:37
St. Johns River		
South Jetty	-0:35	-0:19
Pablo Creek bascule bridge	+1:27	+1:13
Fulton	+0:17	+0:40
Dame Point	+0:34	+0:53
Phoenix Park, (Cummers Mill)	+0:46	+1:23
Jacksonville, (Dredge Depot)	+1:12	+1:48
Jacksonville, (RR bridge)	+1:54	+2:11
Ortega River entrance	+2:15	+2:48
Orange Park	+3:37	+4:12
Green Cove Springs	+5:14	+6:11
East Tocoi	+6:35	+7:16
Bridgeport	+6:46	+7:30
Palatka	+7:14	+8:19
Welaka	+7:34	+8:23
Atlantic Beach	-0:37	-0:20
St. Augustine Inlet	-0:33	-0:03
St. Augustine	+0:02	+0:41
Daytona Beach, (ocean)	-0:45	-0:34

March Spotlight: BLACK DRUM

It is spawning time for giant **black drum** along the jetties in Northeast inlets. Top zones for this bite include St. Augustine Inlet and St. Marys River jetties. Surf fishermen can hook an outsized black drum too when the fish move to piers and shorebreaks. Top bait is a chunk of blue crab, fished with a sliding egg-sinker rig on 15- to 25-pound tackle. Remove the bait's legs and shell and scatter them in the water as chum. Release these big ones; they are too coarse to eat. Small fish are much better.

MAYPORT

SUNDAY	MONDAY	TUESDAY	WEDNESDAY	THURSDAY	FRIDAY	SATURDAY
		1 6:23a 4.5' 6:36p 4.2' 12:13p 0.0'	**2** 7:06a 4.6' 7:19p 4.3' 12:23a -0.2' 12:57p -0.2'	**3 ●** 7:45a 4.5' 7:58p 4.4' 1:08a -0.3'	**4** 8:21a 4.5' 8:35p 4.4' 1:36a -0.3' 1:49a -0.3'	**5** 8:54a 4.4' 9:09p 4.5' 2:11p -0.3' 2:26a -0.3' 2:42p -0.3'
6 9:27a 4.3' 9:42p 4.5' 3:01a -0.2' 3:11p -0.2'	**7** 9:59a 4.2' 10:16p 4.5' 3:33a -0.1' 3:37p -0.1'	**8** 10:33a 4.1' 10:50p 4.5' 4:05a 0.1' 4:06p 0.1'	**9** 11:08a 4.0' 11:27p 4.4' 4:40a 0.3' 4:40p 0.2'	**10** 11:46a 3.9' 5:20a 0.5' 5:21p 0.3'	**11 ◐** 12:09a 4.4' 12:30p 3.8' 6:08a 0.7' 6:11p 0.4'	**12** 12:57a 4.4' 1:21p 3.8' 7:06a 0.8' 7:10p 0.4'
13 1:56a 4.4' 4:23p 3.8' 10:09a 0.7' 10:16p 0.4'	**14** 5:04a 4.4' 5:33p 3.9' 11:13a 0.6' 11:23p 0.2'	**15** 6:13a 4.5' 6:41p 4.1' 12:14p 0.3'	**16** 7:15a 4.7' 7:42p 4.5' 12:29a -0.1' 1:11p -0.1'	**17** 8:11a 4.9' 8:38p 4.8' 1:32a -0.5' 2:04p -0.6'	**18** 9:04a 5.1' 9:31p 5.2' 2:30a -0.9' 2:54p -1.0'	**19 ○** 9:55a 5.1' 10:23p 5.4' 3:24a -1.2' 3:42p -1.2'
20 10:45a 5.1' 11:14p 5.5' 4:16a -1.3' 4:29p -1.3'	**21** 11:36a 5.0' 5:07a -1.2' 5:16p -1.3'	**22** 12:06a 5.5' 12:27p 4.8' 6:00a -1.0' 6:06p -1.0'	**23** 12:59a 5.3' 1:20p 4.6' 6:56a -0.7' 6:59p -0.6'	**24** 1:53a 5.1' 2:14p 4.3' 7:57a -0.3' 7:59p -0.2'	**25 ◑** 2:52a 4.8' 3:14p 4.1' 9:01a 0.1' 9:05p 0.1'	**26** 3:55a 4.6' 4:18p 4.0' 10:04a 0.3' 10:12p 0.4'
27 5:02a 4.5' 5:25p 4.0' 11:05a 0.4' 11:16p 0.5'	**28** 6:06a 4.4' 6:27p 4.1' 12:01p 0.4'	**29** 7:02a 4.4' 7:21p 4.3' 12:15a 0.5' 12:53p 0.4'	**30** 7:50a 4.5' 8:08p 4.4' 1:10a 0.4' 1:40p 0.2'	**31** 8:33a 4.5' 8:50p 4.6' 2:00a 0.2' 2:23p 0.1'		

Fish the creekmouths for flounder.

	March 1	March 15	March 30
SUNRISE	6:53 a.m.	7:37 a.m.	7:18 a.m.
SUNSET	6:25 p.m.	7:35 p.m.	7:44 p.m.

DST Starts on March 13

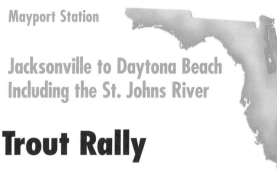

Jacksonville to Daytona Beach Including the St. Johns River

Trout Rally

TIDE CORRECTIONS
For Mayport

	High	Low
Nassau Sound, Ft. George River		
St. Marys, St. Marys River	+1:19	+1:13
Crandall, St. Marys River	+2:08	+2:02
Fernandina Beach, outer coast	-0:30	-0:03
Fernandina Beach, Amelia River	+0:20	+0:14
Chester, Bells River	+0:37	+0:39
SCL RR bridge, Kingsley Creek	+0:47	+0:41
Nassau Sound	-0:15	+0:04
Amelia City, S. Amelia River	+0:42	+1:01
Nassauville, Nassau River	+0:52	+1:35
Mink Creek entrance, Nassau R.	+1:46	+2:30
Halfmoon Island, highway bridge	+2:48	+3:19
Sawpit Creek entrance	-0:14	+0:28
Ft. George Island, Ft.George R.	+0:17	+0:37
St. Johns River		
South Jetty	-0:35	-0:19
Pablo Creek bascule bridge	+1:27	+1:13
Fulton	+0:17	+0:40
Dame Point	+0:34	+0:53
Phoenix Park, (Cummers Mill)	+0:46	+1:23
Jacksonville, (Dredge Depot)	+1:12	+1:48
Jacksonville, (RR bridge)	+1:54	+2:11
Ortega River entrance	+2:15	+2:48
Orange Park	+3:37	+4:12
Green Cove Springs	+5:14	+6:11
East Tocoi	+6:35	+7:16
Bridgeport	+6:46	+7:23
Palatka	+7:14	+8:19
Welaka	+7:34	+8:23
Atlantic Beach	-0:37	-0:20
St. Augustine Inlet	-0:33	-0:03
St. Augustine	+0:02	+0:41
Daytona Beach, (ocean)	-0:45	-0:34

INSHORE

Inlets are amok with **bluefish, sheepshead** and **black drum**. **Spanish mackerel** move in this month as weather warms—spoons and jigs score big in inlets and nearby beaches. **Seatrout** go off this month, and some fat 6-plus-pounders are in the mix; cast topwater plugs along ICW creekmouths at first light. Strive to fish in somewhat clean water that big specks prefer.

Flood tides usher in improving **redfish** numbers. Mud flats with spartina edges are best. Top baits include weedless soft plastics crawled along bottom. **Flounder** take soft baits on the flats too, though some natural bait can close the deal.

OFFSHORE

Bluewater trolling coming on strong now with **dolphin** and **blackfin tuna** joining still plentiful **wahoo**. Standard approach is trolling weedlines, current rips, temperature breaks and pronounced bottom contours. Search for birds, and tuna and dolphin should be on the spot. Frigates and terns shadowing baits on top are golden. Nearshore pogy pods attract **cobia, redfish** and **jack crevalle**. Stick a live pogy on your hook and a bite is all but assured.

April Spotlight: SEATROUT

There are gators in them there waters! **Seatrout** in the 8-pound-plus range and loads of smaller, legal-size fish will shadow bait schools near creekmouths. Fish a running tide around submerged oysters and grassy points that give the fish a current lee and ambush station. Top feeding tides are at the higher stages, especially in the morning. Cast popping, twitch-bait, diving and walking plugs throughout the day for the biggest fish. Fly fishers get in the game with with hard poppers, Gurglers and Dahlberg Divers. Schoolies fall for plastic-tail jigs, plastic shrimp, synthetic scented shrimp, bucktails, or live baits under a float. Let the big breeding size females go to make more tasty schoolies.

SUNDAY	MONDAY	TUESDAY	WEDNESDAY	THURSDAY	FRIDAY	SATURDAY

Hanna Park surf fishing.

1 (Friday): 9:11a 4.4', 9:29p 4.7'; 2:45a 0.1', 3:01p 0.0'
2 (Saturday): 9:48a 4.4', 10:05p 4.8'; 3:26a 0.0', 3:35p -0.1'

● 3 10:23a 4.3', 10:39p 4.8'; 4:03a -0.1', 4:06p -0.1'
4 10:57a 4.3', 11:13p 4.8'; 4:37a 0.0', 4:35p -0.1'
5 11:32a 4.2', 11:47p 4.8'; 5:09a 0.1', 5:02p 0.0'
6 12:07p 4.1', 12:23a 4.8'; 5:41a 0.2', 5:33p 0.1'
7 12:44p 4.1'; 6:14a 0.3', 6:09p 0.2'
8 1:01a 4.7', 1:24p 4.0'; 6:54a 0.5', 6:52p 0.4'
9 1:43a 4.7', 2:09p 4.0'; 7:42a 0.6', 7:44p 0.5'

10 2:32a 4.7', 3:01p 4.0'; 8:38a 0.7', 8:45p 0.5'
◑ 11 3:28a 4.6', 4:02p 4.1'; 9:40a 0.6', 9:53p 0.5'
12 4:33a 4.6', 5:11p 4.3'; 10:43a 0.4', 11:03p 0.3'
13 5:41a 4.7', 6:19p 4.5'; 11:42a 0.1'
14 6:45a 4.8', 7:21p 4.9'; 12:10a 0.0', 12:39p -0.2'
15 7:44a 4.9', 8:18p 5.2'; 1:14a -0.3', 1:34p -0.6'
16 8:40a 4.9', 9:12p 5.5'; 2:14a -0.6', 2:27p -0.9'

17 9:33a 4.9', 10:04p 5.7'; 3:09a -0.9', 3:17p -1.1'
○ 18 10:25a 4.9', 10:56p 5.7'; 4:02a -1.0', 4:06p -1.2'
19 11:17a 4.8', 11:48p 5.6'; 4:53a -1.0', 4:54p -1.1'
20 12:10p 4.7'; 5:45a -0.8', 5:44p -0.8'
21 12:40a 5.4', 1:02p 4.5'; 6:39a -0.5', 6:38p -0.4'
22 1:33a 5.2', 1:55p 4.4'; 7:36a -0.2', 7:37p 0.0'
23 2:27a 4.9', 2:51p 4.2'; 8:37a 0.1', 8:41p 0.4'

24 3:24a 4.7', 3:51p 4.2'; 9:36a 0.3', 9:46p 0.6'
◐ 25 4:23a 4.5', 4:52p 4.2'; 10:33a 0.5', 10:48p 0.7'
26 5:23a 4.4', 5:52p 4.3'; 11:25a 0.5', 11:45p 0.8'
27 6:18a 4.3', 6:45p 4.4'; 12:13p 0.5'
28 7:07a 4.3', 7:32p 4.6'; 12:39a 0.7', 12:59p 0.4'
29 7:51a 4.3', 8:15p 4.7'; 1:30a 0.6', 1:41p 0.3'
30 8:32a 4.2', 8:55p 4.9'; 2:16a 0.4', 2:20p 0.2'

	April 1	April 15	April 30
SUNRISE	7:16 a.m.	7:00 a.m.	6:44 a.m.
SUNSET	7:45 p.m.	7:54 p.m.	8:04 p.m.

Jacksonville to Daytona Beach
Including the St. Johns River

Cobes and Kings

INSHORE

Pier fishing can turn on big time for **kingfish**, **tarpon**, **barracuda**, **jacks** and **sharks**. Stay on top of reports to get in on the bite. For tarpon or kings, fish medium-to-heavy tackle and bait up a snelled circle hook with a live pogy. **Spanish mackerel** and **bluefish** are thick, and clobber jigs, spoons and popular, long-casting Gotcha plugs.

Inlets see good numbers of **sheepshead**, bull **redfish**, **flounder** and tarpon. Standard inlet baits include finger mullet, shrimp, pogies and crabs. High tides put big **trout** and redfish on rock reefs or grassy islands where finger mullet-style plugs are top choice.

OFFSHORE

Cobia are making their move down the beaches. Sight-fishing reigns for the brown bombers that will tail along with manta rays and swim amongst dense bait schools just off the sand. Even pier and partyboat anglers land the cobes this month.

Gulf Stream trolling doesn't get better. **Dolphin**, **blackfin tuna** and holdover **wahoo** are feeding along weedlines at 21 fathoms and deeper. Expect **sailfish** numbers to increase, too. **Kingfish** are on the deep wrecks where a fresh sabikied live pogy will not live long.

May Spotlight: COBIA

Free-swimming and manta-shadowing **cobia** are on the march within miles or even yards of the beach some days. Do your hunting from a high perch wherever bait pods congregate. Cruise at planing speed or slower where signs are prevalent along the beaches when the sun is high enough (from 9 a.m. until 3 p.m.) to help you spot rays and fish from a distance.

Then move in and cast live pogies, eels, or 1-ounce colorful jigs.

Fish of all sizes are possible; cobia must be at least 33 inches to keep. Hooked cobia can come in green, so be ready with the gaff, get your fish in the box and slam that lid!

May 2011

SUNDAY	MONDAY	TUESDAY	WEDNESDAY	THURSDAY	FRIDAY	SATURDAY
1	**2** ●	**3**	**4**	**5**	**6**	**7**
9:11a 4.2' / 9:32p 4.9'	9:50a 4.2' / 10:09p 5.0'	10:28a 4.2' / 10:46p 5.0'	11:06a 4.1' / 11:23p 4.9'	11:45a 4.1' / 12:02p 4.9'	12:25p 4.1' / 12:42a 4.9'	1:08p 4.1'
2:58a 0.3' / 2:56p 0.1'	3:37a 0.2' / 3:30p 0.0'	4:13a 0.1' / 4:01p 0.0'	4:46a 0.1' / 4:33p 0.0'	5:19a 0.2' / 5:07p 0.1'	5:55a 0.2' / 5:47p 0.1'	6:36a 0.3' / 6:33p 0.2'
8	**9** ◑	**10**	**11**	**12**	**13**	**14**
1:26a 4.9' / 1:55p 4.1'	2:15a 4.8' / 2:48p 4.2'	3:08a 4.8' / 3:47p 4.4'	4:08a 4.7' / 4:53p 4.6'	5:13a 4.6' / 5:59p 4.8'	6:18a 4.6' / 7:02p 5.1'	7:20a 4.6' / 8:00p 5.4'
7:24a 0.4' / 7:26p 0.4'	8:18a 0.4' / 8:29p 0.4'	9:17a 0.3' / 9:39p 0.4'	10:17a 0.1' / 10:48p 0.3'	11:14a -0.1' / 11:55p 0.1'	12:11p -0.4'	12:58a -0.2' / 1:07p -0.6'
15	**16** ○	**17**	**18**	**19**	**20**	**21**
8:18a 4.6' / 8:55p 5.5'	9:13a 4.6' / 9:48p 5.6'	10:07a 4.6' / 10:40p 5.6'	11:00a 4.5' / 11:31p 5.5'	11:52a 4.4'	12:22a 5.3' / 12:43p 4.4'	1:11a 5.1' / 1:34p 4.3'
1:58a -0.4' / 2:02p -0.8'	2:55a -0.7' / 2:54p -1.0'	3:48a -0.8' / 3:45p -1.0'	4:39a -0.8' / 4:35p -0.9'	5:29a -0.7' / 5:25p -0.6'	6:20a -0.5' / 6:17p -0.3'	7:13a -0.2' / 7:12p 0.1'
22	**23** ◐	**24**	**25**	**26**	**27**	**28**
1:59a 4.8' / 2:25p 4.2'	2:48a 4.6' / 3:18p 4.2'	3:38a 4.4' / 4:12p 4.2'	4:29a 4.2' / 5:07p 4.3'	5:22a 4.1' / 6:00p 4.4'	6:13a 4.0' / 6:49p 4.6'	7:02a 4.0' / 7:35p 4.7'
8:08a 0.1' / 8:?? 0.4'	9:02a 0.3' / 9:14p 0.7'	9:54a 0.4' / 10:13p 0.8'	10:42a 0.5' / 11:09p 0.9'	11:28a 0.5' / 12:02a 0.9'	12:12p 0.5' / 12:53a 0.8'	12:54p 0.4'
29	**30**	**31**				
7:48a 4.0' / 8:18p 4.8'	8:32a 4.0' / 8:59p 4.9'	9:15a 4.0' / 9:40p 4.9'				
1:41a 0.6' / 1:36p 0.3'	2:26a 0.5' / 2:15p 0.1'	3:07a 0.3' / 2:53p 0.0'				

Set your sights on redfish.

	May 1	May 15	May 30
SUNRISE	6:43 a.m.	6:24 a.m.	6:26 a.m.
SUNSET	8:24 p.m.	8:30 p.m.	8:23 p.m.

MAYPORT

Jacksonville to Daytona Beach
Including the St. Johns River

Blue Battlers

INSHORE

School-size **trout** are at peak numbers on the edges of mud and oyster flats. They will strike most agressively on subsurface hard baits and jigs. For a change of pace, cast at lighted docks for the specks. The specks feed in docklights on tiny shrimp and minnows. Diminutive fly patterns excel but small plastic shrimp take fish when they are hot to feed.

Jumbo **redfish** are in the inlet food line for pogies, jumbo shrimp and crabs. Make an accurate presentation just uptide, or freeline the baits. **Flounder** hunker on creek mud bottoms and along jetty rocks. Tip a jig with a mud minnow and bump it on bottom. Northbound **pompano** raid the surf troughs and run-outs; live sandfleas, cut clams and shrimp on dropper rigs score.

OFFSHORE

Local wrecks hold numbers of **red snapper, grouper, bee-liners** and **amberjack**. Beaches still have summer bait pods hounded by **kingfish**, bull **reds**, **tarpon** and **cobia**.

Dolphin are amassing underneath weedlines. Troll lures and lure/bait combos alongside, or past flotsam and under birds. Send a speed jig or live bait for under structure for **wahoo**. **Blue marlin** pop up in trolling spreads, particularly around the Steeples out of Ponce Inlet.

June Spotlight: DOLPHIN

Reasonably behaved seas and weather allow weekenders in smaller boats to get offshore for **dolphin** dinners. Weedlines and debris could hold 'phins of any size, so be prepared with light casting tackle and medium spin and trolling gear. Troll along weedlines, under diving birds, and near flotsam. Short of fish signs, check for temp breaks, current edges and slicks and put out a spread of both surface and deep offerings. A big billfish underneath schoolies at the stern could bag a billfish or the dolphin of your life. Keep schoolies around by chucking out occasional small handfuls of cutbait or live baits, and mind those liberal limits.

June 2011

SUNDAY	MONDAY	TUESDAY	WEDNESDAY	THURSDAY	FRIDAY	SATURDAY

Grab the bull by the fins.

1
9:58a 4.0' 10:20p 5.0'
3:46a 0.1' 3:30p -0.1'

2
10:41a 4.0' 11:01p 5.0'
4:22a 0.0' 4:08p -0.2'

3
11:24a 4.0' 11:43p 5.0'
4:58a 0.0' 4:47p -0.2'

4
12:08p 4.1'
5:37a 0.0' 5:31p -0.1'

5
12:27a 5.0' 12:55p 4.2'
6:19a 0.0' 6:20p 0.0'

6
1:12a 5.0' 1:44p 4.3'
7:07a 0.0' 7:15p 0.1'

7
2:00a 4.9' 2:37p 4.4'
7:59a -0.1' 8:19p 0.2'

8
2:52a 4.8' 3:34p 4.6'
8:56a -0.1' 9:28p 0.3'

9
3:48a 4.6' 4:37p 4.7'
9:53a -0.2' 10:36p 0.2'

10
4:51a 4.5' 5:42p 4.9'
10:50a -0.3' 11:41p 0.1'

11
5:56a 4.3' 6:46p 5.1'
11:48a -0.5'

12
7:00a 4.3' 7:45p 5.3'
12:44a -0.1' 12:45p -0.6'

13
8:01a 4.3' 8:41p 5.4'
1:44a -0.3' 1:42p -0.7'

14
8:57a 4.3' 9:35p 5.4'
2:40a -0.5' 2:37p -0.8'

15
9:52a 4.3' 10:26p 5.3'
3:33a -0.6' 3:29p -0.8'

16
10:44a 4.3' 11:15a 5.2'
4:23a -0.7' 4:19p -0.7'

17
11:34a 4.2' 12:01a 5.1'
5:11a -0.6' 5:07p -0.5'

18
12:22p 4.2'
5:58a -0.5' 5:56p -0.3'

19
12:45a 4.9' 1:08p 4.2'
6:45a -0.3' 6:46p 0.1'

20
1:28a 4.7' 1:54p 4.2'
7:33a 0.0' 7:39p 0.4'

21
2:09a 4.5' 2:40p 4.2'
8:21a 0.2' 8:36p 0.7'

22
2:51a 4.3' 3:27p 4.2'
9:07a 0.3' 9:33p 0.9'

23
3:35a 4.1' 4:16p 4.3'
9:53a 0.4' 10:28p 1.0'

24
4:23a 4.0' 5:08p 4.4'
10:37a 0.5' 11:20p 1.0'

25
5:16a 3.9' 6:00p 4.5'
11:20a 0.5'

26
6:10a 3.8' 6:51p 4.6'
12:11a 0.9' 12:04p 0.4'

27
7:02a 3.8' 7:39p 4.7'
1:01a 0.8' 12:49p 0.3'

28
7:53a 3.8' 8:25p 4.8'
1:49a 0.6' 1:34p 0.1'

29
8:41a 3.9' 9:10p 4.9'
2:33a 0.4' 2:19p -0.1'

30
9:28a 3.9' 9:55p 5.0'
3:15a 0.1' 3:03p -0.2'

	June 1	June 15	June 30
SUNRISE	6:25 a.m.	6:24 a.m.	6:28 a.m.
SUNSET	8:24 p.m.	8:30 p.m.	8:33 p.m.

Jacksonville to Daytona Beach Including the St. Johns River

The King of Macks

INSHORE

Time to get an early start if **trout** are in your shallow-water gameplan. **Redfishing** is more consistent through midday, and as far inland as freshwater sections of the St. Johns River. **Pompano** cooperate in the surf.

Tarpon rally around the pogy pods along the beach, and in the deeper sections of the ICW. **Flounder** and **black drum** are stalwarts for the jetty crowd, and anglers fishing shrimp along seawalls or under docks and bridges.

OFFSHORE

Nearshore wrecks to about 15 miles out are chockablock with **grouper, snapper** and **kingfish**. Expect more **vermilions** to inhabit deeper structures. **Red snapper** and **snowy grouper** will eat your live or frozen baitfish in 100 feet or more. Trolling a spread should result in **sailfish**, when **cudas** and **bonito** are not beating the spindlebeaks to the punch. Send a live bait out over a reef in 80 to 100 feet of water and you take a **blackfin tuna** home for supper.

TIDE CORRECTIONS For Mayport	High	Low
Nassau Sound, Ft. George River		
St. Marys, St. Marys River	+1:19	+1:13
Crandall, St. Marys River	+2:08	+2:02
Fernandina Beach, outer coast	-0:30	-0:03
Fernandina Beach, Amelia River	+0:20	+0:14
Chester, Bells River	+0:37	+0:39
SCL RR bridge, Kingsley Creek	+0:47	+0:41
Nassau Sound	-0:15	+0:04
Amelia City, S. Amelia River	+0:42	+1:01
Nassauville, Nassau River	+0:52	+1:35
Mink Creek entrance, Nassau R.	+1:46	+2:30
Halfmoon Island, highway bridge	+2:48	+3:19
Sawpit Creek entrance	-0:14	+0:28
Ft. George Island, Ft.George R.	+0:17	+0:37
St. Johns River		
South Jetty	-0:35	-0:19
Pablo Creek bascule bridge	+1:27	+1:13
Fulton	+0:17	+0:40
Dame Point	+0:34	+0:53
Phoenix Park, (Cummers Mill)	+0:46	+1:23
Jacksonville, (Dredge Depot)	+1:12	+1:48
Jacksonville, (RR bridge)	+1:54	+2:11
Ortega River entrance	+2:15	+2:48
Orange Park	+3:37	+4:12
Green Cove Springs	+5:14	+6:11
East Tocoi	+6:35	+7:16
Bridgeport	+6:46	+7:30
Palatka	+7:14	+8:19
Welaka	+7:34	+8:23
Atlantic Beach	-0:37	-0:20
St. Augustine Inlet	-0:33	-0:03
St. Augustine	+0:02	+0:41
Daytona Beach, (ocean)	-0:45	-0:34

July Spotlight: KINGFISH

King mackerel may come out of your kitchen faucet this month. For certain they range wide, from the piers to the Elton Bottom, over the wrecks and live bottom from there back to the inlet mouths. Smokers exceeding 40 pounds are a common occurrence on live baits in 40 feet of water. Try slow-trolling with pogies, mullet, pinfish or croakers just outside the inlets, or if you don't mind burning a bit more gas, troll rigged ribbonfish on a downrigger 100 feet on out. The freshest ribbonfish account for many tournament winners. Serious king rigs are wire rigged with stinger hooks.

July 2011

SUNDAY	MONDAY	TUESDAY	WEDNESDAY	THURSDAY	FRIDAY	SATURDAY

Young angler with spotted seatrout.

1
10:15a 4.0' — 10:39p 5.1'
3:55a -0.1' — 3:47p -0.4'

2
11:02a 4.2' — 11:24p 5.1'
4:35a -0.3' — 4:31p -0.5'

3
11:50a 4.3'
5:16a -0.4' — 5:18p -0.4'

4
12:09a 5.1' — 12:39p 4.5'
5:59a -0.4' — 6:09p -0.3'

5
12:56a 5.1' — 1:29p 4.6'
6:47a -0.4' — 7:06p -0.1'

6
1:44a 4.9' — 2:23p 4.7'
7:38a -0.4' — 8:10p 0.1'

7
2:36a 4.7' — 3:20p 4.8'
8:34a -0.4' — 9:17p 0.2'

8
3:32a 4.5' — 4:22p 4.9'
9:32a -0.4' — 10:24p 0.2'

9
4:34a 4.3' — 5:28p 5.0'
10:31a -0.3' — 11:28p 0.2'

10
5:40a 4.2' — 6:33p 5.1'
11:30a -0.3'

11
6:46a 4.1' — 7:34p 5.2'
12:30a 0.1' — 12:29p -0.4'

12
7:47a 4.2' — 8:30p 5.2'
1:30a 0.0' — 1:27p -0.4'

13
8:44a 4.2' — 9:22p 5.2'
2:26a -0.2' — 2:23p -0.5'

14
9:37a 4.2' — 10:10p 5.2'
3:18a -0.3' — 3:15p -0.5'

15
10:26a 4.3' — 10:55p 5.1'
4:05a -0.4' — 4:03p -0.5'

16
11:13a 4.3' — 11:37p 4.9'
4:49a -0.4' — 4:49p -0.3'

17
11:57a 4.3'
5:31a -0.3' — 5:33p -0.1'

18
12:18a 4.8' — 12:39p 4.3'
6:12a -0.2' — 6:18p 0.2'

19
12:54a 4.6' — 1:19p 4.3'
6:52a 0.0' — 7:05p 0.5'

20
1:31a 4.5' — 2:00p 4.4'
7:33a 0.2' — 7:54p 0.7'

21
2:08a 4.3' — 2:41p 4.4'
8:14a 0.4' — 8:47p 1.0'

22
2:49a 4.2' — 3:26p 4.4'
8:56a 0.6' — 9:41p 1.1'

23
3:33a 4.0' — 4:15p 4.5'
9:40a 0.7' — 10:34p 1.2'

24
4:24a 3.9' — 5:09p 4.5'
10:26a 0.7' — 11:26p 1.1'

25
5:20a 3.9' — 6:05p 4.6'
11:15a 0.6'

26
6:18a 3.9' — 7:00p 4.8'
12:17a 1.0' — 12:05p 0.5'

27
7:15a 4.0' — 7:51p 4.9'
1:08a 0.8' — 12:57p 0.3'

28
8:08a 4.1' — 8:40p 5.1'
1:56a 0.5' — 1:49p 0.0'

29
8:59a 4.2' — 9:28p 5.2'
2:42a 0.2' — 2:39p -0.3'

30
9:49a 4.4' — 10:14p 5.3'
3:26a -0.1' — 3:28p -0.5'

31
10:39a 4.6' — 11:01p 5.4'
4:09a -0.4' — 4:16p -0.6'

Sun, sand and surf fishing.

	July 1	July 15	July 30
SUNRISE	6:28 a.m.	6:35 a.m.	6:44 a.m.
SUNSET	8:33 p.m.	8:30 p.m.	8:22 p.m.

Jacksonville to Daytona Beach Including the St. Johns River

Bow Now, Again!

TIDE CORRECTIONS
For Mayport

	High	Low
Nassau Sound, Ft. George River		
St. Marys, St. Marys River	+1:19	+1:13
Crandall, St. Marys River	+2:08	+2:02
Fernandina Beach, outer coast	-0:30	-0:03
Fernandina Beach, Amelia River	+0:20	+0:14
Chester, Bells River	+0:37	+0:39
SCL RR bridge, Kingsley Creek	+0:47	+0:41
Nassau Sound	-0:15	+0:04
Amelia City, S. Amelia River	+0:42	+1:01
Nassauville, Nassau River	+0:52	+1:35
Mink Creek entrance, Nassau R.	+1:46	+2:30
Halfmoon Island, highway bridge	+2:48	+3:19
Sawpit Creek entrance	+0:14	+0:28
Ft. George Island, Ft.George R.	+0:17	+0:37
St. Johns River		
South Jetty	-0:35	-0:19
Pablo Creek bascule bridge	+1:27	+1:13
Fulton	+0:17	+0:40
Dame Point	+0:34	+0:53
Phoenix Park, (Cummers Mill)	+0:46	+1:23
Jacksonville, (Dredge Depot)	+1:12	+1:48
Jacksonville, (RR bridge)	+1:54	+2:11
Ortega River entrance	+2:15	+2:48
Orange Park	+3:37	+4:12
Green Cove Springs	+5:14	+6:11
East Tocoi	+6:35	+7:16
Bridgeport	+6:46	+7:30
Palatka	+7:14	+8:19
Welaka	+7:34	+8:23
Atlantic Beach	-0:37	-0:20
St. Augustine Inlet	-0:33	-0:03
St. Augustine	+0:02	+0:41
Daytona Beach, (ocean)	-0:45	-0:34

INSHORE

The shrimp run steers inshore action this month.
Redfish and **largemouth bass** both take live shrimp
in the upper reaches of the St. Johns River. **Croakers**, **weakfish** and **seatrout** fall for shrimp fished via popping cork or
freelined with a splitshot. The summer **flounder** bite is off the
hook around docks, rocks and creekmouths. **Tarpon** by the tons
shadow pogies on the beach, in the inlets and the ICW. Toss live
pogies or plug imitators into the fray and hang on! ICW bridges
and docks normally hold a few **snook**, but they will be rarer
than ever since the freeze.

OFFSHORE

King mackerel are right against the beach. Smokers are
swimming with bait in tight; smaller kings are more likely hanging
over nearshore wrecks. Flat seas should allow for trips for **dolphin** along weedlines, rips and flotsam from 21 fathoms out to
the Rolldown. Deeper wrecks will deliver dinner in the form of
sea bass and **beeliners**, **snowy grouper**, **gag grouper**
and **red snapper**.

August Spotlight: TARPON

If you can't hook a Northeast **tarpon**
this month, turn in your tackle! The bite is
about assured around pogy pods, particularly early and late in the day. Run along at
planing speed, look for diving pelicans,
rolling fish, or busts on top, slow down and
sneak into position for a cast or to freeline
livies. Live-baiting below the surface with
circle hooks accounts for most of the hookups, but big soft plastics and plugs will
work when the bite is on. Rig up with at
least 30-pound gear and 80- to 100-pound-test fluoro leader, as beach tarpon are burly
and bruising. Remember the law: Do not drag your poon aboard for "grip-and-grins."

August 2011

SUNDAY	MONDAY	TUESDAY	WEDNESDAY	THURSDAY	FRIDAY	SATURDAY
	1	**2**	**3**	**4**	**5**	**6** ◑
	11:29a 4.8' / 11:49p 5.3'	12:20p 5.0' / 12:37a 5.2'	1:12p 5.1' / 1:27a 5.1'	2:06p 5.2' / 2:20a 4.8'	3:03p 5.2' / 3:17a 4.6'	4:07p 5.2'
	4:51a -0.6' / 5:06p -0.6'	5:36a -0.6' / 5:58p -0.4'	6:23a -0.6' / 6:55p -0.2'	7:15a -0.5' / 7:58p 0.1'	8:12a -0.3' / 9:05p 0.3'	9:12a -0.1' / 10:12p 0.4'
7	**8**	**9**	**10**	**11**	**12** ○	**13**
4:20a 4.4' / 5:14p 5.2'	5:28a 4.3' / 6:21p 5.2'	6:35a 4.3' / 7:21p 5.2'	7:35a 4.4' / 8:16p 5.3'	8:30a 4.5' / 9:05p 5.3'	9:20a 4.5' / 9:49p 5.2'	10:05a 4.6' / 10:31p 5.1'
10:15a 0.0' / 11:16p 0.5'	11:17a 0.1' / 12:17a 0.4'	12:17p 0.1' / 1:15a 0.3'	1:16p 0.0' / 2:09a 0.2'	2:11p 0.0' / 2:58a 0.1'	3:01p -0.1' / 3:42a 0.0'	3:47p -0.1'
14	**15**	**16**	**17**	**18**	**19**	**20**
10:48a 4.6' / 11:09p 5.0'	11:28a 4.7' / 11:45p 4.9'	12:06p 4.7'	12:19a 4.7' / 12:43p 4.7'	12:54a 4.6' / 1:20p 4.7'	1:31a 4.5' / 1:58p 4.8'	2:09a 4.4' / 2:40p 4.8'
4:23a -0.1' / 4:30p 0.0'	5:00a 0.0' / 5:10p 0.2'	5:36a 0.1' / 5:50p 0.4'	6:09a 0.3' / 6:30p 0.7'	6:43a 0.5' / 7:12p 1.0'	7:18a 0.7' / 7:58p 1.2'	7:57a 0.9' / 8:49p 1.4'
21 ◐	**22**	**23**	**24**	**25**	**26**	**27**
2:52a 4.3' / 3:27p 4.8'	3:41a 4.2' / 4:21p 4.8'	4:37a 4.2' / 5:21p 4.9'	5:39a 4.2' / 6:21p 5.0'	6:40a 4.4' / 7:17p 5.2'	7:38a 4.6' / 8:09p 5.4'	8:31a 4.8' / 8:59p 5.6'
8:43a 1.0' / 9:44p 1.5'	9:35a 1.0' / 10:39p 1.4'	10:31a 0.9' / 11:33p 1.3'	11:28a 0.8'	12:27a 1.1' / 12:26p 0.5'	1:18a 0.7' / 1:22p 0.2'	2:08a 0.3' / 2:17p -0.1'
28 ●	**29**	**30**	**31**			
9:23a 5.1' / 9:48p 5.6'	10:15a 5.4' / 10:37p 5.7'	11:06a 5.6' / 11:27p 5.6'	11:59a 5.7'			
2:54a 0.0' / 3:10p -0.3'	3:40a -0.4' / 4:01p -0.5'	4:25a -0.6' / 4:52p -0.5'	5:11a -0.6' / 5:45p -0.3'			

Fishing around structures in Jacksonville.

	August 1	August 15	August 30
SUNRISE	6:45 a.m.	6:54 a.m.	7:02 a.m.
SUNSET	8:20 p.m.	8:08 p.m.	7:52 p.m.

Jacksonville to Daytona Beach
Including the St. Johns River

Tails in the Grass

INSHORE

Huge Autumn tides open shallowest spartina marsh to **redfish** and **sheepshead** hankering for fiddler and mud crabs. Cast flies and weedless jerkbaits to slots in the grass where you see tail tips. Surf fishing comes on with the fall mullet run for **bluefish**. Also **whiting** and **black drum**.

Tarpon hang near inlets feeding on baits both early and late. **Flounder** possible on bottom off jetties; **Spanish mackerel** make inlet raids. **Trout** gather at the creekmouths where they will take jigs and sinking plugs on moving water.

OFFSHORE

Grouper and **snapper** are in the works at the wrecks northeast of Mayport. Off St. Augustine, anglers score on **beeliners** (vermilion snapper), **cobia**, **amberjack** and tasty **triggerfish**. Reefs and wrecks in 70 to 90 feet hold undersize **red snapper** and **gag grouper**, but enough keepers are mixed in. Run offshore of St. Augustine and Ponce inlets and troll ballyhoo/skirt combos for increasing numbers of **sailfish**.

September Spotlight: REDFISH

It's dry land one minute, and a **redfish** flat the next! Reds ride the big tide onto spartina marsh mud flats to feast on fiddler crabs and anything else that gets in their sights. This sets up classic wading with a fly rod or light spinner. Reds are also spawning at the inlets and cruising the surf. Flies and small plastics work best in the marsh. Elsewhere, cast streamers, spoons, suspending plugs, and shrimp to reds in the surf trough, or in the inlet. Those big breeder reds at the inlet are the fishery's future; if you insist on winching one in, release it quickly in good shape.

MAYPORT

SUNDAY	MONDAY	TUESDAY	WEDNESDAY	THURSDAY	FRIDAY	SATURDAY

King of the Jacksonville Pier.

1 — 12:17a 5.4' / 12:52P 5.7'; 5:59a -0.5' / 6:42p 0.0'
2 — 1:10a 5.3' / 1:47p 5.7'; 6:52a -0.3' / 7:44p 0.3'
3 — 2:04a 5.1' / 2:46p 5.6'; 7:50a 0.0' / 8:51p 0.5'

4 — 3:03a 4.9' / 3:50p 5.5'; 8:55a 0.3' / 9:57p 0.7'
5 — 4:07a 4.7' / 4:58p 5.4'; 10:01a 0.5' / 11:00p 0.8'
6 — 5:15a 4.7' / 6:04p 5.4'; 11:05a 0.6' / 12:00A 0.8'
7 — 6:21a 4.7' / 7:03p 5.4'; 12:05P 0.6' / 12:55a 0.7'
8 — 7:20a 4.8' / 7:55p 5.4'; 1:03p 0.6'
9 — 8:11a 4.9' / 8:41p 5.4'; 1:46a 0.6' / 1:56p 0.5'
10 — 8:58a 5.0' / 9:23p 5.3'; 2:32a 0.5' / 2:44p 0.5'

11 — 9:40a 5.1' / 10:01p 5.2'; 3:14a 0.4' / 3:28p 0.4'
12 — 10:20a 5.1' / 10:37p 5.1'; 3:52a 0.4' / 4:09p 0.5'
13 — 10:57a 5.2' / 11:12p 5.0'; 4:26a 0.4' / 4:47p 0.6'
14 — 11:32a 5.2' / 11:46p 4.9'; 4:58a 0.5' / 5:23p 0.7'
15 — 12:07P 5.2'; 5:28a 0.7' / 5:58p 1.0'
16 — 12:21A 4.8' / 12:43P 5.2'; 5:57a 0.8' / 6:35p 1.2'
17 — 12:58A 4.7' / 1:21p 5.2'; 6:30a 1.0' / 7:15p 1.4'

18 — 1:37a 4.6' / 2:02p 5.1'; 7:10a 1.2' / 8:02p 1.6'
19 — 2:19a 4.6' / 2:49p 5.1'; 7:57a 1.3' / 8:57p 1.7'
20 — 3:08a 4.5' / 3:42p 5.2'; 8:53a 1.3' / 9:55p 1.7'
21 — 4:04a 4.6' / 4:42p 5.2'; 9:55a 1.3' / 10:53p 1.5'
22 — 5:07a 4.7' / 5:44p 5.3'; 10:58a 1.1' / 11:48p 1.2'
23 — 6:11a 4.9' / 6:43p 5.5'; 12:00p 0.8'
24 — 7:11a 5.2' / 7:38p 5.6'; 12:42a 0.8' / 1:00p 0.5'

25 — 8:06a 5.5' / 8:31p 5.8'; 1:34a 0.4' / 1:58p 0.2'
26 — 9:00a 5.8' / 9:22p 5.8'; 2:23a 0.0' / 2:53p -0.1'
27 — 9:52a 6.0' / 10:13p 5.8'; 3:11a -0.3' / 3:46p -0.3'
28 — 10:45a 6.2' / 11:05p 5.7'; 3:59a -0.5' / 4:38p -0.3'
29 — 11:38a 6.2' / 11:58p 5.6'; 4:47a -0.5' / 5:31p -0.1'
30 — 12:33p 6.2'; 5:36a -0.3' / 6:27p 0.1'

	September 1	September 15	September 30
SUNRISE	7:03 a.m.	7:11 a.m.	7:19 a.m.
SUNSET	7:49 p.m.	7:32 p.m.	7:13 p.m.

MAYPORT

Jacksonville to Daytona Beach
Including the St. Johns River

Flat Out Good

TIDE CORRECTIONS
For Mayport

	High	Low
Nassau Sound, Ft. George River		
St. Marys, St. Marys River	+1:19	+1:13
Crandall, St. Marys River	+2:08	+2:02
Fernandina Beach, outer coast	-0:30	-0:03
Fernandina Beach, Amelia River	+0:20	+0:14
Chester, Bells River	+0:37	+0:39
SCL RR bridge, Kingsley Creek	+0:47	+0:41
Nassau Sound	-0:15	+0:04
Amelia City, S. Amelia River	+0:42	+1:01
Nassauville, Nassau River	+0:52	+1:35
Mink Creek entrance, Nassau R.	+1:46	+2:30
Halfmoon Island, highway bridge	+2:48	+3:19
Sawpit Creek entrance	-0:14	+0:28
Ft. George Island, Ft.George R.	+0:17	+0:37
St. Johns River		
South Jetty	-0:35	-0:19
Pablo Creek bascule bridge	+1:27	+1:13
Fulton	+0:17	+0:40
Dame Point	+0:34	+0:53
Phoenix Park, (Cummers Mill)	+0:46	+1:23
Jacksonville, (Dredge Depot)	+1:12	+1:48
Jacksonville, (RR bridge)	+1:54	+2:11
Ortega River entrance	+2:15	+2:48
Orange Park	+3:37	+4:12
Green Cove Springs	+5:14	+6:11
East Tocoi	+6:35	+7:16
Bridgeport	+6:46	+7:30
Palatka	+7:14	+8:19
Welaka	+7:34	+8:23
Atlantic Beach	-0:37	-0:20
St. Augustine Inlet	-0:33	-0:03
St. Augustine	+0:02	+0:41
Daytona Beach, (ocean)	-0:45	-0:34

INSHORE

Big doormat **flounder** are here, and stack in the inlets for some social mixers. Soak a mud minnow on a slide sinker rig and wait for the "weight." **Reds** and **trout** hold around oysters and grass. **Bluefish**, **weakfish** and **black drum** are also in the inlet and nearby ICW. Live baits like shrimp and mullet work for all, as do jigs, topwater plugs, suspending baits and shrimp-imitators.

Cooler water perks up the trout topwater bite. Beach fishermen will find **whiting** and **pompano** before fall temps send 'em south. Fish live mullet for the last of the **tarpon** at the inlets.

OFFSHORE

Daytona Beach waters are the place for **sailfish**. They'll ball up bait schools in the blue water this month. It is very visual, and the drill is to get close, shut the engines unless seas are up, and toss baits into the herd. Wrecks within 15 miles of shore hold **grouper** and **snapper**; deeper structures home to **cobia** and **African pompano** for live-baiters. Troll lures near the Ledge and Steeples for **dolphin** and **wahoo**. Out at the Rolldown **blue marlin** are possible.

October Spotlight: FLOUNDER

Ten-pound **flounder** are a fall ritual in Northeast Florida. The doormats pave the bottom at times at inlets when the water temperature falls to 68 degrees. Timing is good, because the mullet migration is underway, too, so there's food for the feast. Best flounder rig includes a sliding egg-sinker with just heavy enough weight to hold bottom. An 8-inch leader will keep the baits near bottom where flounder lay. Top baits include finger mullet and mud minnows. To feel the flounder's subtle take and get it off bottom quickly, choose a medium-heavy spinning or baitcasting outfit to crank a doormat through current. Eddies near rock jetties, dock pilings and scattered riprap are prime lairs.

SUNDAY	MONDAY	TUESDAY	WEDNESDAY	THURSDAY	FRIDAY	SATURDAY

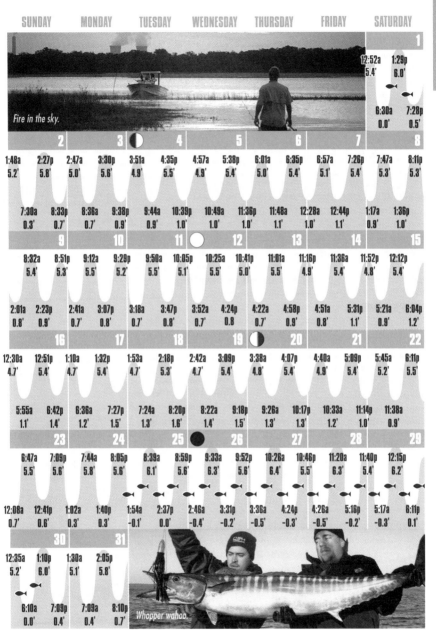

Fire in the sky.

1
12:52a 5.4' | 1:29p 6.0'
6:30a 0.0' | 7:28p 0.5'

2
1:48a 5.2' | 2:27p 5.8'
7:30a 0.3' | 8:33p 0.7'

3 ◐
2:47a 5.0' | 3:30p 5.6'
8:36a 0.7' | 9:38p 0.9'

4
3:51a 4.9' | 4:35p 5.5'
9:44a 0.9' | 10:39p 1.0'

5
4:57a 4.9' | 5:38p 5.4'
10:49a 1.0' | 11:36p 1.0'

6
6:01a 5.0' | 6:35p 5.4'
11:48a 1.1'

7
6:57a 5.1' | 7:26p 5.4'
12:28a 1.0' | 12:44p 1.1'

8
7:47a 5.3' | 8:11p 5.3'
1:17a 0.9' | 1:36p 1.0'

9
8:32a 5.4' | 8:51p 5.3'
2:01a 0.8' | 2:23p 0.9'

10
9:12a 5.5' | 9:29p 5.2'
2:41a 0.7' | 3:07p 0.8'

11 ○
9:50a 5.5' | 10:05p 5.1'
3:18a 0.7' | 3:47p 0.8'

12
10:25a 5.5' | 10:41p 5.0'
3:52a 0.7' | 4:24p 0.8

13
11:01a 5.5' | 11:16p 4.9'
4:22a 0.7' | 4:58p 0.9'

14
11:36a 5.4'
4:51a 0.8' | 5:31p 1.1'

15
11:52a 4.8' | 12:12p 5.4'
5:21a 0.9' | 6:04p 1.2'

16
12:30a 4.7' | 12:51p 5.4'
5:55a 1.1' | 6:42p 1.4'

17
1:10a 4.7' | 1:32p 5.4'
6:36a 1.2' | 7:27p 1.5'

18
1:53a 4.7' | 2:18p 5.3'
7:24a 1.3' | 8:20p 1.6'

19 ◐
2:42a 4.7' | 3:09p 5.4'
8:22a 1.4' | 9:18p 1.5'

20
3:38a 4.8' | 4:07p 5.4'
9:26a 1.3' | 10:17p 1.3'

21
4:40a 4.9' | 5:09p 5.4'
10:33a 1.2' | 11:14p 1.0'

22
5:45a 5.2' | 6:11p 5.5'
11:38a 0.9'

23
6:47a 5.5' | 7:09p 5.6'
12:08a 0.7' | 12:41p 0.6'

24
7:44a 5.8' | 8:05p 5.6'
1:02a 0.3' | 1:40p 0.3'

25 ●
8:39a 6.1' | 8:59p 5.6'
1:54a -0.1' | 2:37p 0.0'

26
9:33a 6.3' | 9:52p 5.6'
2:46a -0.4' | 3:31p -0.2'

27
10:26a 6.4' | 10:46p 5.5'
3:36a -0.5' | 4:24p -0.3'

28
11:20a 6.3' | 11:40p 5.4'
4:26a -0.5' | 5:16p -0.2'

29
12:15p 6.2'
5:17a -0.3' | 6:11p 0.1'

30
12:35a 5.2' | 1:10p 6.0'
6:10a 0.0' | 7:09p 0.4'

31
1:30a 5.1' | 2:05p 5.8'
7:09a 0.4' | 8:10p 0.7'

Whopper wahoo.

	October 1	October 15	October 30
SUNRISE	7:20 a.m.	7:29 a.m.	7:39 a.m.
SUNSET	7:12 p.m.	6:56 p.m.	6:41 p.m.

Jacksonville to Daytona Beach
Including the St. Johns River

Get Your Grouper

TIDE CORRECTIONS
For Mayport

	High	Low
Nassau Sound, Ft. George River		
St. Marys, St. Marys River	+1:19	+1:13
Crandall, St. Marys River	+2:08	+2:02
Fernandina Beach, outer coast	-0:30	-0:03
Fernandina Beach, Amelia River	+0:20	+0:14
Chester, Bells River	+0:37	+0:39
SCL RR bridge, Kingsley Creek	+0:47	+0:41
Nassau Sound	-0:15	+0:04
Amelia City, S. Amelia River	+0:42	+1:01
Nassauville, Nassau River	+0:52	+1:35
Mink Creek entrance, Nassau R.	+1:46	+2:30
Halfmoon Island, highway bridge	+2:48	+3:19
Sawpit Creek entrance	-0:14	+0:28
Ft. George Island, Ft.George R.	+0:17	+0:37
St. Johns River		
South Jetty	-0:35	-0:19
Pablo Creek bascule bridge	+1:27	+1:13
Fulton	+0:17	+0:40
Dame Point	+0:34	+0:53
Phoenix Park, (Cummers Mill)	+0:46	+1:23
Jacksonville, (Dredge Depot)	+1:12	+1:48
Jacksonville, (RR bridge)	+1:54	+2:11
Ortega River entrance	+2:15	+2:48
Orange Park	+3:37	+4:12
Green Cove Springs	+5:14	+6:11
East Tocoi	+6:35	+7:16
Bridgeport	+6:46	+7:30
Palatka	+7:14	+8:19
Welaka	+7:34	+8:23
Atlantic Beach	-0:37	-0:20
St. Augustine Inlet	-0:33	-0:03
St. Augustine	+0:02	+0:41
Daytona Beach, (ocean)	-0:45	-0:34

INSHORE

Time for a cool change, and a fired-up, all-day inshore bite. **Redfish**, **seatrout** and **black drum** lead the charge. Tidal creekmouths, spartina-lined mud-bottom creeks and oyster mounds will all hold these species.

Flounder continue the inlet spawn, with **sheepshead** coming on as well as waters cool. Soak shrimp near jetty rocks for a chance at both species, but go with finger mullet to specifically target flounder. Crabs and sandfleas are tops for sheepshead. The jetty bag may also include big **croakers**. In the surf, crab baits cast to sandbars take **pompano** and **whiting**.

OFFSHORE

Nearshore wrecks and ledges can be reached by small-boaters when seas allow for fast **grouper** and **snapper** fishing. **Gag grouper**, **red snapper**, **vermilion snapper** and **sea bass** will scarf squid, frozen sardines and baitfish over structure 10 to 15 miles offshore, which is 50- to 80-pound rod country. Target **sailfish** out of Ponce Inlet in waters from 100 to 400 feet. Run to the edge of the Gulf Stream and troll a varied spread of lures for **marlin**, **dolphin**, **wahoo** and **yellowfin tuna**.

November Spotlight: GAG GROUPER

Your best chance for a braggin' size **gag grouper** awaits on the wrecks, reefs and ledges in less than 80 feet. For comfort and most effective bait presentation, pick a day between windy fronts. Live baits are best, so load the livewell with pinfish, or mullet and pogies. A stout boat rod in the 50-pound class rigged with a single-hook, sliding-sinker rig consisting of a 6-foot fluorocarbon leader. For **red grouper** fish over patchy hard bottom in 100-plus feet. Limestone holes hold aggressive studs that attack bucktails tipped with bonito strips. **Scamp** and **snowy grouper** hang near deeper wrecks.

November 2011

SUNDAY	MONDAY	TUESDAY	WEDNESDAY	THURSDAY	FRIDAY	SATURDAY
		1 ◐	**2**	**3**	**4**	**5**
		2:28a 5.0' / 3:03p 5.5'	3:28a 4.9' / 4:02p 5.3'	4:30a 4.9' / 5:01p 5.2'	5:31a 5.0' / 5:57p 5.1'	6:27a 5.1' / 6:48p 5.0'
		8:14a 0.7' / 9:12p 0.9'	9:21a 1.0' / 10:11p 1.0'	10:25a 1.2' / 11:04p 1.0'	11:24a 1.2' / 11:54p 1.0'	12:18p 1.2'
6	**7**	**8**	**9** ○	**10**	**11**	**12**
5:16a 5.2' / 5:34p 5.0'	6:00a 5.3' / 6:16p 4.9'	6:41a 5.4' / 6:55p 4.8'	7:19a 5.5' / 7:33p 4.8'	7:56a 5.5' / 8:11p 4.7'	8:33a 5.4' / 8:49p 4.7'	9:10a 5.4' / 9:28p 4.6'
12:40a 0.9' / 11:10a 1.1'	11:24p 0.9' / 11:57a 1.0'	12:05a 0.8' / 12:42p 0.9'	12:43a 0.7' / 1:22p 0.8'	1:18a 0.6' / 2:00p 0.8'	1:51a 0.6' / 2:34p 0.8'	2:22a 0.6' / 3:07p 0.8'
13	**14**	**15**	**16**	**17** ◐	**18**	**19**
9:48a 5.4' / 10:07p 4.6'	10:27a 5.3' / 10:48p 4.5'	11:09a 5.3' / 11:33p 4.6'	11:54a 5.3'	12:21a 4.6' / 12:43p 5.2'	1:16a 4.8' / 1:38p 5.2'	2:17a 4.9' / 2:38p 5.1'
2:54a 0.6' / 3:40p 0.9'	3:30a 0.7' / 4:17p 1.0'	4:12a 0.8' / 5:01p 1.1'	5:01a 0.9' / 5:51p 1.1'	5:59a 1.0' / 6:47p 1.0'	7:04a 1.0' / 7:45p 0.8'	8:13a 0.9' / 8:42p 0.5'
20	**21**	**22**	**23**	**24** ●	**25**	**26**
3:22a 5.2' / 3:42p 5.1'	4:26a 5.4' / 4:44p 5.1'	5:26a 5.7' / 5:44p 5.1'	6:23a 5.9' / 6:40p 5.1'	7:18a 6.0' / 7:36p 5.1'	8:12a 6.1' / 8:30p 5.0'	9:05a 6.0' / 9:24p 5.0'
	🐟	🐟	🐟	🐟	🐟	🐟
9:20a 0.7' / 9:38p 0.3'	10:24a 0.5' / 10:35p 0.0'	11:25a 0.2' / 11:30p -0.3'	12:23p -0.1'	12:25a -0.6' / 1:18p -0.3'	1:18a -0.7' / 2:10p -0.4'	2:09a -0.7' / 3:01p -0.4'
27	**28**	**29**	**30**			
9:58a 5.8' / 10:17p 4.9'	10:49a 5.6' / 11:09p 4.8'	11:39a 5.4' / 12:02p 4.7'	12:30p 5.1'			
🐟	🐟					
3:00a -0.5' / 3:53p -0.2'	3:52a -0.2' / 4:46p 0.0'	4:48a 0.1' / 5:42p 0.3'	5:47a 0.5' / 6:38p 0.5'			

Gaffer dolphin off Ormond Beach.

	November 1	November 15	November 30
SUNRISE	7:41 a.m.	6:52 a.m.	7:05 a.m.
SUNSET	6:39 p.m.	5:30 p.m.	5:26 p.m.

DST Ends on Nov. 6

Jacksonville to Daytona Beach Including the St. Johns River

'Head Games

INSHORE

Sheepshead stack up along dock and bridge pilings where chumming fires the bite. On the beach, good numbers of **whiting** are biting sandfleas and shrimp on fishfinder rigs. **Black drum**, **flounder** and **redfish** join the surf roster, with Flagler and St. Augustine beaches popular with locals.

Seatrout will school up and take both plugs and bottom lures in deeper ICW creeks. The deepest holes and feeder creeks of the St. Johns River hold **weakfish**.

OFFSHORE

Cobia, huge **redfish** and **amberjack** are on hand at near-shore wrecks; best baits to send down include live pogies, mullet and crabs. Local knowledge helps for such wreck trips—find a cluster of them 10 to 15 miles out to shorten the hunt and save gas. **Gag** and **red groupers** and **red snapper** are stationed over nearshore hard bottom. In 100 feet or more, throw **African pompano** into the mix. The Ledge holds **wahoo** for those rigged to fast-troll with one lure down to better determine the hot depth.

TIDE CORRECTIONS For Mayport	High	Low
Nassau Sound, Ft. George River		
St. Marys, St. Marys River	+1:19	+1:13
Crandall, St. Marys River	+2:08	+2:02
Fernandina Beach, outer coast	-0:30	-0:03
Fernandina Beach, Amelia River	+0:20	+0:14
Chester, Bells River	+0:37	+0:39
SCL RR bridge, Kingsley Creek	+0:47	+0:41
Nassau Sound	-0:15	+0:04
Amelia City, S. Amelia River	+0:42	+1:01
Nassauville, Nassau River	+0:52	+1:35
Mink Creek entrance, Nassau R.	+1:46	+2:30
Halfmoon Island, highway bridge	+2:48	+3:19
Sawpit Creek entrance	-0:14	+0:28
Ft. George Island, Ft.George R.	+0:17	+0:37
St. Johns River		
South Jetty	-0:35	-0:19
Pablo Creek bascule bridge	+0:17	+0:40
Fulton	+0:17	+0:40
Dame Point	+0:34	+0:53
Phoenix Park, (Cummers Mill)	+0:46	+1:23
Jacksonville, (Dredge Depot)	+1:12	+1:48
Jacksonville, (RR bridge)	+1:54	+2:11
Ortega River entrance	+2:15	+2:48
Orange Park	+3:37	+4:12
Green Cove Springs	+5:14	+6:11
East Tocoi	+6:35	+7:16
Bridgeport	+6:46	+7:24
Palatka	+7:14	+8:19
Welaka	+7:34	+8:23
Atlantic Beach	-0:37	-0:20
St. Augustine Inlet	-0:33	-0:03
St. Augustine	+0:02	+0:41
Daytona Beach, (ocean)	-0:45	-0:34

December Spotlight: SHEEPSHEAD

Striped bandits, convict fish, 'heads—call 'em what you will—**sheepshead** are numerous all winter, and do have a penchant for stealing your bait. You can catch plenty smack against dock and bridge pilings, or against rocky jetties by soaking a fiddler crab, fresh oyster, shrimp or a sandflea on a small hook and lightest weight possible to hold bottom. But real sheepshead vets chum likely structure with oysters and shovel-scraped barnacles. To increase hookup percentages, use a light-wire hook and braided polyethylene line for a most-sensitive presentation. Wait for the tap-tap and set the hook. Or, strike back just before the bite!

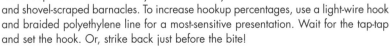

December 2011

SUNDAY	MONDAY	TUESDAY	WEDNESDAY	THURSDAY	FRIDAY	SATURDAY

A red snapper for the photo album.

Week of Dec 1–3

				THURSDAY 1 ◐	FRIDAY 2	SATURDAY 3
				12:56a 4.6' · 1:21p 4.9'	1:52a 4.6' · 2:14p 4.7'	2:49a 4.6' · 8:50a 1.1'
				6:50a 0.8' · 7:33p 0.6'	7:52a 1.0' · 8:24p 0.7'	8:50a 1.1' · 9:12p 0.8'

Week of Dec 4–10

SUNDAY 4	MONDAY 5	TUESDAY 6	WEDNESDAY 7	THURSDAY 8	FRIDAY 9 ○	SATURDAY 10
3:45a 4.7' · 4:00p 4.4'	4:37a 4.8' · 4:50p 4.3'	5:24a 4.9' · 5:37p 4.3'	6:08a 5.0' · 6:21p 4.3'	6:49a 5.1' · 7:03p 4.3'	7:29a 5.1' · 7:44p 4.3'	8:09a 5.1' · 8:24p 4.3'
9:45a 1.1' · 9:58p 0.8'	10:37a 1.1' · 10:43p 0.7'	11:27a 0.9' · 11:26p 0.6'	12:13p 0.8' · 12:07a 0.5'	12:55p 0.6' · 12:46a 0.3'	1:34p 0.5' · 1:23p 0.2'	2:10p 0.4'

Week of Dec 11–17

SUNDAY 11	MONDAY 12	TUESDAY 13	WEDNESDAY 14	THURSDAY 15	FRIDAY 16	SATURDAY 17
8:48a 5.1' · 9:05p 4.3'	9:27a 5.1' · 9:46p 4.3'	10:07a 5.1' · 10:29p 4.3'	10:49a 5.1' · 11:14p 4.4'	11:33a 5.0'	12:03a 4.5' · 12:20p 4.9'	12:56a 4.6' · 1:13p 4.8'
1:58a 0.1' · 2:44p 0.3'	2:34a 0.1' · 3:19p 0.3'	3:12a 0.1' · 3:56p 0.3'	3:55a 0.2' · 4:38p 0.3'	4:45a 0.3' · 5:25p 0.3'	5:42a 0.4' · 6:18p 0.2'	6:47a 0.5' · 7:15p 0.1'

Week of Dec 18–24

SUNDAY 18 ◑	MONDAY 19	TUESDAY 20	WEDNESDAY 21	THURSDAY 22	FRIDAY 23 ●	SATURDAY 24
1:56a 4.8' · 2:13p 4.6'	3:02a 4.9' · 3:18p 4.5'	4:09a 5.1' · 4:25p 4.4'	5:13a 5.3' · 5:28p 4.4'	6:12a 5.4' · 6:27p 4.5'	7:08a 5.5' · 7:23p 4.5'	8:01a 5.5' · 8:16p 4.5'
7:56a 0.5' · 8:14p 0.0'	9:04a 0.4' · 9:13p -0.2'	10:09a 0.2' · 10:13p -0.4'	11:11a 0.0' · 11:12p -0.6'	12:10p -0.3' · 12:10a -0.8'	1:05p -0.5' · 1:04a -0.9'	1:56p -0.6'

Week of Dec 25–31

SUNDAY 25	MONDAY 26	TUESDAY 27	WEDNESDAY 28	THURSDAY 29	FRIDAY 30	SATURDAY 31
8:51a 5.5' · 9:08p 4.5'	9:39a 5.3' · 9:57p 4.5'	10:25a 5.1' · 10:45p 4.4'	11:09a 4.9' · 11:32p 4.4'	11:52a 4.6'	12:19a 4.3' · 12:36p 4.4'	1:07a 4.3' · 1:21p 4.1'
1:56a -0.9' · 2:45p -0.7'	2:46a -0.8' · 3:33p -0.6'	3:35a -0.6' · 4:20p -0.4'	4:24a -0.3' · 5:08p -0.2'	5:17a 0.1' · 5:56p 0.1'	6:13a 0.4' · 6:46p 0.3'	7:12a 0.7' · 7:35p 0.4'

	December 1	December 15	December 30
SUNRISE	7:05 a.m.	7:16 a.m.	7:23 a.m.
SUNSET	5:26 p.m.	5:28 p.m.	5:36 p.m.

MIAMI STATION Ponce Inlet • Cape Canaveral • Sebastian • Vero Beach
Ft. Pierce • Stuart • Jupiter • Palm Beach • Hillsboro
Ft. Lauderdale • Miami • Homestead • Key Largo

Mix it Up Inside and Offshore

Surf fishing is as popular as ever along the Southeast Coast.

Update 2011: This Florida Atlantic coast region is unique in the fact that flats, general inshore, surf and bluewater fisheries are so close in proximity. Check this out for variety: **Bonefishing** in Biscayne Bay and **dolphin** fishing can be done in a half-day from a skiff on a flat summer day. Or, jump winter **tarpon** inside an inlet in the wee hours and then bag a catch of **Spanish mackerel** just outside the inlet mouths. Or, put a **sailfish** in the air just a short boat ride away at the blue edge. And there are many, many other such opportunities. **Spotted seatrout** in good shape throughout the region, with rebounding numbers in Biscayne Bay, and plenty of gators from Stuart to Mosquito Lagoon. **Snook** fishing took a hit from the freeze, but fishable numbers exist from the rivers to the beaches. **Spanish mackerel** fishing is superb along beaches, with lots of summer holdovers. Plenty of migratory **tarpon** on sight fishing flats south of Miami and north on beaches to Cape Canaveral. The winter/spring **sailfishing** was a repeat of recent seasons, with **dolphin** chiming in with numerous slammers in the Upper Keys. **Cobia** provided an intense spring run and **kingfish** remain as strong as ever. Bottom fishing featured good **mangrove snapper** north, and **yellowtails** in Upper Keys.

A light-tackle angler could easily spend two lifetimes learning each nook and cranny in the marvelously diverse waters of this tidal region. There are record-class redfish on the flats of the

Banana River, doormat-size flounder in Sebastian Inlet, mammoth snook in Jupiter Inlet, huge trout in the Indian River, the biggest, most clever bonefish in Biscayne Bay, and slab-sided permit in the Keys— and that's just the start.

Along with boundless inshore possibilities, the warm, fertile waters of the Gulf Stream swing in close here. Offshore and reef opportunities abound, with seasonal runs of sailfish, mackerel, dolphin, tunas and plenty of resident grouper and snapper.

Angling is as much a lifestyle as it is a sport in this region. Much of Florida's sportfishing history is part of local lore in towns like Stuart, Palm Beach, Miami and Islamorada. There are numerous tackle shops, charter docks, fishing tournaments, boat builders, rod builders and fishing

Tides play an important role in nearly all the region's fisheries, and a quick look at the monthly predictions can clue you in to the best bite. Most popular fish bite best with some moving current, but there are some specific times that you'll learn about in each month's fishing report.

The tides for this region are based on measurements from the entrance of Government Cut at the south end of Miami Beach. Keep in mind that for inshore waters like the Indian and Banana rivers, Lake Worth and Biscayne Bay, the tide must pass through narrow inlets, which means the tide stage will follow the ocean by up to several hours.

Many of the bays in this area are served by two or more inlets and since the geography tends to be north-to-south, the currents created by the tide run toward the nearest inlet. Knowing which inlet influences the tide where you're fishing is important. Most gamefish, like redfish, face into the current when hunting food. In the Indian River Lagoon, for example, if you know a certain flat is drained through Fort Pierce Inlet, you can predict the direction of flow for a given tide.

As with the tides at Mayport near Jacksonville, there are two tides daily

Wahoo are commonly caught by anglers trolling deep and fast.

clubs, and they're all here for the same thrills that bring smiles to family anglers each weekend.

Despite a booming population and rapidly growing cities, there's still more than enough good fishing to go around, and plenty of casting room.

from Cape Canaveral southward to Long Key, but local weather conditions can greatly affect the highs and lows. Heavy winds can reduce or enhance tidal ranges and therefore the velocity of the current. This is especially true in shallow lagoons like the Banana River.

Average Tidal Range at Miami: 2.5 feet
Average Range of Spring Tides: 3.0 feet

Cape Canaveral to Islamorada

MIAMI

Spindlebeakin'

INSHORE

Indian River Lagoon anglers can expect influx of **pompano**, **bluefish** and **Spanish mackerel** over shoals and grassflats; **seatrout** best on warm days. Miami's Biscayne Bay shallows see **bonefish** between cold fronts, and **barracuda** take up the slack on coldest days. Surf fishing features pompano, blues and Spanish, with **sheepshead** and small **black drum** at bridges and jetties from Jupiter north. **Tarpon** pile up just inside inlets to feast during shrimp runs between Palm Beach and Miami. Look for **redfish** on IRL flats on warm days.

OFFSHORE

Kitefishing and trolling with dredges is the hot ticket for **sailfish** anglers from Jupiter south in roughly 90 to 200 feet. Same depth over reef will produce **African pompano**, **amberjack** and **cobia**. Season is closed on most **groupers**. Anglers dialed in on **swordfish** catch them night and day, with specimens over 200 pounds fairly commonplace. Cross the Stream to the Bahamas and fast-troll with lures for speedy **wahoo**.

January Spotlight: SAILFISH

Sailfishing comes into its own and can be epic, with multiple catches possible on the tail of cold fronts. From now through spring, most fish will come on trolled natural baits or live baits under kites on the western edge of the Gulf Stream from Fort Pierce through Miami. The key is to fish around concentrations of top sailfish prey such as ballyhoo (from Miami south) sardines and goggle-eyes. Hot action can be had where a north swell and northbound current converge along a distinct blue-green color change. Top that off with a water temp of 73 and above and you'll be flying those release flags.

TIDE CORRECTIONS *For Government Cut*	High	Low
Ponce de Leon Inlet	+0:04	+0:21
Cape Canaveral	-0:43	-0:40
Indian River		
Palm Bay	+3:38	+4:20
Wabasso	+2:46	+3:20
Vero Beach	+3:19	+3:51
Ft. Pierce	+1:06	+1:02
Jensen Beach	+2:38	+3:07
Sebastian Inlet	-0:26	-0:19
Vero Beach, (ocean)	-0:33	-0:24
Ft. Pierce Inlet, south jetty	-0:11	-0:13
St. Lucie River		
N. Fork	+2:48	+3:30
Stuart	+2:35	+3:34
S. Fork	+2:52	+3:35
Sewall Point	+1:33	+2:12
St. Lucie Inlet	-0:32	-0:13
Great Pocket	+1:16	+1:52
Gomez, S. Jupiter Narrows	+1:54	+2:42
Hobe Sound—State Park	+1:44	+2:23
Conch Bar, Jupiter Sound	+1:17	+1:39
Jupiter Sound, south end	+0:44	+0:50
Jupiter Inlet	+0:13	+0:02
Loxahatchee River		
Tequesta	+1:16	+2:03
N. Fork	+1:25	+2:00
Southwest Fork, (spillway)	+1:13	+1:50
Northwest Fork	+1:32	+2:01
Southwest Fork	+1:13	+1:48
Jupiter, Lake Worth Creek	+0:55	+1:17
Donald Ross Bridge	+0:41	+0:55
N. Palm Beach, Lake Worth Creek	+0:03	+0:18
Port of Palm Beach, Lake Worth	-0:02	+0:13
Palm Beach, (ocean)	-0:23	-0:17
W. Palm Beach Canal	+1:06	+1:37
Lake Worth Pier, (ocean)	-0:21	-0:16
Boynton Beach	+1:24	+2:10
Delray Beach	+1:43	+2:10
Yamato	+1:41	+2:00
Boca Raton	+0:45	+1:14
Deerfield Beach	+0:49	+1:08
Hillsboro Beach, Intracoastal Waterway	+0:24	+0:39
Hillsboro Inlet, (inside)	+0:06	+0:07
Lauderdale-By-the-Sea	-0:10	-0:07
Ft. Lauderdale		
Bahia Mar Yacht Club	+0:17	+0:39
Andrews Avenue Bridge, New River	+0:37	+0:57
Port Everglades	-0:08	-0:05
South Port Everglades	-0:02	+0:02
Hollywood Beach	+0:58	+1:09
Golden Beach	+1:34	+2:05
Sunny Isles, Biscayne Creek	+2:21	+2:28
North Miami Beach	-0:06	+0:01
Bakers Haulover Inlet, (inside)	+1:15	+1:36
Indian Creek	+1:34	+1:51
Miami Beach	-0:02	+0:01
Biscayne Bay		
Miami, 79th St. Causeway	+1:43	+2:14
Miami, Marina	+0:54	+1:18
Miami, Causeway(east end)	+1:17	+1:11
Dinner Key Marina	+1:17	+1:51
Cape Florida (west side), Key Biscayne	+0:47	+1:03
Cutler, Biscayne Bay	+1:23	+2:02
Soldier Key	+0:53	+1:20
Fowey Rocks	+0:01	+0:03
Ragged Keys, Biscayne Bay	+1:13	+1:45
Elliott Key, (outside)	-0:04	0:00
Elliott Key Harbor	+2:26	+3:25
Adams Key, Biscayne Bay	+2:48	+2:34
Christmas Point, Elliott Key	+0:35	+0:39
Totten Key, Biscayne Bay	+2:33	+3:26
Totten Key	+2:48	+3:45
Ocean Reef Club, Key Largo	+0:11	+0:20
Garden Cove, Key Largo	+0:34	+1:10
Mosquito Bank	+0:22	+0:31
Molasses Reef	+0:14	+0:12
Pumpkin Key, Card Sound	+3:10	+3:16
Tavernier, Hawk Channel	+0:29	+0:28
Alligator Reef Light	+0:40	+0:34

January 2011

SUNDAY	MONDAY	TUESDAY	WEDNESDAY	THURSDAY	FRIDAY	SATURDAY

Tarpon on the roll.

MIAMI

1
6:07a 6:13p
2.5' 2.3'

11:47a
0.2'

2
7:00a 7:05p
2.5' 2.4'

12:07a 12:38p
-0.4' 0.1'

3 ●
7:47a 7:53p
2.5' 2.4'

12:57a 1:26p
-0.4' 0.0'

4
8:30a 8:37p
2.5' 2.4'

1:43a 2:11p
-0.4' 0.0'

5
9:10a 9:19p
2.5' 2.3'

2:27a 2:54p
-0.3' 0.0'

6
9:49a 10:00p
2.4' 2.3'

3:09a 3:36p
-0.3' 0.0'

7
10:25a 10:40p
2.4' 2.2'

3:50a 4:16p
-0.2' 0.0'

8
11:01a 11:21p
2.3' 2.1'

4:30a 4:56p
0.0' 0.0'

9
11:38a
2.1'

5:10a 5:37p
0.1' 0.1'

10
12:03a 12:16p
2.0' 2.0'

5:51a 6:20p
0.2' 0.1

11 ◗
12:48a 12:57p
1.9' 1.9'

6:37a 7:06p
0.4' 0.2'

12
1:39a 1:43p
1.9' 1.9'

7:28a 7:58p
0.4' 0.2'

13
2:35a 2:36p
1.8' 1.8'

8:25a 8:53p
0.5' 0.1'

14
3:36a 3:35p
1.9' 1.8'

9:25a 9:49p
0.5' 0.0'

15
4:37a 4:37p
1.9' 1.9

10:22a 10:43p
0.4' -0.1'

16
5:35a 5:36p
2.1' 2.0'

11:16a 11:35p
0.3' -0.3'

17
6:28a 6:31p
2.2' 2.1'

12:06p
0.1'

18 ○
7:17a 7:23p
2.4' 2.3'

12:24a 12:54p
-0.4' 0.0'

19
8:04a 8:14p
2.5' 2.4'

1:13a 1:42p
-0.6' -0.2'

20
8:49a 9:04p
2.6' 2.5'

2:00a 2:29p
-0.6' -0.4'

21
9:34a 9:54p
2.7' 2.6'

2:48a 3:16p
-0.7' -0.5'

22
10:20a 10:45p
2.6' 2.6'

3:37a 4:05p
-0.6' -0.6'

23
11:06a 11:38p
2.6' 2.5'

4:28a 4:57p
-0.5' -0.6'

24
11:55a
2.5'

5:21a 5:51p
-0.3' -0.5'

25 ◗
12:34a 12:47p
2.4' 2.3'

6:18a 6:50p
-0.2' -0.5'

26
1:34a 1:45p
2.3' 2.2'

7:20a 7:52p
0.0' -0.4'

27
2:38a 2:48p
2.2' 2.1'

8:26a 8:57p
0.1' -0.3'

28
3:46a 3:55p
2.1' 2.0'

9:32a 10:01p
0.2' -0.3'

29
4:53a 5:00p
2.1' 2.0'

10:35a 11:00p
0.2' -0.3'

30
5:52a 5:59p
2.2' 2.1'

11:32a 11:54p
0.1' -0.3'

31
6:44a 6:51p
2.2' 2.1'

12:24p
0.0'

Dolphin outside Jupiter Inlet.

	January 1	January 15	January 30
SUNRISE	7:08 a.m.	7:09 a.m.	7:05 a.m.
SUNSET	5:42 p.m.	5:52 p.m.	6:03 p.m.

Cape Canaveral to Islamorada

Pumped for Pompano

INSHORE

Pompano begin their run along the beaches and in the Intracoastal Waterway. Steep beaches and grassy, shell shoals are top spots. **Snook** fishing beat on structure: bridges, lighted docks and channel edges. Magic water temp 70 and above. **Seatrout** best on warm afternoons in IRL in three feet or more. Some **reds** take to flats on sunny days. Big **bonefish** and first push of **permit** in Biscayne Bay on mild days.

OFFSHORE

Sailfishing is world-class in 90 to 200 feet. **Amberjack** will test your muscles over wrecks and humps at the same depth. Drop a jig or live bait for the jacks and you might also hook a **wahoo**. Trolling on top produces **blackfin tuna** and **dolphin**. Fish a wreck holding bait and **kingfish** are assured. Keep an eye peeled and a live bait ready to pitch to early **cobia**, and leaping, twisting **spinner sharks** from right off the beach.

February Spotlight: POMPANO

Delicious **pompano** cast a spell on seafood aficionados and anglers of all persuasions. This hard-fighting fish has made a comeback in Florida, and is right at home in not only the surf, but inside inlets, over grassflats and shoals, and at bridges in the Intracostal Waterway. Tackle up with 10- to 10-foot surf rods and heavy sinkers to hold sandfleas, shrimp or clams on bottom when surf is up, and to reach fish on far bars, or lighter tackle when fish are close to the beach. Inshore, watch for fish skipping in your boat wake around sand or shell flats. Traditional pompano jigs, Clouser Minnow flies or similar pomano "jig-flies" are eagerly accepted.

TIDE CORRECTIONS
For Government Cut

	High	Low
Ponce de Leon Inlet	+0:04	+0:21
Cape Canaveral	-0:43	-0:40
Indian River		
Palm Bay	+3:38	+4:20
Wabasso	+2:46	+3:20
Vero Beach	+3:19	+3:51
Ft. Pierce	+1:06	+1:02
Jensen Beach	+2:38	+3:07
Sebastian Inlet	-0:26	-0:19
Vero Beach, (ocean)	-0:33	-0:24
Ft. Pierce Inlet, south jetty	-0:11	-0:13
St. Lucie River		
N. Fork	+2:48	+3:30
Stuart	+2:35	+3:34
S. Fork	+2:52	+3:35
Sewall Point	+1:33	+2:12
St. Lucie Inlet	-0:32	-0:13
Great Pocket	+1:16	+1:52
Gomez, S. Jupiter Narrows	+1:54	+2:42
Hobe Sound — State Park	+1:44	+2:23
Conch Bar, Jupiter Sound	+1:17	+1:39
Jupiter Sound, south end	+0:44	+0:50
Jupiter Inlet	+0:13	+0:02
Loxahatchee River		
Tequesta	+1:16	+2:03
N. Fork	+1:25	+2:00
Southwest Fork, (spillway)	+1:13	+1:50
Northwest Fork	+1:32	+2:11
Southwest Fork	+1:13	+1:48
Jupiter, Lake Worth Creek	+0:55	+1:17
Donald Ross Bridge	+0:41	+0:55
N. Palm Beach, Lake Worth Creek	+0:03	+0:18
Port of Palm Beach, Lake Worth	-0:02	+0:13
Palm Beach, (ocean)	-0:23	-0:17
W. Palm Beach Canal	+1:06	+1:37
Lake Worth Pier, (ocean)	-0:21	-0:16
Boynton Beach	+1:24	+2:10
Delray Beach	+1:43	+2:10
Yamato	+1:41	+2:00
Boca Raton	+0:45	+1:14
Deerfield Beach	+0:49	+1:08
Hillsboro Beach, Intracoastal Waterway	+0:24	+0:39
Hillsboro Inlet, (inside)	+0:06	+0:07
Lauderdale-By-the-Sea	-0:10	-0:07
Ft. Lauderdale		
Bahia Mar Yacht Club	+0:17	+0:39
Andrews Avenue Bridge, New River	+0:37	+0:57
Port Everglades	-0:08	-0:05
South Port Everglades	-0:02	+0:02
Hollywood Beach	+0:58	+1:09
Golden Beach	+1:34	+2:05
Sunny Isles, Biscayne Creek	+2:21	+2:28
North Miami Beach	-0:06	+0:01
Bakers Haulover Inlet, (inside)	+1:15	+1:36
Indian Creek	+1:34	+1:51
Miami Beach	-0:02	+0:01
Biscayne Bay		
Miami, 79th St. Causeway	+1:43	+2:14
Miami, Marina	+0:54	+1:18
Miami, Causeway(east end)	+1:17	+1:11
Dinner Key Marina	+1:17	+1:51
Cape Florida (west side), Key Biscayne	+0:47	+1:03
Cutler, Biscayne Bay	+1:23	+2:02
Soldier Key	+0:53	+1:20
Fowey Rocks	+0:01	+0:03
Ragged Keys, Biscayne Bay	+1:13	+1:05
Elliott Key, (outside)	-0:04	0:00
Elliott Key Harbor	+2:26	+3:25
Adams Key, Biscayne Bay	+2:35	+3:39
Christmas Point, Elliott Key	+0:35	+0:39
Turkey Point, Biscayne Bay	+2:48	+2:34
Totten Key	+2:48	+3:45
Ocean Reef Club, Key Largo	+0:11	+0:20
Garden Cove, Key Largo	+0:34	+1:10
Mosquito Bank	+0:22	+0:31
Molasses Reef	+0:14	+0:12
Pumpkin Key, Card Sound	+3:10	+3:16
Tavernier, Hawk Channel	+0:29	+0:28
Alligator Reef Light	+0:40	+0:34

February 2011

MIAMI

SUNDAY	MONDAY	TUESDAY	WEDNESDAY	THURSDAY	FRIDAY	SATURDAY
		1	**2** ●	**3**	**4**	**5**
		7:29a 2.3' / 7:37p 2.2'	8:09a 2.3' / 8:19p 2.2'	8:46a 2.3' / 8:58p 2.2'	9:20a 2.3' / 9:35p 2.2'	9:54a 2.2' / 10:12p 2.2'
		12:43a -0.4' / 1:10p -0.1'	1:27a -0.4' / 1:52p -0.1'	2:08a -0.4' / 2:31p -0.2'	2:47a -0.3' / 3:09p -0.2'	3:23a -0.2' / 3:44p -0.2'
6	**7**	**8**	**9**	**10**	**11** ◑	**12**
10:27a 2.2' / 10:49p 2.1'	11:01a 2.1' / 11:28p 2.0'	11:36a 2.0' / 12:09a 1.9'	12:13p 1.9' / 12:55a 1.9'	12:56p 1.8' / 1:49a 1.8'	1:48p 1.7' / 2:51a 1.8'	2:51p 1.7'
3:59a -0.1' / 4:19p -0.2'	4:34a 0.0' / 4:54p -0.1'	5:10a 0.1' / 5:31p -0.1'	5:48a 0.2 / 6:12p 0.0'	6:34a 0.3' / 7:02p 0.0'	7:29a 0.4' / 8:01p 0.0'	8:34a 0.4' / 9:05p 0.0'
13	**14**	**15**	**16**	**17**	**18** ○	**19**
3:58a 1.8' / 4:00p 1.8'	5:02a 2.0' / 5:08p 1.9'	5:59a 2.2' / 6:09p 2.1'	6:50a 2.3' / 7:04p 2.4'	7:38a 2.5' / 7:56p 2.5'	8:25a 2.6' / 8:47p 2.7'	9:10a 2.7' / 9:37p 2.8'
9:41a 0.4' / 10:08p -0.1'	10:43a 0.2' / 11:07p -0.3'	11:38a 0.0' / 12:01a -0.4'	12:30p -0.2' / 12:53a -0.6'	1:19p -0.4' / 1:42a -0.7'	2:08p -0.6' / 2:31a -0.7'	2:56p -0.8'
20	**21**	**22**	**23** ◐	**24**	**25**	**26**
9:56a 2.7' / 10:27p 2.7'	10:43a 2.6' / 11:19p 2.6'	11:32a 2.5' / 12:13a 2.5'	12:24p 2.5' / 1:11a 2.3'	1:22p 2.3' / 2:15a 2.2'	2:26p 2.1' / 3:23a 2.0'	3:35p 2.0'
3:20a -0.6' / 3:45p -0.8'	4:10a -0.5' / 4:35p -0.8'	5:02a -0.3' / 5:29p -0.6'	5:58a -0.1' / 6:27p -0.5'	6:58a 0.0' / 7:29p -0.3'	8:04a 0.2' / 8:36p -0.2'	9:12a 0.3' / 9:42p -0.1'
27	**28**					
4:30a 2.0' / 4:43p 2.0'	5:30a 2.1' / 5:42p 2.0'					
10:17a 0.2' / 10:43p -0.1'	11:14a 0.2' / 11:37p -0.1'					

Night fishing payoff.

	February 1	February 15	February 28
SUNRISE	7:05 a.m.	6:56 a.m.	6:45 a.m.
SUNSET	6:05 p.m.	6:14 p.m.	6:22 p.m.

Cape Canaveral to Islamorada

Mack is Back

INSHORE

Spring brings warming water temps that improve the bite for **seatrout**, **snook** and **redfish** on the Indian River Lagoon. Biscayne Bay comes on strong for trophy **bonefish** and **permit**. Hordes of **Spanish mackerel** and **bluefish** will shadow bait schools along beaches, and pour into inlets, and over inside flats and channels. **Bluefish** and **pompano** plentiful in surf throughout region, but rarely mix. Just off the beach, run and look for **cobia** and bruiser **jack crevalle**. Pier and jetty anglers rally for **kingfish** that occasionally raid the structures.

OFFSHORE

Time for **dolphin** of a lifetime, in the 40- to 50-pound class along edge in 100 feet or more, especially around flotsam. Best approach for **sailfish** is to troll rigged baits or livies; kite presentation tops down south. During calmer periods, it's worthwhile to soak baits for **snapper** and **amberjack** on the reefs. **Cobia** hunters run on plane in 30 to 60 feet to spot manta rays and pitch baits or jigs to fish underneath. **Tripletail** are a possbility around floating debris or weed rafts.

March Spotlight: SPANISH MACKEREL

Where aren't **Spanish mackerel** these days? The fishery is tremendous in Florida Bay, Hawks Channel off Miami, Biscayne Bay near Key Biscayne, and Hobe Sound's Peck Lake. One- to 3-pounders are typical, with some fish up to 7 or 8 pounds. Many

methods score: Retrieve spoons or jigs at warp speed, freeline pilchards or live shrimp under a float. Fly rodders mop 'em up on small, flashy baitfish patterns. Signs of fish include diving birds, surface busts and even bait "oil" slicks. To attract fish, soak a chumbag stuffed with blood chum and toss out glass minnows where there's current. Toothy macks call for heavy mono or light wire leader or tippet.

TIDE CORRECTIONS For Government Cut	High	Low
Ponce de Leon Inlet	+0:04	+0:21
Cape Canaveral	-0:43	-0:40
Indian River		
Palm Bay	+3:38	+4:20
Wabasso	+2:46	+3:20
Vero Beach	+3:19	+3:51
Ft. Pierce	+1:06	+1:02
Jensen Beach	+2:38	+3:07
Sebastian Inlet	-0:26	-0:19
Vero Beach, (ocean)	-0:33	-0:24
Ft. Pierce Inlet, south jetty	-0:11	-0:13
St. Lucie River		
N. Fork	+2:48	+3:30
Stuart	+2:35	+3:34
S. Fork	+2:52	+3:35
Sewall Point	+1:33	+2:12
St. Lucie Inlet	-0:32	-0:13
Great Pocket	+1:16	+1:52
Gomez, S. Jupiter Narrows	+1:54	+2:42
Hobe Sound—State Park	+1:44	+2:23
Conch Bar, Jupiter Sound	+1:17	+1:39
Jupiter Sound, south end	+0:44	+0:50
Jupiter Inlet	+0:13	+0:02
Loxahatchee River		
Tequesta	+1:16	+2:03
N. Fork	+1:25	+2:00
Southwest Fork, (spillway)	+1:13	+1:50
Northwest Fork	+1:32	+2:11
Southwest Fork	+1:13	+1:48
Jupiter, Lake Worth Creek	+0:55	+1:17
Donald Ross Bridge	+0:41	+0:55
N. Palm Beach, Lake Worth Creek	+0:03	+0:18
Port of Palm Beach, Lake Worth	-0:02	+0:13
Palm Beach, (ocean)	-0:23	-0:17
W. Palm Beach Canal	+1:06	+1:37
Lake Worth Pier, (ocean)	-0:21	-0:16
Boynton Beach	+1:24	+2:10
Delray Beach	+1:43	+2:10
Yamato	+1:41	+2:00
Boca Raton	+0:45	+1:14
Deerfield Beach	+0:49	+1:08
Hillsboro Beach, Intracoastal Waterway	+0:24	+0:39
Hillsboro Inlet, (inside)	+0:06	+0:07
Lauderdale-By-the-Sea	-0:10	-0:07
Ft. Lauderdale		
Bahia Mar Yacht Club	+0:17	+0:39
Andrews Avenue Bridge, New River	+0:37	+0:57
Port Everglades	-0:08	-0:05
South Port Everglades	-0:02	+0:02
Hollywood Beach	+0:58	+1:09
Golden Beach	+1:34	+2:05
Sunny Isles, Biscayne Creek	+2:21	+2:28
North Miami Beach	-0:06	+0:01
Bakers Haulover Inlet, (inside)	+1:15	+1:36
Indian Creek	+1:34	+1:51
Miami Beach	-0:02	+0:01
Biscayne Bay		
Miami, 79th St. Causeway	+1:43	+2:14
Miami, Marina	+0:54	+1:18
Miami, Causeway(east end)	+1:17	+1:11
Dinner Key Marina	+1:17	+1:51
Cape Florida (west side), Key Biscayne	+0:47	+1:03
Cutler, Biscayne Bay	+1:23	+2:02
Soldier Key	+0:53	+1:20
Fowey Rocks	+0:01	+0:03
Ragged Keys, Biscayne Bay	+1:13	+1:45
Elliott Key, (outside)	-0:04	0:00
Elliott Key Harbor	+2:26	+3:25
Adams Key, Biscayne Bay	+2:48	+2:34
Christmas Point, Elliott Key	+0:35	+0:39
Turkey Point, Biscayne Bay	+2:32	+2:26
Totten Key	+2:48	+3:45
Ocean Reef Club, Key Largo	+0:11	+0:20
Garden Cove, Key Largo	+0:34	+1:10
Mosquito Bank	+0:22	+0:31
Molasses Reef	+0:14	+0:12
Pumpkin Key, Card Sound	+3:10	+3:16
Tavernier, Hawk Channel	+0:29	+0:28
Alligator Reef Light	+0:40	+0:34

March 2011

March is slammer dolphin time.

SUNDAY	MONDAY	TUESDAY	WEDNESDAY	THURSDAY	FRIDAY	SATURDAY
		1 6:21a 2.1' / 6:33p 2.1' — 12:04p 0.1'	**2** 7:03a 2.2' / 7:17p 2.2' — 12:24a -0.2' / 12:48p 0.0'	**3** ● 7:41a 2.2' / 7:57p 2.3' — 1:07a -0.2' / 1:27p -0.1'	**4** 8:16a 2.3' / 8:34p 2.3' — 1:45a -0.2' / 2:04p -0.2'	**5** 8:50a 2.3' / 9:10p 2.3' — 2:22a -0.2' / 2:39p -0.2'
6 9:23a 2.3' / 9:45p 2.3' — 2:57a -0.1' / 3:12p -0.2'	**7** 9:56a 2.2' / 10:21p 2.3' — 3:30a 0.0' / 3:44p -0.2'	**8** 10:29a 2.2' / 10:59p 2.2' — 4:03a 0.0' / 4:17p -0.1'	**9** 11:03a 2.1' / 11:38p 2.1' — 4:36a 0.1' / 4:52p -0.1'	**10** 11:40a 2.1' — 5:13a 0.3' / 5:32p 0.0'	**11** ◐ 12:23a 2.0' / 12:22p 2.0' — 5:57a 0.4' / 6:21p 0.0'	**12** 1:14a 1.9' / 1:14p 1.9' — 6:51a 0.4' / 7:20p 0.1'
13 4:15a 1.9' / 4:19p 1.9' — 9:57a 0.5' / 10:28p 0.1'	**14** 5:22a 2.0' / 6:33p 1.9' — 11:07a 0.4' / 11:37p 0.0'	**15** 6:27a 2.1' / 6:44p 2.1' — 12:12p 0.2'	**16** 7:26a 2.3' / 7:47p 2.3' — 12:40a -0.1' / 1:11p 0.0'	**17** 8:20a 2.4' / 8:44p 2.6' — 1:38a -0.3' / 2:05p -0.3'	**18** 9:10a 2.6' / 9:38p 2.8' — 2:31a -0.4' / 2:55p -0.5'	**19** ○ 9:58a 2.7' / 10:29p 2.9' — 3:23a -0.5' / 3:45p -0.7'
20 10:46a 2.8' / 11:19p 3.0' — 4:12a -0.5' / 4:34p -0.8'	**21** 11:33a 2.8' / 12:09a 2.9' — 5:02a -0.5' / 5:23p -0.8'	**22** 12:21p 2.7' — 5:52a -0.4' / 6:14p -0.7'	**23** 1:00a 2.8' / 1:11p 2.6' — 6:43a -0.2' / 7:07p -0.5'	**24** 1:52a 2.6' / 2:04p 2.4' — 7:38a 0.0' / 8:04p -0.3'	**25** ◑ 2:48a 2.4' / 3:01p 2.2' — 8:38a 0.2' / 9:06p -0.1'	**26** 3:48a 2.2' / 4:03p 2.1' — 9:42a 0.3' / 10:12p 0.1'
27 4:53a 2.1' / 5:11p 2.0' — 10:49a 0.4' / 11:18p 0.1'	**28** 5:57a 2.1' / 6:17p 2.0' — 11:52a 0.4' / 12:18a 0.2'	**29** 6:56a 2.1' / 7:17p 2.1' — 12:48p 0.3'	**30** 7:45a 2.1' / 8:07p 2.2' — 1:11a 0.2' / 1:36p 0.2'	**31** 8:28a 2.2' / 8:50p 2.3' — 1:58a 0.1' / 2:18p 0.1'		

	March 1	March 15	March 30
SUNRISE	6:44 a.m.	7:30 a.m.	7:14 a.m.
SUNSET	6:23 p.m.	7:30 p.m.	7:37 p.m.

DST Starts on March 13

Cape Canaveral to Islamorada

MIAMI

Mahi Mania

INSHORE

Bonefish, **permit** and **tarpon** all on hand to give flats anglers a real chance at a coveted grand slam on light tackle or fly from Biscayne Bay to the Upper Florida Keys. Biggest **seatrout** of the season and **snook** of all sizes target baitfish schools in the Indian River and tributaries and north Biscayne Bay. Top time for **pompano** in the surf, with increasing **whiting** numbers and small permit taken in same zone.

OFFSHORE

Schools of silver mullet, menhaden and thread herring a big draw for smoker **kingfish**. Big **dolphin** and smaller schoolies are on the increase from the edge on out; schoolies may be shadowed by the occasional **blue marlin**. **Yellowfin tuna** are a growing prospect on the far side of the Gulf Stream. **Sailfishing** tends to be overshadowed this month, but the bite is excellent from Miami to the Upper Keys. **Wahoo** bite in 100 to 300 feet of water throughout the region. Bottom fishermen set sights on improving **mutton snapper** bite over reefs and wrecks in 70 to 100 feet.

April Spotlight: DOLPHIN

There is quite a mix of sizes of **dolphin**, from peanuts to chickens to gaffers to slammers on hand from the blue edge on out. Best bet for bagging a bull weighing upward of 40 pounds is to troll either big lures or horse ballyhoo with mono leaders, with or without a dredge at the transom. Run and gun while watching for frigatebirds and put in extra time around solid weedlines, rips or flotsam. Expect fish closer in with favorable easterly winds that help weedlines form. If you hook a slammer while trolling, toss a frisky live bait or a noisy chugger plug to its mate with a beefy spin or conventional rod.

TIDE CORRECTIONS For Government Cut	High	Low
Ponce de Leon Inlet	+0:04	+0:21
Cape Canaveral	-0:43	-0:40
Indian River		
Palm Bay	+3:38	+4:20
Wabasso	+2:46	+3:20
Vero Beach	+3:19	+3:51
Ft. Pierce	+1:06	+1:02
Jensen Beach	+2:38	+3:07
Sebastian Inlet	-0:26	-0:19
Vero Beach, (ocean)	-0:33	-0:24
Ft. Pierce Inlet, south jetty	-0:11	-0:13
St. Lucie River		
N. Fork	+2:48	+3:30
Stuart	+2:35	+3:34
S. Fork	+2:52	+3:35
Sewall Point	+1:33	+2:12
St. Lucie Inlet	-0:32	-0:13
Great Pocket	+1:16	+1:52
Gomez, S. Jupiter Narrows	+1:54	+2:42
Hobe Sound — State Park	+1:44	+2:23
Conch Bar, Jupiter Sound	+1:17	+1:39
Jupiter Sound, south end	+0:44	+0:50
Jupiter Inlet	+0:13	+0:02
Loxahatchee River		
Tequesta	+1:16	+2:03
N. Fork	+1:25	+2:00
Southwest Fork, (spillway)	+1:13	+1:50
Northwest Fork	+1:32	+2:11
Southwest Fork	+1:13	+1:48
Jupiter, Lake Worth Creek	+0:55	+1:17
Donald Ross Bridge	+0:41	+0:55
N. Palm Beach, Lake Worth Creek	+0:03	+0:18
Port of Palm Beach, Lake Worth	-0:02	+0:13
Palm Beach, (ocean)	-0:23	-0:17
W. Palm Beach Canal	+1:06	+1:37
Lake Worth Pier, (ocean)	-0:21	-0:16
Boynton Beach	+1:24	+2:10
Delray Beach	+1:43	+2:10
Yamato	+1:41	+2:00
Boca Raton	+0:45	+1:14
Deerfield Beach	+0:49	+1:08
Hillsboro Beach, Intracoastal Waterway	+0:24	+0:39
Hillsboro Inlet, (inside)	+0:06	+0:07
Lauderdale-By-the-Sea	-0:10	-0:07
Ft. Lauderdale		
Bahia Mar Yacht Club	+0:17	+0:39
Andrews Avenue Bridge, New River	+0:37	+0:57
Port Everglades	-0:08	-0:05
South Port Everglades	-0:02	+0:02
Hollywood Beach	+0:58	+1:09
Golden Beach	+1:34	+2:05
Sunny Isles, Biscayne Creek	+2:21	+2:28
North Miami Beach	-0:06	+0:01
Bakers Haulover Inlet, (inside)	+1:15	+1:36
Indian Creek	+1:34	+1:51
Miami Beach	-0:02	+0:01
Biscayne Bay		
Miami, 79th St. Causeway	+1:43	+2:14
Miami, Marina	+0:54	+1:18
Miami, Causeway(east end)	+1:17	+1:11
Dinner Key Marina	+1:17	+1:51
Cape Florida (west side), Key Biscayne	+0:47	+1:03
Cutler, Biscayne Bay	+1:23	+2:02
Soldier Key	+0:53	+1:20
Fowey Rocks	+0:01	+0:03
Ragged Keys, Biscayne Bay	+1:13	+1:45
Elliott Key, (outside)	-0:04	0:00
Elliott Key Harbor	+2:26	+3:35
Adams Key, Biscayne Bay	+2:48	+2:34
Christmas Point, Elliott Key	+0:35	+0:39
Turkey Point, Biscayne Bay	+2:33	+3:26
Totten Key	+2:48	+3:45
Ocean Reef Club, Key Largo	+0:11	+0:20
Garden Cove, Key Largo	+0:34	+1:10
Mosquito Bank	+0:22	+0:31
Molasses Reef	+0:14	+0:12
Pumpkin Key, Card Sound	+3:10	+3:16
Tavernier, Hawk Channel	+0:29	+0:28
Alligator Reef Light	+0:40	+0:34

April 2011

MIAMI

SUNDAY	MONDAY	TUESDAY	WEDNESDAY	THURSDAY	FRIDAY	SATURDAY

Lady luck shines down.

Week 1

					1 (Fri)	**2** (Sat)
					9:06a 2.3' · 9:30p 2.4'	9:42a 2.3' · 10:07p 2.4'
					2:40a 0.1' · 2:57p 0.0'	3:18a 0.1' · 3:33p -0.1'

Week 2 (● New Moon, 3)

3 (Sun)	**4** (Mon)	**5** (Tue)	**6** (Wed)	**7** (Thu)	**8** (Fri)	**9** (Sat)
10:17a 2.3' · 10:43p 2.5'	10:52a 2.3' · 11:20p 2.5'	11:27a 2.3' · 11:57p 2.4'	12:02p 2.2' · 12:36a 2.4'	12:38p 2.2'	1:16a 2.3' · 1:17p 2.1'	2:01a 2.2' · 2:02p 2.1'
3:54a 0.1' · 4:07p -0.1'	4:29a 0.1' · 4:40p -0.1'	5:02a 0.1' · 5:13p -0.1'	5:36a 0.2' · 5:47p -0.1'	6:10a 0.3' · 6:23p 0.0'	6:49a 0.3' · 7:05p 0.0'	7:34a 0.4' · 7:55p 0.1'

Week 3 (◐ First Quarter, 10)

10 (Sun)	**11** (Mon)	**12** (Tue)	**13** (Wed)	**14** (Thu)	**15** (Fri)	**16** (Sat)
2:51a 2.2' · 2:57p 2.0'	3:48a 2.1' · 4:02p 2.0'	4:50a 2.2' · 5:13p 2.1'	5:53a 2.2' · 6:22p 2.3'	6:53a 2.4' · 7:26p 2.5'	7:49a 2.5' · 8:24p 2.7'	8:42a 2.7' · 9:19p 2.9'
8:28a 0.4' · 8:54p 0.1'	9:33a 0.4' · 10:01p 0.2'	10:41a 0.3' · 11:10p 0.1'	11:45a 0.1'	12:15a 0.0' · 12:44p -0.1'	1:14a -0.1' · 1:39p -0.3'	2:09a -0.2' · 2:31p -0.5'

Week 4 (○ Full Moon, 17)

17 (Sun)	**18** (Mon)	**19** (Tue)	**20** (Wed)	**21** (Thu)	**22** (Fri)	**23** (Sat)
9:33a 2.8' · 10:10p 3.0'	10:22a 2.8' · 11:01p 3.0'	11:11a 2.8' · 11:51p 3.0'	12:01p 2.7'	12:41a 2.8' · 12:51p 2.6'	1:31a 2.7' · 1:43p 2.4'	2:24a 2.5' · 2:38p 2.3'
3:02a -0.3' · 3:22p -0.7'	3:52a -0.3' · 4:12p -0.7'	4:43a -0.3' · 5:02p -0.7'	5:33a -0.2' · 5:53p -0.6'	6:25a 0.0' · 6:46p -0.4'	7:19a 0.1' · 7:42p -0.2'	8:16a 0.2' · 8:41p 0.0'

Week 5 (◑ Last Quarter, 24)

24 (Sun)	**25** (Mon)	**26** (Tue)	**27** (Wed)	**28** (Thu)	**29** (Fri)	**30** (Sat)
3:19a 2.3' · 3:37p 2.2'	4:15a 2.2' · 4:39p 2.1'	5:13a 2.1' · 5:42p 2.1'	6:08a 2.1' · 6:40p 2.1'	6:58a 2.1' · 7:31p 2.2'	7:43a 2.1' · 8:16p 2.3'	8:25a 2.2' · 8:58p 2.4'
9:17a 0.3' · 9:43p 0.2'	10:19a 0.4' · 10:45p 0.3'	11:18a 0.4' · 11:43p 0.4'	12:11p 0.3'	12:36a 0.4' · 12:59p 0.2'	1:23a 0.4' · 1:41p 0.1'	2:06a 0.3' · 2:21p 0.0'

	April 1	April 15	April 30
SUNRISE	7:12 a.m.	6:58 a.m.	6:45 a.m.
SUNSET	7:38 p.m.	7:44 p.m.	7:52 p.m.

Cape Canaveral to Islamorada

Spot-on Specks

INSHORE

Top month for either a gator **seatrout** or gaudy numbers. Fish around baitfish schools over grassflats with mullet-style topwaters, jerkbaits, plastic shrimp or weedless flies and poppers; check out dropoffs and deep potholes as tide falls. Inlet **snook** action heating up; also many fish under bridge and dock lights. **Bonefish** still all-day affair with lots of tailers shallow in Biscayne Bay and Upper Keys. Migratory oceanside **tarpon** moving along Biscayne Bay where flies and swimming plugs score. **Permit** around in fishable numbers, though they start to move offshore to wrecks and reefs; from Jupiter north, they are caught by surf casters and sight casters just off beach.

OFFSHORE

Baitfish come out of the woodwork along beaches and out to the reef. **Kingfish**, **blackfin tuna** and **sailfish** venture into shallow water in hot pursuit. Bluewater action features **dolphin** and **wahoo** for anglers who troll baits shallow and deep to cover the water column. Bottom fishermen should find plenty of **black**, **gag** and **red grouper**.

May Spotlight: SPOTTED SEATROUT

Seatrout fishing is in fine form in the usual haunts: Indian River Lagoon, Biscayne Bay and Florida Bay. Great time for those fat 24- to 30-inchers in shallow water, especially at first light. Action lasts all day in slightly deeper water. Cast to potholes and grassy ridges when current is flowing. Mullet muds, docks, and bridges all top lairs. To catch a mess of schoolies, drift-fish over grassflats in 4 to 6 feet of water. Top offerings include topwater and subsurface plugs, soft plastics, jigs, shrimp or baitfish flies and shrimp-and-cork combo. Wade for the biggest, spooky gators. Keep electric motor use to a minimum, and pole if possible.

TIDE CORRECTIONS *For Government Cut*	High	Low
Ponce de Leon Inlet	+0:04	+0:21
Cape Canaveral	-0:43	-0:40
Indian River		
Palm Bay	+3:38	+4:20
Wabasso	+2:46	+3:20
Vero Beach	+3:19	+3:51
Ft. Pierce	+1:06	+1:02
Jensen Beach	+2:38	+3:07
Sebastian Inlet	-0:26	-0:19
Vero Beach, (ocean)	-0:33	-0:24
Ft. Pierce Inlet, south jetty	-0:11	-0:13
St. Lucie River		
N. Fork	+2:48	+3:30
Stuart	+2:35	+3:34
S. Fork	+2:52	+3:35
Sewall Point	+1:33	+2:12
St. Lucie Inlet	-0:32	-0:13
Great Pocket	+1:16	+1:52
Gomez, S. Jupiter Narrows	+1:54	+2:42
Hobe Sound, Jupiter Sound	+1:44	+2:23
Conch Bar, Jupiter Sound	+1:17	+1:39
Jupiter Sound, south end	+0:44	+0:50
Jupiter Inlet	+0:13	+0:02
Loxahatchee River		
Tequesta	+1:16	+2:03
N. Fork	+1:25	+2:00
Southwest Fork, (spillway)	+1:13	+1:50
Northwest Fork	+1:32	+2:17
Southwest Fork	+1:13	+1:48
Jupiter, Lake Worth Creek	+0:55	+1:17
Donald Ross Bridge	+0:41	+0:55
N. Palm Beach, Lake Worth Creek	+0:03	+0:18
Port of Palm Beach, Lake Worth	-0:02	+0:13
Palm Beach, (ocean)	-0:23	-0:17
W. Palm Beach Canal	+1:06	+1:37
Lake Worth Pier, (ocean)	-0:21	-0:16
Boynton Beach	+1:24	+2:10
Delray Beach	+1:43	+2:10
Yamato	+1:41	+2:00
Boca Raton	+0:45	+1:14
Deerfield Beach	+0:49	+1:08
Hillsboro Beach, Intracoastal Waterway	+0:24	+0:39
Hillsboro Inlet, (inside)	+0:06	+0:07
Lauderdale-By-the-Sea	-0:10	-0:07
Ft. Lauderdale		
Bahia Mar Yacht Club	+0:17	+0:39
Andrews Avenue Bridge, New River	+0:37	+0:57
Port Everglades	-0:08	-0:05
South Port Everglades	-0:02	+0:02
Hollywood Beach	+0:58	+1:09
Golden Beach	+1:34	+2:05
Sunny Isles, Biscayne Creek	+2:21	+2:28
North Miami Beach	-0:06	+0:01
Bakers Haulover Inlet, (inside)	+1:15	+1:36
Indian Creek	+1:34	+1:51
Miami Beach	-0:02	+0:01
Biscayne Bay		
Miami, 79th St. Causeway	+1:43	+2:14
Miami, Marina	+0:54	+1:18
Miami, Causeway(east end)	+1:17	+1:11
Dinner Key Marina	+1:17	+1:51
Cape Florida (west side), Key Biscayne	+0:47	+1:03
Cutler, Biscayne Bay	+1:23	+2:02
Soldier Key	+0:53	+1:20
Fowey Rocks	+0:01	+0:03
Ragged Keys, Biscayne Bay	+1:13	+1:45
Elliott Key, (outside)	-0:04	0:00
Elliott Key Harbor	+2:26	+3:25
Adams Key, Biscayne Bay	+2:48	+2:34
Christmas Point, Elliott Key	+0:35	+0:39
Turkey Point, Biscayne Bay	+2:33	+3:26
Totten Key	+2:48	+3:45
Ocean Reef Club, Key Largo	+0:11	+0:20
Garden Cove, Key Largo	+0:34	+1:10
Mosquito Bank	+0:22	+0:31
Molasses Reef	+0:14	+0:12
Pumpkin Key, Card Sound	+3:10	+3:16
Tavernier, Hawk Channel	+0:29	+0:28
Alligator Reef Light	+0:40	+0:34

MIAMI

SUNDAY	MONDAY	TUESDAY	WEDNESDAY	THURSDAY	FRIDAY	SATURDAY
1	**2** ●	**3**	**4**	**5**	**6**	**7**
9:05a 2.3' / 9:38p 2.4'	9:44a 2.3' / 10:17p 2.5'	10:22a 2.3' / 10:56p 2.5'	11:00a 2.3' / 11:36p 2.5'	11:39a 2.3' / 12:17a 2.5'	12:20p 2.2' / 12:59a 2.4'	1:03p 2.2'

SUNDAY	MONDAY	TUESDAY	WEDNESDAY	THURSDAY	FRIDAY	SATURDAY
2:46a 0.3' / 2:58p 0.0'	3:24a 0.3' / 3:34p -0.1'	4:00a 0.2' / 4:10p -0.1'	4:36a 0.2' / 4:45p -0.1'	5:12a 0.3' / 5:23p -0.1'	5:51a 0.3' / 6:02p -0.1'	6:32a 0.3' / 6:47p 0.0'
8	**9**	**10** ◑	**11**	**12**	**13**	**14**
1:44a 2.4' / 1:52p 2.2'	2:32a 2.3' / 2:47p 2.2'	3:24a 2.3' / 3:49p 2.2'	4:21a 2.3' / 4:56p 2.3'	5:21a 2.3' / 6:02p 2.4'	6:21a 2.4' / 7:06p 2.6'	7:19a 2.5' / 8:05p 2.7'

SUNDAY	MONDAY	TUESDAY	WEDNESDAY	THURSDAY	FRIDAY	SATURDAY
7:20a 0.3' / 7:38p 0.0'	8:14a 0.3' / 8:36p 0.1'	9:15a 0.3' / 9:41p 0.2'	10:18a 0.1' / 10:47p 0.2'	11:21a 0.0' / 11:51p 0.1'	12:20p -0.2'	12:52a 0.1' / 1:16p -0.4'
15	**16** ○	**17**	**18**	**19**	**20**	**21**
8:16a 2.6' / 9:01p 2.8'	9:10a 2.6' / 9:53p 2.9'	10:02a 2.7' / 10:44p 2.9'	10:52a 2.7' / 11:33p 2.9'	11:42a 2.6'	12:21a 2.8' / 12:32p 2.5'	1:09a 2.6' / 1:22p 2.4'

SUNDAY	MONDAY	TUESDAY	WEDNESDAY	THURSDAY	FRIDAY	SATURDAY
1:48a 0.0' / 2:09p -0.5'	2:42a -0.1' / 3:02p -0.6'	3:33a -0.1' / 3:53p -0.6'	4:24a -0.1' / 4:43p -0.6'	5:15a -0.1' / 5:34p -0.5'	6:06a 0.0' / 6:25p -0.3'	6:58a 0.1' / 7:17p -0.1'
22	**23** ◐	**24**	**25**	**26**	**27**	**28**
1:57a 2.5' / 2:13p 2.3'	2:44a 2.3' / 3:06p 2.1'	3:33a 2.2' / 4:01p 2.1'	4:22a 2.1' / 4:57p 2.0'	5:12a 2.0' / 5:53p 2.0'	6:03a 2.0' / 6:47p 2.1'	6:52a 2.0' / 7:37p 2.2'

SUNDAY	MONDAY	TUESDAY	WEDNESDAY	THURSDAY	FRIDAY	SATURDAY
7:51a 0.2' / 8:11p 0.1'	8:46a 0.3' / 9:07p 0.2'	9:42a 0.3' / 10:04p 0.4'	10:36a 0.3' / 11:00p 0.4'	11:27a 0.3' / 11:52p 0.5'	12:15p 0.2'	12:42a 0.5' / 1:00p 0.1'
29	**30**	**31**				
7:40a 2.1' / 8:23p 2.3'	8:26a 2.1' / 9:08p 2.3'	9:10a 2.2' / 9:51p 2.4'	*Pucker up for mutton snapper.*			
1:27a 0.4' / 1:42p 0.0'	2:10a 0.4' / 2:23p 0.0'	2:51a 0.3' / 3:03p -0.1'				

	May 1	May 15	May 30
SUNRISE	6:44 a.m.	6:35 a.m.	6:30 a.m.
SUNSET	7:52 p.m.	8:00 p.m.	8:07 p.m.

Cape Canaveral to Islamorada

Bow to the King

INSHORE

Catch-and-release **snook** fishing peaks. Spawning inlet fish should be handled carefully; linesiders also at bridges, docks, grassflats, and the surf. Surf also holds tasty **whiting** in the trough. At first light, cast to **tarpon** in bait schools close to the sand. Snook, **trout** and **reds** headline the Indian River fishery. Action best early with plugs and soft-plastics. Pick a spring tide for Biscayne Bay **bonefish**. Tarpon numbers explode along Biscayne and Upper Keys oceanside flats.

OFFSHORE

Bottom fishing for **mangrove** and **yellowtail snapper** excellent night and day over natural bottom in 40 to 100 feet. Also **mutton snapper** from 100 to 200 feet over wrecks and artificial reefs. A top time for small boaters to range out for **dolphin** due to calmer seas. If you run and gun, watch for flotsam and frigatebirds and then troll lures or rigged baits on the spot to check for fish. Otherwise troll weedlines, rips, slicks and temp changes. Anglers heading to far edge of Stream can troll or chunk for **yellowfin tuna**.

June Spotlight: TARPON

Tarpon action is hot on all fronts. From Miami to the Upper Keys, sight fishing with fly and light tackle for 70- to 100-pound-plus fish is the main game. Anglers either stake out or pole their skiffs along travel routes from first light through middle of the day. Tarpon take flies, soft plastics and swimming plugs presented in a natural manner. Bait fishermen score in bridge channels from the Upper Keys to Biscayne Bay. June sees best bite at night, for giants and juvenile fish. Top baits include mullet and pinfish, crabs and hand-picked shrimp, fished on 15- to 25-pound tackle. Beaches from Broward County to Canaveral hold cruisers for sight casting, too.

TIDE CORRECTIONS
For Government Cut

	High	Low
Ponce de Leon Inlet	+0:04	+0:21
Cape Canaveral	-0:43	-0:40
Indian River		
Palm Bay	+3:38	+4:20
Wabasso	+2:46	+3:20
Vero Beach	+3:19	+3:51
Ft. Pierce	+1:06	+1:02
Jensen Beach	+2:38	+3:07
Sebastian Inlet	-0:26	-0:19
Vero Beach, (ocean)	-0:33	-0:24
Ft. Pierce Inlet, south jetty	-0:11	-0:13
St. Lucie River		
N. Fork	+2:48	+3:30
Stuart	+2:35	+3:34
S. Fork	+2:52	+3:35
Sewall Point	+1:33	+2:12
St. Lucie Inlet	-0:32	-0:13
Great Pocket	+1:16	+1:52
Gomez, S. Jupiter Narrows	+1:54	+2:42
Hobe Sound, (ocean)	+1:44	+2:23
Conch Bar, Jupiter Sound	+1:17	+1:39
Jupiter Sound, south end	+0:44	+0:50
Jupiter Inlet	+0:13	+0:02
Loxahatchee River		
Tequesta	+1:16	+2:03
N. Fork	+1:25	+2:00
Southwest Fork, (spillway)	+1:13	+1:50
Northwest Fork	+1:32	+2:11
Southwest Fork	+1:13	+1:48
Jupiter, Lake Worth Creek	+0:55	+1:17
Donald Ross Bridge	+0:41	+0:55
N. Palm Beach, Lake Worth Creek	+0:03	+0:18
Port of Palm Beach, Lake Worth	-0:02	+0:13
Palm Beach, (ocean)	-0:23	-0:17
W. Palm Beach Canal	+1:06	+1:37
Lake Worth Pier, (ocean)	-0:21	-0:16
Boynton Beach	+1:24	+2:10
Delray Beach	+1:43	+2:10
Yamato	+1:41	+2:00
Boca Raton	+0:45	+1:14
Deerfield Beach	+0:49	+1:08
Hillsboro Beach, Intracoastal Waterway	+0:24	+0:39
Hillsboro Inlet, (inside)	+0:06	+0:07
Lauderdale-By-the-Sea	-0:10	-0:07
Ft. Lauderdale		
Bahia Mar Yacht Club	+0:17	+0:39
Andrews Avenue Bridge, New River	+0:37	+0:57
Port Everglades	-0:08	-0:05
South Port Everglades	-0:02	+0:02
Hollywood Beach	+0:58	+1:09
Golden Beach	+1:34	+2:05
Sunny Isles, Biscayne Creek	+2:21	+2:28
North Miami Beach	-0:06	+0:01
Bakers Haulover Inlet, (inside)	+1:15	+1:36
Indian Creek	+1:34	+1:51
Miami Beach	-0:02	+0:01
Biscayne Bay		
Miami, 79th St. Causeway	+1:43	+2:14
Miami, Marina	+0:54	+1:18
Miami, Causeway(east end)	+1:17	+1:11
Dinner Key Marina	+1:17	+1:51
Cape Florida (west side), Key Biscayne	+0:47	+1:03
Cutler, Biscayne Bay	+1:23	+2:02
Soldier Key	+0:53	+1:20
Fowey Rocks	+0:01	+0:03
Ragged Keys, Biscayne Bay	+1:13	+1:45
Elliott Key, (outside)	-0:04	0:00
Elliott Key Harbor	+2:26	+3:25
Adams Key, Biscayne Bay	+2:33	+3:26
Christmas Point, Elliott Key	+0:35	+0:39
Turkey Point, Biscayne Bay	+2:33	+3:26
Totten Key	+2:48	+3:45
Ocean Reef Club, Key Largo	+0:11	+0:20
Garden Cove, Key Largo	+0:34	+1:10
Mosquito Bank	+0:22	+0:31
Molasses Reef	+0:14	+0:12
Pumpkin Key, Card Sound	+3:10	+3:16
Tavernier, Hawk Channel	+0:29	+0:28
Alligator Reef Light	+0:40	+0:34

June 2011

MIAMI

SUNDAY	MONDAY	TUESDAY	WEDNESDAY	THURSDAY	FRIDAY	SATURDAY

Hold on!

1 (new moon)
9:54a 2.2' / 10:34p 2.5'
3:31a 0.3' / 3:42p -0.2'

2
10:37a 2.3' / 11:16p 2.5'
4:11a 0.2' / 4:22p -0.2'

3
11:20a 2.3' / 11:59p 2.5'
4:51a 0.2' / 5:03p -0.2'

4
12:05p 2.3'
5:33a 0.2' / 5:46p -0.2'

5
12:42a 2.5' / 12:52p 2.3'
6:18a 0.1' / 6:33p -0.2'

6
1:26a 2.5' / 1:42p 2.3'
7:07a 0.1' / 7:24p -0.1'

7
2:13a 2.4' / 2:37p 2.3'
8:00a 0.0' / 8:21p 0.0'

8 (first quarter)
3:02a 2.4' / 3:36p 2.3'
8:57a 0.0' / 9:22p 0.1'

9
3:56a 2.3' / 4:39p 2.3'
9:57a -0.1' / 10:26p 0.1'

10
4:53a 2.3' / 5:44p 2.4'
10:58a -0.2' / 11:30p 0.2'

11
5:54a 2.3' / 6:48p 2.5'
11:58a -0.3'

12
6:55a 2.4' / 7:48p 2.6'
12:31a 0.1' / 11:56a -0.4'

13
7:55a 2.4' / 8:45p 2.7'
12:29a 0.1' / 12:51p -0.5'

14 (full moon)
8:51a 2.5' / 9:38p 2.7'
1:24a 0.0' / 1:44p -0.6'

15
9:45a 2.5' / 10:28p 2.7'
2:16a 0.0' / 2:36p -0.5'

16
10:35a 2.5' / 11:15p 2.7'
3:07a 0.0' / 3:26p -0.5'

17
11:24a 2.5' / 12:00a 2.6'
3:56a 0.0' / 4:14p -0.4'

18
12:11p 2.4'
4:45a 0.0' / 5:02p -0.3'

19
12:43a 2.5' / 12:58p 2.3'
6:33a 0.0' / 6:50p -0.1'

20
1:25a 2.4' / 1:44p 2.2'
7:21a 0.1' / 7:37p 0.1'

21
2:07a 2.3' / 2:30p 2.1'
8:09a 0.1' / 8:26p 0.2'

22 (last quarter)
2:48a 2.2' / 3:19p 2.0'
8:58a 0.2' / 9:17p 0.4'

23
3:31a 2.1' / 4:10p 2.0'
9:47a 0.2' / 10:10p 0.5'

24
4:17a 2.0' / 5:03p 2.0'
10:38a 0.2' / 11:03p 0.5'

25
5:07a 1.9' / 5:59p 2.0'
11:27a 0.2' / 11:55p 0.5'

26
6:00a 1.9' / 6:55p 2.0'
12:16p 0.1' / 12:45p 0.5'

27
6:55a 2.0' / 7:48p 2.1'
1:03p 0.0' / 1:33a 0.4'

28
7:47a 2.0' / 8:37p 2.3'
1:48p -0.1' / 2:18a 0.4'

29
8:38a 2.1' / 9:24p 2.4'
2:32p -0.2' / 3:02a 0.3'

30
9:27a 2.2' / 10:09p 2.5'
3:16p -0.2'

	June 1	June 15	June 30
SUNRISE	6:29 a.m.	6:29 a.m.	6:33 a.m.
SUNSET	8:08 p.m.	8:14 p.m.	8:16 p.m.

Miami Station

Cape Canaveral to Islamorada

MIAMI

King Mack Attack

INSHORE

Biscayne Bay flats fishing for **bonefish** is at its best early due to high water temps. **Permit** more heat tolerant and provide all-day sight fishing on strong tides. **Redfish** school up and tail in Mosquito Lagoon and northern Indian River Lagoon. **Tarpon** still on the move; get out at first light to spot fish to cast at. **Snook** and **seatrout** is a dawn deal on Indian River; night shift heads to dock lights. IRL also holds small to medium tarpon on flats and residential canals. Fish an outgoing inlet tide for permit and tarpon. First great month for snook in the surf; sight fishing is best under high sun at high tide.

OFFSHORE

Trollers will need to run a bit farther, to at least 200 to 300 feet to target both **wahoo** and **dolphin.** Smaller 'phins are the rule but thorough hunting may find a big pair under a bird or board. Hard-fighting **bonito** plentiful at southern end of the region, with bonus **blackfin tuna** for anglers who live-chum over structure and hard bottom. Kingfish are thick along northern beaches, and reefs in 100 feet or more out front of Miami. **Yellowtail**, **lane** and **mangrove snapper** night bite is excellent.

July Spotlight: KING MACKEREL

The days of **king mackerel** shortages are a distant memory, with current stocks at yesteryear levels. It's time for the midsummer run, with migratory smokers under bait pods off northern beaches, from roughly Stuart north. Smaller resident fish will feed best morning and late afternoon along the southern reef from Jupiter to the upper Keys. Live bait is the ticket; blue runners, mullet and herring are smoker candy. Schoolies are quick to snap up a dead sardine, or a jig or baitfish fly pattern fished with a sinking line. Chum or cast over the reef, after you mark fish, find bait, or spot kings busting bait at the surface.

TIDE CORRECTIONS
For Government Cut

	High	Low
Ponce de Leon Inlet	+0:04	+0:21
Cape Canaveral	-0:43	-0:40
Indian River		
Palm Bay	+3:38	+4:20
Wabasso	+2:46	+3:20
Vero Beach	+3:19	+3:51
Ft. Pierce	+1:06	+1:02
Jensen Beach	+2:38	+3:07
Sebastian Inlet	-0:26	-0:19
Vero Beach, (ocean)	-0:33	-0:24
Ft. Pierce Inlet, south jetty	-0:11	-0:13
St. Lucie River		
N. Fork	+2:48	+3:30
Stuart	+2:35	+3:34
S. Fork	+2:52	+3:35
Sewall Point	+1:33	+2:12
St. Lucie Inlet	-0:32	-0:13
Great Pocket	+1:16	+1:52
Gomez, S. Jupiter Narrows	+1:54	+2:42
Hobe Sound — State Park	+1:44	+2:23
Conch Bar, Jupiter Sound	+1:17	+1:39
Jupiter Sound, south end	+0:44	+0:50
Jupiter Inlet	+0:13	+0:02
Loxahatchee River		
Tequesta	+1:16	+2:03
N. Fork	+1:25	+2:00
Southwest Fork, (spillway)	+1:13	+1:50
Northwest Fork	+1:32	+2:11
Southwest Fork	+1:13	+1:48
Jupiter, Lake Worth Creek	+0:55	+1:17
Donald Ross Bridge	+0:41	+0:55
N. Palm Beach, Lake Worth Creek	+0:03	+0:18
Port of Palm Beach, Lake Worth	-0:02	+0:13
Palm Beach, (ocean)	-0:23	-0:17
W. Palm Beach Canal	+1:06	+1:37
Lake Worth Pier, (ocean)	-0:21	-0:16
Boynton Beach	+1:24	+2:10
Delray Beach	+1:43	+2:10
Yamato	+1:41	+2:00
Boca Raton	+0:45	+1:14
Deerfield Beach	+0:49	+1:08
Hillsboro Inlet, Intracoastal Waterway	+0:24	+0:39
Hillsboro Inlet, (inside)	+0:06	+0:07
Lauderdale-By-the-Sea	-0:10	-0:07
Ft. Lauderdale		
Bahia Mar Yacht Club	+0:17	+0:39
Andrews Avenue Bridge, New River	+0:37	+0:57
Port Everglades	-0:08	-0:05
South Port Everglades	-0:02	+0:02
Hollywood Beach	+0:58	+1:09
Golden Beach	+1:34	+2:05
Sunny Isles, Biscayne Creek	+2:21	+2:28
North Miami Beach	-0:06	+0:01
Bakers Haulover Inlet, (inside)	+1:15	+1:36
Indian Creek	+1:34	+1:51
Miami Beach	-0:02	+0:01
Biscayne Bay		
Miami, 79th St. Causeway	+1:43	+2:14
Miami, Marina	+0:54	+1:18
Miami, Causeway(east end)	+1:17	+1:11
Dinner Key Marina	+1:17	+1:51
Cape Florida (west side), Key Biscayne	+0:47	+1:03
Cutler, Biscayne Bay	+1:23	+2:02
Soldier Key	+0:53	+1:20
Fowey Rocks	+0:01	+0:03
Ragged Keys, Biscayne Bay	+1:13	+1:45
Elliott Key, (outside)	-0:04	0:00
Elliott Key Harbor	+2:26	+3:25
Adams Key, Biscayne Bay	+2:48	+2:34
Christmas Point, Elliott Key	+0:35	+0:39
Turkey Point, Biscayne Bay	0:00	0:06
Totten Key	+2:48	+3:45
Ocean Reef Club, Key Largo	+0:11	+0:20
Garden Cove, Key Largo	+0:34	+1:10
Mosquito Bank	+0:22	+0:31
Molasses Reef	+0:14	+0:12
Pumpkin Key, Card Sound	+3:10	+3:16
Tavernier, Hawk Channel	+0:29	+0:28
Alligator Reef Light	+0:40	+0:34

SUNDAY	MONDAY	TUESDAY	WEDNESDAY	THURSDAY	FRIDAY	SATURDAY

Fine mangrove snapper. Night fishing is excellent this month.

MIAMI

1 ●
10:14a 2.3' · 10:53p 2.5' · 11:01a 2.4' · 11:37p 2.6'
3:46a 0.2' · 4:00p -0.3' · 4:29a 0.1' · 4:44p -0.3'

2

3
11:49a 2.4' · 12:20a 2.6'
5:14a 0.0' · 5:30p -0.3'

4
12:38p 2.5' · 1:05a 2.6'
6:00a -0.1' · 6:18p -0.3'

5
1:29p 2.5' · 1:51a 2.5'
6:49a -0.2' · 7:10p -0.2'

6
2:23p 2.4' · 2:40a 2.5'
7:41a -0.2' · 8:05p 0.0'

7
3:20p 2.4' · 3:33a 2.4'
8:37a -0.2' · 9:04p 0.1'

8 ◐
4:22p 2.4' · 4:31a 2.3'
9:37a -0.3' · 10:07p 0.2'

9
5:26p 2.4'
10:39a -0.3' · 11:12p 0.2'

10
5:33a 2.3' · 6:31p 2.4'
11:40a -0.3' · 12:14a 0.2'

11
6:38a 2.3' · 7:34p 2.5'
12:40p -0.3' · 1:13a 0.2'

12
7:40a 2.3' · 8:31p 2.5'
1:37p -0.4' · 2:09a 0.1'

13
8:37a 2.4' · 9:23p 2.6'
2:30p -0.4' · 3:01a 0.1'

14
9:30a 2.4' · 10:10p 2.6'
3:21p -0.4' · 3:50a 0.0'

15 ○
10:19a 2.5' · 10:54p 2.6'
4:08p -0.3' · 4:36a 0.0'

16
11:05a 2.5' · 11:34p 2.6'
4:53p -0.2'

17
11:48a 2.4' · 12:13a 2.5'
5:20a 0.0' · 5:37p -0.1'

18
12:30p 2.4' · 12:51a 2.4'
6:03a 0.0' · 6:19p 0.0'

19
1:11p 2.3' · 1:27a 2.3'
6:45a 0.1' · 7:01p 0.1'

20
1:53p 2.2' · 2:05a 2.2'
7:27a 0.1' · 7:43p 0.3'

21
2:37p 2.1' · 2:45a 2.1'
8:09a 0.2' · 8:28p 0.4'

22 ◑
3:24p 2.1' · 3:28a 2.0'
8:55a 0.2' · 9:16p 0.5'

23
4:16p 2.0'
9:44a 0.3' · 10:10p 0.6'

24
4:17a 2.0' · 5:13p 2.0'
10:37a 0.3' · 11:06p 0.7'

25
5:13a 2.0' · 6:13p 2.1'
11:31a 0.2' · 12:03a 0.6'

26
6:13a 2.0' · 7:12p 2.2'
12:25p 0.2' · 12:56a 0.5'

27
7:13a 2.1' · 8:06p 2.3'
1:15p 0.0' · 1:46a 0.4'

28
8:09a 2.2' · 8:55p 2.5'
2:04p -0.1' · 2:34a 0.3'

29 ●
9:02a 2.4' · 9:42p 2.6'
2:51p -0.2' · 3:20a 0.1'

30
9:52a 2.5' · 10:27p 2.7'
3:38p -0.3'

31
10:41a 2.6' · 11:11p 2.8'
4:05a 0.0' · 4:25p -0.3'

Haulover Canal, northeast of Titusville.

	July 1	July 15	July 30
SUNRISE	6:33 a.m.	6:39 a.m.	6:46 a.m.
SUNSET	8:16 p.m.	8:15 p.m.	8:08 p.m.

Cape Canaveral to Islamorada

Tuna Tug of War

INSHORE

Baitfish schools are nearing summertime peak along ICW and beaches, attracting numbers of **snook**, **seatrout** and **tarpon**. Glass minnows and finger mullet stream into the surf as month closes; that's prime time for giant tarpon, snook, **ladyfish**, **mackerel**, **jack crevalle** and more. Get out at dawn for flats action, or after thunderstorms abate. Heat of the day fishing worthwhile for heat-tolerant **permit** or **redfish**. Biscayne Bay permit cruise flats edge channels on spring tides. Nighttime dock fishing from Miami to Vero Beach with small lures and flies is excellent for snook, trout and small tarpon.

OFFSHORE

Night fishing is comfortable and productive for **snapper** and **swordfish**. Best shot at **wahoo** is fast-trolling at first light or at sunset. **Kingfish** will cooperate for anglers getting out early in the day or in late afternoon along northern beaches; fish around bait pods or where you mark fish. Top time for **bonito** and **blackfins** on the reefline and **yellowfins** are farther offshore where radar-equipped anglers search for birds.

August Spotlight: TUNA

Bluewater anglers are increasingly dialed-in to tuna along the East Central to Southeast Florida coast. **Blackfin**, **skipjack** and **little tunny** (a.k.a. bonito), are favorites among the small-boating, light-tackle crowd. Top methods include trolling, casting and chumming. While running stay on the lookout for surface busts, then stop and drift into range and cast small jigs, spoons, plugs or flies. Trollers hook up then live chum to fire up the bite. **Yellowfin**, **big-eye** and **bluefin tuna** take trolled big lures. A federal HMS vessel permit is mandatory should you land one of the regulated tuna species.

TIDE CORRECTIONS
For Government Cut

	High	Low
Ponce de Leon Inlet	+0:04	+0:21
Cape Canaveral	-0:43	-0:40
Indian River		
Palm Bay	+3:38	+4:20
Wabasso	+2:46	+3:20
Vero Beach	+3:19	+3:51
Ft. Pierce	+1:06	+1:02
Jensen Beach	+2:38	+3:07
Sebastian Inlet	-0:26	-0:19
Vero Beach, (ocean)	-0:33	-0:24
Ft. Pierce Inlet, south jetty	-0:11	-0:13
St. Lucie River		
N. Fork	+2:48	+3:30
Stuart	+2:35	+3:34
S. Fork	+2:52	+3:35
Sewall Point	+1:33	+2:12
St. Lucie Inlet	-0:32	-0:13
Great Pocket	+1:16	+1:52
Gomez, S. Jupiter Narrows	+1:54	+2:42
Hobe Sound—State Park	+1:44	+2:23
Conch Bar, Jupiter Sound	+1:17	+1:39
Jupiter Sound, south end	+0:44	+0:50
Jupiter Inlet	+0:13	+0:02
Loxahatchee River		
Tequesta	+1:16	+2:03
N. Fork	+1:25	+2:00
Southwest Fork, (spillway)	+1:13	+1:50
Northwest Fork	+1:32	+2:11
Southwest Fork	+1:13	+1:48
Jupiter, Lake Worth Creek	+0:55	+1:17
Donald Ross Bridge	+0:41	+0:55
N. Palm Beach, Lake Worth Creek	+0:03	+0:18
Port of Palm Beach, Lake Worth	-0:02	+0:13
Palm Beach, (ocean)	-0:23	-0:17
W. Palm Beach Canal	+1:06	+1:37
Lake Worth Pier, (ocean)	-0:21	-0:16
Boynton Beach	+1:24	+2:10
Delray Beach	+1:43	+2:10
Yamato	+1:41	+2:00
Boca Raton	+0:45	+1:14
Deerfield Beach	+0:49	+1:08
Hillsboro Beach, Intracoastal Waterway	+0:24	+0:39
Hillsboro Inlet, (inside)	+0:06	+0:07
Lauderdale-By-the-Sea	-0:10	-0:07
Ft. Lauderdale		
Bahia Mar Yacht Club	+0:17	+0:39
Andrews Avenue Bridge, New River	+0:37	+0:57
Port Everglades	-0:08	-0:05
South Port Everglades	-0:02	+0:02
Hollywood Beach	+0:58	+1:09
Golden Beach	+1:34	+2:05
Sunny Isles, Biscayne Creek	+2:21	+2:28
North Miami Beach	-0:06	+0:01
Bakers Haulover Inlet, (inside)	+1:15	+1:36
Indian Creek	+1:34	+1:51
Miami Beach	-0:02	+0:01
Biscayne Bay		
Miami, 79th St. Causeway	+1:43	+2:14
Miami, Marina	+0:54	+1:18
Miami, Causeway(east end)	+1:17	+1:11
Dinner Key Marina	+1:17	+1:51
Cape Florida (west side), Key Biscayne	+0:47	+1:03
Cutler, Biscayne Bay	+1:23	+2:02
Soldier Key	+0:53	+1:20
Fowey Rocks	+0:01	+0:03
Ragged Keys, Biscayne Bay	+1:13	+1:45
Elliott Key, (outside)	-0:04	0:00
Elliott Key Harbor	+2:26	+3:25
Adams Key, Biscayne Bay	+2:48	+2:34
Christmas Point, Elliott Key	+0:35	+0:39
Turkey Point, Biscayne Bay	+2:33	+3:26
Totten Key	+2:40	+0:13
Ocean Reef Club, Key Largo	+0:11	+0:20
Garden Cove, Key Largo	+0:34	+1:10
Mosquito Bank	+0:22	+0:31
Molasses Reef	+0:14	+0:12
Pumpkin Key, Card Sound	+3:10	+3:16
Tavernier, Hawk Channel	+0:29	+0:28
Alligator Reef Light	+0:40	+0:34

August 2011

MIAMI

SUNDAY	MONDAY	TUESDAY	WEDNESDAY	THURSDAY	FRIDAY	SATURDAY
	1	**2**	**3**	**4**	**5**	**6**
	11:30a 2.7' 11:55p 2.8'	12:20p 2.8' 12:41a 2.8'	1:11p 2.8' 1:28a 2.7'	2:05p 2.7' 2:18a 2.6'	3:02p 2.6' 3:13a 2.5'	4:04p 2.5'
	4:52a -0.2' 5:12p -0.3'	5:39a -0.3' 6:01p -0.2'	6:28a -0.3' 6:52p -0.1'	7:20a -0.3' 7:47p 0.1'	8:17a -0.2' 8:46p 0.2'	9:18a -0.2' 9:50p 0.4'
7	**8**	**9**	**10**	**11**	**12**	**13**
4:13a 2.4' 5:10p 2.5'	5:19a 2.4' 6:16p 2.5'	6:25a 2.4' 7:19p 2.5'	7:28a 2.4' 8:15p 2.6'	8:25a 2.5' 9:04p 2.6'	9:15a 2.6' 9:48p 2.7'	10:00a 2.6' 10:28p 2.7
10:22a -0.1' 10:56p 0.4'	11:26a 0.0' 12:01a 0.4'	12:28p 0.0' 1:01a 0.4'	1:25p 0.0' 1:55a 0.3'	2:17p 0.0' 2:45a 0.3'	3:04p 0.0' 3:30a 0.2'	3:48p 0.0'
14	**15**	**16**	**17**	**18**	**19**	**20**
10:42a 2.6' 11:05p 2.7'	11:22a 2.6' 11:40p 2.6'	12:00p 2.6' 12:14a 2.6'	12:38p 2.5' 12:49a 2.5'	1:17p 2.4' 1:25a 2.4'	1:58p 2.4' 2:03a 2.3'	2:43p 2.3'
4:12a 0.1' 4:30p 0.0'	4:51a 0.1' 5:09p 0.1'	5:29a 0.1' 5:47p 0.2'	6:06a 0.2' 6:24p 0.4'	6:43a 0.3' 7:01p 0.5'	7:21a 0.3' 7:41p 0.6'	8:03a 0.4' 8:25p 0.7'
21	**22**	**23**	**24**	**25**	**26**	**27**
2:46a 2.2' 3:34p 2.2'	3:35a 2.2' 4:32p 2.2'	4:34a 2.2' 5:35p 2.2'	5:39a 2.2' 6:36p 2.4'	6:43a 2.3' 7:33p 2.5'	7:43a 2.5' 8:24p 2.7'	8:38a 2.7' 9:12p 2.9'
8:51a 0.5' 9:18p 0.8'	9:47a 0.5' 10:19p 0.9'	10:48a 0.5' 11:22p 0.8'	11:48a 0.4' 12:21a 0.7'	12:45p 0.3' 1:15a 0.6'	1:37p 0.1' 2:05a 0.3'	2:27p 0.0'
28	**29**	**30**	**31**	Great fishing and reading.		
9:30a 2.9' 9:58p 3.0'	10:21a 3.1' 10:43p 3.1'	11:10a 3.2' 11:29p 3.1'	12:01p 3.2'			
2:53a 0.1' 3:16p -0.1'	3:40a -0.1' 4:04p -0.1'	4:27a -0.2' 4:52p -0.1'	5:15a -0.3' 5:42p 0.0'			

	August 1	August 15	August 30
SUNRISE	6:47 a.m.	6:54 a.m.	7:01 a.m.
SUNSET	8:07 p.m.	7:56 p.m.	7:41 p.m.

Cape Canaveral to Islamorada

MIAMI

The Cadillac Jack

INSHORE

The fall bait run creates a major buzz among anglers. Small silver mullet stream south along the beaches and pour into inlets and the ICW. **Snook, sharks, jacks, tarpon, seatrout, bluefish** and more go on the feed, with the surf, jetties, flats, seawalls and bridges are holding hungry predators. Live baits assure a hookup, though plenty of fish take plugs, spooons, jigs and flies around bait schools. Trophy **bonefish** show on Biscayne Bay and the Keys around month's end, with excellent **permit** numbers on channel-edge flats. Wide-open spillways after heavy rains attract hungry snook and tarpon.

OFFSHORE

Anglers make longer runs offshore to find weedlines holding **dolphin** and **blue marlin**. The reefline may be a better bet with enough **kingfish** and **blackfin tuna** to put some fish on ice. Good month for day or night trips for **snapper**, with **muttons** moving in shallow to beaches after squally tropical weather and **cuberas** making a move in the Upper Keys.

September Spotlight: PERMIT

Permit are at their best on the flats from Key Biscayne to Islamorada. Pole over "crunchy" oceanside flats, or over grassy shallows just inside Biscayne Bay on strongest tides. Flats edges in three or four feet are ideal, but big high tides prompt them to feed over shallower crowns where they sometimes tail up. Watch for "floaters" in main Biscayne Bay channels. Windy days take the edge off of these wary gamefish. Top bait is a live, half dollar-size blue crab. Live shrimp is a good alternative, with skimmer jigs and fast-sinking crab flies other options. Also try inlet jetties and wrecks close to shore.

TIDE CORRECTIONS
For Government Cut

	High	Low
Ponce de Leon Inlet	+0:04	+0:21
Cape Canaveral	-0:43	-0:40
Indian River		
Palm Bay	+3:38	+4:20
Wabasso	+2:46	+3:20
Vero Beach	+3:19	+3:51
Ft. Pierce	+1:06	+1:02
Jensen Beach	+2:38	+3:07
Sebastian Inlet	-0:26	-0:19
Vero Beach, (ocean)	-0:33	-0:24
Ft. Pierce Inlet, south jetty	-0:11	-0:13
St. Lucie River		
N. Fork	+2:48	+3:30
Stuart	+2:35	+3:34
S. Fork	+2:52	+3:35
Sewall Point	+1:33	+2:12
St. Lucie Inlet	-0:32	-0:13
Great Pocket	+1:16	+1:52
Gomez, S. Jupiter Narrows	+1:54	+2:42
Hobe Sound—State Park	+1:44	+2:23
Conch Bar, Jupiter Sound	+1:17	+1:39
Jupiter Sound, south end	+0:44	+0:50
Jupiter Inlet	+0:13	+0:02
Loxahatchee River		
Tequesta	+1:16	+2:03
N. Fork	+1:25	+2:00
Southwest Fork, (spillway)	+1:13	+1:50
Northwest Fork	+1:32	+2:11
Southwest Fork	+1:13	+1:48
Jupiter, Lake Worth Creek	+0:55	+1:17
Donald Ross Bridge	+0:41	+0:55
N. Palm Beach, Lake Worth Creek	+0:03	+0:18
Port of Palm Beach, Lake Worth	-0:02	+0:13
Palm Beach, (ocean)	-0:23	-0:17
W. Palm Beach Canal	+1:06	+1:37
Lake Worth Pier, (ocean)	-0:21	-0:16
Boynton Beach	+1:24	+2:10
Delray Beach	+1:43	+2:10
Yamato	+1:41	+2:00
Boca Raton	+0:45	+1:14
Deerfield Beach	+0:49	+1:08
Hillsboro Beach, Intracoastal Waterway	+0:24	+0:39
Hillsboro Inlet, (inside)	+0:06	+0:07
Lauderdale-By-the-Sea	-0:10	-0:07
Ft. Lauderdale		
Bahia Mar Yacht Club	+0:17	+0:39
Andrews Avenue Bridge, New River	+0:37	+0:57
Port Everglades	-0:08	-0:05
South Port Everglades	-0:02	+0:02
Hollywood Beach	+0:58	+1:09
Golden Beach	+1:34	+2:05
Sunny Isles, Biscayne Creek	+2:21	+2:28
North Miami Beach	-0:06	+0:01
Bakers Haulover Inlet, (inside)	+1:15	+1:36
Indian Creek	+1:34	+1:51
Miami Beach	-0:02	+0:01
Biscayne Bay		
Miami, 79th St. Causeway	+1:43	+2:14
Miami, Marina	+0:54	+1:18
Miami, Causeway(east end)	+1:17	+1:11
Dinner Key Marina	+1:17	+1:51
Cape Florida (west side), Key Biscayne	+0:47	+1:03
Cutler, Biscayne Bay	+1:23	+2:02
Soldier Key	+0:53	+1:20
Fowey Rocks	+0:01	+0:03
Ragged Keys, Biscayne Bay	+1:13	+1:45
Elliott Key, (outside)	-0:04	0:00
Elliott Key Harbor	+2:26	+3:25
Adams Key, Biscayne Bay	+2:48	+2:34
Christmas Point, Elliott Key	+0:35	+0:39
Totten Point, Biscayne Bay	+2:33	+3:26
Totten Key	+2:48	+3:45
Ocean Reef Club, Key Largo	+0:11	+0:20
Garden Cove, Key Largo	+0:34	+1:10
Mosquito Bank	+0:22	+0:31
Molasses Reef	+0:14	+0:12
Pumpkin Key, Card Sound	+3:10	+3:16
Tavernier, Hawk Channel	+0:29	+0:28
Alligator Reef Light	+0:40	+0:34

September 2011

SUNDAY	MONDAY	TUESDAY	WEDNESDAY	THURSDAY	FRIDAY	SATURDAY

Surf bait runs lead to snook.

Thursday 1 — 12:16a 3.1', 12:52p 3.1', 6:06a -0.3', 6:33p 0.1'

Friday 2 — 1:05a 3.0', 1:46p 3.0', 6:59a -0.2', 7:28p 0.3'

Saturday 3 — 1:57a 2.9', 2:43p 2.9', 7:56a 0.0', 8:28p 0.5'

Sunday 4 — 2:55a 2.7', 3:45p 2.7', 8:59a 0.1', 9:34p 0.6'

Monday 5 — 3:58a 2.6', 4:51p 2.7', 10:05a 0.3', 10:42p 0.7'

Tuesday 6 — 5:05a 2.6', 5:58p 2.6', 11:12a 0.3', 11:47p 0.7'

Wednesday 7 — 6:13a 2.6', 7:00p 2.7', 12:15p 0.4'

Thursday 8 — 7:15a 2.6', 7:53p 2.7', 12:46a 0.6', 1:11p 0.4'

Friday 9 — 8:09a 2.7', 8:39p 2.8', 1:38a 0.5', 2:00p 0.3'

Saturday 10 — 8:56a 2.8', 9:20p 2.8', 2:24a 0.5', 2:45p 0.3'

Sunday 11 — 9:38a 2.8', 9:57p 2.8, 3:05a 0.4', 3:25p 0.4'

Monday 12 — 10:17a 2.9', 10:32p 2.8', 3:44a 0.3', 4:03p 0.4'

Tuesday 13 — 10:54a 2.9', 11:05p 2.8', 4:20a 0.3', 4:40p 0.4'

Wednesday 14 — 11:30a 2.9', 11:39p 2.7', 4:55a 0.3', 5:15p 0.5'

Thursday 15 — 12:06p 2.8', 5:29a 0.4', 5:50p 0.6'

Friday 16 — 12:14a 2.7', 12:44p 2.7', 6:03a 0.4', 6:24p 0.7'

Saturday 17 — 12:50p 2.6', 1:25p 2.6', 6:39a 0.5', 7:02p 0.9'

Sunday 18 — 1:28a 2.5', 2:09p 2.6', 7:19a 0.6', 7:44p 1.0'

Monday 19 — 2:11a 2.4', 3:00p 2.5', 8:06a 0.7', 8:37p 1.0'

Tuesday 20 — 3:02a 2.4', 3:57p 2.5', 9:03a 0.7', 9:40p 1.1'

Wednesday 21 — 44:03a 2.4', 4:59p 2.5', 10:09a 0.7', 10:47p 1.0'

Thursday 22 — 5:11a 2.5', 6:01p 2.6', 11:15a 0.7', 11:50p 0.8'

Friday 23 — 6:18a 2.6', 6:58p 2.8', 12:16p 0.5'

Saturday 24 — 7:19a 2.8', 7:50p 2.9', 12:45p 0.6', 1:11p 0.4'

Sunday 25 — 8:16a 3.1', 8:40p 3.1', 1:37a 0.4', 2:03p 0.3'

Monday 26 — 9:09a 3.3', 9:28p 3.2', 2:26a 0.1', 2:53p 0.2'

Tuesday 27 — 10:00a 3.4', 10:15p 3.3', 3:15a -0.1', 3:43p 0.1'

Wednesday 28 — 10:50a 3.5', 11:03p 3.3', 4:03a -0.2', 4:32p 0.1'

Thursday 29 — 11:41a 3.5', 11:53p 3.3', 4:53a -0.2', 5:22p 0.2'

Friday 30 — 12:33p 3.4', 5:44a -0.2', 6:14p 0.4'

	September 1	September 15	September 30
SUNRISE	7:01 a.m.	7:07 a.m.	7:13 a.m.
SUNSET	7:40 p.m.	7:25 p.m.	7:09 p.m.

Cape Canaveral to Islamorada

Close to the Bone

INSHORE

Fall bait run still holding **jacks**, **tarpon** and **snook** in the surf, though blustery winds makes fishing tougher. Numbers of larger **mackerel**, **bluefish** and **pompano** on the rise as water cools. Surf and piers top spots. Cooling water also improves the **seatrout** bite over grass-flats of IRL and Biscayne Bay. Try topwaters at first light; soft-plastics, jigs and shrimp under a cork at other times. **Flounder** run just getting underway around jetties and bridge and dock pilings near northern inlets. Top month for 10-pound-plus **bonefish** from Miami to Islamorada flats. Also, good **permit** month.

OFFSHORE

Migrating **kingfish** join up with resident fish to improve the bite. **Spanish mackerel** numbers are up and some fish enter Biscayne Bay and the ICW. Good **dolphin** action in blue water from 100 feet on out, with slammers available. Prime time for **mutton** and **mangrove snapper** over southern reefs to the Keys; bridges, patch reefs in 20 or 30 feet of water and wrecks in 100 feet are best bets.

October Spotlight: BONEFISH

October ushers in as many big **bonefish** as March and April. Biscayne Bay and Upper Keys flats are awash in 9- to 12-pounders, with occasional "teener." Enjoy all-day fishing now that water temps are ideal, and typical breezy October days make it possible to sneak a bit closer for accurate presentations. Especially windy days makes schools mud aggressively along flats edges. Shrimp, small blue crabs, skimmer jigs and crab flies are big-fish favorites. Fish low water for tailers, or mudders on the edges. Fish are available on oceanside and bayside flats. Fish adequate tackle for the biggest fish.

TIDE CORRECTIONS For Government Cut	High	Low
Ponce de Leon Inlet	+0:04	+0:21
Cape Canaveral	-0:43	-0:40
Indian River		
Palm Bay	+3:38	+4:20
Wabasso	+2:46	+3:20
Vero Beach	+3:19	+3:51
Ft. Pierce	+1:06	+1:02
Jensen Beach	+2:38	+3:07
Sebastian Inlet	-0:26	-0:19
Vero Beach, (ocean)	-0:33	-0:24
Ft. Pierce Inlet, south jetty	-0:11	-0:13
St. Lucie River		
N. Fork	+2:48	+3:30
Stuart	+2:35	+3:34
S. Fork	+2:52	+3:35
Sewall Point	+1:33	+2:12
St. Lucie Inlet	-0:32	-0:13
Great Pocket	+1:16	+1:52
Gomez, S. Jupiter Narrows	+1:54	+2:42
Hobe Sound	+1:44	+2:23
Conch Bar, Jupiter Sound	+1:17	+1:39
Jupiter Sound, south end	+0:44	+0:50
Jupiter Inlet	+0:13	+0:02
Loxahatchee River		
Tequesta	+1:16	+2:03
N. Fork	+1:25	+2:00
Southwest Fork, (spillway)	+1:13	+1:50
Northwest Fork	+1:32	+2:11
Southwest Fork	+1:13	+1:48
Jupiter, Lake Worth Creek	+0:55	+1:17
Donald Ross Bridge	+0:41	+0:55
N. Palm Beach, Lake Worth Creek	+0:03	+0:18
Port of Palm Beach, Lake Worth	-0:02	+0:13
Palm Beach, (ocean)	-0:23	-0:17
W. Palm Beach Canal	+1:06	+1:37
Lake Worth Pier, (ocean)	-0:21	-0:16
Boynton Beach	+1:24	+2:10
Delray Beach	+1:43	+2:10
Yamato	+1:41	+2:00
Boca Raton	+0:45	+1:14
Deerfield Beach	+0:49	+1:08
Hillsboro Beach, Intracoastal Waterway	+1:24	+2:09
Hillsboro Inlet, (inside)	+0:06	+0:07
Lauderdale-By-the-Sea	-0:10	-0:07
Ft. Lauderdale		
Bahia Mar Yacht Club	+0:17	+0:39
Andrews Avenue Bridge, New River	+0:37	+0:57
Port Everglades	-0:08	-0:05
South Port Everglades	-0:02	+0:02
Hollywood Beach	+0:58	+1:09
Golden Beach	+1:34	+2:05
Sunny Isles, Biscayne Creek	+2:21	+2:28
North Miami Beach	-0:06	+0:01
Bakers Haulover Inlet, (inside)	+1:15	+1:36
Indian Creek	+1:34	+1:51
Miami Beach	-0:02	+0:01
Biscayne Bay		
Miami, 79th St. Causeway	+1:43	+2:14
Miami, Marina	+0:54	+1:18
Miami, Causeway(east end)	+1:17	+1:11
Dinner Key Marina	+1:17	+1:51
Cape Florida (west side), Key Biscayne	+0:47	+1:03
Cutler, Biscayne Bay	+1:23	+2:02
Soldier Key	+0:53	+1:20
Fowey Rocks	+0:01	+0:03
Ragged Keys, Biscayne Bay	+1:13	+1:45
Elliott Key, (outside)	-0:04	0:00
Elliott Key Harbor	+2:26	+3:25
Adams Key, Biscayne Bay	+2:48	+3:24
Christmas Point, Elliott Key	+0:35	+0:39
Turkey Point, Biscayne Bay	+2:33	+3:26
Totten Key	+2:48	+3:45
Ocean Reef Club, Key Largo	+0:11	+0:20
Garden Cove, Key Largo	+0:34	+1:10
Mosquito Bank	+0:22	+0:31
Molasses Reef	+0:14	+0:12
Pumpkin Key, Card Sound	+3:10	+3:16
Tavernier, Hawk Channel	+0:29	+0:28
Alligator Reef Light	+0:40	+0:34

October 2011

SUNDAY	MONDAY	TUESDAY	WEDNESDAY	THURSDAY	FRIDAY	SATURDAY

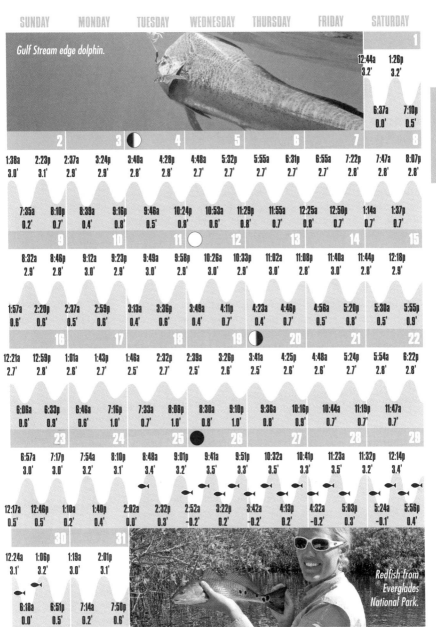

Gulf Stream edge dolphin.

1
12:44a 3.2' | 1:26p 3.2'
6:37a 0.0' | 7:10p 0.5'

2
1:38a 3.0' | 2:23p 3.1'
7:35a 0.2' | 8:10p 0.7'

3
2:37a 2.9' | 3:24p 2.9'
8:39a 0.4' | 9:16p 0.8'

4
3:40a 2.8' | 4:28p 2.8'
9:46a 0.5' | 10:24p 0.8'

5
4:48a 2.7' | 5:32p 2.7'
10:53a 0.6' | 11:29p 0.8'

6
5:55a 2.7' | 6:31p 2.7'
11:55a 0.7'

7
6:55a 2.7' | 7:22p 2.8'
12:25a 0.8' | 12:50p 0.7'

8
7:47a 2.8' | 8:07p 2.8'
1:14a 0.7' | 1:37p 0.7'

9
8:32a 2.9' | 8:46p 2.8'
1:57a 0.6' | 2:20p 0.6'

10
9:12a 3.0' | 9:23p 2.9'
2:37a 0.5' | 2:59p 0.6'

11
9:49a 3.0' | 9:58p 2.9'
3:13a 0.4' | 3:36p 0.6'

12
10:26a 3.0' | 10:33p 2.9'
3:49a 0.4' | 4:11p 0.7'

13
11:02a 3.0' | 11:08p 2.8'
4:23a 0.4' | 4:46p 0.7'

14
11:40a 3.0'
4:56a 0.5' | 5:20p 0.8'

15
11:44p 2.8' | 12:18p 2.9'
5:30a 0.5' | 5:55p 0.9'

16
12:21a 2.7' | 12:59p 2.8'
6:06a 0.6' | 6:33p 0.9'

17
1:01a 2.6' | 1:43p 2.7'
6:46a 0.6' | 7:16p 1.0'

18
1:46a 2.5' | 2:32p 2.7'
7:33a 0.7' | 8:08p 1.0'

19
2:39a 2.5' | 3:26p 2.6'
8:30a 0.8' | 9:10p 1.0'

20
3:41a 2.5' | 4:25p 2.6'
9:36a 0.8' | 10:16p 0.9'

21
4:48a 2.6' | 5:24p 2.7'
10:44a 0.7' | 11:19p 0.7'

22
5:54a 2.8' | 6:22p 2.8'
11:47a 0.7'

23
6:57a 3.0' | 7:17p 3.0'
12:17a 0.5' | 12:46p 0.5'

24
7:54a 3.2' | 8:10p 3.1'
1:10a 0.2' | 1:40p 0.4'

25
8:48a 3.4' | 9:01p 3.2'
2:02a 0.0' | 2:32p 0.3'

26
9:41a 3.5' | 9:51p 3.3'
2:52a -0.2' | 3:22p 0.2'

27
10:32a 3.5' | 10:41p 3.3'
3:42a -0.2' | 4:13p 0.2'

28
11:23a 3.5' | 11:32p 3.2'
4:32a -0.2' | 5:03p 0.3'

29
12:14p 3.4'
5:24a -0.1' | 5:56p 0.4'

30
12:24a 3.1' | 1:06p 3.2'
6:18a 0.0' | 6:51p 0.5'

31
1:19a 3.0' | 2:01p 3.1'
7:14a 0.2' | 7:50p 0.6'

Redfish from Everglades National Park.

	October 1	October 15	October 30
SUNRISE	7:13 a.m.	7:20 a.m.	7:28 a.m.
SUNSET	7:07 p.m.	6:53 p.m.	6:41p.m.

MIAMI

Cape Canaveral to Islamorada

MIAMI

Grouper Grab

INSHORE

Cooling waters bring on the **sheepshead** bite around bridge and dock pilings in ICW. Those after **flounder** head to favorite mud-bottom flats just inside inlets, particularly close to jetties and docks pilings. **Spanish mackerel** are widely available now, along beach, inside inlets and around ICW bridges. Indian River Lagoon and north Biscayne Bay **seatrout** bite is excellent, mainly for schoolies. **Pompano** numbers improve along northern surf, and grassy and shelly shoals in ICW. Good **bonefish** month (mainly between windy fronts) in Biscayne Bay and Keys.

OFFSHORE

Head out to 50- to 150-foot depth **kingfish**; a trolled spoon or rigged bait pulled deep via planer or downrigger, or a drift-fished live or dead bait will bend a rod. **Blackfin tuna** are on deepwater humps or inshore reef edge. **Cero mackerel** are on southern patch reefs, along with **mutton snapper**.

November Spotlight: GROUPER

Grab the heavy gear and soak live baits or do some deep-jigging over wrecks and reefs for **grouper**. **Reds** will be scattered throughout this region; fish north of Miami if you want to bag a **gag**. Along the Keys reef tract, **blacks** rule the roost. Check with authorities for updates on harvest regulations that change year to year. To cover maximum ground on southern ledges, troll a lipped plugs for black grouper. Don't be shocked to hook a keeper-size gag or two on a lipped lure in the Intracoastal Waterway. Keeper gags also live along undercut mangrove shorelines and deepholes around boat docks. **Goliath grouper** still fully protected from harvest; it is illegal to boat one, even for a quick photo.

	High	Low
Ponce de Leon Inlet	+0:04	+0:21
Cape Canaveral	-0:43	-0:40
Indian River		
Palm Bay	+3:38	+4:20
Wabasso	+2:46	+3:20
Vero Beach	+3:19	+3:51
Ft. Pierce	+1:06	+1:02
Jensen Beach	+2:38	+3:07
Sebastian Inlet	-0:26	-0:19
Vero Beach, (ocean)	-0:33	-0:24
Ft. Pierce Inlet, south jetty	-0:11	-0:13
St. Lucie River		
N. Fork	+2:48	+3:30
Stuart	+2:35	+3:34
S. Fork	+2:52	+3:35
Sewall Point	+1:33	+2:12
St. Lucie Inlet	-0:32	-0:13
Great Pocket	+1:16	+1:52
Gomez, S. Jupiter Narrows	+1:54	+2:42
Hobe Sound — State Park	+1:44	+2:23
Conch Bar, Jupiter Sound	+1:17	+1:39
Jupiter Sound, south end	+0:44	+0:50
Jupiter Inlet	+0:13	+0:02
Loxahatchee River		
Tequesta	+1:16	+2:03
N. Fork	+1:25	+2:00
Southwest Fork, (spillway)	+1:13	+1:50
Northwest Fork	+1:32	+2:11
Southwest Fork	+1:13	+1:48
Jupiter, Lake Worth Creek	+0:55	+1:17
Donald Ross Bridge	+0:41	+0:55
N. Palm Beach, Lake Worth Creek	+0:03	+0:18
Port of Palm Beach, Lake Worth	-0:02	+0:13
Palm Beach, (ocean)	-0:23	-0:17
W. Palm Beach Canal	+1:06	+1:37
Lake Worth Pier, (ocean)	-0:21	-0:16
Boynton Beach	+1:24	+2:10
Delray Beach	+1:43	+2:10
Yamato	+1:41	+2:00
Boca Raton	+0:45	+1:14
Deerfield Beach	+0:49	+1:08
Hillsboro Beach, Intracoastal Waterway	+0:24	+0:39
Hillsboro Inlet, (inside)	+0:06	+0:07
Lauderdale-By-the-Sea	-0:10	-0:07
Ft. Lauderdale		
Bahia Mar Yacht Club	+0:17	+0:39
Andrews Avenue Bridge, New River	+0:37	+0:57
Port Everglades	-0:08	-0:05
South Port Everglades	-0:02	+0:02
Hollywood Beach	+0:58	+1:09
Golden Beach	+1:34	+2:05
Sunny Isles, Biscayne Creek	+2:21	+2:28
North Miami Beach	-0:06	+0:01
Bakers Haulover Inlet, (inside)	+1:15	+1:36
Indian Creek	+1:34	+1:51
Miami Beach	-0:02	+0:01
Biscayne Bay		
Miami, 79th St. Causeway	+1:43	+2:14
Miami, Marina	+0:54	+1:18
Miami, Causeway(east end)	+1:17	+1:11
Dinner Key Marina	+1:17	+1:51
Cape Florida (west side), Key Biscayne	+0:47	+1:03
Cutler, Biscayne Bay	+1:23	+2:02
Soldier Key	+0:53	+1:20
Fowey Rocks	+0:01	+0:03
Ragged Keys, Biscayne Bay	+1:13	+1:45
Elliott Key, (outside)	-0:04	0:00
Elliott Key Harbor	+2:26	+3:25
Adams Key, Biscayne Bay	+2:48	+2:34
Christmas Point, Elliott Key	+0:35	+0:39
Turkey Point, Biscayne Bay	+2:33	+3:26
Totten Key	+2:48	+3:45
Ocean Reef Club, Key Largo	+0:11	+0:20
Garden Cove, Key Largo	+0:34	+1:10
Mosquito Bank	+0:22	+0:31
Molasses Reef	+0:14	+0:12
Pumpkin Key, Card Sound	+3:10	+3:16
Tavernier, Hawk Channel	+0:29	+0:28
Alligator Reef Light	+0:40	+0:34

MIAMI

SUNDAY	MONDAY	TUESDAY	WEDNESDAY	THURSDAY	FRIDAY	SATURDAY
		1 ◑	**2**	**3**	**4**	**5**
		2:16a 2.8' / 2:57p 2.9'	3:17a 2.7' / 3:55p 2.7'	4:21a 2.6' / 4:54p 2.7'	5:25a 2.6' / 5:50p 2.6'	6:24a 2.6' / 6:41p 2.6'
		8:15a 0.4' / 8:54p 0.7'	9:20a 0.6' / 9:58p 0.8'	10:24a 0.7' / 10:59p 0.7'	11:25a 0.8' / 11:54p 0.7'	12:19p 0.8'
6	**7**	**8**	**9** ○	**10**	**11**	**12**
5:16a 2.7' / 5:26p 2.6'	6:01a 2.8' / 6:08p 2.7'	6:42a 2.8' / 6:47p 2.7'	7:22a 2.9' / 7:26p 2.7'	8:00a 2.9' / 8:03p 2.7'	8:38a 2.9' / 8:42p 2.7'	9:17a 2.9' / 9:20p 2.6'
12:42a 0.6' / 11:07a 0.8'	11:25a 0.5' / 11:50p 0.7'	12:05a 0.4' / 12:30p 0.7'	12:43a 0.4' / 1:08p 0.7'	1:19a 0.3' / 1:44p 0.7'	1:54a 0.3' / 2:20p 0.7'	2:29a 0.3' / 2:56p 0.7'
13	**14**	**15**	**16**	**17** ◑	**18**	**19**
9:57a 2.8' / 10:00p 2.6'	10:38a 2.8' / 10:42p 2.5'	11:22a 2.7' / 11:29p 2.5'	12:08p 2.6'	12:22a 2.5' / 12:58p 2.6'	1:21a 2.5' / 1:52p 2.6'	2:26a 2.5' / 2:49p 2.6'
3:05a 0.3' / 3:32p 0.7'	3:42a 0.4' / 4:12p 0.7'	4:24a 0.4' / 4:56p 0.8'	5:11a 0.5' / 5:47p 0.7'	6:06a 0.6' / 6:45p 0.7'	7:09a 0.6' / 7:48p 0.6'	8:15a 0.6' / 8:50p 0.4'
20	**21**	**22**	**23**	**24** ●	**25**	**26**
3:32a 2.7' / 3:48p 2.7'	4:35a 2.8' / 4:47p 2.8'	5:35a 3.0' / 5:44p 2.9'	6:31a 3.1' / 6:38p 3.0'	7:24a 3.2' / 7:32p 3.0'	8:16a 3.3' / 8:24p 3.0'	9:06a 3.2' / 9:15p 3.0'
9:20a 0.6' / 9:50p 0.2'	10:21a 0.5' / 10:46p 0.0'	11:18a 0.4' / 11:40p -0.2'	12:12p 0.3'	12:33a -0.3' / 1:04p 0.2'	1:24a -0.4' / 1:56p 0.1'	2:15a -0.4' / 2:47p 0.2'
27	**28**	**29**	**30**			
9:56a 3.1' / 10:07p 2.9'	10:45a 3.0' / 10:59p 2.8'	11:34a 2.8' / 11:52p 2.6'	12:24p 2.7'			
3:07a -0.3' / 3:38p 0.2'	3:59a -0.1' / 4:31p 0.3'	4:52a 0.1' / 5:26p 0.4'	5:47a 0.3' / 6:23p 0.4'			

Gator fan.

	November 1	November 15	November 30
SUNRISE	7:29 a.m.	6:39 a.m.	6:50 a.m.
SUNSET	6:39 p.m.	5:32 p.m.	5:29 p.m.

DST Ends on Nov. 6

Cape Canaveral to Islamorada

MIAMI

Fatty Flatties

INSHORE

Hooking a **Spanish mackerel** is easy this month, whether you fish the surf, inlet, or the ICW bridges and shoals. Choose between trolling or casting with silver spoons or flashy jigs. Chum or drift-fish and cast over schools. Fly fishers hook up with flashy minnow patterns. **Snook** are in river headwaters. Otherwise, docks and bridges see a decent night bite. **Flounder** are on the move inside inlets, jetties and mud flats; top bait is a live finger mullet or tipped jig. **Pompano** numbers increase inshore, in surf, and around ICW bridges and over grassflats and shoals. **Redfish** abundant on Indian River Lagoon flats.

OFFSHORE

Sailfishing improves with each cold front passage. Twenty— to 40-pound fish are plentiful, so troll smaller baits such as strips and plastics designed for **dolphin**. A live pilchard is a top small sail bait. Expect to hook **kingfish** and dolphin on reef edge, too. **Grouper** fishing improves, with large **gags** migrating into the region and resident **blacks** and **reds** moving a bit shallower and feeding more aggressively.

December Spotlight: FLOUNDER

As the water cools, the seaward spawning migration of **southern flounder** gets into gear. Flounder specialists target those doormats over 10 pounds from Fort Pierce to Sebastian Inlet. It's hard to top a live finger mullet on a fishfinder rig. Prime lies for the big ones include ICW flats and spoil islands. It calls for patient fishing smack on bottom with finger mullet, shrimp or synthetic bait tipped on jigs. Do not pass up current-swept bottoms at culverts and drainage ditches.

TIDE CORRECTIONS *For Government Cut*	High	Low
Ponce de Leon Inlet	+0:04	+0:21
Cape Canaveral	-0:43	-0:40
Indian River		
Palm Bay	+3:38	+4:20
Wabasso	+2:46	+3:20
Vero Beach	+3:19	+3:51
Ft. Pierce	+1:06	+1:02
Jensen Beach	+2:38	+3:07
Sebastian Inlet	-0:26	-0:19
Vero Beach, (ocean)	-0:33	-0:24
Ft. Pierce Inlet, south jetty	-0:11	-0:13
St. Lucie River		
N. Fork	+2:48	+3:30
Stuart	+2:35	+3:34
S. Fork	+2:52	+3:35
Sewall Point	+1:33	+2:12
St. Lucie Inlet	-0:32	-0:13
Great Pocket	+1:16	+1:52
Gomez, S. Jupiter Narrows	+1:54	+2:42
Hobe Sound	+1:44	+2:23
Conch Bar, Jupiter Sound	+1:17	+1:39
Jupiter Sound, south end	+0:44	+0:50
Jupiter Inlet	+0:13	+0:02
Loxahatchee River		
Tequesta	+1:16	+2:03
N. Fork	+1:25	+2:00
Southwest Fork, (spillway)	+1:13	+1:50
Northwest Fork	+1:32	+2:11
Southwest Fork	+1:13	+1:48
Jupiter, Lake Worth Creek	+0:55	+1:17
Donald Ross Bridge	+0:41	+0:55
N. Palm Beach, Lake Worth Creek	+0:03	+0:18
Port of Palm Beach, Lake Worth	-0:02	+0:13
Palm Beach, (ocean)	-0:23	-0:17
W. Palm Beach Canal	+1:06	+1:37
Lake Worth Pier, (ocean)	-0:21	-0:16
Boynton Beach	+1:24	+2:10
Delray Beach	+1:43	+2:10
Yamato	+1:41	+2:00
Boca Raton	+0:45	+1:14
Deerfield Beach	+0:49	+1:08
Hillsboro Beach, Intracoastal Waterway	+0:24	+0:39
Hillsboro Inlet, (inside)	+0:06	+0:07
Lauderdale-By-the-Sea	-0:10	-0:07
Ft. Lauderdale		
Bahia Mar Yacht Club	+0:17	+0:39
Andrews Avenue Bridge, New River	+0:37	+0:57
Port Everglades	-0:08	-0:05
South Port Everglades	-0:02	+0:02
Hollywood Beach	+0:58	+1:09
Golden Beach	+1:34	+2:05
Sunny Isles, Biscayne Creek	+2:21	+2:28
North Miami Beach	-0:06	+0:01
Bakers Haulover Inlet, (inside)	+1:15	+1:36
Indian Creek	+1:34	+1:51
Miami Beach	-0:02	+0:01
Biscayne Bay		
Miami, 79th St. Causeway	+1:43	+2:14
Miami, Marina	+0:54	+1:18
Miami, Causeway(east end)	+1:17	+1:11
Dinner Key Marina	+1:17	+1:51
Cape Florida (west side), Key Biscayne	+0:47	+1:03
Cutler, Biscayne Bay	+1:23	+2:02
Soldier Key	+0:53	+1:20
Fowey Rocks	+0:01	+0:03
Ragged Keys, Biscayne Bay	+1:13	+1:45
Elliott Key, (outside)	-0:04	0:00
Elliott Key Harbor	+2:26	+3:25
Adams Key, Biscayne Bay	+2:48	+2:34
Christmas Point, Elliott Key	+0:35	+0:39
Turkey Point, Biscayne Bay	+2:33	+3:26
Totten Key	+2:48	+3:45
Ocean Reef Club, Key Largo	+0:11	+0:20
Garden Cove, Key Largo	+0:34	+1:01
Mosquito Bank	+0:22	+0:31
Molasses Reef	+0:14	+0:12
Pumpkin Key, Card Sound	+3:10	+3:16
Tavernier, Hawk Channel	+0:29	+0:28
Alligator Reef Light	+0:40	+0:34

December 2011

SUNDAY	MONDAY	TUESDAY	WEDNESDAY	THURSDAY	FRIDAY	SATURDAY
				1 ◑	**2**	**3**
				12:47a 2.5' / 1:15p 2.5'	1:44a 2.4' / 2:06p 2.4'	2:43a 2.3' / 2:58p 2.3'
				6:45a 0.4' / 7:21p 0.5'	7:45a 0.6' / 8:18p 0.5'	8:43a 0.7' / 9:12p 0.5'

Lobsters for the holidays.

SUNDAY	MONDAY	TUESDAY	WEDNESDAY	THURSDAY	FRIDAY	SATURDAY
4	**5**	**6**	**7**	**8**	**9** ○	**10**
3:41a 2.3' / 3:49p 2.3'	4:35a 2.3' / 4:39p 2.3'	5:25a 2.4' / 5:27p 2.3'	6:11a 2.5' / 6:12p 2.3'	6:54a 2.5' / 6:55p 2.4'	7:36a 2.6' / 7:38p 2.4'	8:17a 2.6' / 8:19p 2.4'
9:38a 0.7' / 10:02p 0.4'	10:29a 0.7' / 10:48p 0.3'	11:16a 0.6' / 11:31p 0.2'	11:59a 0.6'	12:12a 0.2' / 12:40p 0.5'	12:51a 0.1' / 1:19p 0.5'	1:29a 0.0' / 1:57p 0.4'

SUNDAY	MONDAY	TUESDAY	WEDNESDAY	THURSDAY	FRIDAY	SATURDAY
11	**12**	**13**	**14**	**15**	**16**	**17**
8:57a 2.7' / 9:01p 2.4'	9:38a 2.6' / 9:43p 2.4'	10:19a 2.6' / 10:27p 2.4'	11:00a 2.6' / 11:15p 2.4'	11:44a 2.5'	12:06a 2.4' / 12:30p 2.5'	1:03a 2.4' / 1:21p 2.4'
2:07a 0.0' / 2:35p 0.4'	2:45a 0.0' / 3:14p 0.4'	3:24a 0.0' / 3:54p 0.3'	4:07a 0.0' / 4:39p 0.3'	4:54a 0.1' / 5:27p 0.2'	5:46a 0.2' / 6:22p 0.2'	6:45a 0.3' / 7:21p 0.1'

SUNDAY	MONDAY	TUESDAY	WEDNESDAY	THURSDAY	FRIDAY	SATURDAY
18 ◐	**19**	**20**	**21**	**22**	**23** ●	**24**
2:04a 2.4' / 2:18p 2.4'	3:10a 2.4' / 3:19p 2.4'	4:15a 2.5' / 4:22p 2.4'	5:18a 2.6' / 5:23p 2.5'	6:16a 2.7' / 6:22p 2.6'	7:11a 2.8' / 7:18p 2.6'	8:02a 2.9' / 8:10p 2.7'
7:49a 0.3' / 8:23p 0.0'	8:55a 0.3' / 9:25p -0.2'	9:59a 0.3' / 10:25p -0.3'	10:59a 0.2' / 11:23p -0.4'	11:56a 0.1'	12:18a -0.5' / 12:50p 0.0'	1:10a -0.6' / 1:41p -0.1'

SUNDAY	MONDAY	TUESDAY	WEDNESDAY	THURSDAY	FRIDAY	SATURDAY
25	**26**	**27**	**28**	**29**	**30**	**31**
8:50a 2.8' / 9:00p 2.7'	9:37a 2.8' / 9:49p 2.6'	10:21a 2.7' / 10:37p 2.5'	11:05a 2.5' / 11:24p 2.4'	11:47a 2.4'	12:12a 2.2' / 12:30p 2.2'	1:01a 2.1' / 1:14p 2.1'
2:01a -0.5' / 2:31p -0.1'	2:51a -0.5' / 3:21p -0.1'	3:39a -0.3' / 4:09p -0.1'	4:27a -0.2' / 4:57p 0.0'	5:16a 0.0' / 5:46p 0.1'	6:05a 0.2' / 6:36p 0.1'	6:57a 0.3' / 7:28p 0.2'

	December 1	December 15	December 30
SUNRISE	6:50 a.m.	7:00 a.m.	7:07 a.m.
SUNSET	5:29 p.m.	5:32 p.m.	5:40 p.m.

KEY WEST STATION

- Chatham River
- Florida Bay
- Marathon
- Key West

Island Time

Update 2011: Most photos in Florida Keys travel brochures have sunrise shots of skiffs being poled for good reason. The flats fishery is alive and well, and the heralded **tarpon** spring migration was very strong in 2010. Many fly fishers reported a good bite along oceanside travel routes and on Florida Bay backcountry banks. Keys bridges were hot both night and day for bait-soakers. The January freeze put a dent in backcountry fishing, and **snook** stocks, but by spring, anglers were catching enough linesiders to signal that the fish will

rebound. **Redfish** and **seatrout** fishing from Cape Sable to the Flamingo poling flats was very good. Deep Everglades back-country haunts saw a slight decrease in snook and tarpon numbers, but **mangrove snapper**, **goliath grouper** (which have not been open to harvest yet) and small to medium **gag grouper** are plentiful in coastal rivers.

The numbers of **Spanish mackerel** were off the charts in Florida Bay with many **bluefish** mixed in. Anglers targeting tasty **tripletail** found worthwhile numbers, with an increasing influx of juvenile fish in places, indicating possible upswing in the action to come.

Big **bonefish** and **permit** were plentiful in the Upper and Middle Keys, with good numbers of smaller bones on the southernmost flats down to Key West. Fly fishers and light-tackle anglers discovered that **barracudas** ruled the winter flats during the most bitter cold fronts.

The Keys recreational **swordfish** fleet has their game dialed in, as evidenced by the steady numbers of fish taken during daylight hours. Day or night, the action is best in 1,500 feet on out on rigged squid

Florida Keys daytime swordfishing is no longer an oddity.

or live baitfish. **Kingfish** action was as good as ever, with plenty of smokers scored in numerous tournaments. **Blackfin tuna** were numerous at times on the popular humps and wrecks. **Cobia** numbers are holding their own in Florida Bay, from Sandy Key out to Gulf-edge wrecks. The winter **sailfish** season delivered in the Upper Keys by December, and by April the bite was best off the Lower Keys.

Dolphin season saw plenty of slammers taken from late May through June from the reef and out to 1,200 feet. **Yellowtail** fishing remains red-hot in the Keys over the reef in 50 to 90 feet. Night fishing is best for flags, but chumming at ledges bagged limits during the day, too.

Summer dolphin runs were strong in 2010.

An incredible array of migratory gamefish shows up in the southernmost Keys and Key West each winter, with everything from kingfish to sailfish. Tarpon, permit and bonefish cruise over clear, shallow flats all year, affording the perfect sight-casting venue. Just offshore, there are miles of coral reefs with snapper, grouper, mackerel and a host of other species. It's no wonder Key West is home to more world records than any other U.S. port.

The Everglades and the Ten Thousand Islands region are renowned for redfish, snook, trout and tarpon, all in the kind of wilderness found nowhere else. Much of this is remote country; at times the only company you'll find will be wading birds and alligators. There are no malls, hotels or subdivisions—only lush mangroves lining the creeks that twist into lonesome, fishy back bays.

One tricky aspect of fishing here involves figuring out how and when the tides will move around numerous islands and channels. Tides influenced by the Gulf and Atlantic are typically delayed the farther you get from open water, and it takes a little getting used to. If you are fishing out of Flamingo in Everglades National Park, for instance, and want to find a low, incoming tide for redfish, you can find that stage at the westernmost Keys near the Gulf, even though the tide may be falling in Snake Bight to the east.

Tides also affect offshore fishing in the Lower Keys. Outgoing tides flush baitfish over the reef into deeper water, where mackerel, tunas and other gamefish feed. There may be a well-defined color change at the edge of the tidal flow—often the focus of feeding activity. Tide corrections are based on Key West measurements, and cover a broad expanse from Long Key, around the Atlantic coast and northward in the Gulf of Mexico to Everglades City, including Florida Bay and much of the backcountry.

In the Gulf from Cape Sable northward, two tidal stages each day are mixed, meaning that one high and one low will be stronger than the other.

Average Tidal Range at Key West: 1.1 feet

Average Range of Spring Tides: 1.7 feet

Long Key to Chatham River

New Year Bites

TIDE CORRECTIONS
For Key West

	High	Low
Florida Bay		
Channel Five, east	-0:55	-0:42
Channel Five, west	-0:59	-0:40
Long Key Channel, east	-1:10	-1:07
Long Key Channel, west	+5:58	+5:40
Duck Key	-1:11	-0:40
Grassy Key, north	+5:38	+6:47
Grassy Key, south	-1:07	-0:40
Flamingo	+5:35	+7:28
Fat Deer Key	+5:09	+6:26
Vaca Key, Boot Key Harbor	-1:04	-0:37
Sombrero Key	-1:01	-0:38
Knight Key Channel	+0:17	-0:18
Pigeon Key, south side	-1:09	-0:39
Pigeon Key, inside	-0:17	+0:18
Molasses Key	-0:50	-0:11
Money Key	+0:56	+1:42
Bahia Honda Key, (bridge)	-0:39	-0:22
No Name Key, (east side)	+1:43	+1:28
Big Spanish Key	+3:26	+4:35
Cudjoe Key, west side (bridge)	+3:58	+2:59
Bird Key, (highway bridge)	-0:19	+1:00
Sand Key Light	-0:55	-0:38
Dry Tortugas	+0:35	+0:40
Channel Key	+3:15	+3:14
Cape Sable, East Cape	+3:56	+4:43
Shark River entrance	+3:20	+4:38
Lostmans River entrance	+3:22	+4:42
Onion Key, Lostmans River	+5:32	+7:46
Chatham River entrance	+3:22	+4:46

INSHORE

Keys: Southernmost flats hold some fish on coldest days; the action soars both on the oceanside and over Gulfside banks for **permit**, **bonefish** and occasional **tarpon** during sunny, warm snaps between fronts. Flats ruled by **sharks** and **barracuda** when all else stays deep on cold days. **Reds**, **trout** and **Spanish mackerel** best on backcountry bets.

Everglades: The winter mixed bag will include **trout, pompano, Spanish mackerel, ladyfish** and **jack crevalle** over grassflats and adjacent channels. Warm, sunny days in Whitewater Bay should prompt snook, reds and small tarpon to strap on the feed bag.

OFFSHORE

The reef and Hawk Channel should be alive with **Spanish mackerel**. The color change is the place for **sailfish** and **cobia**. Fish in 120 to 250 feet along the reefline and keep an eye peeled for both species on top. Chum up **blackfin tuna** with live pilchards over the wrecks and cast streamer flies, metal jigs or freeline live baits. **Black grouper** are at their seasonal peak right now.

January Spotlight: SPANISH MACKEREL

Break in a new angler, or thrill the kids with voracious, hard-fighting **Spanish mackerel** this month. They are widespread from the Hawk Channel patches to the sand-and-grass bottoms or shallow wrecks in Florida Bay. Unless sure signs like dipping birds and bait busts at the surface show you the schools, chum at a spot while the current is strong for 20 minutes

or so at anchor. Move on if fish fail to show. Troll spoons between chum spots. Live shrimp or pilchards under a cork, flashy jigs and spoons and streamer flies all work, though artificials are best in cloudy water. Macks have razor-sharp teeth, so bite leader is a must. Tie on a 6-inch trace of 50-pound mono or fluorocarbon in clear water. Try heavier mono or light wire in cloudy conditions.

January 2011

SUNDAY	MONDAY	TUESDAY	WEDNESDAY	THURSDAY	FRIDAY	SATURDAY

Heavy-handed wahoo.

KEY WEST

1
8:21a 7:25p
0.9'   1.9'
1:30a 12:22p
-0.3' 0.4'

2
9:07a 8:15p
0.9' 1.9'
2:20a 1:14p
-0.4' 0.3'

3 ●
9:47a 9:00p
0.9' 1.9'
3:05a 2:04p
-0.4' 0.3'

4
10:23a 9:42p
1.0'   1.9'
3:45a 2:51p
-0.4' 0.2'

5
10:56a 10:20p
1.0'   1.8'
4:23a 3:37p
-0.3' 0.2'

6
11:27a 10:58p
1.1'   1.8'
4:58a 4:22p
-0.2' 0.2'

7
11:58a 11:37p
1.2'   1.6'
5:33a 5:09p
-0.2' 0.2'

8
12:30p
1.2'
6:07a 5:57p
-0.1' 0.3'

9
12:17a 1:03p
1.5'   1.3'
6:40a 6:50a
0.1' 0.3'

10
1:02a 1:38p
1.3' 1.3'
7:12a 7:50p
0.2' 0.3'

11 ◐
1:54a 2:18p
1.1' 1.3'
7:46a 8:59p
0.3' 0.2'

12
2:58a 3:04p
0.9' 1.3'
8:23a 10:12p
0.4' 0.1'

13
4:20a 3:56p
0.8' 1.4'
9:07a 11:21p
0.4' 0.0'

14
5:52a 4:55p
0.7' 1.4'
10:01a 12:21a
0.5'   -0.1'

15
7:07a 5:54p
1.7' 1.5'
11:00a
0.5'

16
8:00a 6:51p
0.8' 1.7'
1:12a 11:56a
-0.2' 0.4'

17
8:43a 7:44p
0.8' 1.8'
1:57a 12:49p
-0.4' 0.3'

18 ○
9:21a 8:33a
0.9' 1.9'
2:39a 1:40p
-0.5' 0.2'

19
9:58a 9:22p
1.0' 2.0'
3:18a 2:31p
-0.5' 0.1'

20
10:34a 10:11p
1.1'   2.0'
3:57a 3:22p
-0.5' 0.0'

21
11:09a 11:00p
1.2'   1.9'
4:35a 4:16p
-0.5' -0.1'

22
11:46p 11:52p
1.4'   1.7'
5:13a 5:12p
-0.4' -0.1'

23
12:24p
1.5'
5:51a 6:12p
-0.2' -0.2'

24
12:47a 1:06p
1.4'   1.5'
6:30a 7:18p
-0.1' -0.2'

25 ◐
1:48a 1:53p
1.1' 1.6'
7:12a 8:31a
0.1' -0.2'

26
3:01a 2:48p
0.9' 1.6'
7:57p 9:51a
0.2' -0.2'

27
4:32a 3:54p
0.7' 1.6'
8:50p 11:12a
0.3' -0.2'

28
6:07a 5:08p
0.6' 1.6'
11:12a 9:54p
0.3'   0.3'

29
7:20a 6:20p
0.7' 1.6'
12:25a 11:03a
-0.3' 0.3'

30
8:12a 7:21p
0.7' 1.7'
1:25a 12:09p
-0.3' 0.3'

31
8:53a 8:12p
0.8' 1.7'
2:13a 1:07p
-0.3' 0.2'

Tarpon tango.

	January 1	January 15	January 30
SUNRISE	7:11 a.m.	7:13 a.m.	7:10 a.m.
SUNSET	5:50 p.m.	6:00 p.m.	6:11 p.m.

Long Key to Chatham River

Cuda Coup

INSHORE

Keys: The biggest **barracuda** of the year invade the flats on coldest days. Otherwise, trophy **bonefish** mud on flats edges and even crawl up skinny during warm snaps. The backcountry features **snook**, **trout**, **pompano** and **redfish** in good numbers. **Spanish mackerel**, **kingfish** and **cobia** are numerous over Gulf wrecks.

Everglades: Run the crab pot lines and markers and search for **cobia** and **tripletail**. Shallow wrecks and ledges are magnets for **mackerel, cobia, tripletail, sharks, grouper, yellowtail, pompano** and more. The bite is best when current is strong; chum to fire up the bite.

OFFSHORE

Sailfishing is just coming into seasonal peak in Middle Keys where slow-trolling or kitefishing with live baits prevails. **Mutton snapper**, **yellowtail** and **kingfish** plentiful for the cooler over the reefs where live baitfish are a deal-closer. If you are out for a workout, big **amberjack** will oblige over humps and wrecks. Serious divers will have the deeper reefs to themselves, where plenty of sizable **spiny lobsters** are the payoff.

TIDE CORRECTIONS For Key West	High	Low
Florida Bay		
Channel Five, east	-0:55	-0:42
Channel Five, west	-0:59	-0:40
Long Key Channel, east	-1:10	-1:07
Long Key Channel, west	+5:58	+5:40
Duck Key	-1:11	-0:40
Grassy Key, north	+5:38	+6:47
Grassy Key, south	-1:07	-0:40
Flamingo	+5:35	+7:28
Fat Deer Key	+5:09	+6:26
Vaca Key, Boot Key Harbor	-1:04	-0:37
Sombrero Key	-1:01	-0:38
Knight Key Channel	+0:17	-0:18
Pigeon Key, south side	-1:09	-0:39
Pigeon Key, inside	-0:17	+0:18
Molasses Key	-0:50	-0:11
Money Key	+0:56	+1:42
Bahia Honda Key, (bridge)	-0:39	-0:22
No Name Key, (east side)	+1:43	+1:28
Big Spanish Key	+3:26	+4:35
Cudjoe Key, west side (bridge)	+3:58	+2:59
Bird Key, (highway bridge)	-0:19	+1:00
Sand Key Light	-0:55	-0:38
Dry Tortugas	+0:35	+0:40
Channel Key	+3:15	+3:14
Cape Sable, East Cape	+3:56	+4:43
Shark River entrance	+3:20	+4:38
Lostmans River entrance	+3:22	+4:42
Onion Key, Lostmans River	+5:32	+7:46
Chatham River entrance	+3:22	+4:46

February Spotlight: BARRACUDA

If you have never tangled with ol' snaggletooth on the flats, this is prime time. **Barracuda** as long as your leg sun themselves over grassy flats on the coldest days. They are there to eat, too, so will run down a tube lure, topwater plug, flyrod streamer or popper. Average size is 10 to 25 pounds and they will make sizzling runs and heart-stopping leaps. Keep your distance and cast your artificials way in front of a sharp-eyed stationary fish and crank at warp speed. Big cudas are wary so stalk them quietly. They are easier to fool on cloudy, windy days.

KEY WEST

February 2011

SUNDAY	MONDAY	TUESDAY	WEDNESDAY	THURSDAY	FRIDAY	SATURDAY
		1 9:27a 0.9' 8:55P 1.7' 2:52a -0.3' 1:59p 0.1'	**2** (new moon) 9:57a 1.0' 9:33p 1.7' 3:26a -0.3' 2:46p 0.1'	**3** 10:24 1.1' 10:08p 1.6' 3:57a -0.3' 3:30p 0.0'	**4** 10:50a 1.2' 10:43p 1.6' 4:27a -0.2' 4:12p 0.0'	**5** 11:16a 1.2' 11:19p 1.4' 4:56a -0.2' 4:53p 0.0'
6 11:43a 1.3' 11:57p 1.3' 5:24a -0.1' 5:35p 0.0'	**7** 12:12p 1.3' 5:50a 0.0' 6:19 0.0'	**8** 12:38a 1.1' 12:44p 1.3' 6:17a 0.1' 7:08p 0.0	**9** 1:24a 1.0' 1:20p 1.3' 6:45a 0.2' 8:05 0.0'	**10** 2:20a 0.8' 2:03p 1.3' 7:17a 0.3' 9:14p 0.0'	**11** (moon) 3:35a 0.6' 2:57p 1.3' 7:58a 0.4' 10:31 -0.1'	**12** 5:15a 0.6' 4:05p 1.4' 8:58a 0.4' 11:43 -0.1'
13 6:39a 0.6' 5:20p 1.5' 10:15a 0.4' 12:42p -0.3'	**14** 7:34a 0.7' 6:29p 1.6' 11:28a 0.4' 1:30a -0.3'	**15** 8:14a 0.8' 7:29p 1.7' 12:32p 0.2' 2:12a -0.4	**16** 8:50a 1.0' 8:24p 1.8' 1:30p 0.1' 2:50a -0.4'	**17** (full moon) 9:24a 1.1' 9:16p 1.9' 2:24p -0.1' 3:27a -0.4'	**18** 9:57a 1.3' 10:06p 1.8' 3:18p -0.3' 4:03a -0.3'	**19** 10:32a 1.5' 10:56p 1.7' 4:11p -0.4'
20 11:08a 1.6' 11:48p 1.5' 4:40a -0.2' 5:06p -0.5'	**21** 11:46a 1.7' 12:41a 1.2' 5:16a -0.1' 6:03p -0.5'	**22** 12:28p 1.7' 1:39a 1.0' 5:54a 0.0' 7:05p -0.4'	**23** (moon) 1:16p 1.7' 2:48a 0.8' 6:35a 0.1' 8:13p -0.3'	**24** 2:41p 1.6' 4:17a 0.6' 7:21a 0.2' 9:30 -0.2'	**25** 3:26p 1.5' 5:51a 0.6' 8:18a 0.3' 10:53p -0.2'	**26** 4:51p 1.5' 9:32a 0.4'
27 7:01a 0.7' 6:11p 1.5' 12:08a -0.2' 10:53 0.3'	**28** 7:49a 0.8' 7:13p 1.5' 1:06a -0.1' 12:06p 0.3'					

KEY WEST

You don't have to leave the dock for snapper.

	February 1	February 15	February 28
SUNRISE	7:09 a.m.	7:01 a.m.	7:10 a.m.
SUNSET	6:13 p.m.	6:22 p.m.	6:30 p.m.

Long Key to Chatham River

Flats on Fire

TIDE CORRECTIONS
For Key West

	High	Low
Florida Bay		
Channel Five, east	-0:55	-0:42
Channel Five, west	-0:59	-0:40
Long Key Channel, east	-1:10	-1:07
Long Key Channel, west	+5:58	+5:40
Duck Key	-1:11	-0:40
Grassy Key, north	+5:38	+6:47
Grassy Key, south	-1:07	-0:40
Flamingo	+5:35	+7:28
Fat Deer Key	+5:09	+6:26
Vaca Key, Boot Key Harbor	-1:04	-0:37
Sombrero Key	-1:01	-0:38
Knight Key Channel	+0:17	-0:18
Pigeon Key, south side	-1:09	-0:39
Pigeon Key, inside	-0:17	+0:18
Molasses Key	-0:50	-0:11
Money Key	+0:56	+1:42
Bahia Honda Key, (bridge)	-0:39	-0:22
No Name Key, (east side)	+1:43	+1:28
Big Spanish Key	+3:26	+4:35
Cudjoe Key, west side (bridge)	+3:58	+2:59
Bird Key, (highway bridge)	-0:19	+1:00
Sand Key Light	-0:55	-0:38
Dry Tortugas	+0:35	+0:40
Channel Key	+3:15	+3:14
Cape Sable, East Cape	+3:56	+4:43
Shark River entrance	+3:20	+4:43
Lostmans River entrance	+3:22	+4:42
Onion Key, Lostmans River	+5:32	+7:46
Chatham River entrance	+3:22	+4:46

KEY WEST

INSHORE

Keys: March ushers in big **bonefish** and **permit** and first of **tarpon** migration in backcountry basins when water temps reach 74 degrees. Target the battling brown bomber, **cobia**, which should be trailing rays. Backcountry waters offer variety with **pompano**, **seatrout**, **redfish** and **snook** at the top of the list.

Everglades: Baitfish such as mullet and pilchards in great supply, so expect **snook**, big **seatrout** and an increasing number of **redfish** to stage up in flats potholes out front of Flamingo and to the south in Florida Bay. Everglades National Park boundary banks such as Schooner, Oxfoot and First National see first of big tarpon run.

OFFSHORE

Keys Gulf wrecks are hopping this month for **cobia**, **kings** and **permit**. **Amberjack** and ever-present **goliath grouper** crash the party at times and will swipe baits, or your hooked fish, if you do not get 'em aboard quickly. If you want to hook an AJ tease 'em to the top with live baits at the shallower structures. Head for Atlantic-side outer reef and wrecks for **African pompano** and **mutton snapper**. **Sailfishing** is off the charts, and chances of bagging a bull **dolphin** grow daily.

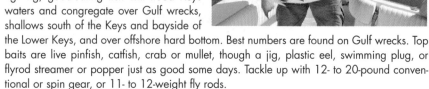

March Spotlight: COBIA

Unlike most other sight-fishing species, **cobia** are relatively easy to fool, endearing them to many anglers. These hardfighting, good-eating fish will flood Keys waters and congregate over Gulf wrecks, shallows south of the Keys and bayside of the Lower Keys, and over offshore hard bottom. Best numbers are found on Gulf wrecks. Top baits are live pinfish, catfish, crab or mullet, though a jig, plastic eel, swimming plug, or flyrod streamer or popper just as good some days. Tackle up with 12- to 20-pound conventional or spin gear, or 11- to 12-weight fly rods.

Pleasing permit.

SUNDAY	MONDAY	TUESDAY	WEDNESDAY	THURSDAY	FRIDAY	SATURDAY
		1	**2**	**3** ●	**4**	**5**
		8:25a 0.9' · 8:03p 1.6'	8:55a 1.0' · 8:44p 1.6'	9:21a 1.2' · 9:21p 1.6'	9:44a 1.3' · 9:55p 1.5'	10:08a 1.4' · 10:29p 1.4'
6	**7**	**8**	**9**	**10**	**11**	**12** ◑
1:49a -0.1' · 1:05p 0.2'	2:24a -0.1' · 1:56p 0.1'	2:54a -0.1' · 2:40p 0.0'	3:22a -0.1' · 3:20p -0.1'	3:49a 0.0' · 3:59p -0.1'		
10:32a 1.4' · 11:04p 1.3'	10:59a 1.5' · 11:41p 1.2'	11:27a 1.5'	12:21a 1.1' · 11:58a 1.5'	1:06a 0.9' · 12:34p 1.5'	1:59a 0.8' · 1:16p 1.4'	3:10a 0.7' · 2:12p 1.4'
13	**14**	**15**	**16**	**17**	**18** ○	**19**
4:15a 0.0' · 4:36p -0.2'	4:40a 0.1' · 5:13p -0.2'	5:05a 0.2' · 5:52p -0.2'	5:31a 0.2' · 6:36a -0.2'	5:59a 0.3' · 7:27p -0.1'	6:32a 0.4' · 8:30p -0.1'	7:16a 0.4' · 9:45p -0.1'
20	**21**	**22**	**23**	**24**	**25**	**26** ◐
6:41a 0.7' · 5:25p 1.4'	8:01a 0.7' · 6:50p 1.5'	8:54a 0.9' · 8:09p 1.6'	9:34a 1.0' · 9:16p 1.7'	10:09a 1.2'	10:15 1.8' · 10:43a 1.4'	11:09p 1.8' · 11:18a 1.6'
10:22a 0.5' · 1:00a -0.1'	11:50a 0.5' · 2:02a -0.1'	1:13p 0.4' · 2:51a -0.2'	2:23p 0.2' · 3:34a -0.2'	3:2p 0.0' · 4:13a -0.1' 🐟	4:19p -0.3' · 4:50a -0.1' 🐟	5:12p -0.5'
27	**28**	**29**	**30**	**31**		
12:01a 1.7' · 11:54a 1.8'	12:51a 1.5' · 12:32p 1.9'	1:42a 1.3' · 1:13p 2.0'	2:34a 1.1' · 1:58p 1.9'	3:29a 0.9' · 2:48p 1.8'	4:34a 0.8' · 3:47p 1.7'	5:54a 0.7' · 5:00p 1.5'
5:27a 0.0' 🐟 · 6:05p -0.6'	6:04a 0.0' 🐟 · 6:57p -0.6'	6:42a 0.1' 🐟 · 7:52p -0.6'	7:22a 0.2' 🐟 · 8:50p -0.5'	8:05a 0.2' · 9:54p -0.3'	8:55a 0.3' · 11:06p -0.1'	9:59a 0.4'
7:19a 0.8' · 6:27p 1.4'	8:24a 0.9' · 7:50p 1.4'	9:09a 1.0' · 8:55p 1.4'	9:43a 1.2' · 9:45p 1.4'	10:11a 1.3' · 10:28p 1.4'		
12:22a 0.0' · 11:22a 0.5'	1:30a 0.0' · 12:49p 0.4'	2:25a 0.1' · 2:02p 0.4'	3:06a 0.1' · 3:00p 0.3'	3:41a 0.1' · 3:48p 0.1'		

KEY WEST

	March 1	March 15	March 30
SUNRISE	6:50 a.m.	7:36 a.m.	7:21 a.m.
SUNSET	5:30 p.m.	7:36 p.m.	7:43 p.m.

DST Starts on March 13

Long Key to Chatham River

Set for Sails

TIDE CORRECTIONS
For Key West

	High	Low
Florida Bay		
Channel Five, east	-0:55	-0:42
Channel Five, west	-0:59	-0:40
Long Key Channel, east	-1:10	-1:07
Long Key Channel, west	+5:58	+5:40
Duck Key	-1:11	-0:40
Grassy Key, north	+5:38	+6:47
Grassy Key, south	-1:07	-0:40
Flamingo	+5:35	+7:28
Fat Deer Key	+5:09	+6:26
Vaca Key, Boot Key Harbor	-1:04	-0:37
Sombrero Key	-1:01	-0:38
Knight Key Channel	+0:17	-0:18
Pigeon Key, south side	-1:09	-0:39
Pigeon Key, inside	-0:17	+0:18
Molasses Key	-0:50	-0:11
Money Key	+0:56	+1:42
Bahia Honda Key, (bridge)	-0:39	-0:22
No Name Key, (east side)	+1:43	+1:28
Big Spanish Key	+3:26	+4:35
Cudjoe Key, west side (bridge)	+3:58	+2:59
Bird Key, (highway bridge)	-0:19	+1:00
Sand Key Light	-0:55	-0:38
Dry Tortugas	+0:35	+0:40
Channel Key	+3:15	+3:14
Cape Sable, East Cape	+3:56	+4:33
Shark River entrance	+3:20	+4:38
Lostmans River entrance	+3:22	+4:42
Onion Key, Lostmans River	+5:32	+7:46
Chatham River entrance	+3:22	+4:46

INSHORE

Keys: Spring means all-day flats action, with water temps ideal for big **bonefish**, **tarpon**, **permit** or **redfish**. As a plus, typical spring winds help take the edge off wary fish that can be hard to approach in dead of summer. Scan flats edges for tarpon and permit, and biggest, mudding bones.

Everglades: **Redfish** and **seatrout** take to shallow grassflats on high water, and stage at channel edges and runouts on falling tide. **Snook** and seatrout stack up along beaches from East Cape to Northwest Cape, and nearby ditches and creeks. **Tarpon** are flooding into basins throughout Florida Bay. Top time for **tripletail** along crabtrap floats.

OFFSHORE

Great month for that **dolphin** of a lifetime right at the color change over the reef. Watch for flyingfish showers and get baits on the spot. That feeding action also attracts **blue marlin** so have a big rod ready when you work a bunch of schoolies. The **yellowtail** bite is good at night, and **muttons** will hold deeper in the chumline.

April Spotlight: SAILFISH

Sailfishing is terrific this month, with numerous sailfish tourneys slated. Spindlebeaks of all sizes will be moving along color changes, pushing into the current, mainly in the 90- to

200-foot depth range. It is a common, visual treat to spot free-jumpers. Keep a sharp eye out for tailers on wave crests, and then get a pitch bait to the fish immediately. Tailing is most common when east winds buck eastbound current. Kitefishing is most common with the tournament crowd but live baiting with pilchards on flatlines will produce good numbers of bites, too. While out for sails, chances are excellent that you will hook blackfin tuna, bonito, and possibly kingfish and wahoo, even at the surface. Keep a rig in the water with wire for that reason.

KEY WEST

April 2011

SUNDAY	MONDAY	TUESDAY	WEDNESDAY	THURSDAY	FRIDAY	SATURDAY
					1	**2**
					10:36a 1.4' 11:06p 1.4' 4:11a 0.2' 4:29p 0.0'	11:00a 1.5' 11:41p 1.4' 4:39a 0.2' 5:07p -0.1'

Artificial reefs provide recreational diving and fishing.

SUNDAY	MONDAY	TUESDAY	WEDNESDAY	THURSDAY	FRIDAY	SATURDAY
3 ●	**4**	**5**	**6**	**7**	**8**	**9**
11:25a 1.6'	12:16a 1.3' 11:52a 1.7'	12:52a 1.3' 12:20p 1.7'	1:30a 1.2' 12:51p 1.7'	2:11p 1.1' 1:24p 1.7'	2:57a 1.0' 2:01p 1.6'	3:50a 0.9' 2:47p 1.6'
5:06a 0.2' 5:42p -0.2'	5:32a 0.3' 6:17p -0.3'	5:58a 0.3' 6:53p -0.3'	6:25a 0.3' 7:31p -0.3'	6:54a 0.4' 8:14p -0.2'	7:26a 0.4' 9:03p -0.2'	8:05a 0.5' 10:01p -0.1'

SUNDAY	MONDAY	TUESDAY	WEDNESDAY	THURSDAY	FRIDAY	SATURDAY
10	**11** ◐	**12**	**13**	**14**	**15**	**16**
4:56a 0.8' 3:44p 1.6'	6:09a 0.9' 4:59p 1.5'	7:14a 1.0' 6:27p 1.5'	8:04a 1.1' 7:52p 1.5'	8:46a 1.3' 9:04p 1.6'	9:24a 1.6' 10:07p 1.6'	10:02a 1.8' 11:03p 1.5'
8:57a 0.5' 11:08p 0.0'	10:12a 0.6' 12:14a 0.0'	11:43a 0.5' 1:14a 0.0'	1:06p 0.4' 2:04a 0.1'	2:16p 0.1' 2:48a 0.1'	3:17p 0.1' 3:30a -0.1'	3:30a 0.1' 4:12p -0.4'

SUNDAY	MONDAY	TUESDAY	WEDNESDAY	THURSDAY	FRIDAY	SATURDAY
17 ○	**18**	**19**	**20**	**21**	**22**	**23**
10:41a 2.0' 11:56p 1.4'	11:21a 2.1' 12:46a 1.3'	12:03p 2.1' 1:35a 1.2'	12:48p 2.1' 2:24a 1.1'	1:35p 2.0' 3:16a 1.0'	2:26p 1.9' 4:14a 0.9'	3:23p 1.7'
4:10a 0.2' 5:05p -0.6'	4:49a 0.2' 5:56p -0.7'	5:29a 0.2' 6:47p -0.7'	6:11a 0.2' 7:40p -0.6'	6:54a 0.3' 8:34p -0.4'	7:42a 0.3' 9:32p -0.2'	8:37a 0.4' 10:35p -0.1'

SUNDAY	MONDAY	TUESDAY	WEDNESDAY	THURSDAY	FRIDAY	SATURDAY
24 ◑	**25**	**26**	**27**	**28**	**29**	**30**
5:20a 0.9' 4:29p 1.5'	6:29a 1.0' 5:48p 1.4'	7:28a 1.1' 7:10p 1.3'	8:13a 1.2' 8:22p 1.3'	8:48a 1.4' 9:19p 1.3'	9:18a 1.5' 10:06p 1.3'	9:47a 1.6' 10:48p 1.3'
9:46a 0.5' 11:38p 0.1'	11:12a 0.6' 12:37a 0.2'	12:37p 0.5' 1:28a 0.3'	1:48p 0.4' 2:10a 0.3'	2:45p 0.3' 2:47a 0.4'	3:32p 0.1' 3:20a 0.4'	4:13p 0.0'

	April 1	April 15	April 30
SUNRISE	7:19 a.m.	7:05 a.m.	6:53 a.m.
SUNSET	7:43 p.m.	7:49 p.m.	7:56 p.m.

Key West Station

Long Key to Chatham River

May-hem

KEY WEST

INSHORE

Keys: Peak of the **tarpon** migration is here, with bridges and flats equally productive. All-day **bonefishing** is excellent throughout the Keys for both tailers and mudding schools. Night bridge bite excellent for tarpon, **snook**, and **mangrove snapper**. **Permit** dependable on channel-edge flats from Upper to Middle Keys to the Marquesas and Key West flats.

Everglades: **Snook** are on the feed for baitfish along the Cape Sable beaches and coastal creeks and rivermouths to the west. Structure is covered with pre-spawn aggregations of **mangrove snapper**. **Trout** school up in mullet muds in backcountry lakes; tailing **reds** more active over Flamingo mud flats on lower ends of the tide. Look for **snook** in potholes on same flats.

OFFSHORE

Dolphin fishing is a best bet anywhere from the reef out to 1,800 feet from upper Key Largo to the Tortugas. Get intel from your tackle shop while picking up baits, and monitor VHF radio chatter for tips about hot depths. Fish bottom baits around the reef for **mutton snapper**; fish live shrimp or pilchards on long leaders. A 20- to 30-mile run north from the Lower and Middle Keys into the Gulf will put you in **blackfin tuna** country—fish near shrimp boats culling the night's catch.

TIDE CORRECTIONS
For Key West

	High	Low
Florida Bay		
Channel Five, east	-0:55	-0:42
Channel Five, west	-0:59	-0:40
Long Key Channel, east	-1:10	-1:07
Long Key Channel, west	+5:58	+5:40
Duck Key	-1:11	-0:40
Grassy Key, north	+5:38	+6:47
Grassy Key, south	-1:07	-0:40
Flamingo	+5:35	+7:28
Fat Deer Key	+5:09	+6:26
Vaca Key, Boot Key Harbor	-1:04	-0:37
Sombrero Key	-1:01	-0:38
Knight Key Channel	+0:17	-0:18
Pigeon Key, south side	-1:09	-0:39
Pigeon Key, inside	-0:17	+0:18
Molasses Key	-0:50	-0:11
Money Key	+0:56	+1:42
Bahia Honda Key, (bridge)	-0:39	-0:22
No Name Key, (east side)	+1:43	+1:28
Big Spanish Key	+3:26	+4:35
Cudjoe Key, west side (bridge)	+3:58	+2:59
Bird Key, (highway bridge)	-0:19	+1:00
Sand Key Light	-0:55	-0:38
Dry Tortugas	+0:35	+0:40
Channel Key	+3:15	+3:14
Cape Sable, East Cape	+3:56	+4:43
Shark River entrance	+3:20	+4:38
Lostmans River entrance	+3:22	+4:42
Onion Key, Lostmans River	+5:32	+7:46
Chatham River entrance	+3:22	+4:46

May Spotlight: PERMIT

Catching a **permit** in May boils down to choosing between two fisheries—the flats or the wrecks. Permit stick to mainly flats edges due to their size and the strongest current, but will tail up very shallow on flood tides. Pole quietly, cast live crabs, shrimp, or jigs with 10-pound spin gear, or crab flies with a 10-weight flyrod. Check bridge channel tidelines where sargassum attracts surface-feeding fish that are hunting

for crabs. Permit can be easiest to hook over wrecks unless they are hard-pounded by boat traffic. Approach quietly and look for surface schools, and cast from a distance with the aforementioned baits. Chumming wrecks with crushed crabs can bring out the jack in a permit.

May 2011

KEY WEST

	SUNDAY	MONDAY	TUESDAY	WEDNESDAY	THURSDAY	FRIDAY	SATURDAY
Date	**1**	**2** (new moon)	**3**	**4**	**5**	**6**	**7**
	10:15a 1.7'	10:45a 1.7'	11:17a 1.8'	11:50a 1.8'	12:25p 1.8'	1:02p 1.8'	1:44p 1.8'
	11:26p 1.2'	12:04a 1.2'	12:42a 1.2'	1:22a 1.1'	2:04a 1.1'	2:50a 1.0'	
	3:50a 0.4'	4:20a 0.4'	4:49a 0.4'	5:19a 0.4'	5:51a 0.4'	6:25a 0.4'	7:05a 0.5'
	4:50p -0.2'	5:25p -0.3'	6:00p -0.3'	6:37p -0.3'	7:16p -0.3'	7:59p -0.3'	8:46p -0.2'

	SUNDAY	MONDAY	TUESDAY	WEDNESDAY	THURSDAY	FRIDAY	SATURDAY
Date	**8**	**9** (first quarter)	**10**	**11**	**12**	**13**	**14**
	3:41a 1.0'	4:35a 1.0'	5:31a 1.1'	6:24a 1.2'	7:12a 1.4'	7:58a 1.6'	8:42a 1.8'
	2:32p 1.7'	3:31p 1.6'	4:44p 1.5'	6:10p 1.4'	7:37p 1.3'	8:55p 1.3'	10:01p 1.3'
	7:53a 0.5'	8:55a 0.6'	10:14a 0.6'	11:40a 0.4'	12:24a 0.2'	1:14a 0.2'	2:01a 0.3'
	9:38p -0.1'	10:33p 0.0'	11:30p 0.1'		1:00p 0.2'	2:10p 0.0'	3:10p -0.3'

	SUNDAY	MONDAY	TUESDAY	WEDNESDAY	THURSDAY	FRIDAY	SATURDAY
Date	**15**	**16** (full moon)	**17**	**18**	**19**	**20**	**21**
	9:27a 2.0'	10:12a 2.1'	10:57a 2.2'	11:44a 2.2'	12:31p 2.1'	2:07p 1.9'	2:07p 1.7'
	10:59p 1.2'	11:50p 1.2'	12:38a 1.1'	1:25a 1.1'	2:10p 1.0'	2:57a 1.0'	
	2:47a 0.3'	3:31a 0.3'	4:15a 0.3'	5:00a 0.3'	5:46a 0.3'	6:33a 0.3'	7:25a 0.4'
	4:05p -0.5'	4:58p -0.6'	5:48p -0.6'	6:37p -0.6'	7:27p -0.5'	9:06p -0.2'	9:06p -0.2'

	SUNDAY	MONDAY	TUESDAY	WEDNESDAY	THURSDAY	FRIDAY	SATURDAY
Date	**22**	**23** (last quarter)	**24**	**25**	**26**	**27**	**28**
	3:46a 1.0'	4:37a 1.1'	5:29a 1.2'	6:18a 1.3'	7:03a 1.4'	7:43a 1.5'	8:21a 1.6'
	2:59p 1.7'	3:55p 1.5'	5:00p 1.3'	6:15p 1.2'	7:35p 1.1'	8:44p 1.1'	9:41p 1.0'
	8:23a 0.5'	9:32a 0.5'	10:51a 0.5'	12:11p 0.5'	12:23a 0.3'	1:07a 0.4'	1:47a 0.5'
	9:57p 0.0'	10:47p 0.1'	11:37p 0.2'		1:21p 0.4'	2:20p 0.2'	3:09p 0.0'

	SUNDAY	MONDAY	TUESDAY
Date	**29**	**30**	**31**
	8:57a 1.6'	9:34a 1.7'	10:12a 1.8'
	10:28p 1.0'	11:10p 1.0'	11:50p 1.0'
	2:24a 0.5'	2:59a 0.5'	3:34a 0.5'
	3:51p -0.1'	4:30p -0.2'	5:08 -0.3'

Dolphin smiles.

	May 1	May 15	May 30
SUNRISE	6:52 a.m.	6:44 a.m.	6:39 a.m.
SUNSET	7:57 p.m.	8:04 p.m.	8:11 p.m.

Long Key to Chatham River

In Tune with June

INSHORE

Keys: **Bonefishing** is excellent both early and late in the day due to rising water temps. Best tailing action is at first light and at dusk after thunderstorms abate. The oceanside **tarpon** run is underway, but backcountry fish tend to bite better. Bridge channel tarpon fishing is best at night or first light for anglers fishing live crabs and pinfish.

Everglades: Head for grass-and-sand bottom in Florida Bay from the national park boundary west where **mangrove snapper** are schooled and ready to pounce on fresh pinfish steaks, whole, small pinfish or squid-tipped jigs. Either drift-fish the baits with splitshot on the line, or chum the snappers at anchor. Big **tarpon** are moving in Sandy Key Basin, and along Nine Mile, Oxfoot and Schooner banks. Flats slams of **reds**, **snook** and baby tarpon are a good bet over most Florida Bay flats. Deeper basins hold larger, rolling tarpon at dawn.

OFFSHORE

Dolphin are widespread from the edge out to 1,000 feet or more. Hunt for signs such as frigatebirds, flotsam or distinct rips with temp changes rather than blindly trolling in open water. Weedlines set up with calmer weather, and you can troll this structure with either small lures and feathers, slow-troll livies or cast at fish sighted under weeds, or where baitfish are gathered. **Sailfish**, **wahoo** and **swordfish** also demand some bluewater time.

June Spotlight: TARPON

If you can't find **tarpon** this month, you should switch to a different quarry! The oceanside sightfishing flats hold great numbers but those fish see a lot of boats and are toughest to feed most days. Best bites occur on small 1/0 flies fished with 10- to 12-weight rods and small lures over darker bottoms during low light primarily. Backcountry basins hold "laid-up" fish that will eat a fly or soft plastic if approached quietly. Most fish, and some very big fish, are hooked in bridge channels both day and night on 12- to 30-pound spin and conventional tackle rigged with 60- to 100-pound bite leaders. Spring tides find silver kings in a chow line containing crabs, shrimp and baitfish.

TIDE CORRECTIONS		
For Key West		
	High	Low
Florida Bay		
Channel Five, east	-0:55	-0:42
Channel Five, west	-0:59	-0:40
Long Key Channel, east	-1:10	-1:07
Long Key Channel, west	+5:58	+5:40
Duck Key	-1:11	-0:40
Grassy Key, north	+5:38	+6:47
Grassy Key, south	-1:07	-0:40
Flamingo	+5:35	+7:28
Fat Deer Key	+5:09	+6:26
Vaca Key, Boot Key Harbor	-1:04	-0:37
Sombrero Key	-1:01	-0:38
Knight Key Channel	+0:17	-0:18
Pigeon Key, south side	-1:09	-0:39
Pigeon Key, inside	-0:17	+0:18
Molasses Key	-0:50	-0:11
Money Key	+0:56	+1:42
Bahia Honda Key, (bridge)	-0:39	-0:22
No Name Key, (east side)	+1:43	+1:28
Big Spanish Key	+3:26	+4:35
Cudjoe Key, west side (bridge)	+3:58	+2:59
Bird Key, (highway bridge)	-0:19	+1:00
Sand Key Light	-0:55	-0:38
Dry Tortugas	+0:35	+0:40
Channel Key	+3:15	+3:14
Cape Sable, East Cape	+3:56	+4:43
Shark River entrance	+3:20	+4:38
Lostmans River entrance	+3:22	+4:42
Onion Key, Lostmans River	+5:32	+7:46
Chatham River entrance	+3:22	+4:46

June 2011

KEY WEST

SUNDAY	MONDAY	TUESDAY	WEDNESDAY	THURSDAY	FRIDAY	SATURDAY

Queen snapper.

Week 1

			1 (new moon)	2	3	4
			10:50a 1.9' / 12:30a 1.0'	11:28a 1.9' / 1:10a 1.0'	12:08p 1.9' / 1:52a 1.0'	12:51p 1.9'
			4:09a 0.4' / 5:45p -0.4'	4:46a 0.4' / 6:23p -0.4'	5:25a 0.4' / 7:02p -0.4'	6:07a 0.4' / 7:43p -0.3'

Week 2

5	6	7	8 (first quarter)	9	10	11
2:34a 1.1' / 1:36p 1.9'	3:18a 1.1' / 2:27p 1.8'	4:02a 1.2' / 3:26p 1.6'	4:48a 1.3' / 4:35p 1.4'	5:36a 1.5' / 5:58p 1.2'	6:25a 1.6' / 7:28p 1.1'	7:17a 1.8' / 8:50p 1.0'
6:56a 0.4' / 8:27p -0.3'	7:51a 0.4' / 9:11p -0.2'	8:57a 0.4' / 9:58p 0.0'	10:14a 0.4' / 10:46p 0.1'	11:35a 0.2' / 11:36p 0.2'	12:53p 0.1'	12:26a 0.3' / 2:02p -0.2'

Week 3

12	13	14	15 (full moon)	16	17	18
8:09a 1.9' / 9:58p 1.0'	9:02a 2.0' / 10:54p 1.0'	0:54a 2.1' / 11:43p 1.0'	10:45a 2.1' / 12:27p 1.0'	11:33a 2.1' / 1:09a 1.0'	12:19p 2.0' / 1:49a 1.0'	1:04p 1.9'
1:18a 0.4' / 3:04p -0.3'	2:09a 0.4' / 4:00p -0.5'	2:59a 0.3' / 4:52p -0.5'	3:49a 0.3' / 5:40p -0.5'	4:39a 0.3' / 6:26p -0.5'	5:29a 0.3' / 7:09p -0.4'	6:19a 0.3' / 7:52p -0.3'

Week 4

19	20	21	22	23 (last quarter)	24	25
2:28a 1.1' / 1:48p 1.8'	3:07a 1.2' / 2:33p 1.6'	3:46a 1.2' / 3:20p 1.4'	4:26a 1.3' / 4:15p 1.2'	5:07a 1.4' / 5:20p 1.1'	5:51a 1.4' / 6:39p 0.9'	6:37a 1.5' / 8:02p 0.9'
7:11a 0.4' / 8:33p -0.1'	8:08a 0.4' / 9:13p 0.0'	9:10a 0.4' / 9:53p 0.1'	10:19a 0.4' / 10:34p 0.3'	11:32a 0.4' / 11:15p 0.4'	12:43p 0.3' / 11:58p 0.5'	1:45p 0.2'

Week 5

26	27	28	29	30		
7:25a 1.6' / 9:12p 0.9'	8:13a 1.6' / 10:06p 0.9'	9:00a 1.7' / 10:51p 0.9'	9:46a 1.8' / 11:32p 1.0'	10:30a 1.9'		
12:42a 0.5' / 2:40p 0.0'	1:26p 0.5' / 3:27a -0.1'	2:11a 0.5' / 4:10p -0.2'	2:54a 0.5' / 4:49p -0.3'	3:38p 0.4' / 5:27p -0.3'		

	June 1	June 15	June 30
SUNRISE	6:38 a.m.	6:38 a.m.	6:42 a.m.
SUNSET	8:12 p.m.	8:17 p.m.	8:20 p.m.

Long Key to Chatham River

Roll Out Early

TIDE CORRECTIONS
For Key West

Florida Bay	High	Low
Channel Five, east	-0:55	-0:42
Channel Five, west	-0:59	-0:40
Long Key Channel, east	-1:10	-1:07
Long Key Channel, west	+5:58	+5:40
Duck Key	-1:11	-0:40
Grassy Key, north	+5:38	+6:47
Grassy Key, south	-1:07	-0:40
Flamingo	+5:35	+7:28
Fat Deer Key	+5:09	+6:26
Vaca Key, Boot Key Harbor	-1:04	-0:37
Sombrero Key	-1:01	-0:38
Knight Key Channel	+0:17	-0:18
Pigeon Key, south side	-1:09	-0:39
Pigeon Key, inside	-0:17	+0:18
Molasses Key	-0:50	-0:11
Money Key	+0:56	+1:42
Bahia Honda Key, (bridge)	-0:39	-0:22
No Name Key, (east side)	+1:43	+1:28
Big Spanish Key	+3:26	+4:35
Cudjoe Key, west side (bridge)	+3:58	+2:59
Bird Key, (highway bridge)	-0:19	+1:00
Sand Key Light	-0:55	-0:38
Dry Tortugas	+0:35	+0:40
Channel Key	+3:15	+3:14
Cape Sable, East Cape	+3:56	+4:43
Shark River entrance	+3:20	+4:38
Lostmans River entrance	+3:22	+4:42
Onion Key, Lostmans River	+5:32	+7:46
Chatham River entrance	+3:22	+4:46

INSHORE

Keys: Sleep in and you'll miss it all. Flats bites are strictly first light 'til "clock in" time, and right at dusk. Rainy, overcast days offer respite for **bonefishermen**, but mudding fish in 2 to 4 feet are the best bet. Bridge **tarpon** are best at night now. Fish live crabs or dredge with bushy dark flies.

Everglades: Great time for tailing **redfish** mainly on low water and early in the day from Sandy Key east to Snake Bight out front of Flamingo. **Tarpon** from 5 to 80 pounds roll and will take flies and plastics on flats at high tide and in basins on low water. Cast to **snook** in flats potholes and in channels around mangrove islands. **Mangrove snapper** are at peak in numbers over Florida Bay grass and sand bottom.

OFFSHORE

Reef fishing is excellent at night, or early and late in the day. Chumming will draw **mangrove**, **yellowtail**, and **mutton snapper**. **Red** and **black grouper** equally abundant over ledges. Look for **blackfin tuna** at the Islamorada and Marathon humps. **Dolphin** are farther offshore and require run-and-gun hunting. The two-day **lobster** sport season takes place late in the month.

July Spotlight: DOLPHIN

Small-boat anglers can range out for **dolphin** now that seas are flat. Weedlines gather well, and allow for concentrated trolling both at the surface and deep under flotsam. After the sun is high in the sky, try dropping a jig. Better yet, fish a live bait deep under weed rafts or boards and similar flotsam for dolphin when the surface is quiet. Keep an eye out for building thunderstorms and head inshore if the threat arises. Ask your bait shop personnel about hot depths and listen to VHF radio chatter. Live chumming may get a bite from hard-fished schoolies.

July 2011

SUNDAY	MONDAY	TUESDAY	WEDNESDAY	THURSDAY	FRIDAY	SATURDAY

The Vandenberg is now a Keys artificial reef.

					1 ●	**2**
					12:10a 11:14a 1.0' 2.0'	12:48a 11:58a 1.1' 2.0'
					4:23a 6:05p 0.4' -0.4'	5:09a 6:43p 0.4' -0.4'

3	**4**	**5**	**6**	**7** ◑	**8**	**9**
1:26a 12:44p 1.2' 2.0'	2:04a 1:32p 1.3' 1.9'	2:42a 2:24p 1.4' 1.7'	3:22a 3:23p 1.5' 1.5'	4:05a 4:30p 1.6' 1.3'	4:52a 5:51p 1.7' 1.0'	5:46a 7:23p 1.8' 0.9'
5:58a 7:21p 0.3' -0.3'	6:52a 8:00p 0.3' -0.2'	7:50a 8:39p 0.3' -0.1'	8:55a 9:21p 0.2' 0.1'	10:08a 10:05p 0.2' 0.2'	11:25a 10:52p 0.1' 0.3'	12:43p 11:46p 0.0' 0.4'

10	**11**	**12**	**13**	**14** ○	**15**	**16**
6:47a 8:47p 1.9' 0.9'	7:50a 9:53p 1.9' 0.9'	8:52a 10:45p 2.0' 0.9'	9:49a 11:29p 2.1' 1.0'	10:40a 2.1'	12:08a 11:26a 1.0' 2.1'	12:43a 12:08p 1.1' 2.0'
1:56a 12:43a -0.2' 0.4'	3:00p 1:43a -0.3' 0.4'	3:56p 2:41a -0.3' 0.4'	4:45p 3:36a -0.3' 0.3'	5:28p 4:28a -0.3' 0.3'	6:07p 5:19a -0.3' 0.3'	6:44p -0.2'

17	**18**	**19**	**20**	**21**	**22** ◐	**23**
1:17a 12:48p 1.2' 1.9'	1:48a 1:27p 1.3' 1.8'	2:20a 2:07p 1.4' 1.6'	2:52a 2:50p 1.4' 1.4'	3:26a 3:38p 1.5' 1.3'	4:04a 4:36p 1.5' 1.1'	4:47a 5:48p 1.5' 0.9'
6:08a 7:19p 0.3' -0.1'	6:57a 7:53p 0.3' 0.0'	7:47a 8:26p 0.4' 0.1'	8:40a 8:58p 0.4' 0.3'	9:39a 9:31p 0.4' 0.4'	10:44a 10:07p 0.4' 0.5'	11:54a 10:47p 0.4' 0.6'

24	**25**	**26**	**27**	**28**	**29** ●	**30**
5:38a 7:18p 1.6' 0.9'	6:35a 8:41p 1.6' 0.9'	7:35a 9:41p 1.7' 0.9'	8:32a 10:25p 1.8' 1.0'	9:25a 11:04p 1.9' 1.1'	10:15a 11:39p 2.1' 1.2'	11:02a 2.1'
1:04p 11:36p 0.2' 0.6'	2:07p 12:33a 0.1' 0.6'	3:00p 0.0'	1:31a 3:45p 0.6' -0.1'	2:26a 4:25p -0.1'	3:18a 5:02p 0.5' -0.2'	4:09a 5:38p 0.4' -0.2'

31						
12:14a 11:50a 1.3' 2.1'						
5:00a 6:14p 0.3' -0.2'						

Sailfish caught on live bait.

KEY WEST

	July 1	July 15	July 30
SUNRISE	6:42 a.m.	6:48 a.m.	6:55 a.m.
SUNSET	8:20 p.m.	8:18 p.m.	8:12 p.m.

FISHING PLANNER 75

Long Key to Chatham River

Bugs Alive!

KEY WEST

INSHORE

Keys: Flats anglers have a short window for **bonefish** but **permit** don't mind hot water. Plan a permit trip on spring tides, and maybe fish for bones as the ice-breaker. Rainy, cloudy days can be super for tailing bonefish through midday. Look for laid-up **tarpon** in Florida Bay close to Overseas Highway, and cast flies at oceanside fish, that are not as pressured as they were earlier in summer. Dive for **lobsters** to beat the midday heat.

Everglades: Tailing **redfish** are common on Flamingo flats. **Snook** stage in flats potholes, and at flats runouts on falling water. **Goliath**, **gag** and **red grouper** available on Gulf wrecks and mouths of Everglades rivers and channels. Good mixed-bag fishing for **mangrove snapper** and **seatrout** at channels outside Flamingo.

OFFSHORE

You need a fast boat to range far offshore this time of year in order to beat it in before thunderstorms form. Bottom fishing is generally better than trolling for pelagics. Anchor at the reef at night for comfort and **mangrove** and **yellowtail snappers**. If you are geared for deep-dropping, **snowy grouper** and other deep dwellers are abundant.

TIDE CORRECTIONS For Key West		
	High	Low
Florida Bay		
Channel Five, east	-0:55	-0:42
Channel Five, west	-0:59	-0:40
Long Key Channel, east	-1:10	-1:07
Long Key Channel, west	+5:58	+5:40
Duck Key	-1:11	-0:40
Grassy Key, north	+5:38	+6:47
Grassy Key, south	-1:07	-0:40
Flamingo	+5:35	+7:28
Fat Deer Key	+5:09	+6:26
Vaca Key, Boot Key Harbor	-1:04	-0:37
Sombrero Key	-1:01	-0:38
Knight Key Channel	+0:17	-0:18
Pigeon Key, south side	-1:09	-0:39
Pigeon Key, inside	-0:17	+0:18
Molasses Key	-0:50	-0:11
Money Key	+0:56	+1:42
Bahia Honda Key, (bridge)	-0:39	-0:22
No Name Key, (east side)	+1:43	+1:28
Big Spanish Key	+3:26	+4:35
Cudjoe Key, west side (bridge)	+3:58	+2:59
Bird Key, (highway bridge)	-0:19	+1:00
Sand Key Light	-0:55	-0:38
Dry Tortugas	+0:35	+0:40
Channel Key	+3:15	+3:14
Cape Sable, East Cape	+3:56	+4:43
Shark River entrance	+3:20	+4:38
Lostmans River entrance	+3:22	+4:42
Onion Key, Lostmans River	+5:32	+7:46
Chatham River entrance	+3:22	+4:46

August Spotlight: LOBSTER

Sport divers who are ready for their second go-round (since the July 2-day mini season) can get their **lobster** fix starting August 6th. It is a relatively quiet time to dive (unlike the mini-season circus)! Look for lobsters in sandy holes on the seafloor, around coral, and around bridge pilings. Be sure to check the local and state regulations before taking lobsters.

August 2011

KEY WEST

SUNDAY	MONDAY	TUESDAY	WEDNESDAY	THURSDAY	FRIDAY	SATURDAY
	1 12:49a 1.5' / 12:38p 2.1' · 5:52a 0.2' / 6:50p -0.1'	**2** 1:24a 1.6' / 1:28p 1.9' · 6:47a 0.3' / 7:26p 0.0'	**3** 2:01a 1.7' / 2:21p 1.7' · 7:45a 0.1' / 8:04p 0.2'	**4** 2:40a 1.8' / 3:19p 1.5' · 8:47a 0.1' / 8:43p 0.3'	**5** ◑ 3:24a 1.9' / 4:25p 1.2' · 9:56a 0.1' / 9:26p 0.4'	**6** 4:16a 2.0' / 5:46p 1.0' · 11:13a 0.1' / 10:16p 0.5'
7 5:17a 2.0' / 7:19p 0.9' · 12:33a 0.3' / 11:16p 0.6'	**8** 6:29a 2.0' / 8:41p 0.9' · 1:49p 0.0' / 12:24a 0.6'	**9** 7:43a 2.0' / 9:41p 1.0' · 2:55p 0.0' / 1:33a 0.6'	**10** 8:50a 2.0' / 10:27p 1.1' · 3:47p 0.0' / 2:36a 0.5'	**11** 9:47a 2.1' / 11:05p 1.2' · 4:29p 0.0' / 3:33a 0.5'	**12** ○ 10:35a 2.1' / 11:38p 1.3' · 5:05p 0.0' / 4:24a 0.4'	**13** 11:17a 2.1' · 5:38p 0.1'
14 12:08a 1.4' / 11:55p 2.0' · 5:11a 0.4' / 6:09p 0.2'	**15** 12:35a 1.5' / 12:31p 1.9' · 5:56a 0.4' / 6:39p 0.2'	**16** 1:02a 1.6' / 1:07p 1.8' · 6:40a 0.3' / 7:08p 0.3'	**17** 1:29a 1.7' / 1:45p 1.7' · 7:23a 0.3' / 7:37p 0.4'	**18** 1:59a 1.7' / 2:25p 1.5' · 8:08a 0.4' / 8:05p 0.5'	**19** 2:31a 1.7' / 3:10p 1.4' · 8:58a 0.4' / 8:34p 0.6'	**20** 3:08a 1.7' / 4:03p 1.2' · 9:54a 0.4' / 9:05p 0.7'
21 ◐ 3:52a 1.7' / 5:12p 1.1' · 11:02a 0.4' / 9:44p 0.8'	**22** 4:46a 1.7' / 6:42p 1.0' · 12:18p 0.4' / 10:40p 0.8'	**23** 5:51a 1.8' / 8:10p 1.0' · 1:29p 0.4' / 11:53p 0.8'	**24** 7:02a 1.9' / 9:08p 1.1' · 2:26p 0.3' / 1:06a 0.8'	**25** 8:08a 2.0' / 9:50p 1.2' · 3:12p 0.2' / 2:09a 0.7'	**26** 9:07a 2.1' / 10:25p 1.4' · 3:51p 0.1' / 3:07a 0.6'	**27** 10:01a 2.2' / 10:59p 1.5' · 4:27p 0.1'
28 ● 10:52a 2.3' / 11:32p 1.7' · 4:00a 0.4' / 5:02p 0.1'	**29** 11:42a 2.2' / 12:06a 1.9' · 4:53a 0.2' / 5:37p 0.2'	**30** 12:32p 2.1' / 12:41a 2.1' · 5:45a 0.1' / 6:13p 0.3'	**31** 1:22p 2.0' · 6:39a 0.0' / 6:49p 0.4'			

Yellowtail snapper for the keeping.

	August 1	August 15	August 30
SUNRISE	6:56 a.m.	7:02 a.m.	7:08 a.m.
SUNSET	8:11 p.m.	8:01 p.m.	7:48 p.m.

Long Key to Chatham River

Fall Guys

INSHORE

Keys: Among the best **permit** months, on oceanside and bayside flats edges alike. **Bonefish** still best early and late and month's end sees bigger fish throughout Keys tract. Bridge **tarpon** fishing excellent at night. **Yellowtail snapper** come to chum on patches; good time for nightime **mangrove snapper**.

Everglades: Small to medium **tarpon** on Flamingo flats in basins early and late afternoon, also along Cape Sable beaches. **Reds** are at their tailing best until month's end from Sandy Key east to Flamingo islands and mainland bights. **Snook** numerous on Florida Bay flats, under Keys bridges, island moats, Cape beaches and rivermouths.

OFFSHORE

Trolling is best in deeper water for **dolphin**, and in lesser numbers, **wahoo**. Get some local knowledge regarding top depths for 'hoos and 'phins. Consider making a nightime reef trip to chum up **yellowtail**, which are red-hot in September. Big flags bite best when the tide is strong over deep side of reef, and **mangrove snapper** will chime in, too.

KEY WEST

TIDE CORRECTION For Key West	High	Low
Florida Bay		
Channel Five, east	-0:55	-0:42
Channel Five, west	-0:59	-0:40
Long Key Channel, east	-1:10	-1:07
Long Key Channel, west	+5:58	+5:40
Duck Key	-1:11	-0:40
Grassy Key, north	+5:38	+6:47
Grassy Key, south	-1:07	-0:40
Flamingo	+5:35	+7:28
Fat Deer Key	+5:09	+6:26
Vaca Key, Boot Key Harbor	-1:04	-0:37
Sombrero Key	-1:01	-0:38
Knight Key Channel	+0:17	-0:18
Pigeon Key, south side	-1:09	-0:39
Pigeon Key, inside	-0:17	+0:18
Molasses Key	-0:50	-0:11
Money Key	+0:56	+1:42
Bahia Honda Key, (bridge)	-0:39	-0:22
No Name Key, (east side)	+1:43	+1:28
Big Spanish Key	+3:26	+4:35
Cudjoe Key, west side (bridge)	+3:58	+2:59
Bird Key, (highway bridge)	-0:19	+1:00
Sand Key Light	-0:55	-0:38
Dry Tortugas	+0:35	+0:40
Channel Key	+3:15	+3:14
Cape Sable, East Cape	+3:56	+4:43
Shark River entrance	+3:20	+4:38
Lostmans River entrance	+3:22	+4:42
Onion Key, Lostmans River	+5:32	+7:46
Chatham River entrance	+3:22	+4:46

September Spotlight: SWORDFISH

Swordfishing has been publicized and fine-tuned to the point that it is easier than ever to strike out on your own or hire out a charter captain who swordfishes out of various marinas from Islamorada to Key West. Night and daytime success is being had by plumbing the same deep dropoffs with live baits on heavy gear. Stocks are rebounding due to longline limitations, and a growing conservation ethic to release the smallest of legal fish.

September 2011

SUNDAY	MONDAY	TUESDAY	WEDNESDAY	THURSDAY	FRIDAY	SATURDAY

Greetings from the Seven Mile Bridge.

1
1:19a 2.2' / 2:16p 1.7'
2:02a 2.2' / 3:13p 1.5'
2
2:50a 2.2' / 4:19p 1.3'
3

7:35a 0.0' / 7:27p 0.5'
8:35a 0.0' / 8:08p 0.6'
9:42a 0.1' / 8:53p 0.7'

4
3:47a 2.2' / 5:39p 1.1'
5
4:56a 2.1' / 7:09p 1.1'
6
6:18a 2.1' / 8:24p 1.2'
7
7:38a 2.1' / 9:17p 1.3'
8
8:46a 2.1' / 9:58p 1.4'
9
9:40a 2.1' / 10:31p 1.6'
10
10:25a 2.1' / 11:00p 1.7'

10:57a 0.2' / 9:49p 0.7'
12:19p 0.3' / 11:00 0.8'
1:35p 0.3' / 12:20a 0.8'
2:36p 0.3' / 1:35a 0.8'
3:22p 0.4' / 2:39a 0.7'
3:59p 0.4' / 3:33a 0.6'
4:31p 0.4'

11
12
13
14
15
16
17

11:04a 2.1 / 11:25p 1.8'
11:40a 2.0' / 11:50p 1.9'
12:14p 1.9' / 12:14a 2.0'
12:49p 1.8' / 12:41a 2.0'
1:26p 1.7' / 1:11a 2.0'
2:06p 1.6' / 1:44a 2.0'
2:50p 1.5'

4:20a 0.5' / 5:00p 0.5'
5:02a 0.5' / 5:28p 0.5'
5:42a 0.4' / 5:56p 0.6'
6:20a 0.4' / 6:23p 0.6'
6:59a 0.3' / 6:50p 0.7'
7:39a 0.4' / 7:17p 0.8'
8:23a 0.4' / 7:45p 0.8'

18
19
20
21
22
23
24

2:21a 2.0' / 3:42p 1.3'
3:06a 1.9' / 4:49p 1.2'
4:02a 1.9' / 6:14p 1.2'
5:12a 1.9' / 7:32p 1.3'
6:31a 2.0' / 8:26p 1.4'
7:45a 2.1' / 9:06p 1.6'
8:50a 2.2' / 9:41p 1.8'

9:14a 0.5' / 8:17p 0.9'
10:17a 0.5' / 9:00p 1.0'
11:31a 0.6' / 10:03p 1.0'
12:43p 0.5' / 11:30p 1.0''
1:42p 0.5' / 12:52a 1.0'
2:28p 0.5' / 2:00a 0.8'
3:08p 0.5'

25
26
27
28
29
30

9:48a 2.2' / 10:14p 2.0'
10:42a 2.2' / 10:49 2.2'
11:34a 2.2' / 11:25p 2.3'
12:25p 2.1' / 12:03a 2.5'
1:16p 1.9' / 12:45a 2.5'
2:08p 1.7'

2:59a 0.6' / 3:46p 0.5'
3:53a 0.3' / 4:22p 0.5'
4:45a 0.1' / 4:58p 0.5'
5:37a 0.0' / 5:35p 0.6'
6:29a -0.1' / 6:14p 0.6'
7:24a -0.1' / 6:54p 0.7'

	September 1	September 15	September 30
SUNRISE	7:08 a.m.	7:13 a.m.	7:19 a.m.
SUNSET	7:46 p.m.	7:31 p.m.	7:15 p.m.

Key West Station

Long Key to Chatham River

Chill Out

INSHORE

Keys: Day-long **bonefishing** is at hand with cooler water temps, and some of the biggest fish, often weighing in the teens, show up in better numbers. They prefer big flies, or small live crabs presented at flats edges. **Permit** still around in September numbers. Resident **tarpon** bite well at the bridges at night on live crabs, mullet, pinfish, swimbaits or bushy flies.

Everglades: Head to a wreck in Florida Bay to wrestle with everything from **goliath grouper** to **cobia** to **permit** to **Spanish mackerel**. The fall bait run fires up the bite by **snook**, **reds** and **tarpon** from the Flamingo flats to Everglades coastal rivers. **Seatrout** come on strong in shallower waters, and **pompano** make first showing on sandy beaches.

OFFSHORE

Blue marlin can become more than a dream this month for those who dedicate the time and tackle up accordingly for the 400- to 600-pounders out near the Wall, the Cracks and Floyd's Wall. Big **swordfish** and **dolphin** share the spotlight along with **cero mackerel** over the deeper outer reefs. First of **cobia** also move along inner reefline.

TIDE CORRECTIONS *For Key West*	High	Low
Florida Bay		
Channel Five, east	-0:55	-0:42
Channel Five, west	-0:59	-0:40
Long Key Channel, east	-1:10	-1:07
Long Key Channel, west	+5:58	+5:40
Duck Key	-1:11	-0:40
Grassy Key, north	+5:38	+6:47
Grassy Key, south	-1:07	-0:40
Flamingo	+5:35	+7:28
Fat Deer Key	+5:09	+6:26
Vaca Key, Boot Key Harbor	-1:04	-0:37
Sombrero Key	-1:01	-0:38
Knight Key Channel	+0:17	-0:18
Pigeon Key, south side	-1:09	-0:39
Pigeon Key, inside	-0:17	+0:18
Molasses Key	-0:50	-0:11
Money Key	+0:56	+1:42
Bahia Honda Key, (bridge)	-0:39	-0:22
No Name Key, (east side)	+1:43	+1:28
Big Spanish Key	+3:26	+4:35
Cudjoe Key, west side (bridge)	+3:58	+2:59
Bird Key, (highway bridge)	-0:19	+1:00
Sand Key Light	-0:55	-0:38
Dry Tortugas	+0:35	+0:40
Channel Key	+3:15	+3:14
Cape Sable, East Cape	+3:56	+4:43
Shark River entrance	+3:20	+4:38
Lostmans River entrance	+3:22	+4:42
Onion Key, Lostmans River	+5:32	+7:46
Chatham River entrance	+3:22	+4:46

October Spotlight: BONEFISH

October ranks right up there with March as a giant **bonefish** month. Oceanside and backcountry flats see the big boys, mainly at the edges where singles tail occasionally, and mostly plow up muds in groups of three to five fish. Islamorada sees the best numbers of 9- to 13-pounders. And a little wind goes a long way to mask your presence when stalking the fish. Live crabs and shrimp, skimmer jigs and crab flies are all effective.

October 2011

SUNDAY	MONDAY	TUESDAY	WEDNESDAY	THURSDAY	FRIDAY	SATURDAY

Pair-a-sailing.

1
1:32a 2.5' / 3:04p 1.5'
8:22a 0.0' / 7:38p 0.8'

2
2:24a 2.4' / 4:08p 1.4'
9:26a 0.2' / 8:28p 0.8'

3
3:24a 2.3' / 5:23p 1.3'
10:38a 0.3' / 9:32p 0.9'

4
4:37a 2.2' / 6:44p 1.3'
11:54a 0.5' / 10:54p 1.0'

5
6:01a 2.1' / 7:51p 1.4'
1:03p 0.6' / 12:22a 1.0'

6
7:24a 2.0' / 8:40p 1.6'
1:58p 0.6' / 1:37a 0.9'

7
8:31a 2.0' / 9:18p 1.7'
2:41p 0.7' / 2:38a 0.8'

8
9:25a 2.0' / 9:49p 1.9'
3:17p 0.7'

9
10:10a 2.0' / 10:16p 2.0'
3:28a 0.6' / 3:48p 0.7'

10
10:49a 1.9' / 10:41p 2.1'
4:11a 0.5' / 4:18p 0.7'

11
11:25a 1.9' / 11:06p 2.1'
4:49a 0.4' / 4:46p 0.8'

12
12:00n 1.8' / 11:33p 2.2'
5:26a 0.3' / 5:13p 0.8'

13
12:35p 1.8' / 12:02a 2.2'
6:01a 0.3' / 5:41p 0.8'

14
1:12p 1.7' / 12:34a 2.2'
6:38a 0.3' / 6:08p 0.8'

15
1:52p 1.6'
7:16a 0.3' / 6:37p 0.9'

16
1:08a 2.2' / 2:37p 1.5'
7:57a 0.3' / 7:08p 0.9'

17
1:47a 2.1' / 3:29p 1.4'
8:45a 0.4' / 7:46p 1.0'

18
2:32a 2.1' / 4:32p 1.4'
9:42a 0.5' / 8:36p 1.1'

19
3:28a 2.0' / 5:41p 1.4'
10:46a 0.6' / 9:48p 1.1'

20
4:39a 2.0' / 4:45p 1.5'
11:52a 0.6' / 11:18p 1.1'

21
6:02a 2.0' / 7:35p 1.6'
12:49p 0.6' / 12:42a 0.9'

22
7:24a 2.0' / 8:16p 1.8'
1:38p 0.6'

23
8:35a 2.0' / 8:54p 2.0'
1:51a 0.7' / 2:21p 0.6'

24
9:38a 2.0' / 9:32p 2.2'
2:50a 0.4' / 3:02p 0.7'

25
10:35a 2.0' / 10:11p 2.4'
3:45a 0.1' / 3:41p 0.7'

26
11:28a 1.9' / 10:52p 2.6'
4:37a -0.1' / 4:21p 0.7'

27
12:18p 1.8' / 11:35p 2.6'
5:28a -0.2' / 5:01p 0.7'

28
1:08p 1.7' / 12:22a 2.6'
6:20a -0.2' / 5:43p 0.7'

29
1:58p 1.5'
7:13a -0.1' / 6:27p 0.7'

30
1:11a 2.6' / 2:51p 1.4'
8:08a 0.0' / 7:15p 0.8'

31
2:05a 2.4' / 3:48p 1.4'
9:07a 0.2' / 8:11p 0.8'

Sugarloaf Key permit.

KEY WEST

	October 1	October 15	October 30
SUNRISE	7:19 a.m.	7:25 a.m.	7:33 a.m.
SUNSET	7:14 p.m.	7:00 p.m.	6:48 p.m.

Long Key to Chatham River

Blaze for the Blue

KEY WEST

INSHORE

Keys: Nearshore fishing revs up for winter season. Migratory species flood Keys waters lead by **Spanish mackerel**, **kingfish** and **bluefish**. Flats anglers hook up on **permit** and **bonefish** between fronts. Still lots of **mangrove** and **yellowtail snapper** to chum up over nearshore patch reefs in Hawk Channel.

Everglades: Florida Bay mixed-bag fishing features **trout**, **Spanish mackerel**, and **bluefish** over mixed sand and grass bottom west of Everglades National Park boundary markers. Same waters have **cobia** on markers and wrecks and **tripletail** on crab floats or free-floating on swift tides.

OFFSHORE

The bait run is shadowed by **cobia**, **kings** and **sailfish** from the deep reef out to blue water. If up for a mixed-bag trip, head for Hawk Channel to chum up **yellowtails**, **muttons** and **grouper**. Trollers target increasing numbers of **blackfin tuna** and **wahoo** by dragging lures both shallow and deep. **Sailfishing** starts its winter uptick, and only gets better in time.

TIDE CORRECTIONS For Key West		
	High	Low
Florida Bay		
Channel Five, east	-0:55	-0:42
Channel Five, west	-0:59	-0:40
Long Key Channel, east	-1:10	-1:07
Long Key Channel, west	+5:58	+5:40
Duck Key	-1:11	-0:40
Grassy Key, north	+5:38	+6:47
Grassy Key, south	-1:07	-0:40
Flamingo	+5:35	+7:28
Fat Deer Key	+5:09	+6:26
Vaca Key, Boot Key Harbor	-1:04	-0:37
Sombrero Key	-1:01	-0:38
Knight Key Channel	+0:17	-0:18
Pigeon Key, south side	-1:09	-0:39
Pigeon Key, inside	-0:17	+0:18
Molasses Key	-0:50	-0:11
Money Key	+0:56	+1:42
Bahia Honda Key, (bridge)	-0:39	-0:22
No Name Key, (east side)	+1:43	+1:28
Big Spanish Key	+3:26	+4:35
Cudjoe Key, west side (bridge)	+3:58	+2:59
Bird Key, (highway bridge)	-0:19	+1:00
Sand Key Light	-0:55	-0:38
Dry Tortugas	+0:35	+0:40
Channel Key	+3:15	+3:14
Cape Sable, East Cape	+3:56	+4:43
Shark River entrance	+3:20	+4:38
Lostmans River entrance	+3:22	+4:42
Onion Key, Lostmans River	+5:32	+7:46
Chatham River entrance	+3:22	+4:46

November Spotlight: WAHOO

The photos don't lie! Keys anglers are clued in to great **wahoo** runs along the Keys reefline beginning in November. Best tactic is to run-and-gun to score in 120- to 200-foot depths with a wide variety of techniques. Some anglers like to drop jigs to the middle of the water column, and still others swear by downriggers and weighted baits trolled just below the surface to cover more ground and thus catch more 'hoos. Typical Keys fish

weigh between 15 to 30 pounds, but fish up to 60 pounds are caught each year. Ice this dark-meat fish well, and baste frequently on the grill.

November 2011

SUNDAY	MONDAY	TUESDAY	WEDNESDAY	THURSDAY	FRIDAY	SATURDAY

1 ◑
- 3:04a 2.2' / 4:53p 1.4'
- 10:10a 0.4' / 9:21p 0.9'

2
- 4:12a 2.1' / 6:00p 1.4'
- 11:14a 0.5' / 10:46p 0.9'

3
- 5:30a 1.9' / 7:01p 1.6'
- 12:14p 0.6' / 12:14a 0.9'

4
- 6:52a 1.8' / 7:50p 1.7'
- 1:06p 0.7' / 1:28a 0.8'

5
- 8:05a 1.7' / 8:29p 1.8'
- 1:49p 0.7'

6
- 7:04a 1.7' / 7:01p 1.9'
- 1:27a 0.6' / 12:28p 0.8'

7
- 7:52a 1.7' / 7:30p 2.0'
- 1:15a 0.5' / 1:02p 0.8'

8
- 8:33a 1.6' / 7:59p 2.1'
- 1:57a 0.4' / 1:34p 0.8'

9
- 9:11a 1.6' / 8:29p 2.1'
- 2:34a 0.2' / 2:04p 0.8'

10 ○
- 9:46a 1.6' / 9:01p 2.2'
- 3:10a 0.2' / 2:34p 0.8'

11
- 10:23a 1.5' / 9:34p 2.2'
- 3:45a 0.1' / 3:04p 0.8'

12
- 11:00a 1.5' / 10:09p 2.2'
- 4:21a 0.1' / 3:35p 0.8'

13
- 11:41a 1.4' / 10:46p 2.1'
- 4:59a 0.1' / 4:08p 0.8'

14
- 12:25p 1.4' / 11:27p 2.1'
- 5:39a 0.2' / 4:46p 0.8'

15
- 1:13p 1.4' / 12:13a 2.0'
- 6:23a 0.2' / 5:31p 0.9'

16
- 2:05p 1.4' / 1:08a 1.9'
- 7:12a 0.3' / 6:28p 0.9'

17 ◑
- 2:59p 1.4' / 2:16a 1.8'
- 8:05a 0.4' / 7:43p 0.9'

18
- 3:51p 1.5' / 3:38a 1.7'
- 9:00a 0.5' / 9:08p 0.8'

19
- 4:40p 1.7'
- 9:53a 0.5' / 10:30p 0.6'

20
- 5:05a 1.6' / 5:26p 1.9'
- 10:45a 0.6' / 11:41p 0.3'

21
- 6:24a 1.6' / 6:11p 2.1'
- 11:33a 0.6' / 12:42a 0.1'

22
- 7:32a 1.6' / 6:56p 2.2'
- 12:19p 0.6' / 1:38a -0.2'

23
- 8:30a 1.5' / 7:43p 2.4'
- 1:04p 0.6' / 2:30a -0.3'

24 ●
- 19:23a 1.5' / 8:31p 2.5'
- 1:49p 0.6' / 3:21a -0.4'

25
- 10:11a 1.4' / 9:19p 2.5'
- 2:34p 0.5' / 4:11a -0.4'

26
- 10:58a 1.3' / 10:08p 2.5'
- 3:21p 0.5'

27
- 11:43a 1.3' / 10:58p 2.4'
- 5:01a -0.3' / 4:09p 0.5'

28
- 12:30p 1.3' / 11:49p 2.2'
- 5:51a -0.1' / 5:02p 0.6'

29
- 1:18p 1.3' / 12:42a 2.0'
- 6:41a 0.0' / 6:00p 0.6'

30
- 2:09p 1.3'
- 7:32a 0.2' / 7:07p 0.7'

Bonefish on the flats.

	November 1	November 15	November 30
SUNRISE	7:34 a.m.	6:43 a.m.	6:54 a.m.
SUNSET	6:47 p.m.	5:40 p.m.	5:38 p.m.

DST Ends on Nov. 6

KEY WEST

Long Key to Chatham River

TIDE CORRECTIONS
For Key West

	High	Low
Florida Bay		
Channel Five, east	-0:55	-0:42
Channel Five, west	-0:59	-0:40
Long Key Channel, east	-1:10	-1:07
Long Key Channel, west	+5:58	+5:40
Duck Key	-1:11	-0:40
Grassy Key, north	+5:38	+6:47
Grassy Key, south	-1:07	-0:40
Flamingo	+5:35	+7:28
Fat Deer Key	+5:09	+6:26
Vaca Key, Boot Key Harbor	-1:04	-0:37
Sombrero Key	-1:01	-0:38
Knight Key Channel	+0:17	-0:18
Pigeon Key, south side	-1:09	-0:39
Pigeon Key, inside	-0:17	+0:18
Molasses Key	-0:50	-0:11
Money Key	+0:56	+1:42
Bahia Honda Key, (bridge)	-0:39	-0:22
No Name Key, (east side)	+1:43	+1:28
Big Spanish Key	+3:26	+4:35
Cudjoe Key, west side (bridge)	+3:58	+2:59
Bird Key, (highway bridge)	-0:19	+1:00
Sand Key Light	-0:55	-0:38
Dry Tortugas	+0:35	+0:40
Channel Key	+3:15	+3:14
Cape Sable, East Cape	+3:56	+4:43
Shark River entrance	+3:20	+4:38
Lostmans River entrance	+3:22	+4:42
Onion Key, Lostmans River	+5:32	+7:46
Chatham River entrance	+3:22	+4:46

Xmas Xcitement

INSHORE

Keys: Backcountry shallows come on this month, where **snook**, **seatrout** and **redfish** go shallow on warmer days, particularly on flats in island lees. **Bonefish** crawl into shallows between windy fronts. Expect **barracuda** to rule on chilly, bluebird cold front days.

Everglades: Florida Bay proper will hold **tripletail**, **Spanish mackerel**, **bluefish**, and incresing numbers of **sharks**. **Snook**, **reds** and **trout** moving inland to hunker down in upper Everglades rivers and creeks. Look for **pompano** to share the sandy shoals and grass beds with trout from Northwest Cape north.

OFFSHORE

December sees the arrival of migrating bait schools this month, followed closely by pelagics such as **blackfin tuna**, **sailfish**, **cobia** and **kingfish**. Take them by trolling, drift-fishing, live-baiting or chunking. Prospects are best over bottom structure and around color changes.

December Spotlight: BLACK GROUPER

Shallow patch reefs are the place this month to nail a **black grouper**. Otherwise, this brawny battler sets up camp over the the main reef and out west at the Marquesas and Tortugas. Live baits excel at tempting a black, but bait-tipped lures, such as a jig baited with ballyhoo, is a great alternative. Or go with a baited Carolina rig or a big-lipped trolling plug. Anglers concerned about the fishery's future have been known to keep smaller, legal blacks and releasing the occasional 60-plus-pounder. Biggest fish are the males so vital for spawning, and are not nearly as good to eat as the younger, more tender fish. The time-proven drill is to either anchor up or drift over their rocky lairs. Heavy boat tackle is a must if you hope to boat the biggest black groupers.

KEY WEST

Sharks like kingfish too.

SUNDAY	MONDAY	TUESDAY	WEDNESDAY	THURSDAY	FRIDAY	SATURDAY
				1 ◑	**2**	**3**
				1:40a 1.8' / 3:02p 1.4'	2:46a 1.6' / 3:54p 1.5'	4:03a 1.4' / 4:43p 1.6'
				8:22a 0.4' / 8:26p 0.7'	9:13a 0.5' / 9:49p 0.7'	10:02a 0.6' / 11:03p 0.5'
4	**5**	**6**	**7**	**8**	**9**	**10** ○
5:24a 1.3' / 5:27p 1.7'	6:35a 1.3' / 6:07p 1.7'	7:31a 1.2' / 6:46p 1.8'	8:17a 1.2' / 7:23p 1.9'	8:57a 1.2' / 8:01p 1.9'	9:34a 1.2' / 8:39p 2.0'	10:10a 1.2' / 9:17p 2.0'
10:49a 0.6' / 12:04a 0.4'	11:33a 0.7' / 12:55a 0.2'	12:13p 0.7' / 1:39a 0.1'	12:50p 0.7' / 2:19a 0.0'	1:26p 0.6' / 2:56a -0.1'	2:00p 0.6' / 3:32a -0.1'	2:35p 0.6'
11	**12**	**13**	**14**	**15**	**16**	**17**
10:47a 1.2' / 9:55p 2.0'	11:26a 1.2' / 10:35p 2.0'	12:05p 1.2' / 11:17p 2.0'	12:46p 1.3' / 12:04a 1.9'	1:27p 1.3' / 12:57a 1.7'	2:11p 1.4' / 2:02a 1.5'	2:56p 1.5'
4:07a -0.2' / 3:12p 0.5'	4:44a -0.2' / 3:52p 0.5'	5:21a -0.1' / 4:36p 0.5'	6:00a -0.1' / 5:27p 0.5'	6:41a 0.0' / 6:26p 0.5'	7:25a 0.1' / 7:37p 0.5'	8:11a 0.3' / 8:56p 0.4'
18 ◐	**19**	**20**	**21**	**22**	**23** ●	**24**
3:21a 1.3' / 3:46p 1.6'	4:51a 1.2' / 4:40p 1.8'	6:18a 1.1' / 5:36p 1.9'	7:30a 1.1' / 6:33p 2.0'	8:28a 1.0' / 7:29p 2.2'	9:17a 1.0' / 8:22p 2.2'	10:01a 1.1' / 9:13p 2.2'
9:01a 0.4' / 10:16p 0.2'	9:53a 0.5' / 11:29p 0.0'	10:47a 0.5' / 12:35a -0.2'	11:42a 0.5' / 1:33a -0.4'	12:35p 0.4' / 2:26a -0.5'	1:27p 0.4' / 3:15a -0.5'	2:18p 0.3'
25	**26**	**27**	**28**	**29**	**30**	**31**
10:42a 1.1' / 10:01p 2.2'	11:22a 1.1' / 10:48p 2.1'	12:00p 1.2' / 11:33p 1.9'	12:39p 1.2' / 12:18a 1.7'	1:17p 1.3' / 1:06a 1.5'	1:57p 1.3' / 1:59a 1.3'	2:39p 1.4'
4:01a -0.5' / 3:09p 0.2'	4:45a -0.4' / 4:00p 0.2'	5:27a -0.3' / 4:52p 0.3'	6:08a -0.1' / 5:47p 0.3'	6:48a 0.0' / 6:47p 0.32'	7:28a 0.2' / 7:54p 0.4'	8:09a 0.3' / 9:07p 0.3'

	December 1	December 15	December 30
SUNRISE	6:54 a.m.	7:04 a.m.	7:11 a.m.
SUNSET	5:38 p.m.	5:41 p.m.	5:49 p.m.

Apalachicola • St. George
Tampa • St. Petersburg
Punta Gorda • Ft. Myers

ST. PETERSBURG

Gulf Grab Bag

Hopefully, snook stocks will rebound quickly from the 2010 freeze.

Update 2011: *Some of the best comeback kids on the Gulf coast include* **seatrout** *and* **pompano**. *The trout size average is excellent throughout Tampa Bay, and pompano are no longer an oddity in the bay systems.* **Sheepshead** *and* **redfish** *fishing remains strong, and sight fishing for* **snook**, **tarpon** *and reds is fairing well.* **Spanish mackerel** *are the family favorites from the beaches to the bays, and numbers are even good in summer months.*

Four **grouper** *per person is the new aggregate bag limit, down from five. There is a February 1 through March 31 closed season for all shallow-water grouper species, including* **red**, **black**, **gag**, **yellowmouth**, **yellowfin**, **rock hind**, **red hind** *and* **scamp**. *However anglers are allowed up to two* **red grouper** *in their aggregate bag limit of 4 grouper per day,*

so the fish fry is not a thing of the past. **Tarpon** *fans can count on great stocks again in 2011, but remember that breakaway jigs are illegal in spring and early summer, and boats may not fish with more than three lines in the water.* **Cobia** *runs continue strong along northwest beaches and* **kingfish** *provided great spring and fall fishing against the beaches.* **Tripletail** *sight fishing was strong around crab pots on calm winter days, and trout and reds held the fort in most coastal bays.*

Finding good current is the name of the game along Florida's west coast, and there are many ways to capitalize on the tides. Redfish of all sizes follow the incoming tide onto grassflats and oyster bars. On an outgoing tide, snook pull out of the deep, dark recesses of mangrove islands and take up feeding stations in holes. Spanish mackerel move in and out of passes, slashing through schools of sardines and glass minnows. Trout become more aggressive as the current picks up. And the list goes on.

The visiting angler will want to acquaint himself with the tide predictions on the following pages, and with the accompanying monthly fishing prospects. Also, be aware that snook are not found in the Apalachicola region, and that tarpon are present there only in the warmest months.

St. Petersburg tide measurements are used to calculate the tides for much of the Gulf Coast from Fort Myers northward to Tampa, plus St. George Sound and Apalachicola Bay. St. Petersburg is also the southernmost location where the two daily tides can disappear, being replaced by a single, diurnal set that features only one high and low each day. On some days, highs and lows are the same or very nearly the same height; these step tides are simply a slack period that occurs over the course of a daylong tide change.

The rest of the region's tides are generally mixed, featuring two tides daily, one of which will offer a lower low and higher high. Usually, the most extreme of the tides offers the best fishing simply because more water is being moved about. Stronger flows often stimulate the appetites of such gamefish as snook and trout.

There are a number of large, shallow bays in this region, including Tampa Bay, Charlotte Harbor, Sarasota Bay and Pine Island Sound, where wind can be a major factor in determining the amount of water you'll find covering your favorite redfish flat. Wind has the capability of pushing enormous amounts of water in front of it, so it's a good idea when fishing the bays to listen to the weather forecast and adjust your plans accordingly.

If there's a strong northeast wind, water can be pushed out of the bays, producing a lower low. Conversely, strong winds from the west push more water into the bays and therefore tides will be higher than forecast.

The farther you go toward the headwaters of any of these bays, the later the tide. That makes it possible for an angler to follow the tide to fish the stage he likes. For instance, someone hunting for redfish in Tampa Bay can catch the early incoming tide near Rattlesnake Key and when the water becomes too deep there, move northwest to the mouth of the Manatee River and find the tidal stage ideal once again.

All smiles for red grouper.

Average Tidal Range at St. Pete: 1.8 feet

Average Range of Spring Tides: 2.6 feet

Estero Bay to Tampa, Including Apalachicola area

Trout for Starters

INSHORE

Want a winter fish dinner? Then **sheepshead** will oblige. Soak live shrimp, fiddler crabs or sandfleas around shell bars, rockpiles and pilings. **Redfish** and **trout** fishing will be best on mild days between fronts on the flats, with channels a better bet when cold. Look for **gag grouper** on bottom structure along channel edges in passes and bays.

OFFSHORE

Groupers and **amberjack** are the main players this time of year, when winter water temps push reef fish out to deeper water. The fish are slow to eat, however, so fresh-dead bait usually works very well. Wrecks will hold **flounder** and **sea bass**, both of which will scarf a jig tipped with squid, shrimp or cutbait. Don't be surprised when your rod doubles over, signaling the arrival of a decent **red grouper**.

TIDE CORRECTIONS For St. Petersburg		
	High	Low
Estero Bay		
Little Hickory Island	-0:58	-1:05
Coconut Point	-0:47	-0:40
Carlos Point	-1:08	-1:28
Mantanzas Pass, (fixed br.) Estero Isl	-1:10	-1:34
Point Ybel, Sand Carlos Bay entrance	-1:50	-1:12
Punta Rassa, San Carlos Bay	-1:01	-1:19
Caloosahatchee River		
Iona Shores	+1:08	+1:40
Cape Coral Bridge	+1:15	+2:02
Ft. Myers	+2:08	+2:44
Pine Island, St. James City	-0:30	-0:44
Galt Island, Pine Island Sound	-0:25	+0:16
Captiva Island, (outside)	-2:20	-2:28
Captiva Island, Pine Island Sound	-0:46	-0:20
Redfish Pass, Captiva I (north end)	-0:55	-1:14
Tropical Homesites Landing, Pine.	-0:08	+0:22
Matlacha Pass, (bascule bridge)	+0:43	+1:24
Pineland, Pine Island	-0:19	+0:26
Boca Grande, Charlotte Harbor	-1:12	-1:56
Punta Gorda, Charlotte Harbor	+1:06	+1:58
Shell Point, Peace River	+1:52	+2:30
El Jobean, Myakka River	+1:38	+1:56
Placida, Gasparilla Sound	-1:27	-0:59
Englewood, Lemon Bay	-0:57	-0:40
Venice Inlet, (inside)	-2:02	-1:38
Sarasota, Sarasota Bay	-1:38	-0:58
Cortez, Sarasota Bay	-2:00	-1:25
Egmont Key, Egmont Channel	-2:27	-2:24
Anna Maria	-2:07	-2:31
Bradenton, Manatee River	-1:24	-0:55
Redfish Point, Manatee River	-0:30	+0:14
Mullet Key Channel, (Skyway)	-2:22	-1:58
Shell Point	+0:08	+0:17
Point Pinellas	-0:22	-0:29
Tampa Bay, Hillsborough Bay	+0:07	+0:26
Safety Harbor, Old Tampa Bay	+1:38	+1:55
Boca Ciega Bay		
Pass-a-Grille Beach	-1:34	-1:30
Gulfport	-1:32	-1:08
St. Petersburg Beach Causeway	-1:18	-0:44
Johns Pass	-2:14	-2:04
Madeira Beach Causeway	-1:40	-1:18
St. George Sound		
Dog Island, west end	+0:07	+0:06
Carrabelle, Carrabelle River	+0:35	+0:31
St. George Island, East End	-0:15	+0:06
St. George Island, Rattlesnake Cove	+0:47	+1:19
St. George Island, Sikes Cut	+0:49	+1:32
Apalachicola Bay		
Cat Point	+1:20	+1:27
Apalachicola	+2:00	+2:44
Lower Anchorage	+1:43	+2:09
West Pass	+1:33	+2:17

January Spotlight: SEATROUT

Speckled trout are dependable winter quarry, though they hunker in creeks, canals and deeper flats edges down in this region during extreme cold. During warm snaps, grassflats in skinny water will produce on sunny afternoons. Check out sandy potholes where they stage up to ambush prey. Mud bottoms are best for fish willing to strike artificials such as spoons, jigs and plastic swimbaits. When all else fails, grab a bucket of live shrimp and a few rattling corks, or hang a plastic shrimp under that float and chug away. Clear winter water is common now, but some mullet mud can be ideal.

ST. PETERSBURG

January 2011

SUNDAY	MONDAY	TUESDAY	WEDNESDAY	THURSDAY	FRIDAY	SATURDAY

Pompano take to the beaches and flats.

1
10:57p 2.3'
6:29a -0.7'

2
11:45p 2.3'
7:15a -0.8'

3 ●
3:34p 12:29a 1.1' 2.3'
7:56a 5:56p -0.8' 1.1'

4
3:52p 1:11a 1.1' 2.2'
8:31a 6:48p -0.7' 1.0'

5
4:07p 1.2'
9:03a 7:40p -0.6' 0.9'

6
1:52a 4:21p 2.1' 1.2'
9:32a 8:32p -0.5' 0.8'

7
2:33a 4:38p 2.0' 1.3'
10:00a 9:26p -0.4' 0.7'

8
3:16a 4:58p 1.8' 1.4'
10:27a 10:24p -0.2' 0.6'

9
4:04a 5:23p 1.5' 1.5'
10:55a 11:27p 0.0' 0.5'

10
5:00a 5:52p 1.3' 1.6'
11:24a 12:36p 0.2' 0.4'

11 ◐
6:11a 6:26p 1.1' 1.7'
11:53a 1:52a 0.4' 0.2'

12
7:49a 7:05p 0.9' 1.8'
12:21p 0.6'

13
10:10a 7:50p 0.8' 1.9'
3:08a 12:47p 0.0' 0.8'

14
8:42p 1.9'
4:18a -0.2'

15
9:37p 2.0'
5:17a -0.4'

16
10:32p 2.2'
6:08a -0.6'

17
2:43p 11:25p 1.1' 2.3'
6:53a 4:47p -0.8' 1.0'

18 ○
3:00p 12:17a 1.1' 2.3'
7:35a 5:48p -0.9' 1.0'

19
3:17p 1.1'
8:13a 6:45p -0.9' 0.8'

20
1:07a 3:34p 2.3' 1.1'
8:50a 7:41p -0.8' 0.7'

21
1:58a 3:53p 2.3' 1.2'
9:25a 8:40p -0.7' 0.5'

22
2:51a 4:16p 2.1' 1.4'
9:59a 9:42p -0.4' 0.3'

23
3:47a 4:43p 1.8' 1.5'
10:31a 10:49p -0.2' 0.2'

24
4:51a 5:14p 1.5' 1.7'
11:00a 12:05a 0.1' 0.0'

25 ◑
6:09a 5:52p 1.1' 1.9'
11:27a 0.4'

26
8:06a 6:38p 0.9' 2.0'
1:30a 11:48a -0.1' 0.7'

27
7:34p 2.0'
3:01a -0.3'

28
8:42p 2.0'
4:23a -0.4'

29
9:54p 2.0'
5:30a -0.6'

30
10:59p 2.1'
6:23a -0.7'

31
2:37p 11:53p 1.1' 2.1'
7:05a 5:28p -0.7' 1.0'

Skinny water redfish.

	January 1	January 15	January 30
SUNRISE	7:22 a.m.	7:23 a.m.	7:18 a.m.
SUNSET	5:47 p.m.	5:58 p.m.	6:10 p.m.

ST. PETERSBURG

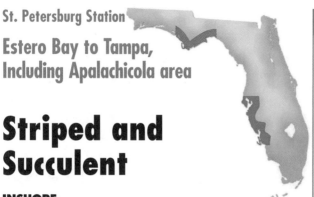

Estero Bay to Tampa, Including Apalachicola area

Striped and Succulent

ST. PETERSBURG

INSHORE

Tasty **sheepshead** are widespread this month. West Central anglers seek **snook** way up in brackish and freshwater creeks. **Redfish**, **trout** and **flounder** prefer creeks and rivers when cold, but slip onto grassflats and oyster bars on warm, sunny days. Grassflats, shoals and channel edges from Tampa Bay south offer up **pompano**.

OFFSHORE

Pick a warm day and troll lipped lures and bait-sweetened jigs along nearshore ledges and bay channels for **snapper** and **sea bass**, which go for cutbait or squid on dropper rigs. Or, go for flatter fare, **flounder**, by plying the oyster bars in headwaters or residential canal mud bottoms. **Amberjack** headline the action at most deeper wrecks while the **grouper** and **red snapper** season is closed.

TIDE CORRECTIONS For St. Petersburg	High	Low
Estero Bay		
Little Hickory Island	-0:58	-1:05
Coconut Point	-0:47	-0:40
Carlos Point	-1:08	-1:28
Mantanzas Pass, (fixed br.) Estero Isl	-1:10	-1:34
Point Ybel, Sand Carlos Bay entrance	-1:50	-1:12
Punta Rassa, San Carlos Bay	-1:01	-1:19
Caloosahatchee River		
Iona Shores	+1:08	+1:40
Cape Coral Bridge	+1:15	+2:02
Ft. Myers	+2:08	+2:44
Pine Island, St. James City	-0:30	-0:44
Galt Island, Pine Island Sound	-0:25	+0:16
Captiva Island, (outside)	-2:20	-2:28
Captiva Island, Pine Island Sound	-0:46	-0:20
Redfish Pass, Captiva I (north end)	-0:55	-1:14
Tropical Homesites Landing, Pine.	-0:08	+0:22
Matlacha Pass, (bascule bridge)	+0:43	+1:28
Pineland, Pine Island	-0:19	+0:26
Boca Grande, Charlotte Harbor	-1:12	-1:56
Punta Gorda, Charlotte Harbor	+1:06	+1:27
Shell Point, Peace River	+1:52	+2:30
El Jobean, Myakka River	+1:38	+1:56
Placida, Gasparilla Sound	-1:27	-0:59
Englewood, Lemon Bay	-0:57	-0:40
Venice Inlet, (inside)	-2:02	-1:38
Sarasota, Sarasota Bay	-1:38	-0:58
Cortez, Sarasota Bay	-2:00	-1:25
Egmont Key, Egmont Channel	-2:27	-2:24
Anna Maria	-2:07	-2:31
Bradenton, Manatee River	-1:24	-0:55
Redfish Point, Manatee River	-0:30	+0:14
Mullet Key Channel, (Skyway)	-2:22	-1:58
Shell Point	+0:08	+0:17
Point Pinellas	-0:22	-0:39
Tampa Bay, Hillsborough Bay	+0:07	+0:26
Safety Harbor, Old Tampa Bay	+1:38	+1:55
Boca Ciega Bay		
Pass-a-Grille Beach	-1:34	-1:30
Gulfport	-1:32	-1:05
St. Petersburg Beach Causeway	-1:18	-0:44
Johns Pass	-2:14	-2:04
Madeira Beach Causeway	-1:40	-1:18
St. George Sound		
Dog Island, west end	+0:07	+0:06
Carrabelle, Carrabelle River	+0:35	+0:31
St. George Island, East End	-0:15	+0:06
St. George Island, Rattlesnake Cove	+0:47	+1:19
St. George Island, Sikes Cut	+0:49	+1:32
Apalachicola Bay		
Cat Point	+1:20	+1:27
Apalachicola	+2:00	+2:44
Lower Anchorage	+1:43	+2:09
West Pass	+1:33	+2:17

February Spotlight: SHEEPSHEAD

Sheepshead taste good because most of their favorite foods (shrimp, crabs and oysters) taste good. These nibbling, striped delicacies do their dining under bridges, around channel markers, oyster bars and barnacle encrusted pilings. Many serious 'head anglers chum on the spot by scraping barnacles and small oysters off pilings into the water column with a

shovel. To increase chances of detecting a bite and getting a hookup, fish with a light-wire hook and no-stretch braided polyethylene line. And, set the hook just before they bite!

February 2011

SUNDAY	MONDAY	TUESDAY	WEDNESDAY	THURSDAY	FRIDAY	SATURDAY
		1	**2** ●	**3**	**4**	**5**
		2:49p 1.1' 7:40a -0.6'	12:39a 2.0' 2:59p 1.2' 6:25p 0.9'	1:19a 2.0' 3:08p 1.2' 8:09p -0.6' 7:12p 0.7'	1:57a 1.9' 3:18p 1.3' 8:34a -0.4' 7:55p 0.6'	2:34a 1.7' 3:31p 1.5' 8:56a -0.3' 8:36p 0.5'

(Additional tide data follows per day below)

6	7	8	9	10	11 ◐	12
3:13a 1.6' 3:49p 1.6'	3:56a 1.4' 4:12p 1.7'	4:45a 1.2' 4:40p 1.8'	5:46a 1.0' 5:14p 1.9'	7:13a 0.8' 5:55p 1.9'	6:46p 1.9'	7:51p 1.9'
9:18a -0.2' 9:18p 0.3'	9:39a 0.0' 10:04p 0.2'	10:01a 0.2' 10:53p 0.1'	10:23a 0.3' 11:49p 0.0'	10:43a 0.5' 12:57a 0.0' 10:58a 0.7'	2:16a -0.1'	3:37a -0.2'

13	14	15	16	17	18 ○	19
9:06p 2.0'	10:19p 2.1'	1:53p 1.1' 11:23p 2.2'	2:04p 1.2' 12:20a 2.2'	2:18p 1.3' 1:14a 2.2'	2:34p 1.4' 2:07a 2.1'	2:53p 1.6'
4:47a -0.4'	5:42a -0.6'	6:29a -0.7' 5:00p 1.0'	7:09a -0.7' 6:03p 0.8'	7:46a -0.7' 6:59p 0.5'	8:19a -0.5' 7:52p 0.3'	8:50a -0.3' 8:45p 0.1'

Sheep head TOURNAMENT

20	21	22	23 ◑	24	25	26
3:01a 1.9' 3:16p 1.7'	3:58a 1.6' 3:44p 1.9'	5:02a 1.3' 4:17p 2.1'	6:26a 1.0' 4:56p 2.1'	5:45p 2.1'	6:50p 2.0'	8:20p 1.9'
9:18a 0.0' 9:41p -0.1'	9:43a 0.3' 10:42p -0.2'	10:05a 0.5' 11:50p -0.3'	10:20a 0.7' 1:09a -0.3'	2:39a -0.3'	4:04a -0.3'	

27	28					
9:53p 1.9'	1:30p 1.2' 11:06p 1.9'					
5:10a -0.4'	5:59a -0.4' 4:52p 1.1'					

Trout tandem.

	February 1	February 15	February 28
SUNRISE	7:17 a.m.	7:08 a.m.	6:56 a.m.
SUNSET	6:11 p.m.	6:22 p.m.	6:31 p.m.

St. Petersburg Station

Estero Bay to Tampa, Including Apalachicola area

Fish on the March

INSHORE

Surf fishing picks up along West Central beaches. Your catch can include **bluefish, whiting, Spanish mackerel** and **pompano**. **Trout** and **redfish** become more active as the water warms, and head to grassflats for increasing baitfish schools. **Snook** follow suit, and also head for structure near passes by late month where they take live baits or artificials. **Sheepshead** active around bridges and inshore structure; pompano raid the bayside grassflats.

OFFSHORE

Northerly migrations are underway along the beaches. **Cobia** and **Spanish mackerel** are in close, with **kingfish** increasing by month's end over nearshore reefs. Freelining herring, sardines and cigar minnows on light wire rigs works best for kings. Don't forget about the **sea bass** and **flounder**. They're still out there and pressure will be lighter on them as most anglers have their eyes on the surface for the migratory fish. **Tripletail** numbers increase in the vicinity of markers and crab pots.

ST. PETERSBURG

TIDE CORRECTIONS
For St. Petersburg

	High	Low
Estero Bay		
Little Hickory Island	-0:58	-1:05
Coconut Point	-0:47	-0:40
Carlos Point	-1:08	-1:28
Mantanzas Pass, (fixed br.) Estero Isl	-1:10	-1:34
Point Ybel, Sand Carlos Bay entrance	-1:50	-1:12
Punta Rassa, San Carlos Bay	-1:01	-1:19
Caloosahatchee River		
Iona Shores	+1:08	+1:40
Cape Coral Bridge	+1:15	+2:02
Ft. Myers	+2:08	+2:44
Pine Island, St. James City	-0:30	-0:44
Galt Island, Pine Island Sound	-0:25	+0:16
Captiva Island, (outside)	-2:20	-2:28
Captiva Island, Pine Island Sound	-0:46	-0:20
Redfish Pass, Captiva I (north end)	-0:55	-1:14
Tropical Homesites Landing, Pinel.	-0:08	+0:22
Matlacha Pass, (bascule bridge)	+0:43	+1:28
Pineland, Pine Island	-0:19	+0:26
Boca Grande, Charlotte Harbor	-1:12	-1:56
Punta Gorda, Charlotte Harbor	+1:06	+1:27
Shell Point, Peace River	+1:52	+2:30
El Jobean, Myakka River	+1:38	+1:56
Placida, Gasparilla Sound	-1:27	-0:59
Englewood, Lemon Bay	-0:57	-0:40
Venice Inlet, (inside)	-2:02	-1:38
Sarasota, Sarasota Bay	-1:38	-0:58
Cortez, Sarasota Bay	-2:00	-1:25
Egmont Key, Egmont Channel	-2:27	-2:24
Anna Maria	-2:07	-2:31
Bradenton, Manatee River	-1:24	-0:55
Redfish Point, Manatee River	-0:30	+0:14
Mullet Key Channel, (Skyway)	-2:22	-1:58
Shell Point	+0:08	+0:17
Point Pinellas	-0:22	-0:29
Tampa Bay, Hillsborough Bay	+0:07	+0:26
Safety Harbor, Old Tampa Bay	+1:38	+1:55
Boca Ciega Bay		
Pass-a-Grille Beach	-1:34	-1:30
Gulfport	-1:32	-1:05
St. Petersburg Beach Causeway	-1:18	-0:44
Johns Pass	-2:14	-2:04
Madeira Beach Causeway	-1:40	-1:18
St. George Sound		
Dog Island, west end	+0:07	+0:06
Carrabelle, Carrabelle River	+0:35	+0:31
St. George Island, East End	-0:15	+0:06
St. George Island, Rattlesnake Cove	+0:47	+1:19
St. George Island, Sikes Cut	+0:49	+1:32
Apalachicola Bay		
Cat Point	+1:20	+1:27
Apalachicola	+2:00	+2:44
Lower Anchorage	+1:43	+2:09
West Pass	+1:33	+2:17

March Spotlight: COBIA

Word spreads quickly when **cobia** are on the move. The brown bomber prefers 70- to 72- degree water. Keep a close tab on water temps while you are on the water or listen up for reports from neighboring waters. St. Patrick's Day is the traditional kickoff in northern waters, and West Central anglers encounter them sooner than that. Keep rods rigged and ready with an eel, eel imitation or jig. Check for fish on markers and buoys. Stout tackle is a must around structure.

March 2011

SUNDAY	MONDAY	TUESDAY	WEDNESDAY	THURSDAY	FRIDAY	SATURDAY
		1	**2**	**3** ●	**4**	**5**
		1:39p 1.3' / 12:00a 1.9'	1:50p 1.4' / 12:45a 1.9'	1:58p 1.4' / 1:24a 1.8'	2:08p 1.5' / 2:00a 1.7'	2:17p 1.7' / 1.7'

		6:37a -0.4' 5:55p 0.9'	7:08a -0.3' 6:41p 0.7'	7:33a -0.2' 7:20p 0.5'	7:55a 0.0' 7:55p 0.3'	8:14a 0.1' 8:29p 0.2'
6	**7**	**8**	**9**	**10**	**11** ◑	**12**
2:36a 1.6' 2:31p 1.8'	3:13a 1.5' 2:50p 1.9'	3:53a 1.4' 3:14p 2.1'	4:39a 1.2' 3:44p 2.1'	5:37a 1.1' 4:19p 2.1'	7:06a 0.9' 5:03p 2.1'	5:58p 2.1'

		8:32a 0.3' 9:05p 0.0'	8:50a 0.4' 9:43p -0.1'	9:08a 0.5' 10:26p -0.1'	9:27a 0.6' 11:16p -0.1'	9:43a 0.8' 12:18a -0.1' 9:50a 0.9' 1:34a -0.1'
13	**14**	**15**	**16**	**17**	**18** ○	**19**
9:13p 2.0'	10:44p 2.0'	2:35p 1.3' 12:10a 2.1'	2:45p 1.4' 1:21a 2.1'	2:59p 1.5' 2:23a 2.1'	3:15p 1.6'	3:21a 2.0' 3:34p 1.8'

BONAIRE → (handwritten)

		4:55a -0.2'	6:07a -0.3'	7:05a -0.4' 5:56p 1.1'	7:52a -0.4' 7:12p 0.8'	8:32a -0.3' 8:10p 0.5' 9:07a -0.1' 9:03p 0.2' 9:38a 0.1' 9:53p -0.1'
20	**21**	**22**	**23**	**24**	**25** ◑	**26**
4:16a 1.9' 3:57p 2.1'	5:12a 1.7' 4:24p 2.2'	6:11a 1.5' 4:56p 2.4'	7:20a 1.2' 5:32p 2.4'	9:00a 1.1' 6:13p 2.4'	7:04p 2.2'	8:15p 2.0'

		10:05a 0.4' 10:44p -0.3'	10:29a 0.6' 11:36p -0.4'	10:50a 0.8' 12:32a -0.4'	11:06a 0.9' 1:35a -0.4'	11:07a 1.0' 2:47a -0.3' 4:08a -0.2'
27	**28**	**29**	**30**	**31**		
10:01p 1.9'	2:12p 1.4' 11:45p 1.8'	2:21p 1.5' 1:00a 1.8'	2:34p 1.6' 1:57a 1.8'	2:46p 1.7'		
5:25a -0.1'	6:26a -0.1' 5:47p 1.2'	7:13a 0.0' 7:06p 1.0'	7:51a 0.1' 7:57p 0.7'	8:21a 0.2' 8:38p 0.5'		

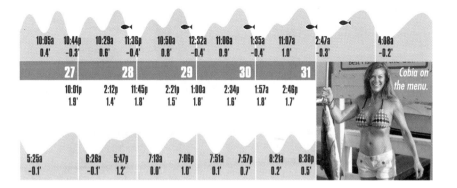

Cobia on the menu.

	March 1	March 15	March 30
SUNRISE	6:55 a.m.	7:40 a.m.	7:23 a.m.
SUNSET	6:31 p.m.	7:39 p.m.	7:47 p.m.

DST Starts on March 13

Estero Bay to Tampa, Including Apalachicola area

Macks and More

INSHORE

Simply put, **Spanish mackerel** are where you look for them. Beaches and bays have schools galore. **Snook** continue to move toward the passes, so action is picking up over coastal grassflats, oyster bars and structure day and night. Topwaters, swimming plugs, soft-plastics and baitfish flies will score in all venues. Stout **seatrout** are in abundance both in northern and central Gulf region; throw topwater plugs and soft baits around sandy holes and along flats edges for the biggest trout. In the surf, **pompano** come on strong for the spring run.

OFFSHORE

Kingfish and **cobia** are hot as a pistol in entire region. For kings, live baitfish slow-trolled are deadly, but spoons on planers and jigs score, too. For cobes, scout from high in the boat if you do not have a tower. Cast eel imitations, jigs or a live baitfish. **Mangrove snapper** bite well over nearshore reefs and rockpiles. **Permit** school up in big numbers at wrecks and rockpiles. Approach structure quietly and cast live crabs or crab-tipped jigs to fish sighted. They can be chummed into a biting mood, and will then take crab flies and pure jigs well.

ST. PETERSBURG

TIDE CORRECTIONS
For St. Petersburg

	High	Low
Estero Bay		
Little Hickory Island	-0:58	-1:05
Coconut Point	-0:47	-0:40
Carlos Point	-1:08	-1:28
Mantanzas Pass, (fixed br.) Estero Isl	-1:10	-1:34
Point Ybel, Sand Carlos Bay entrance	-1:50	-1:12
Punta Rassa, San Carlos Bay	-1:01	-1:19
Caloosahatchee River		
Iona Shores	+1:08	+1:40
Cape Coral Bridge	+1:15	+2:02
Ft. Myers	+2:08	+2:44
Pine Island, St. James City	-0:30	-0:44
Galt Island, Pine Island Sound	-0:25	+0:16
Captiva Island, (outside)	-2:20	-2:28
Captiva Island, Pine Island Sound	-0:46	-0:20
Redfish Pass, Captiva I (north end)	-0:55	-1:14
Tropical Homesites Landing, Pine1.	-0:08	+0:22
Matlacha Pass, (bascule bridge)	+0:43	+1:38
Pineland, Pine Island	-0:19	-0:57
Boca Grande, Charlotte Harbor	-1:12	-1:56
Punta Gorda, Charlotte Harbor	+1:06	+1:27
Shell Point, Peace River	+1:52	+2:30
El Jobean, Myakka River	+1:38	+1:56
Placida, Gasparilla Sound	-1:27	-0:59
Englewood, Lemon Bay	-0:57	-0:40
Venice Inlet, (inside)	-2:02	-1:38
Sarasota, Sarasota Bay	-1:38	-0:58
Cortez, Sarasota Bay	-2:00	-1:25
Egmont Key, Egmont Channel	-2:27	-2:24
Anna Maria	-2:07	-2:31
Bradenton, Manatee River	-1:24	-0:55
Redfish Point, Manatee River	-0:30	+0:14
Mullet Key Channel, (Skyway)	-2:22	-1:58
Shell Point	+0:08	+0:17
Point Pinellas	-0:22	-0:29
Tampa Bay, Hillsborough Bay	+0:07	+0:26
Safety Harbor, Old Tampa Bay	+1:38	+1:55
Boca Ciega Bay		
Pass-a-Grille Beach	-1:34	-1:30
Gulfport	-1:32	-1:05
St. Petersburg Beach Causeway	-1:18	-0:44
Johns Pass	-2:14	-2:04
Madeira Beach Causeway	-1:40	-1:18
St. George Sound		
Dog Island, west end	+0:07	+0:06
Carrabelle, Carrabelle River	+0:35	+0:31
St. George Island, East End	-0:15	+0:06
St. George Island, Rattlesnake Cove	+0:47	+1:19
St. George Island, Sikes Cut	+0:49	+1:32
Apalachicola Bay		
Cat Point	+1:20	+1:27
Apalachicola	+2:00	+2:44
Lower Anchorage	+1:43	+2:09
West Pass	+1:33	+2:17

April Spotlight: SPANISH MACKEREL

Give the family a treat on a school of **Spanish mackerel**. They're easy to catch, fight to the finish and are great fresh on the table. Look for birds dipping over bait schools where macks attack from below. Drift into casting range from upwind or uptide and cast flashy white or green jigs, small silver spoons or streamer flies. Or, anchor and chum them to the boat to keep the bite going. Rig with heavy mono or light wire.

April 2011

handwritten: Long bar Trout a Snook 2 reds

SUNDAY	MONDAY	TUESDAY	WEDNESDAY	THURSDAY	FRIDAY	SATURDAY
Tarpon revival.					**1**	**2**
					2:45a 1.7' / 2:57p 1.8'	3:27a 1.7' / 3:08p 1.9' *Reel Tony*
					8:46a 0.3' / 9:13p 0.3'	9:06a 0.5' / 9:46p 0.1'
3	**4**	**5**	**6**	**7**	**8**	**9**
4:05a 1.6' / 3:21p 2.1'	4:41a 1.5' / 3:38p 2.2'	5:18a 1.4' / 4:01p 2.3'	5:58a 1.4' / 4:29p 2.4'	6:45a 1.3' / 5:02p 2.4'	7:48a 1.2' / 5:42p 2.4'	6:29p 2.3'
9:25a 0.6' / 10:18p 0.0'	9:41a 0.7' / 10:51p -0.2'	9:58a 0.8' / 11:28p -0.2'	10:16a 0.9'	12:09a -0.2' / 10:34a 1.0'	12:58a -0.2' / 10:52a 1.0' *SHAKE OUT Boat*	1:56a -0.2'
10	**11**	**12**	**13**	**14**	**15**	**16**
Jersey Boys Schmidt 2:29p 2.2'	8:51p 2.1'	1:00p 1.4' / 10:30p 2.0'	1:15p 1.5' / 12:03a 2.0' *Fish Egmont*	1:33p 1.7' / 1:21a 1.9'	1:54p -1.9' / 2:29a 1.9' *Fish Reskin*	2:17p 2.1'
3:04a -0.1'	4:15a -0.1'	5:20a -0.1' / 4:29p 1.2'	6:16a 0.0' / 6:06p 1.0'	7:03a 0.1' / 7:14p 0.6'	7:43a 0.3' / 8:10p 0.3'	8:17a 0.5' / 9:02p -0.1'
17	**18**	W **19**	W **20**	W **21**	**22**	**23**
3:31a 1.8' / 2:42p 2.3'	4:30a 1.7' / 3:11p 2.5'	5:30a 1.5' / 3:43p 2.7' W	6:33a 1.4' / 4:20p 2.7' W	7:48a 1.2' / 5:00p 2.6' W	*Pump* 5:45p 2.5'	6:38p 2.3' *Fish Anna Maria Long Boat*
8:46a 0.7' / 9:51p -0.3'	9:12a 0.9' / 10:40p -0.5'	9:34a 1.0' / 11:31p -0.5'	9:53a 1.1'	12:24a -0.5' / 10:08a 1.2'	1:20a -0.4'	2:22a -0.2'
24	**25**	**26**	**27**	**28**	**29**	**30**
Easter 7:49p 2.0'	12:33p 1.5' / 9:31p 1.8'	12:46p 1.6' / 11:18p 1.7' *Work*	1:04p 1.7' *Work*	12:41a 1.6' / 1:22p 1.9' *Work*	1:46a 1.6' / 1:39p 2.0' *Book*	2:42a 1.6' / 1:55p 2.1' *Pack*
3:26a -0.1'	4:27a 0.1' / 3:48p 1.4'	5:22a 0.2' / 5:43p 1.1'	6:08a 0.3' / 6:52p 0.9'	6:47a 0.5' / 7:42p 0.6'	7:20a 0.6' / 8:22p 0.3'	7:47a 0.8' / 8:59p 0.1'

handwritten: Tarpon Shows week of 24 Apr 11

ST. PETERSBURG

	April 1	April 15	April 30
SUNRISE	7:21 a.m.	7:06 a.m.	6:52 a.m.
SUNSET	7:48 p.m.	7:56 p.m.	8:04 p.m.

Estero Bay to Tampa, Including Apalachicola area

Reds are Ready

INSHORE

Tarpon are stacked in the southern passes, along with **snook** that are staging for spawning. **Cobia** widespread but a bit tougher to fool by month's end; search for free-swimmers and those shadowing channel markers and crab pots. The northern surf is alive with **pompano** and **Spanish mackerel** that are ravaging bait pods, with **kingfish** close by in entire region.

Sight fishing is improving for **redfish** over the bay grassflats and oyster bars as water warms. **Trout** fishing nears a peak, particularly for gators.

OFFSHORE

For **grouper** and **snapper** head for the nearshore wrecks and rockpiles. Your best **red grouper** shot is on limestone ledges from St. Petersburg north. In fair seas, it's worth a run for **dolphin**, **blackfin tuna** and **sailfish**. Otherwise, consider targeting **king mackerel** in about 60 feet of water where slow-trolling with live threadfins and sardines is deadly, or just rig dead baits such as cigar minnows and ribbonfish.

ST. PETERSBURG

TIDE CORRECTIONS
For St. Petersburg

	High	Low
Estero Bay		
Little Hickory Island	-0:58	-1:05
Coconut Point	-0:47	-0:40
Carlos Point	-1:08	-1:28
Mantanzas Pass, (fixed br.) Estero Isl	-1:10	-1:34
Point Ybel, Sand Carlos Bay entrance	-1:50	-1:12
Punta Rassa, San Carlos Bay	-1:01	-1:19
Caloosahatchee River		
Iona Shores	+1:08	+1:40
Cape Coral Bridge	+1:15	+2:02
Ft. Myers	+2:08	+2:44
Pine Island, St. James City	-0:30	-0:44
Galt Island, Pine Island Sound	-0:25	+0:16
Captiva Island, (outside)	-2:20	-2:28
Captiva Island, Pine Island Sound	-0:46	-0:20
Redfish Pass, Captiva I (north end)	-0:55	-1:14
Tropical Homesites Landing, Pinel.	-0:08	+0:22
Matlacha Pass, (bascule bridge)	+0:43	+1:28
Pineland, Pine Island	-0:19	+0:26
Boca Grande, Charlotte Harbor	-1:12	-1:05
Punta Gorda, Charlotte Harbor	+1:06	+1:27
Shell Point, Peace River	+1:52	+2:30
El Jobean, Myakka River	+1:38	+1:56
Placida, Gasparilla Sound	-1:27	-0:59
Englewood, Lemon Bay	-0:57	-0:40
Venice Inlet, (inside)	-2:02	-1:38
Sarasota, Sarasota Bay	-1:38	-0:58
Cortez, Sarasota Bay	-2:00	-1:15
Egmont Key, Egmont Channel	-2:27	-2:24
Anna Maria	-2:07	-2:31
Bradenton, Manatee River	-1:24	-0:55
Redfish Point, Manatee River	-0:30	+0:14
Mullet Key Channel, (Skyway)	-2:22	-1:38
Shell Point	+0:08	+0:17
Point Pinellas	-0:22	-0:09
Tampa Bay, Hillsborough Bay	+0:07	+0:26
Safety Harbor, Old Tampa Bay	+1:38	+1:55
Boca Ciega Bay		
Pass-a-Grille Beach	-1:34	-1:30
Gulfport	-1:32	-1:05
St. Petersburg Beach Causeway	-1:18	-0:44
Johns Pass	-2:14	-2:04
Madeira Beach Causeway	-1:40	-1:18
St. George Sound		
Dog Island, west end	+0:07	+0:06
Carrabelle, Carrabelle River	+0:35	+0:31
St. George Island, East End	-0:15	+0:06
St. George Island, Rattlesnake Cove	+0:47	+1:19
St. George Island, Sikes Cut	+0:49	+1:32
Apalachicola Bay		
Cat Point	+1:20	+1:27
Apalachicola	+2:00	+2:44
Lower Anchorage	+1:43	+2:09
West Pass	+1:33	+2:17

May Spotlight: REDFISH

Though the summer peak is yet to come, May offers classic **redfish** sight casting for those who practice stealth by poling or wading to tailers and waking schools. Time up an early morning with an ebbing tide to spot signs of fish. At higher tides, fish drop off the flats, or hunker under mangrove cover. Toss real or scented shrimp or crab baits, soft-plastic jerkbaits, flies, spoons or cutbait.

May 2011

SUNDAY	MONDAY	TUESDAY	WEDNESDAY	THURSDAY	FRIDAY	SATURDAY
1	**2** ●	**3**	**4**	**5**	**6**	**7**

SUNDAY	MONDAY	TUESDAY	WEDNESDAY	THURSDAY	FRIDAY	SATURDAY
3:31a 2:12p 1.6' 2.2'	4:15a 2:31p 1.5' 2.4'	4:55a 2:55p 1.5' 2.5'	5:35a 3:24p 1.4' 2.6'	6:18a 3:58p 1.3' 2.6'	7:08a 4:37p 1.3' 2.6'	8:10a 5:21p 1.3' 2.6'

ITALY

8:10a 9:33p 0.9' -0.1'	8:29a 10:07p 1.0' -0.2'	8:47a 10:41p 1.1' -0.3'	9:04a 11:19p 1.2' -0.3'	9:25a 12:01a 1.2' -0.3'	9:49a 12:48a 1.2' -0.3'	10:20a 1.2'
8	**9** ◑	**10**	**11**	**12**	**13**	**14**
6:14p 2.4'	10:22a 7:18p 1.4' 2.3'	10:59a 8:41p 1.5' 2.0'	11:30a 10:21p 1.6' 1.8'	11:58a 12:00a 1.8' 1.7'	12:27a 1:27a 2.0' 1.7'	12:56p 2.3'

1:40a -0.2'	2:37a 12:42p -0.2' 1.3'	3:34a 2:48p -0.1' 1.3'	4:29a 4:39p 0.1' 1.1'	5:19a 6:04p 0.3' 0.7'	6:05a 7:11p 0.5' 0.3'	6:44a 8:08p 0.8' 0.0'
15	**16** ○	**17**	**18**	**19**	**20**	**21**
2:44a 1:28p 1.6' 2.5'	3:52a 2:01p 1.5' 2.7'	4:56a 2:38p 1.5' 2.8'	5:58a 3:17p 1.4' 2.8'	7:00a 3:58p 1.3' 2.8'	4:42p 2.7'	5:29p 2.5'

7:18a 9:00p 1.0' -0.3'	7:48a 9:50p 1.1' -0.5'	8:14a 10:39p 1.2' -0.6'	8:38a 11:26p 1.3' -0.5'	9:03a 12:14a 1.3' -0.4'	1:01a -0.3'	
22	**23** ◑	**24**	**25**	**26**	**27**	**28**
9:40a 6:22p 1.4' 2.2'	10:13a 7:28p 1.5' 2.0'	10:43a 8:54p 1.6' 1.7'	11:12a 10:36p 1.8' 1.5'	11:39a 12:12a 1.9' 1.4'	12:06p 2.0'	1:33a 12:31p 1.4' 2.2'

1:49a 11:48a -0.1' 1.4'	2:36a 1:38p 0.0' 1.4'	3:22a 3:32p 0.2' 1.2'	4:07a 5:08p 0.4' 1.0'	4:50a 6:19p 0.6' 0.7'	5:31a 7:13p 0.8' 0.4'	6:07a 7:59p 1.0' 0.2'
29	**30**	**31**				
2:41a 12:57p 1.4' 2.3'	3:41a 1:24p 1.4' 2.4'	4:33a 1:54p 1.4' 2.5'				
6:39a 8:41p 1.1' 0.0'	7:05a 9:19p 1.2' -0.2'	7:29a 9:57p 1.3' -0.3'				

Hit the reefs for grouper.

	May 1	May 15	May 30
SUNRISE	6:51 a.m.	6:41 a.m.	6:35 a.m.
SUNSET	8:05 p.m.	8:13 p.m.	8:21 p.m.

ST. PETERSBURG

FISHING PLANNER 97

Estero Bay to Tampa, Including Apalachicola area

Jumps in June

INSHORE

Tarpon season is in full swing, with fish of all sizes widely distributed throughout the region. Beaches to north see some, but the best bite is in central Gulf passes, along beaches close to passes, and around bridges. If looking for smaller game, how about **Spanish mackerel**, **snook** (catch and release), **black** and **red drum**, and **trout**? Early starts and incoming tides bring in the coolest water, which is ideal. **Mangrove snapper** stack up around docks and bridges, too.

OFFSHORE

June means flatter seas for running during open season on **red snapper** and **grouper**, plus there's a good shot at **yellowfin tuna**, **dolphin** and **wahoo** for those willing to run farther offshore. But June is the one month of the year when **blue marlin** are almost dependable out at the deep canyons, and **dolphin** are more available now than any other time.

ST. PETERSBURG

TIDE CORRECTIONS
For St. Petersburg

	High	Low
Estero Bay		
Little Hickory Island	-0:58	-1:05
Coconut Point	-0:47	-0:40
Carlos Point	-1:08	-1:28
Mantanzas Pass, (fixed br.) Estero Isl	-1:10	-1:34
Point Ybel, Sand Carlos Bay entrance	-1:50	-1:12
Punta Rassa, San Carlos Bay	-1:01	-1:19
Caloosahatchee River		
Iona Shores	+1:08	+1:40
Cape Coral Bridge	+1:15	+2:02
Ft. Myers	+2:08	+2:44
Pine Island, St. James City	-0:30	-0:44
Galt Island, Pine Island Sound	-0:25	+0:16
Captiva Island, (outside)	-2:20	-2:28
Captiva Island, Pine Island Sound	-0:46	-0:20
Redfish Pass, Captiva I (north end)	-0:55	-1:14
Tropical Homesites Landing, Pinel.	-0:08	+0:22
Matlacha Pass, (bascule bridge)	+0:43	+1:28
Pineland, Pine Island	-0:19	+0:26
Boca Grande, Charlotte Harbor	-1:12	-1:56
Punta Gorda, Charlotte Harbor	+1:06	+1:27
Shell Point, Peace River	+1:52	+2:30
El Jobean, Myakka River	+1:38	+1:56
Placida, Gasparilla Sound	-1:27	-0:59
Englewood, Lemon Bay	0:57	-0:40
Venice Inlet, (inside)	-2:02	-1:38
Sarasota, Sarasota Bay	-1:38	-0:58
Cortez, Sarasota Bay	-2:00	-1:25
Egmont Key, Egmont Channel	-2:27	-2:24
Anna Maria	-2:07	-2:31
Bradenton, Manatee River	-1:24	-0:55
Redfish Point, Manatee River	-0:30	+0:14
Mullet Key Channel, (Skyway)	-2:22	-1:58
Shell Point	+0:08	+0:17
Point Pinellas	-0:22	-0:29
Tampa Bay, Hillsborough Bay	+0:07	+0:26
Safety Harbor, Old Tampa Bay	+1:38	+1:55
Boca Ciega Bay		
Pass-a-Grille Beach	-1:34	-1:30
Gulfport	-1:32	-1:05
St. Petersburg Beach Causeway	-1:18	-1:01
Johns Pass	-2:14	-2:04
Madeira Beach Causeway	-1:40	-1:18
St. George Sound		
Dog Island, west end	+0:07	+0:06
Carrabelle, Carrabelle River	+0:35	+0:31
St. George Island, East End	-0:15	+0:06
St. George Island, Rattlesnake Cove	+0:47	+1:19
St. George Island, Sikes Cut	+0:49	+1:32
Apalachicola Bay		
Cat Point	+1:20	+1:27
Apalachicola	+2:00	+2:44
Lower Anchorage	+1:43	+2:09
West Pass	+1:33	+2:17

June Spotlight: TARPON

Yes, there is always the **tarpon** "rodeo" in Boca Grande Pass, so now's the time to try combat fishing for thousands of tarpon in the 75- to 200-pound class. But other options exist. For example, sight fishing over shoals outside Gulf passes, or up north over grass bottoms of the eastern Panhandle. Standard baits include a live crab or pinfish, flies and soft plastics. Approach rolling fish with an electric motor from a distance, then drift in to cast live crabs, whitebaits or flies.

Trout 14ft Area Grassy

June 2011

SUNDAY	MONDAY	TUESDAY	WEDNESDAY	THURSDAY	FRIDAY	SATURDAY

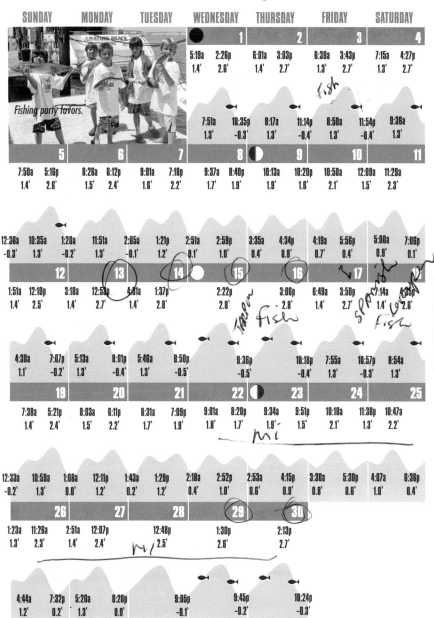

Fishing party favors.

1 ●
5:19a 2:26p
1.4' 2.6'
7:51a 10:35p
1.3' -0.3'

2
6:01a 3:03p
1.4' 2.7'
8:17a 11:14p
1.3' -0.4'

fish

3
6:39a 3:43p
1.3' 2.7'
8:50a 11:54p
1.3' -0.4'

4
7:15a 4:27p
1.3' 2.7'
9:36a
1.3'

5
7:50a 5:16p
1.4' 2.6'

6
8:26a 6:12p
1.5' 2.4'

7
9:01a 7:18p
1.6' 2.2'

8 ◑
9:37a 8:40p
1.7' 1.9'

9
10:13a 10:20p
1.9' 1.6'

10
10:50a 12:09a
2.1' 1.5'

11
11:29a
2.3'

12
12:36a 10:35a
-0.3' 1.3'
1:51a 12:10p
1.4' 2.5'

13
1:20a 11:51a
-0.2' 1.3'
3:18a 12:55p
1.4' 2.7'

14 ○
2:05a 1:21p
-0.1' 1.2'
4:31a 1:37p
1.4' 2.8'

15
2:51a 2:59p
0.1' 1.0'
2:22p
2.8'

Taram fish

16
3:35a 4:34p
0.4' 0.8'
3:06p
2.8'

fish

17
4:19a 5:56p
0.7' 0.4'
6:49a 3:50p
1.4' 2.7'

Spanish fish

18
5:00a 7:06p
0.9' 0.1'
7:14a 4:35p
1.4' 2.6'

19
4:38a 7:07p
1.1' -0.2'

20
5:13a 8:01p
1.3' -0.4'

21
5:46a 8:50p
1.3' -0.5'

22 ◑
9:36p
-0.5'

23
10:18p
-0.4'

24
7:55a 10:57p
1.3' -0.3'

25
8:54a
1.3'

26
7:38a 5:21p
1.4' 2.4'
12:33a 10:59a
-0.2' 1.3'
1:23a 11:26a
1.3' 2.3'

27
8:03a 6:11p
1.5' 2.2'
1:08a 12:11p
0.0' 1.2'
2:51a 12:07p
1.4' 2.4'

mi

28
8:31a 7:09p
1.7' 1.9'
1:43a 1:29p
0.2' 1.2'
12:48p
2.5'

29
9:01a 8:20p
1.8' 1.7'
2:18a 2:52p
0.4' 1.0'
1:30p
2.6'

mi

30
9:34a 9:51p
1.9' 1.5'
2:53a 4:15p
0.6' 0.9'
2:13p
2.7'

(continued lower rows)
10:10a 11:38p
2.1' 1.3'
3:30a 5:30p
0.8' 0.6'
4:44a 7:32p
1.2' 0.2'

10:47a
2.2'
4:07a 6:36p
1.0' 0.4'
5:20a 8:20p
1.3' 0.0'

9:05p
-0.1'

9:45p
-0.2'

10:24p
-0.3'

	June 1	June 15	June 30
SUNRISE	6:35 a.m.	6:34 a.m.	6:38 a.m.
SUNSET	8:22 p.m.	8:28 p.m.	8:31 p.m.

Estero Bay to Tampa, Including Apalachicola area

Go for Grouper

INSHORE

Set that alarm clock for serious fishing, it's an early bite in many cases. Surf fishing centers around sight casting for **snook** with flies and small lures when the sun is bright and still in the morning sky. **Redfish** raid the flats and are best seen on lower water, especially around oyster bars. Northwest Florida sees a big effort for **scallops**.

OFFSHORE

Kings are peaking along Northwest beaches and finding bait means hooking up. Bottom fans turn their attention to **red snapper** and **red grouper**, both of which are quick to snap up a live baitfish or squid-tipped jig over limestone hard bottom. **Cobia** and **tripletail** are shadowing markers and buoys, and free-swimming at the surface in the region. Pick a sunny morning and be the first boat on the structure to present a live pinfish, shrimp, crab, jig or fly.

ST. PETERSBURG

TIDE CORRECTIONS For St. Petersburg	High	Low
Estero Bay		
Little Hickory Island	-0:58	-1:05
Coconut Point	-0:47	-0:40
Carlos Point	-1:08	-1:28
Mantanzas Pass, (fixed br.) Estero Isl	-1:10	-1:34
Point Ybel, Sand Carlos Bay entrance	-1:50	-1:12
Punta Rassa, San Carlos Bay	-1:01	-1:19
Caloosahatchee River		
Iona Shores	+1:08	+1:40
Cape Coral Bridge	+1:15	+2:02
Ft. Myers	+2:08	+2:44
Pine Island, St. James City	-0:30	-0:44
Galt Island, Pine Island Sound	-0:25	+0:16
Captiva Island, (outside)	-2:20	-2:28
Captiva Island, Pine Island Sound	-0:46	-0:20
Redfish Pass, Captiva I (north end)	-0:55	-1:14
Tropical Homesites Landing, Pinel.	-0:08	+0:22
Matlacha Pass, (bascule bridge)	+0:43	+1:28
Pineland, Pine Island	-0:19	+0:26
Boca Grande, Charlotte Harbor	-1:12	-1:56
Punta Gorda, Charlotte Harbor	+1:06	+1:27
Shell Point, Peace River	+1:52	+2:30
El Jobean, Myakka River	+1:38	+1:56
Placida, Gasparilla Sound	-1:27	-0:59
Englewood, Lemon Bay	-0:57	-0:40
Venice Inlet, (inside)	-2:02	-1:38
Sarasota, Sarasota Bay	-1:38	-0:58
Cortez, Sarasota Bay	-2:00	-1:25
Egmont Key, Egmont Channel	-2:27	-2:24
Anna Maria	-2:07	-2:31
Bradenton, Manatee River	-1:24	-0:55
Redfish Point, Manatee River	-0:30	+0:14
Mullet Key Channel, (Skyway)	-2:22	-1:58
Shell Point	+0:08	+0:17
Point Pinellas	-0:22	-0:39
Tampa Bay, Hillsborough Bay	+0:07	+0:26
Safety Harbor, Old Tampa Bay	+1:38	+1:55
Boca Ciega Bay		
Pass-a-Grille Beach	-1:34	-1:30
Gulfport	-1:32	-1:05
St. Petersburg Beach Causeway	-1:18	-0:44
Johns Pass	-2:14	-2:04
Madeira Beach Causeway	-1:40	-1:18
St. George Sound		
Dog Island, west end	+0:07	+0:06
Carrabelle, Carrabelle River	+0:35	+0:31
St. George Island, East End	-0:15	+0:06
St. George Island, Rattlesnake Cove	+0:47	+1:19
St. George Island, Sikes Cut	+0:49	+1:32
Apalachicola Bay		
Cat Point	+1:20	+1:27
Apalachicola	+2:00	+2:44
Lower Anchorage	+1:43	+2:09
West Pass	+1:33	+2:17

July Spotlight: RED GROUPER

Red grouper are among the easiest groupers to catch, and by now are moving inshore, close to the beach. Drift-fish over hard bottom and limestone ledges which are abundant off St. Petersburg and Clearwater beaches in only 30 to 50 feet. Live baits can be caught on sabiki rigs at most ledges; drop fresh baits down, or fresh squid when baits are scarce, to bottom with on 20-pound-class tackle. Deep-jigging with tipped bucktails is an option.

July 201

SUNDAY	MONDAY	TUESDAY	WEDNESDAY	THURSDAY	FRIDAY	SATURDAY

Big backwater redfish.

1 ●
5:51a 2:56p
1.4' 2.8'
8:05a 11:01p
1.3' -0.3'

2
6:10a 3:41p
1.4' 2.8'
8:59a 11:38p
1.3' -0.3'

3
6:30a 4:29p
1.5' 2.7'
8:58a 11:15p
1.2' -0.2'

4
6:53a 5:21p
1.5' 2.6'
10:02a 11:51p
1.1' 0.0'

5
7:20a 6:18p
1.7' 2.3'
11:11a
1.0'

6
7:50a 7:24p
1.8' 2.0'
12:28a 12:29p
0.2' 0.9'

7
8:26a 8:46p
2.0' 1.7'
1:04a 1:53p
0.5' 0.7'

8 ◗
9:06a 10:34p
2.2' 1.4'
1:39a 3:22p
0.8' 0.5'

9
9:52a
2.4'
2:13a 4:48p
1.0' 0.3'

10
12:45a 10:45a
1.3' 2.5'
3:46a 7:03p
1.2' 0.0'

11
11:41a
2.7'
Fish
Red
8:07p
-0.1'

12
12:39p
2.7'
9:00p
-0.3'

13
1:33p
2.8'
9:46p
-0.3'

14
5:20a 2:23p
1.4' 2.8'
7:24a 10:24p
1.4' -0.2'

15 ○
5:37a 3:09p
1.5' 2.7'
8:25a 10:58p
1.3' -0.1'

16
5:52a 3:52p
1.5' 2.6'
9:20a 11:28p
1.3' 0.0'

17
6:06a 4:33p
1.6' 2.5'
10:14a 11:55p
1.2' 0.1'

18
6:21a 5:15p
1.7' 2.3'
11:07a
1.1'

19
6:41a 6:01p
1.8' 2.1'
12:21a 12:03p
0.3' 1.0'

20
7:04a 6:52p
1.9' 1.9'
12:48a 1:01p
0.5' 0.9'

21
7:33a 7:53p
2.0' 1.7'
1:16a 2:06p
0.7' 0.8'

22 ◖
8:07a 9:13p
2.1' 1.5'
1:45a 3:17p
0.9' 0.7'

23
8:47a 11:07p
2.2' 1.4'
Fish
trout
S pot
mangos
2:14a 4:35p
1.0' 0.6'

24
9:34a
2.3'
2:42a 5:52p
1.2' 0.5'

25
10:28a
2.4'
7:00p
0.3'

26
11:27a
2.5'
7:56p
0.1'

27
12:25p
2.6'
8:43p
0.0'

28
3:07a 1:50p
3.1' 3.7'
7:51a 9:24p
1.9' -0.1'

29
4:38a 2:09p
1.5' 2.8'
7:27a 10:01p
1.4' -0.1'

30 ●
4:53a 2:57p
1.5' 2.8'
fish
8:24a 10:36p
1.3' -0.1'
Bad
Tide
notion

31
5:08a 3:46p
1.6' 2.8'
9:18a 11:09p
1.1' 0.0'

Kayaking the Weedon Island Preserve.

ST. PETERSBURG

	July 1	July 15	July 30
SUNRISE	6:38 a.m.	6:45 a.m.	6:53 a.m.
SUNSET	8:31 p.m.	8:29 p.m.	8:21 p.m.

Bay to Tampa,
including Apalachicola area

Summer Finish

INSHORE

Tarpon in decent numbers in the passes, along beaches and bays north and south; juveniles thick in rivers. **Snook** numbers soar in the surf, with others on bayside structure, and lighted docks. **Gulf flounder** make a showing, with mud minnows and finger mullet top baits in Northwest Florida. Find birds and bait and you are into **Spanish mackerel**. Schooling **reds** are at a summer peak, with over-slot specimens common on flats and bars, and along mangrove shorelines. Soft plastics, scented baits, spoons, topwaters, live crabs and cut mullet are all top producers. **Trout** are a good bet at first light.

OFFSHORE

The bluewater scene is dominated by **dolphin**, **wahoo** and **blackfin tuna** around far offshore weedlines, rips and floating debris. **Blue marlin** may show in 600 feet or more for long-range boaters fast-trolling lure spreads and teasers. Then there's **king mackerel**, **cobia** for sight fishing, and a variety of **grouper** for bottom fans.

ST. PETERSBURG

TIDE CORRECTIONS
For St. Petersburg

	High	Low
Estero Bay		
Little Hickory Island	-0:58	-1:05
Coconut Point	-0:47	-0:40
Carlos Point	-1:08	-1:28
Mantanzas Pass, (fixed br.) Estero Isl	-1:10	-1:34
Point Ybel, Sand Carlos Bay entrance	-1:50	-1:12
Punta Rassa, San Carlos Bay	-1:01	-1:19
Caloosahatchee River		
Iona Shores	+1:08	+1:40
Cape Coral Bridge	+1:15	+2:02
Ft. Myers	+2:08	+2:44
Pine Island, St. James City	-0:30	-0:44
Galt Island, Pine Island Sound	-0:25	+0:16
Captiva Island, (outside)	-2:20	-2:28
Captiva Island, Pine Island Sound	-0:46	-0:20
Redfish Pass, Captiva I (north end)	-0:55	-1:14
Tropical Homesites Landing, Pinel.	-0:08	+0:22
Matlacha Pass, (bascule bridge)	+0:43	+1:28
Pineland, Pine Island	-0:19	+0:26
Boca Grande, Charlotte Harbor	-1:12	-1:56
Punta Gorda, Charlotte Harbor	+1:06	+1:27
Shell Point, Peace River	+1:52	+2:30
El Jobean, Myakka River	+1:38	+1:56
Placida, Gasparilla Sound	-1:27	-0:59
Englewood, Lemon Bay	-0:57	-0:40
Venice Inlet, (inside)	-2:02	-1:38
Sarasota, Sarasota Bay	-1:38	-0:58
Cortez, Sarasota Bay	-2:00	-1:25
Egmont Key, Egmont Channel	-2:27	-2:24
Anna Maria	-2:07	-2:31
Bradenton, Manatee River	-1:24	-0:55
Redfish Point, Manatee River	-0:30	+0:14
Mullet Key Channel, (Skyway)	-2:22	-1:58
Shell Point	+0:08	+0:17
Point Pinellas	-0:22	-0:29
Tampa Bay, Hillsborough Bay	+0:07	+0:26
Safety Harbor, Old Tampa Bay	+1:38	+1:55
Boca Ciega Bay		
Pass-a-Grille Beach	-1:34	-1:30
Gulfport	-1:32	-1:05
St. Petersburg Beach Causeway	-1:18	-0:44
Johns Pass	-2:14	-2:04
Madeira Beach Causeway	-1:40	-1:18
St. George Sound		
Dog Island, west end	+0:07	+0:06
Carrabelle, Carrabelle River	+0:35	+0:31
St. George Island, East End	-0:15	+0:06
St. George Island, Rattlesnake Cove	+0:47	+1:19
St. George Island, Sikes Cut	+0:49	+1:32
Apalachicola Bay		
Cat Point	+1:20	+1:27
Apalachicola	+2:00	+2:44
Lower Anchorage	+1:43	+2:09
West Pass	+1:33	+2:17

August Spotlight: REDFISH

It's time to nail that big tailer on a Central Gulf or Northwest bay flat. Pick a big ebb tide, and you will stand the best chance of seeing waking schools, or those bronzish orange flags. The fish are spooky on the flattest sunny days, so look for that favorable tide during low light hours, and pole or wade into casting range. Deliver a live shrimp, crab, soft plastic or crab fly. High tide calls for "combing the bushes."

August 2011

(handwritten) full Moon Sat JULY 30
(handwritten) Great Day Fishing
(handwritten) Friday FISH

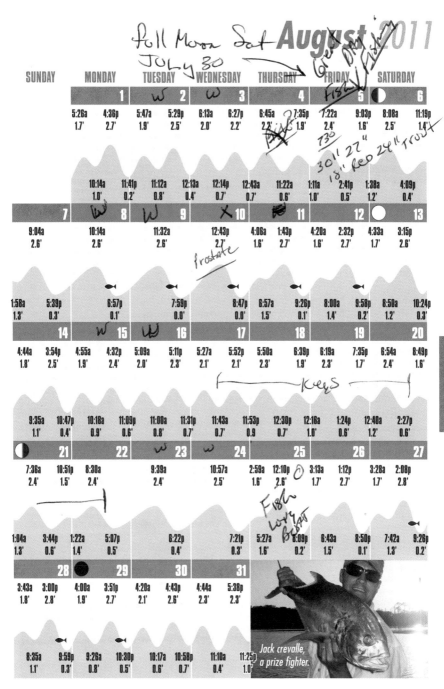

SUNDAY	MONDAY	TUESDAY	WEDNESDAY	THURSDAY	FRIDAY	SATURDAY
	1	**2** *(W)*	**3** *(W)*	**4**	**5**	**6**
	5:26a 4:36p	5:47a 5:29p	6:13a 6:27p	6:45a 7:35p	7:22a 9:03p	8:08a 11:19p
	1.7' 2.7'	1.9' 2.5'	2.0' 2.2'	2.2' 1.9'	2.4' 1.6'	2.5' 1.4'

(handwritten: 730, 30" 27", 18" RED 24" TROUT)

7	**8** *(W)*	**9** *(W)*	**10** *(X)*	**11**	**12** ○	**13**
	10:14a 11:41p	11:12a 12:13a	12:14p 12:43a	11:22a 1:11a	2:41p 1:38a	4:09p
	1.0' 0.2'	0.8' 0.4'	0.7' 0.7'	0.6' 1.0'	0.5' 1.2'	0.4'

9:04a	10:14a	11:32a	12:43p	4:06a 1:43p	4:20a 2:32p	4:33a 3:15p
2.6'	2.6'	2.6'	2.7'	1.6' 2.7'	1.6' 2.7'	1.7' 2.6'

(handwritten: Prostate)

14	**15** *(W)*	**16** *(W)*	**17**	**18**	**19**	**20**
1:58a 5:39p	6:57p	7:59p	8:47p	6:57a 9:26p	8:00a 9:58p	8:50a 10:24p
1.3' 0.3'	0.1'	0.0'	0.0'	1.5' 0.1'	1.4' 0.2'	1.2' 0.3'

4:44a 3:54p	4:55a 4:32p	5:09a 5:11p	5:27a 5:52p	5:50a 6:39p	6:19a 7:35p	6:54a 8:49p
1.8' 2.5'	1.9' 2.4'	2.0' 2.3'	2.1' 2.1'	2.3' 1.9'	2.3' 1.7'	2.4' 1.6'

(handwritten: Keys)

21	**22**	**23** *(W)*	**24** *(W)*	**25**	**26**	**27**
9:35a 10:47p	10:18a 11:09p	11:00a 11:31p	11:43a 11:53p	12:30p	12:16a 1:24p	12:40a 2:27p
1.1' 0.4'	0.9' 0.6'	0.8' 0.7'	0.7' 0.9	0.7'	1.0' 0.6'	1.2' 0.6'

7:36a 10:51p	8:30a	9:39a	10:57a	2:59a 12:10p ☉	3:13a 1:12p	3:26a 2:08p
2.4' 1.5'	2.4'	2.4'	2.5'	1.6' 2.6'	1.7' 2.7'	1.7' 2.8'

(handwritten: Fish Lots Baby)

28	**29** ●	**30**	**31**			
1:04a 3:44p	1:22a 5:07p	6:22p	7:21p	5:27a 8:09p	6:43a 8:50p	7:42a 9:26p
1.3' 0.6'	1.4' 0.5'	0.4'	0.3'	1.6' 0.2'	1.5' 0.1'	1.3' 0.2'

3:43a 3:00p	4:00a 3:51p	4:20a 4:43p	4:44a 5:38p			
1.8' 2.8'	1.9' 2.7'	2.1' 2.6'	2.3' 2.3'			

8:35a 9:59p	9:26a 10:30p	10:17a 10:58p	11:10a	11:25p		
1.1' 0.3'	0.8' 0.5'	0.6' 0.7'	0.4'	1.0'		

Jack crevalle, a prize fighter.

	August 1	August 15	August 30
SUNRISE	6:54 a.m.	7:01 a.m.	7:09 a.m.
SUNSET	8:20 p.m.	8:09 p.m.	7:54 p.m.

ST. PETERSBURG

Estero Bay to Tampa, Including Apalachicola area

Linesider Rebound

INSHORE

Traditionally, **snook** harvest opens at the beginning of the month. Check regulations for 2011 season. Take great care in releasing fish, due to the winter's dent in the stocks. They're in the surf, passes, and on flats and inshore structure. Northwest anglers enjoy a great **trout** bite over grassflats and around oysters. Great time for **redfish** over grassflats and oyster bars—watch for wakes on calm surface, and tails early and late. **Pompano** are active on Northwest beaches and in bays.

OFFSHORE

Grouper are stacked up on wrecks and reefs in southern region. Both **kingfish** and **Spanish** shadow copious bait pods throughout region. Live baits and lipped lures are tops for kingfish; Spanish clobber small spoons and jigs retrieved at warp speed. **Dolphin**, **blackfin tuna** and **wahoo** prowl offshore weedlines and rips. **Cobia** start heading south along Gulf beaches ahead of fall's arrival.

TIDE CORRECTIONS
For St. Petersburg

	High	Low
Estero Bay		
Little Hickory Island	-0:58	-1:05
Coconut Point	-0:47	-0:40
Carlos Point	-1:08	-1:28
Mantanzas Pass, (fixed br.) Estero Isl	-1:10	-1:34
Point Ybel, Sand Carlos Bay entrance	-1:50	-1:12
Punta Rassa, San Carlos Bay	-1:01	-1:19
Caloosahatchee River		
Iona Shores	+1:08	+1:40
Cape Coral Bridge	+1:15	+2:02
Ft. Myers	+2:08	+2:44
Pine Island, St. James City	-0:30	-0:44
Galt Island, Pine Island Sound	-0:25	+0:16
Captiva Island, (outside)	-2:20	-2:28
Captiva Island, Pine Island Sound	-0:46	-0:20
Redfish Pass, Captiva I (north end)	-0:55	-1:14
Tropical Homesites Landing, Pinel.	-0:08	+0:22
Matlacha Pass, (bascule bridge)	+0:43	+1:38
Pineland, Pine Island	-0:19	+0:26
Boca Grande, Charlotte Harbor	-1:12	-1:56
Punta Gorda, Charlotte Harbor	+1:06	+1:27
Shell Point, Peace River	+1:52	+2:30
El Jobean, Myakka River	+1:38	+1:56
Placida, Gasparilla Sound	-1:27	-0:59
Englewood, Lemon Bay	-0:57	-0:40
Venice Inlet, (inside)	-2:02	-1:38
Sarasota, Sarasota Bay	-1:38	-0:58
Cortez, Sarasota Bay	-2:00	-1:25
Egmont Key, Egmont Channel	-2:27	-2:24
Anna Maria	-2:07	-2:31
Bradenton, Manatee River	-1:24	-0:55
Redfish Point, Manatee River	-0:30	+0:14
Mullet Key Channel, (Skyway)	-2:22	-1:58
Shell Point	+0:08	+0:17
Point Pinellas	-0:22	-0:29
Tampa Bay, Hillsborough Bay	+0:07	+0:26
Safety Harbor, Old Tampa Bay	+1:38	+1:55
Boca Ciega Bay		
Pass-a-Grille Beach	-1:34	-1:30
Gulfport	-1:32	-1:05
St. Petersburg Beach Causeway	-1:18	-0:41
Johns Pass	-2:14	-2:04
Madeira Beach Causeway	-1:40	-1:18
St. George Sound		
Dog Island, west end	+0:07	+0:06
Carrabelle, Carrabelle River	+0:35	+0:31
St. George Island, East End	-0:15	+0:06
St. George Island, Rattlesnake Cove	+0:47	+1:19
St. George Island, Sikes Cut	+0:49	+1:32
Apalachicola Bay		
Cat Point	+1:20	+1:27
Apalachicola	+2:00	+2:44
Lower Anchorage	+1:43	+2:09
West Pass	+1:33	+2:17

September Spotlight: SNOOK

Snook fishing is a lock this month. Freelined live baits are deadly around bridges or in passes day and night, though jigs rolled on bottom compare favorably. Still some fish cruising the sand, but most are on bayside structure. Fish flies, plugs and jigs under docks and at bridges.

September 2011

SUNDAY	MONDAY	TUESDAY	WEDNESDAY	THURSDAY	FRIDAY	SATURDAY

Blacktip, handle with care.

1
5:13a 6:39p
2.5' 2.1'
11:08a 10:50p
0.3' 1.2'

2
5:47a 7:54p
2.6' 1.8'
12:12p
0.3'

3
6:28a 9:44p
2.7' 1.6'
11:12p 1:27p
1.4' 0.3'

4
7:19a
2.7'
12:26a 3:54p
1.5' 0.3'

5
8:26a
2.6'
5:23p
0.3'

6
9:59a
2.5'
6:37p
0.3'

7
2:37a 11:36a
1.7' 2.5'
4:42a 7:33p
1.7' 0.3'

8
2:45a 12:52p
1.8' 2.5'
6:24a 8:15p
1.5' 0.4'

9
3:00a 1:50p
1.8' 2.5'
7:29a 8:49p
1.3' 0.5'

10
3:14a 2:38p
1.9' 2.5'
8:18a 9:16p
1.1' 0.6'

11
3:27a 3:19p
2.0' 2.4'
8:59a 9:39p
1.0' 0.7'

12
3:37a 3:57p
2.1' 2.4'
9:35a 9:59p
0.8' 0.9'

13
3:49a 4:33p
2.2' 2.3'
10:10a 10:18p
0.6' 1.0'

14
4:04a 5:09p
2.4' 2.1'
10:45a 10:37p
0.5' 1.1'

15
4:23a 5:49p
2.5' 2.0'
11:22a 10:57p
0.4' 1.3'

16
4:49a 6:33p
2.6' 1.9'
12:04a 11:18p
0.4' 1.3'

17
5:19a 7:27p
2.6' 1.7'
12:52p 11:39p
0.4' 1.4'

18
5:56a 8:44p
2.6' 1.6'
1:50p 12:01a
0.5' 1.5'

19
6:41a
2.6'
3:02p
0.5'

20
7:40a
2.5'
4:23p
0.5'

21
8:59a
2.4'
5:36p
0.5'

22
1:26a 10:32a
1.7' 2.4'
4:07a 6:35p
1.7' 0.4'

23
1:43a 11:56a
1.8' 2.5'
5:44a 7:23p
1.5' 0.4'

24
2:00a 1:06p
1.9' 2.6'
6:51a 8:04p
1.3' 0.5'

25
2:18a 2:06p
2.0' 2.6'
7:46a 8:40p
1.0' 0.6'

26
2:37a 3:03p
2.2' 2.6'
8:36a 9:12p
0.7' 0.8'

27
2:58a 3:58p
2.3' 2.5'
9:25a 9:41p
0.4' 1.0'

28
3:22a 4:53p
2.5' 2.3'
10:14a 10:07p
0.1' 1.2'

29
3:51a 5:52p
2.7' 2.1'
11:05a 10:31p
0.0' 1.4'

30
4:24a 6:59p
2.8' 1.9'
12:01p 10:52p
0.0' 1.5'

ST. PETERSBURG

	September 1	September 15	September 30
SUNRISE	7:09 a.m.	7:16 a.m.	7:23 a.m.
SUNSET	7:51 p.m.	7:35 p.m.	7:18 p.m.

Estero Bay to Tampa, Including Apalachicola area

Pomp Romp!

INSHORE

Redfish in good supply on the flats, with outsized specimens common in fall; check grassflats on lower tides, head to mangrove shorelines on the flood. Spoons, soft plastics and crab flies all effective. **Pompano** in the Northwest surf; schools heading south this month. **Trout** bite improves as water cools, drift grass beds with topwaters and plastic shrimp, or live shrimp under corks. **Gag grouper** inside Sarasota and Tampa bays will bang troll lipped lures and jigs near structure. Cast swimming plugs, jigs and plastics for bridge and flats **snook**.

OFFSHORE

Southbound bait pods are shadowed by **kingfish**, **tarpon** and **cobia** on the "reverse" migration. Look for **Spanish mackerel** under glass minnows on beach, in bays. **Gag grouper** and **red grouper** mainly in shallows 20 feet and less, ready to head inside bays. Soak live pinfish or troll lipped plugs over hard bottom.

ST. PETERSBURG

TIDE CORRECTIONS
For St. Petersburg

	High	Low
Estero Bay		
Little Hickory Island	-0:58	-1:05
Coconut Point	-0:47	-0:40
Carlos Point	-1:08	-1:28
Mantanzas Pass, (fixed br.) Estero Isl	-1:10	-1:34
Point Ybel, Sand Carlos Bay entrance	-1:50	-1:12
Punta Rassa, San Carlos Bay	-1:01	-1:19
Caloosahatchee River		
Iona Shores	+1:08	+1:40
Cape Coral Bridge	+1:15	+2:02
Ft. Myers	+2:08	+2:44
Pine Island, St. James City	-0:30	-0:44
Galt Island, Pine Island Sound	-0:25	+0:16
Captiva Island, (outside)	-2:20	-2:28
Captiva Island, Pine Island Sound	-0:46	-0:20
Redfish Pass, Captiva I (north end)	-0:55	-1:14
Tropical Homesites Landing, Pinel.	-0:08	+0:22
Matlacha Pass, (bascule bridge)	+0:43	+1:28
Pineland, Pine Island	-0:19	+0:26
Boca Grande, Charlotte Harbor	-1:12	-1:56
Punta Gorda, Charlotte Harbor	+1:06	+1:27
Shell Point, Peace River	+1:52	+2:30
El Jobean, Myakka River	+1:38	+1:56
Placida, Gasparilla Sound	-1:27	-0:59
Englewood, Lemon Bay	-0:57	-0:40
Venice Inlet, (inside)	-2:02	-1:38
Sarasota, Sarasota Bay	-1:38	-0:58
Cortez, Sarasota Bay	-2:00	-1:25
Egmont Key, Egmont Channel	-2:27	-2:24
Anna Maria	-2:07	-2:31
Bradenton, Manatee River	-1:24	-0:55
Redfish Point, Manatee River	-0:30	+0:14
Mullet Key Channel, (Skyway)	-2:22	-1:58
Shell Point	+0:08	+0:17
Point Pinellas	-0:22	-0:29
Tampa Bay, Hillsborough Bay	+0:07	+0:26
Safety Harbor, Old Tampa Bay	+1:38	+1:55
Boca Ciega Bay		
Pass-a-Grille Beach	-1:34	-1:30
Gulfport	-1:32	-1:05
St. Petersburg Beach Causeway	-1:18	-0:44
Johns Pass	-2:14	-2:04
Madeira Beach Causeway	-1:40	-1:18
St. George Sound		
Dog Island, west end	+0:07	+0:06
Carrabelle, Carrabelle River	+0:35	+0:31
St. George Island, East End	-0:15	+0:06
St. George Island, Rattlesnake Cove	+0:47	+1:19
St. George Island, Sikes Cut	+0:49	+1:32
Apalachicola Bay		
Cat Point	+1:20	+1:27
Apalachicola	+2:00	+2:44
Lower Anchorage	+1:43	+2:09
West Pass	+1:33	+2:17

October Spotlight: POMPANO

The **pompano** parade begins by midmonth as cold fronts pass through regularly. Many fish are summer holdovers, signaling a stock rebound in Florida waters. Northwest surf anglers had them all summer, and now central Gulf coasters will fish

for them on the beach early on, and by month's end, over grassflats and shoals just inside passes. On the beach, either cast jigs with light tackle, or soak sand fleas, shrimp or clams on dropper rigs. Flies take them, too, on inside waters.

October 2011

SUNDAY	MONDAY	TUESDAY	WEDNESDAY	THURSDAY	FRIDAY	SATURDAY

Mackerel will be on the hunt.

1
5:02a 2.9' | 8:27p 1.7'
1:02p 0.1' | 11:07p 1.6'

2
5:46a 2.8'
2:13p 0.2'

3
6:41a 2.7'
3:32p 0.3'

4
7:58a 2.5'
4:50p 0.4'

5
9:48a 2.3'
5:55p 0.5'

6
1:20a 1.8' | 11:33a 2.3'
5:26a 1.6' | 6:46p 0.5'

7
1:37p 1.9' | 12:49p 2.2'
6:42a 1.3' | 7:26p 0.7'

8
1:54a 2.0' | 1:49p 2.2'
7:35a 1.0' | 7:58p 0.8'

9
2:10a 2.1' | 2:38p 2.2'
8:17a 0.8' | 8:25p 0.9'

10
2:24a 2.2' | 3:22p 2.1'
8:54a 0.6' | 8:47p 1.1'

11
2:37a 2.4' | 4:02p 2.1'
9:27a 0.4' | 9:07p 1.2'

12
2:51a 2.5' | 4:39p 2.0'
9:59a 0.3' | 9:25p 1.3'

13
3:10a 2.6' | 5:16p 1.9'
10:32a 0.2' | 9:42p 1.4'

14
3:33a 2.6' | 5:54p 1.8'
11:07a 0.1' | 10:01p 1.4'

15
4:02a 2.7' | 6:38p 1.7'
11:46a 0.1' | 10:22p 1.5'

16
4:36a 2.7' | 7:35p 1.6'
12:32p 0.2' | 10:46p 1.5'

17
5:16a 2.6' | 8:54p 1.6'
1:27p 0.2' | 11:16p 1.6'

18
6:04a 2.6'
2:31p 0.3'

19
7:06a 2.4'
3:39p 0.3'

20
11:32p 1.7' | 8:30a 2.3'
2:21a 1.6' | 4:44p 0.4'

21
12:02a 1.8' | 10:11a 2.2'
4:22a 1.5' | 5:41p 0.4'

22
12:27a 1.9' | 11:44a 2.2'
5:46a 1.2' | 6:29p 0.6'

23
12:51a 2.0' | 1:02p 2.2'
6:49a 0.8' | 7:11p 0.7'

24
1:14a 2.2' | 2:10p 2.2'
7:43a 0.5' | 7:47p 0.9'

25
1:39a 2.4' | 3:12p 2.6'
8:33a 0.1' | 8:19p 1.1'

26
2:06a 2.6' | 4:12p 2.0'
9:22a -0.2' | 8:47p 1.3'

27
2:37a 2.8' | 5:11p 1.9'
10:11a -0.3' | 9:12p 1.4'

28
3:11a 2.9' | 6:14p 1.7'
11:02a -0.4' | 9:35p 1.5'

29
3:50a 2.9' | 7:26p 1.6'
11:55a -0.3' | 9:56p 1.5'

30
4:32a 2.9'
12:51p -0.2'

31
5:20a 2.7'
1:52p 0.0'

Oversize snook gets a kiss goodbye.

	October 1	October 15	October 30
SUNRISE	7:23 a.m.	7:31 a.m.	7:40 a.m.
SUNSET	7:17 p.m.	7:02 p.m.	6:48 p.m.

Estero Bay to Tampa, Including Apalachicola area

Holy Smoker!

INSHORE

Flounder numbers will increase; runs are hard to predict, but 2010 was good from Tampa south, and in Northwest waters. Fish mud minnows, finger mullet and tipped jigs on bottom near oysters and manmade structure.

Trout bite is fast on surface plugs until midmorning; jigs, weighted plastics and shrimp best through midday. **Redfish** target mullet run in bays, and aggressively eat live baits or subsurface plugs, spoons and baitfish flies. Or, cut mullet soaked under mangroves.

OFFSHORE

King mackerel school up over limestone ledges, where the drill is to freeline or slow-troll a live blue runner, mullet or small mackerel. Another option is a rigged **Spanish mackerel** or ribbonfish for the biggest kings. Offshore bait pods hold some **blackfin tuna**. Expect **gag grouper** to move to hard bottom closer to shore where a live bait-tipped jig will score.

ST. PETERSBURG

November Spotlight: KINGFISH

King mackerel flood nearshore waters, and basically make their way south along with migrating bait schools. A 20-pounder is typical, and lots of 30- to 40-pounders, and occasional 50s hit the docks. Kings school where there's food—over limestone ledges, hard bottom, near-shore wrecks, and sometimes right against the beach. Slow-troll live threadfins or sardines, or pull spoons and plugs at 4 to 6 knots. Wire leader is a must.

TIDE CORRECTIONS
For St. Petersburg

	High	Low
Estero Bay		
Little Hickory Island	-0:58	-1:05
Coconut Point	-0:47	-0:40
Carlos Point	-1:08	-1:28
Mantanzas Pass, (fixed br.) Estero Isl	-1:10	-1:34
Point Ybel, Sand Carlos Bay entrance	-1:50	-1:12
Punta Rassa, San Carlos Bay	-1:01	-1:19
Caloosahatchee River		
Iona Shores	+1:08	+1:40
Cape Coral Bridge	+1:15	+2:02
Ft. Myers	+2:08	+2:44
Pine Island, St. James City	-0:30	-0:44
Galt Island, Pine Island Sound	-0:25	+0:16
Captiva Island, (outside)	-2:20	-2:28
Captiva Island, Pine Island Sound	-0:46	-0:20
Redfish Pass, Captiva I (north end)	-0:55	-1:14
Tropical Homesites Landing, Pinel.	-0:08	+0:22
Matlacha Pass, (bascule bridge)	+0:43	+1:28
Pineland, Pine Island	-0:19	+0:26
Boca Grande, Charlotte Harbor	-1:12	-1:56
Punta Gorda, Charlotte Harbor	+1:06	+1:27
Shell Point, Peace River	+1:52	+2:30
El Jobean, Myakka River	+1:38	+1:56
Placida, Gasparilla Sound	-1:27	-0:59
Englewood, Lemon Bay	-0:57	-0:40
Venice Inlet, (inside)	-2:02	-1:38
Sarasota, Sarasota Bay	-1:38	-0:58
Cortez, Sarasota Bay	-2:00	-1:25
Egmont Key, Egmont Channel	-2:27	-2:24
Anna Maria	-2:07	-2:31
Bradenton, Manatee River	-1:24	-0:55
Redfish Point, Manatee River	-0:30	+0:14
Mullet Key Channel, (Skyway)	-2:22	-1:58
Shell Point	+0:08	+0:17
Point Pinellas	-0:22	-0:29
Tampa Bay, Hillsborough Bay	+0:07	+0:26
Safety Harbor, Old Tampa Bay	+1:38	+1:55
Boca Ciega Bay		
Pass-a-Grille Beach	-1:34	-1:30
Gulfport	-1:32	-1:05
St. Petersburg Beach Causeway	-1:18	-0:44
Johns Pass	-2:14	-2:04
Madeira Beach Causeway	-1:40	-1:18
St. George Sound		
Dog Island, west end	+0:07	+0:06
Carrabelle, Carrabelle River	+0:35	+0:31
St. George Island, East End	-0:15	+0:06
St. George Island, Rattlesnake Cove	+0:47	+1:19
St. George Island, Sikes Cut	+0:49	+1:32
Apalachicola Bay		
Cat Point	+1:20	+1:27
Apalachicola	+2:00	+2:44
Lower Anchorage	+1:43	+2:09
West Pass	+1:33	+2:17

November 2011

SUNDAY	MONDAY	TUESDAY	WEDNESDAY	THURSDAY	FRIDAY	SATURDAY
		1 ◑ 6:18a 2.5' 2:55p 0.2'	**2** 7:35a 2.2' 3:57p 0.3'	**3** 11:39a 1.7' / 9:24a 2.0' 3:44a 1.5' / 4:53p 0.5'	**4** 12:02a 1.8' / 11:12a 1.8' 5:27a 1.2' / 5:40p 0.6'	**5** 12:25a 2.0' / 12:36p 1.8' 6:34a 0.9' / 6:21p 0.8'
6 12:46a 2.1' / 11:43a 1.8' 5:23a 0.6' / 4:56p 1.0'	**7** 11:06p 2.2' / 12:39a 1.8' 6:04a 0.3' / 5:26p 1.1'	**8** 11:25p 2.3' / 1:29p 1.7' 6:41a 0.1' / 5:51p 1.2'	**9** ○ 11:44p 2.4' / 2:14p 1.7' 7:15a 0.0' / 6:13p 1.3'	**10** 12:05a 2.5' / 2:55p 1.6' 7:48a -0.1' / 6:31p 1.4'	**11** 🐟 12:30a 2.6' / 3:33p 1.6' 8:22a -0.2' / 6:50p 1.4'	**12** 🐟 12:59a 2.6' / 4:11p 1.5' 8:58a -0.2' / 7:12p 1.4'
13 🐟 1:33a 2.6' / 4:53p 1.5' 9:37a -0.2' / 7:41p 1.4'	**14** 🐟 2:11a 2.6' / 5:41p 1.5' 10:20a -0.2' / 8:20p 1.4'	**15** 🐟 2:55a 2.5' / 6:34p 1.5' 11:08a -0.1' / 9:19p 1.4'	**16** 3:47a 2.4' / 7:24p 1.5' 12:00n 0.0' / 10:48p 1.4'	**17** ◐ 4:50a 2.2' / 8:06p 1.6' 12:54p 0.1'	**18** 6:13a 2.0' / 8:42p 1.8' 12:37a 1.3' / 1:49p 0.3' *JERRY*	**19** 7:55a 1.8' / 9:14p 1.9' 2:18a 1.0' / 2:40p 0.4'
20 9:38a 1.7' / 9:46p 2.1' 3:38a 0.7' / 3:28p 0.7' *20 Reds*	**21** 11:07a 1.6' / 10:18p 2.3' 4:42a 0.3' / 4:11p 0.9'	**22** 12:25p 1.6' / 10:52p 2.5' 5:39a -0.1' / 4:49p 1.1'	**23** 🐟 1:34p 1.6' / 11:28p 2.7' 6:31a -0.4' / 5:22p 1.2'	**24** ● 2:38p 1.5' / 12:07a 2.8' 7:21a -0.6' / 5:52p 1.3'	**25** 🐟 3:39p 1.5' / 12:49a 2.8' 8:10a -0.7' / 6:21p 1.3' *Jimmy Reds*	**26** 🐟 4:36p 1.4' 8:59a -0.7' / 6:53p 1.3'
27 🐟 1:33a 2.8' / 5:28p 1.3' 9:47a -0.6' / 7:33p 1.3'	**28** 2:19a 2.6' / 6:14p 1.3' 10:34a -0.4' / 8:32p 1.3'	**29** 3:09a 2.4' / 6:53p 1.4' 11:21a -0.2' / 9:53p 1.3'	**30** 4:05a 2.1' / 7:27p 1.5' 12:06n 0.0' / 11:36p 1.2'			

Flounder will be congregating near natural and manmade structure.

	November 1	November 15	November 30
SUNRISE	7:42 a.m.	6:52 a.m.	7:03 a.m.
SUNSET	6:47 p.m.	5:38 p.m.	5:35 p.m.

DST Ends on Nov. 6

Estero Bay to Tampa, Including Apalachicola area

Gag in the Bag

ST. PETERSBURG

INSHORE

Winter patterns for **redfish**, **snook** and **trout** are set. Snook are out of season but you will release plenty by fishing upper estuary waters with manmade structure. Reds soak up the sun on flats, and many trout head for creeks and canals where bottom baits and lures score. **Pompano** fishing is red-hot in south region, over grassflats and bars. Try soaking a live baitfish or bounce a mullet-tipped jig over shell bottom or near docks and bridge pilings for **flounder**.

OFFSHORE

Kings, **Spanish mackerel** and **bluefish** will be easy to find; look for birds and bait busts. Late-season **tripletail** still possible along West Central region. **Gag grouper** are the best bet for bottom fishermen. Frozen sardines and squid produce just as well as live bait during winter. Though they are shallow, stout tackle is best for winching them from structure.

December Spotlight: GAG GROUPER

TIDE CORRECTIONS
For St. Petersburg

	High	Low
Estero Bay		
Little Hickory Island	-0:58	-1:05
Coconut Point	-0:47	-0:40
Carlos Point	-1:08	-1:28
Mantanzas Pass, (fixed br.) Estero Isl	-1:10	-1:34
Point Ybel, Sand Carlos Bay entrance	-1:50	-1:12
Punta Rassa, San Carlos Bay	-1:01	-1:19
Caloosahatchee River		
Iona Shores	+1:08	+1:40
Cape Coral Bridge	+1:15	+2:02
Ft. Myers	+2:08	+2:44
Pine Island, St. James City	-0:30	-0:44
Galt Island, Pine Island Sound	-0:25	+0:16
Captiva Island, (outside)	-2:20	-2:28
Captiva Island, Pine Island Sound	-0:46	-0:20
Redfish Pass, Captiva I (north end)	-0:55	-1:14
Tropical Homesites Landing, Pinel.	-0:08	+0:22
Matlacha Pass, (bascule bridge)	+0:43	+1:28
Pineland, Pine Island	-0:19	+0:26
Boca Grande, Charlotte Harbor	-1:12	-1:56
Punta Gorda, Charlotte Harbor	+1:06	+1:27
Shell Point, Peace River	+1:52	+2:30
El Jobean, Myakka River	+1:38	+1:56
Placida, Gasparilla Sound	-1:27	-0:59
Englewood, Lemon Bay	-0:57	-0:40
Venice Inlet, (inside)	-2:02	-1:38
Sarasota, Sarasota Bay	+1:38	-0:58
Cortez, Sarasota Bay	-2:00	-1:25
Egmont Key, Egmont Channel	-2:27	-2:24
Anna Maria	-2:07	-2:31
Bradenton, Manatee River	-1:24	-0:55
Redfish Point, Manatee River	-0:30	+0:14
Mullet Key Channel, (Skyway)	-2:22	-1:58
Shell Point	+0:08	+0:17
Point Pinellas	-0:22	-0:29
Tampa Bay, Hillsborough Bay	+0:07	+0:26
Safety Harbor, Old Tampa Bay	+1:38	+1:55
Boca Ciega Bay		
Pass-a-Grille Beach	-1:34	-1:30
Gulfport	-1:32	-1:05
St. Petersburg Beach Causeway	-1:18	-0:44
Johns Pass	-2:14	-2:04
Madeira Beach Causeway	-1:40	-1:18
St. George Sound		
Dog Island, west end	+0:07	+0:06
Carrabelle, Carrabelle River	+0:35	+0:31
St. George Island, East End	-0:15	+0:06
St. George Island, Rattlesnake Cove	+0:47	+1:19
St. George Island, Sikes Cut	+0:49	+1:32
Apalachicola Bay		
Cat Point	+1:20	+1:27
Apalachicola	+2:00	+2:44
Lower Anchorage	+1:43	+2:09
West Pass	+1:33	+2:17

Prime winter habitat for great **gag grouper** catches include bridge pilings and structure in Tampa Bay and high-relief channel edges east and west of the Skyway Bridge. Troll lipped plugs or bucktail jigs just off the bottom to locate grouper lairs. Hammer down your drag—a hooked gag heads for holes and structure. Grouper can be marked on rockpiles before fishing; find a few fish and then send down a crushed frozen sardine into their lair. Winter gags aren't energetic, so fresh, smelly baits outfish live bait.

December 2011

SUNDAY	MONDAY	TUESDAY	WEDNESDAY	THURSDAY	FRIDAY	SATURDAY

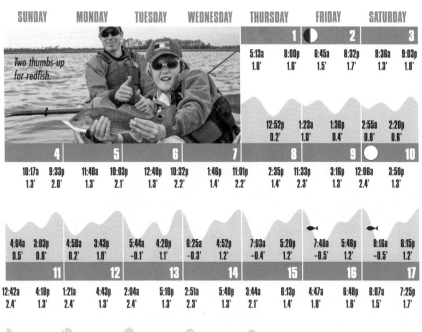

Two thumbs-up for redfish.

1 ◑
5:13a 1.8' 8:00p 1.6' 6:45a 1.5' 8:32p 1.7'
12:52p 0.2' 1:23a 1.0' 1:36p 0.4'

2
8:36a 1.3' 9:03p 1.8'
2:55a 0.8' 2:20p 0.6'

3

4
10:17a 1.3' 9:33p 2.0'

5
11:40a 1.3' 10:03p 2.1'

6
12:48p 1.3' 10:32p 2.2'

7
1:46p 1.4' 11:01p 2.2'

8
2:35p 1.4' 11:33p 2.3'

9
3:16p 1.3' 12:06a 2.4'

10 ○
3:50p 1.3'

11
4:04a 0.5' 3:03p 0.8'
12:42a 2.4' 4:18p 1.3'

12
4:58a 0.2' 3:43p 1.0'
1:21a 2.4' 4:43p 1.3'

13
5:44a -0.1' 4:20p 1.1'
2:04a 2.4' 5:10p 1.3'

14
6:25a -0.3' 4:52p 1.2'
2:51a 2.3' 5:40p 1.3'

15
7:03a -0.4' 5:20p 1.2'
3:44a 2.1' 6:13p 1.4'

16
7:40a -0.5' 5:46p 1.2'
4:47a 1.8' 6:48p 1.6'

17
8:16a -0.5' 6:15p 1.2'
6:07a 1.5' 7:25p 1.7'

18 ◐
8:51a -0.5' 6:52p 1.2'
7:48a 1.3' 8:05p 1.9'

19
9:28a -0.5' 7:38p 1.1'
9:46a 1.2' 8:47p 2.1'

20
10:06a -0.5' 8:35p 1.1'
11:36a 1.1' 9:32p 2.3'

21
10:45a -0.4' 9:43p 1.0'
1:06p 1.2' 10:19p 2.4'

22
11:26a -0.2' 11:03p 0.9'
2:17p 1.2' 11:07p 2.5'

23
12:08p 0.0' 12:32a 0.7'
3:10p 1.2' 11:56p 2.6'

24 ●
12:51p 0.2'
3:49p 1.2'

25
2:02a 0.5' 1:35p 0.5'
12:44a 2.5' 4:17p 1.2'

26
3:24a 0.1' 2:18p 0.7'
1:31a 2.4' 4:41p 1.2'

27
4:35a -0.2' 3:01p 0.9'
2:17a 2.3' 5:03p 1.2'

28
5:37a -0.5' 3:42p 1.1'
3:05a 2.0' 5:26p 1.3'

29
6:32a -0.7' 4:25p 1.1'
3:56a 1.8' 5:52p 1.4'

30
7:23a -0.9' 5:11p 1.2'
4:54a 1.5' 6:22p 1.5'

31
8:09a -0.9' 6:01p 1.1'
6:08a 1.2' 6:55p 1.6'

8:52a -0.8' 6:56p 1.0'
9:30a -0.7' 7:55p 1.0'
10:06a -0.5' 8:58p 0.9'
10:40a -0.3' 10:05p 0.8'
11:12a -0.1' 11:19p 0.7'
11:44a 0.1' 12:39a 0.6' 12:17p 0.3'

	December 1	December 15	December 30
SUNRISE	7:04 a.m.	7:14 a.m.	7:21 a.m.
SUNSET	5:35 p.m.	5:38 p.m.	5:46 p.m.

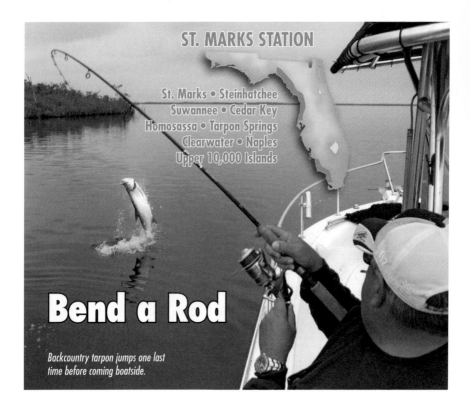

St. Marks • Steinhatchee
Suwannee • Cedar Key
Homosassa • Tarpon Springs
Clearwater • Naples
Upper 10,000 Islands

Bend a Rod

Backcountry tarpon jumps one last
time before coming boatside.

ST. MARKS

Update 2011: Inshore anglers enjoy many improved fisheries, among them **seatrout**, **tarpon** and **redfish**. Anglers from St. Marks to St. Joseph Sound catch more 4- to 6-pound specks now on topwater plugs and soft-plastic baits. Come spring, **grouper** fishing commands attention, there's an early summer **tarpon** run, and by late summer **scallops** bring families from all corners to hunt for the tasty bivalves.

On the subject of tarpon, Homosassa still has the giants (a 190-pounder fell to a fly angler last spring). They are tougher to spot and approach over deep flats, different than fish in other places such as much of the southwest coast from Clearwater south. New tarpon fisheries are being developed around St. George Island over light-sand shoals reminding one of the Keys.

Redfish numbers are stable and schools of the big spawners are hooked by anglers fishing nearshore wrecks. Wade-fishing is especially popular on hard-bottom creeks and bars around Horseshoe Beach and other ports.

Offshore, stabilizing gas prices prompt anglers to make long runs out to blue water for **dolphin**, **wahoo** and **tuna**. This is big-boat stuff for anglers putting in long days, but the payoff can be great in some of the state's least-fished deep Gulf waters.

Reef fisheries have been troubled by ever-tightening limits, including a short open season for **red snapper**, which, by most accounts of veteran anglers, seem more and more abundant in recent years. **Red grouper** limits loosened some from 1 to 2 per person, reflecting managers' view of upward tick in population. Grouper season closed two months, Feb. 1 through Mar. 31, for **gags**, **reds** and other shallow-water groupers.

Permit are regularly targeted on the nearshore wrecks from Naples south to Chokoloskee, and despite conservative bag limits, there's still talk about a possible kill tag. For now, data must be collected to prove a need for it. At present, **goliath grouper** are still federally protected, and numbers are strong, or too strong, if you consider the number of hooked **cobia**, permit and snapper that this predator steals from anglers.

Artificial reef development has been strong in the northern sector, with the Mexico Beach Artificial Reef Association and county authorities deploying a number of sites.

Minimal red tides and tropical storms in 2008 and 2009 promise consistent fisheries for 2011. Let's hope the pattern holds.

Widely diverse in geography and climate, Florida's Big Bend and Upper Ten Thousand Islands are grouped in the same tide region. It's one of nature's quirks that corrections for both waters are based on measurements from the entrance of the St. Marks River south of Tallahassee. This unusual matchup is where the similarities end.

These regions hold some of Florida's last real fishing secrets. In the Big Bend, literally thousands of unnamed and largely unfished tidal creeks flow into numerous bays and some of the state's best-known coastal rivers, such as the Suwannee and Steinhatchee. Roads are few, and fish are plentiful. Trout and redfish are among the residents, joined seasonally by mackerel,

tarpon and cobia, which migrate along the Gulf coastline and hold on wrecks.

In the Upper Ten Thousand Islands, from the bustling city of Naples through the tiny isle of Chokoloskee, gateway to Everglades National Park, much is as it was hundreds of years ago—including the great fishing. Most of the same fish found in the Big Bend reside here, with the notable addition of snook and permit.

Mixed tides along these stretches of coastline mean the highs and lows of the twice-daily sets usually differ in range, and many knowledgeable anglers elect to fish the stronger of the two for such species as redfish and snook.

To determine the strongest daily tide, compare the average tidal ranges (given below) to the daily tides in the charts on the following pages. It's even easier to keep an eye out for the fish symbols, which point the way to good current and good fishing.

If you're targeting redfish in the Big Bend tidal creeks, for instance, try to fish the stronger tides, paying particular attention to the lower stages. The fish are more concentrated at these times, and easier to find. With a rising tide, redfish will push water as they scurry onto oyster bars and grassflats.

Snook in the Ten Thousand Islands are particularly sensitive to strong current. They take up ambush stations along mangrove shorelines, waiting for food that's swept along by the tide.

For some fish, slack tide or lower tidal ranges are the best times to fish. If you are hunting tripletail at the markers off Apalachicola Bay, for instance, choose times and tides where little water is moving. These odd gamesters often bite better then.

ST. MARKS

Average Tidal Range at St. Marks: 2.6 feet

Average Range of Spring Tides: 3.5 feet

Florida's Big Bend, plus Naples and the Upper Ten Thousand Islands

Family Favorites

TIDE CORRECTIONS
For St. Marks

	High	Low
Pavilion Key	-0:57	-0:43
Chokoloskee	+0:14	+1:07
Everglades City, Barron River	+0:23	+1:18
Indian Key	-1:05	-0:48
Round Key	-1:06	-0:55
Pumpkin Bay	+0:39	+1:00
Coon Key	-0:45	-0:36
Cape Romano	-1:17	-1:03
Marco, Big Marco River	-1:04	-1:08
Naples, (outer coast)	-1:59	-2:04
Indian Rocks Beach, (inside)	-1:29	-1:25
Clearwater	-2:20	-2:07
Dunedin, St Joseph Sound	-2:22	-2:17
Anclote Keys, south end	-2:19	-2:28
TarponSprings, Anclote River	-1:20	-1:13
Indian Bay	-0:46	-0:09
Bayport	-0:59	-0:42
Withlacoochee River entrance	-0:25	+0:23
Cedar Key	-0:29	-0:30
Suwannee River entrance	-0:26	-0:14
Pepperfish Keys	-0:20	-0:08
Steinhatchee R., Ent. Deadman Bay	-0:15	-0:03
Fishermans Rest	-0:14	-0:02
Spring Warrior Creek	-0:09	+0:03
Rock Islands	-0:03	+0:04
Apalachee Bay		
Aucilla River entrance	+0:03	+0:05
St. Marks, St Marks River	+0:36	+1:04
Bald Point, Ochlockonee Bay	+0:20	+0:28
Turkey Point, St James Island	-0:12	-0:18

INSHORE

Big Bend: Fish fry fans savor **sheepshead** and **white trout** and they both bite this month. The striped porgies spawn on nearshore rubble piles and around navigational markers. Live fiddler crabs are a super, but hard-to-find bait, so substitute with live shrimp on a light sliding sinker or knocker rig. **Redfish** warm up in shallow water in rivers. Sunny, warm periods put a few more **seatrout** on the flats, but most stick to deep holes in coastal rivers such as the Aucilla and Steinhatchee.

10,000 Islands: A mixed bag can be had on grassflats of outside waters. **Seatrout**, **pompano**, **mackerel** and **bluefish** all take jigs, plugs and spoons where water is not too clear. West winds can muddy the water too much and kill the action, so pick your days. **Snook** and **tarpon** are in the backcountry for the most part, where they take plugs and topwater flies or streamers.

OFFSHORE

Great time to nab your **gag grouper**, starting in about 30 feet of water. Dead cigar minnows, squid or jigs work well on these winter fish. **Sheepshead** stack up on many wrecks out 10 or 20 miles. In southern region, **kingfish** and **Spanish mackerel** in good numbers. Reef fishermen count on **mangrove**, **lane** and other **snappers**.

ST. MARKS

January Spotlight: WHITE TROUT

White seatrout, or sand seatrout, provide family fun and small, but tasty fillets. This cousin of the spotted seatrout schools up in deep bays and channels, as well as within a mile or so of the beach. Top methods for catching a mess include soaking shrimp, small bits

of cutbait, or synthetic bait strips on bottom with a fishfinder rig. Or, tip a small bucktail with bait. Let it sit, or bounce it along lightly. This fish seldom exceeds one pound so have fun with ultralight spinning gear and take only what you plan to eat at one sitting.

January 2011

SUNDAY	MONDAY	TUESDAY	WEDNESDAY	THURSDAY	FRIDAY	SATURDAY

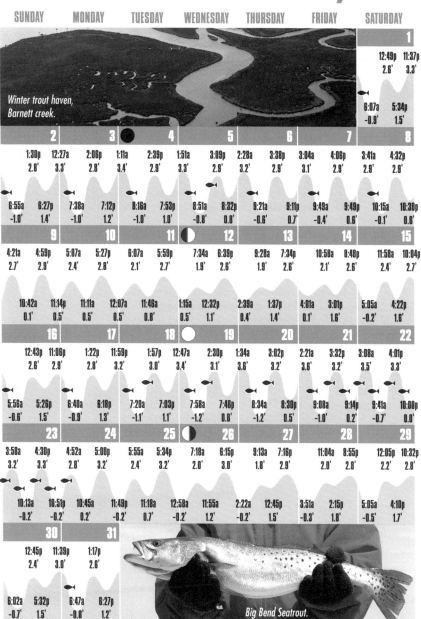

Winter trout haven, Barnett creek.

1
12:49p 11:37p
2.6' 3.3'
6:07a 5:34p
-0.9' 1.5'

2
1:30p 12:27a
2.8' 3.3'
6:55a 6:27p
-1.0' 1.4'

3 ●
2:06p 1:11a
2.8' 3.4'
7:38a 7:12p
-1.0' 1.2'

4
2:39p 1:51a
2.9' 3.3'
8:16a 7:53p
-1.0' 1.0'

5
3:09p 2:28a
2.9' 3.2'
8:51a 8:32p
-0.8' 0.8'

6
3:38p 3:04a
2.9' 3.1'
9:21a 9:11p
-0.6' 0.7'

7
4:06p 3:41a
2.9' 2.9'
9:49a 9:49p
-0.4' 0.6'

8
4:32p
2.9'
10:15a 10:30p
-0.1' 0.6'

9
4:21a 4:59p
2.7' 2.9'
10:42a 11:14p
0.1' 0.5'

10
5:07a 5:27p
2.4' 2.8'
11:11a 12:07a
0.5' 0.5'

11 ◐
6:07a 5:59p
2.1' 2.7'
11:46a
0.8'

12
7:34a 6:39p
1.9' 2.6'
1:15a 12:32p
0.5' 1.1'

13
9:28a 7:34p
1.9' 2.6'
2:39a 1:37p
0.4' 1.4'

14
10:58a 8:48p
2.1' 2.6'
4:01a 3:01p
0.1' 1.6'

15
11:58a 10:04p
2.4' 2.7'
5:05a 4:22p
-0.2' 1.6'

16
12:43p 11:06p
2.6' 2.9'
5:56a 5:26p
-0.6' 1.5'

17
1:22p 11:59p
2.8' 3.2'
6:40a 6:18p
-0.9' 1.3'

18 ○
1:57p
3.0'
7:20a 7:03p
-1.1' 1.1'

19
12:47a 2:30p
3.4' 3.1'
7:58a 7:46p
-1.2' 0.8'

20
1:34a 3:02p
3.6' 3.2'
8:34a 8:30p
-1.2' 0.5'

21
2:21a 3:32p
3.6' 3.2'
9:08a 9:14p
-1.0' 0.2'

22
3:08a 4:01p
3.5' 3.3'
9:41a 10:00p
-0.7' 0.0'

23
3:58a 4:30p
3.2' 3.3'
10:13a 10:51p
-0.2' -0.2'

24
4:52a 5:00p
2.8' 3.2'
10:45a 11:49p
0.2' -0.2'

25 ◐
5:55a 5:34p
2.4' 3.2'
11:18a 12:58a
0.7' -0.2'

26
7:18a 6:15p
2.0' 3.0'
11:55a
1.2'

27
9:13a 7:16p
1.8' 2.9'
2:22a 12:45p
-0.2' 1.5'

28
11:04a 8:55p
2.0' 2.8'
3:51a 2:15p
-0.3' 1.8'

29
12:05p 10:32p
2.2' 2.8'
5:05a 4:10p
-0.5' 1.7'

30
12:45p 11:39p
2.4' 3.0'
6:02a 5:32p
-0.7' 1.5'

31
1:17p
2.6'
6:47a 6:27p
-0.8' 1.2'

Big Bend Seatrout.

ST. MARKS

	January 1	January 15	January 30
SUNRISE	7:15 a.m.	7:16 a.m.	7:12 a.m.
SUNSET	5:47 p.m.	5:57 p.m.	6:09 p.m.

Florida's Big Bend, plus Naples and the Upper Ten Thousand Islands

Up a Creek

INSHORE

Big Bend: **Seatrout** are closed to harvest this month north of Pasco/Pinellas county line. **Redfish** take up the slack in the marsh creeks, from Spring Creek in Apalachee Bay, to the Withlacoochee River. Give sight fishing a shot for St. Joseph Sound redfish; clear water makes the spotting easy. **Sheepshead** are in good numbers over hard bottom and rockpiles off the ocast.

10,000 Islands: A fine time for numbers of **pompano** in southwest coast and northern Everglades bays and outside grassflats. Oyster and sand bars are top hangouts. Bump small nylon-skirted jigs on bottom to find schools, then break out fly-rods and Clouser Minnows. Mixed-bag backcountry catch can include **sheepshead**, **drum**, **snapper** and **seatrout**. A good all-round offering is a jighead or bucktail tipped with fresh shrimp, or live shrimp on a small jighead. **Tarpon** may show in Everglades bays from Chokoloskee south on warm snaps. Baby poons and **snook** are in headwaters of coastal rivers.

OFFSHORE

Though **gag grouper** feed well this month through spring, the closure begins February 1. Be sure to check regulations for possible updates. **Sea bass**, **flounder** and **amberjack** are northern alternatives for the ice chest, as are **snappers** and **cobia** out of Naples and Marco Island.

February Spotlight: REDFISH

Redfish change their feeding behavior as winter temps clear up the water and push bait-fish out. Reds turn to crustaceans for the most part, so fish with live shrimp and crabs or arti-ficial lures and flies patterned after them. Top winter redfish spots include oyster bars and warm, sheltered mud-bottom coastal creeks and rivermouths that harbor shrimp. In both north and south tidal region, think backcountry to find the fish.

February 2011

SUNDAY	MONDAY	TUESDAY	WEDNESDAY	THURSDAY	FRIDAY	SATURDAY
		1	**2** ●	**3**	**4**	**5**
		12:29a 1:46p 3.1' 2.8'	1:11a 2:13p 3.2' 2.9'	1:48a 2:38p 3.2' 3.0'	2:22a 3:03p 3.2' 3.1'	2:55a 3:26p 3.1' 3.2'
		7:25a 7:10p -0.8' 0.9'	7:57a 7:47p -0.7' 0.6'	8:26a 8:23p -0.6' 0.4'	8:51a 8:57p -0.5' 0.3'	9:14a 9:30p -0.3' 0.1'
6	**7**	**8**	**9**	**10**	**11** ◗	**12**
3:29a 3:48p 2.9' 3.2'	4:05a 4:10p 2.8' 3.1'	4:45a 4:33p 2.5' 3.1'	5:35a 5:00p 2.3' 3.0'	6:44a 5:33p 2.0' 2.8'	8:32a 6:20p 1.9' 2.7'	10:27a 7:37p 2.0' 2.6'
9:37a 10:04p -0.1' 0.1'	10:01a 10:41p 0.1' 0.1'	10:28a 11:22p 0.4' 0.2	10:59a 12:15a 0.7' 0.2'	11:37a 1.1'	1:31a 12:33p 0.3' 1.5'	3:08a 2:04p 0.1' 1.7'
13	**14**	**15**	**16**	**17** ○	**18**	**19**
11:36a 9:25p 2.4' 2.7'	12:21p 10:50p 2.6' 2.9'	12:57p 11:52p 2.9' 3.2'	1:30p 3.1'	12:45a 2:00p 3.5' 3.3'	1:34a 2:28p 3.6' 3.4'	2:22a 2:56p 3.6' 3.5'
4:30a 3:50p -0.2' 1.7'	5:30a 5:09p -0.5' 1.5'	6:17a 6:05p -0.8' 1.2'	6:58a 6:52p -1.0' 0.8'	7:36a 7:36p -1.0' 0.3'	8:11a 8:20p -0.8' -0.1'	8:44a 9:03p -0.6' -0.4'
20	**21**	**22**	**23** ◗	**24**	**25**	**26**
3:10a 3:23p 3.5' 3.5'	3:58a 3:49p 3.2' 3.6'	4:49a 4:17p 2.8' 3.5'	5:47a 4:46p 2.4' 3.4'	7:03a 5:22p 2.0' 3.1'	9:05a 6:14p 1.8' 2.8'	11:13a 8:26p 2.0' 2.6'
9:15a 9:48p -0.2' -0.6'	9:44a 10:36p 0.2' -0.7'	10:11a 11:29p 0.7' -0.5'	10:38a 12:34a 1.1' -0.3'	11:05a 1.4'	1:58a 11:40a -0.1' 1.7'	3:34a 1:22p -0.1' 1.9'
27	**28**					
11:56a 10:36p 2.2' 2.7'	12:25p 11:42p 2.5' 2.9'					
4:52a 4:16p -0.1' 1.8'	5:48a 5:39p -0.2' 1.4'					

Cobia, a welcome catch.

	February 1	February 15	February 28
SUNRISE	7:11 a.m.	7:03 a.m.	6:52 a.m.
SUNSET	6:10 p.m.	6:20 p.m.	6:28 p.m.

ST. MARKS

Florida's Big Bend, plus Naples and the Upper Ten Thousand Islands

Macks a Million

TIDE CORRECTIONS
For St. Marks

	High	Low
Pavilion Key	-0:57	-0:43
Chokoloskee	+0:14	+1:07
Everglades City, Barron River	+0:23	+1:18
Indian Key	-1:05	-0:48
Round Key	-1:06	-0:55
Pumpkin Bay	+0:39	+1:00
Coon Key	-0:45	-0:36
Cape Romano	-1:17	-1:03
Marco, Big Marco River	-1:04	-1:08
Naples, (outer coast)	-1:59	-2:04
Indian Rocks Beach, (inside)	-1:29	-1:25
Clearwater	-2:20	-2:07
Dunedin, St Joseph Sound	-2:22	-2:17
Anclote Keys, south end	-2:19	-2:28
TarponSprings, Anclote River	-1:20	-1:13
Indian Bay	-0:46	-0:09
Bayport	-0:59	-0:42
Withlacoochee River entrance	-0:25	+0:23
Cedar Key	-0:29	-0:30
Suwannee River entrance	-0:26	-0:14
Pepperfish Keys	-0:20	-0:08
Steinhatchee R., Ent. Deadman Bay	-0:15	-0:03
Fishermans Rest	-0:14	-0:02
Spring Warrior Creek	-0:09	+0:03
Rock Islands	-0:03	+0:04
Apalachee Bay		
Aucilla River entrance	+0:03	+0:05
St. Marks, St Marks River	+0:36	+1:04
Bald Point, Ochlockonee Bay	+0:20	+0:28
Turkey Point, St James Island	-0:12	-0:18

INSHORE

Big Bend: **Trout** are legal to keep and most anglers fish the outside grassflats for keeper-size fish; jigs or shrimp-and-popping cork combos are tops. Big single fish can be found in creekmouth shallows, and some will remain in coastal rivers. Schooling **sheepshead**, **black drum** and **redfish** can be caught at hotspots such as Horseshoe Beach.

10,000 Islands: Time for classic backcountry fly fishing and plugging, particularly now that waters are warming. Fish along undercut shorelines and points where birds congregate. Big **tarpon** are laid-up in bays, sunning near the surface; they are suckers for bushy flies, suspending plugs and soft plastics. **Trout** fishing is excellent on both inside and outside grassflats. **Spanish mackerel** raid outside flats and also enter river-mouths and passes.

OFFSHORE

Reef fishermen in this region begin to switch gears as offshore grouper closures will end on April 1 for **red**, **gag** and **black grouper**. **Triggerfish** and **amberjack** are worthy targets on deep reefs. **Red snapper** closed. Baitfish pods will have **kingfish** and **cobia** in tow, mainly over wrecks and reefs. **Tripletail** will be on the increase in southern region around markers and crabtrap buoys.

March Spotlight: SPANISH MACKEREL

It's hard not to like **Spanish mackerel**; this spunky speedster thrills kids and veteran anglers alike. They are present throughout the region right now, and hooking up entails trolling or casting small spoons or jigs on light spinning tackle, or casting streamers on fly gear. Or, chum fish into a frenzy at the stern. Average fish is 2 pounds, max is around 7.

ST. MARKS

March 2011

SUNDAY	MONDAY	TUESDAY	WEDNESDAY	THURSDAY	FRIDAY	SATURDAY

Putting in at Shired Island boat ramp.

1
12:51p 2.7' 12:28a 3.0'
6:29a -0.3' 6:25p 1.0'

2
1:15p 2.9' 1:06a 3.1'
7:02a -0.3' 7:02p 0.7'

3 ●
1:39p 3.1' 1:40a 3.2'
7:30a -0.2' 7:36p 0.4'

4
2:02p 3.3' 1:55a -0.1'... 7:55a -0.1' 8:08p 0.1'

5
2:12a 3.2' 2:24p 3.4'
8:18a 0.0' 8:39p 0.0'

6
2:44a 3.1' 2:45p 3.4'
8:40a 0.1' 9:10p -0.1'

7
3:16a 3.1' 3:06p 3.5'
9:03a 0.2' 9:40p -0.2'

8
3:51a 3.0' 3:27p 3.4'
9:28a 0.4' 10:12p -0.2'

9
4:29a 2.8' 3:51p 3.4'
9:56a 0.7' 10:49p -0.1'

10
5:15a 2.5' 4:19p 3.3'
10:27a 0.9' 11:35p 0.0'

11
6:17a 2.3' 4:53p 3.2'
11:06a 1.3'

12 ◐
7:49a 2.1' 5:40p 3.0'
12:41a 0.1' 12:00p 1.6'

13
11:42a 2.2' 8:57p 2.8'
1:43p 2.8' 12:36a 3.0'

14
12:56p 2.5' 10:58p 2.8'
2:19p 3.1' 1:45a 3.3'

15
12:36a 3.0' 2:19p 3.1'
2:51p 3.3' 2:41a 3.6'

16
1:45a 3.3' 2:51p 3.3'
3:21p 3.5' 3:32a 3.7'

17
2:41a 3.6' 3:21p 3.5'
3:50p 3.7'

18 ○
3:32a 3.7' 3:50p 3.7'

19

20
4:13a 0.2' 3:31p 1.8'
4:21a 3.7' 4:18p 3.8'

21
5:44a 0.0' 5:25p 1.8'
5:08a 3.5' 4:46p 3.9'

22
6:52a -0.2' 6:50p 1.4'
5:55a 3.3' 5:14p 3.9'

23
7:44a -0.4' 7:49p 0.9'
6:44a 2.9' 5:43p 3.8'

24
8:28a -0.4' 8:38p 0.4'
7:37a 2.5' 6:13p 3.6'

25 ◐
9:07a -0.4' 9:23p -0.1'
8:46a 2.1' 6:48p 3.3'

26
9:43a -0.1' 10:07p -0.6'
10:30a 2.0' 7:36p 2.9'

27
10:16a 0.2' 10:51p -0.9'
12:26a 2.1' 10:04p 2.5'
5:00a 0.3' 3:17p 2.0'

28
10:47a 0.5' 11:35p -0.9'
1:15p 2.4' 12:28a 2.6'
6:20a 0.4' 6:18p 1.8'

29
11:15a 0.9' 12:22a -0.8'
1:45p 2.6' 1:33a 2.8'
7:15a 0.4' 7:30p 1.4'

30
11:42a 1.2' 1:13a -0.6' 12:09p 1.4'
2:12p 2.9' 2:18a 3.0'
7:56a 0.4' 8:12p 0.9'

31
2:13a -0.2' 12:38p 1.6'
2:37p 3.1'
8:28a 0.4' 8:47p 0.5'

ST. MARKS

	March 1	March 15	March 30
SUNRISE	6:51 a.m.	7:37 a.m.	7:20 a.m.
SUNSET	6:29 p.m.	7:36 p.m.	7:43 p.m.

DST Starts on March 13

Florida's Big Bend, plus Naples and the Upper Ten Thousand Islands

Silver Slabs!

TIDE CORRECTIONS		
For St. Marks		
	High	Low
Pavilion Key	-0:57	-0:43
Chokoloskee	+0:14	+1:07
Everglades City, Barron River	+0:23	+1:18
Indian Key	-1:05	-0:48
Round Key	-1:06	-0:55
Pumpkin Bay	+0:39	+1:00
Coon Key	-0:45	-0:36
Cape Romano	-1:17	-1:03
Marco, Big Marco River	-1:04	-1:08
Naples, (outer coast)	-1:59	-2:04
Indian Rocks Beach, (inside)	-1:29	-1:25
Clearwater	-2:20	-2:07
Dunedin, St Joseph Sound	-2:22	-2:17
Anclote Keys, south end	-2:19	-2:28
TarponSprings, Anclote River	-1:20	-1:13
Indian Bay	-0:46	-0:09
Bayport	-0:59	-0:42
Withlacoochee River entrance	-0:25	+0:23
Cedar Key	-0:29	-0:30
Suwannee River entrance	-0:26	-0:14
Pepperfish Keys	-0:20	-0:08
Steinhatchee R., Ent. Deadman Bay	-0:15	-0:03
Fishermans Rest	-0:14	-0:02
Spring Warrior Creek	-0:09	+0:03
Rock Islands	-0:03	+0:04
Apalachee Bay		
Aucilla River entrance	+0:03	+0:05
St. Marks, St Marks River	+0:36	+1:04
Bald Point, Ochlockonee Bay	+0:20	+0:28
Turkey Point, St James Island	-0:12	-0:18

INSHORE

Big Bend: **Trout** fishing is super on coastal grassflats from Apalachee Bay to St. Joseph Sound. Live-baiters go with pinfish or shrimp but all you really need is soft-plastic jigs or plugs. Sight-cast to **redfish** over shallow grasflats, oyster bars and at rivermouths. **Black drum** are in the spartina grass shallows around Cedar Key. Giant **tarpon** hunters begin their trek to Homosassa late this month.

10,000 Islands: Great time to hook a "silver slab," the renown **permit**! Head for nearshore wrecks and cast to spotted fish and hang on. Last month of **snook** fishing before summer conditions take hold. Slot-size fish moving toward the Gulf to spawn and occasionally feed in the passes; otherwise, fish can be hooked at mangrove points, seawalls and canals in residential areas of Naples and Marco Island. **Tarpon** migration reaches beaches in this region, and lower bays hold some laid-up giants, too.

OFFSHORE

Current regulations have **grouper** season reopening this month, and rockpiles of the Big Bend and offshore ledges in 10,000 Islands region should deliver nicely. Watch for bait and surface signs of **kingfish** as well as **cobia** when fishing wrecks and bait pods. **Bonito** and **blackfin tuna** should appear offshore. If you're up for a long jaunt offshore, chances of hooking **dolphin** and **wahoo** are good.

April Spotlight: PERMIT

If you thought **permit** were strictly flats and surf fish, think again. Big slabs in the 25- to 35-pound class congregate on wrecks between Naples and Chokoloskee, some as far out as 20 miles. The northernmost range is roughly Clearwater, and wrecks as far south as Florida Bay are prime. Approach wrecks quietly, and cast from a distance. Anchor upcurrent and freeline live crabs, or drop a few with a splitshot sinker on stout tackle. If calm you may spot their dorsals and tails. They eat well, (limit is one over 20 inches, with 2-fish boat limit) but most are released.

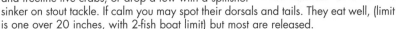

ST. MARKS

April 2011

Last cast for the day.

SUNDAY	MONDAY	TUESDAY	WEDNESDAY	THURSDAY	FRIDAY	SATURDAY

Fri 1 — 2:55a 3.1' / 3:01p 3.3'; 8:55a 0.4' / 9:20p 0.2'
Sat 2 — 3:29a 3.2' / 3:23p 3.5'; 9:19a 0.5' / 9:51p 0.0'

Sun 3 (●) — 4:01a 3.2' / 3:45p 3.6'; 9:43a 0.6' / 10:21p -0.2'
Mon 4 — 4:33a 3.2' / 4:07p 3.7'; 10:08a 0.6' / 10:50p -0.3'
Tue 5 — 5:06a 3.2' / 4:29p 3.7'; 10:33a 0.7' / 11:20p -0.3'
Wed 6 — 5:41a 3.1' / 4:53p 3.7'; 11:01a 0.9' / 11:52p -0.3'
Thu 7 — 6:19a 3.0' / 5:20p 3.7'; 11:32a 1.0'
Fri 8 — 7:05a 2.8' / 5:52p 3.6'; 12:29a -0.2' / 12:07p 1.3'
Sat 9 — 8:02a 2.7' / 6:31p 3.5'; 1:13a -0.1' / 12:50p 1.5'

Sun 10 — 9:17a 2.5' / 7:23p 3.2'; 2:12a 0.0' / 1:49p 1.7'
Mon 11 (◗) — 10:46a 2.6' / 8:44p 3.0'; 3:27a 0.2' / 3:18p 1.9'
Tue 12 — 11:58a 2.8' / 10:41p 2.9'; 4:49a 0.2' / 5:03p 1.7'
Wed 13 — 12:50p 3.0' / 12:23a 3.1'; 6:02a 0.2' / 6:27p 1.2'
Thu 14 — 1:30p 3.3' / 1:36a 3.3'; 7:00a 0.2' / 7:29p 0.6'
Fri 15 — 2:06p 3.6' / 2:35a 3.5'; 7:49a 0.3' / 8:21p 0.0'
Sat 16 — 2:40p 3.8'; 8:32a 0.5' / 9:08p -0.5'

Sun 17 (○) — 3:28a 3.7' / 3:12p 4.0'; 9:11a 0.7' / 9:54p -0.9'
Mon 18 — 4:18a 3.6' / 3:44p 4.1'; 9:47a 0.9' / 10:39p -1.0'
Tue 19 — 5:05a 3.5' / 4:16p 4.1'; 10:20a 1.2' / 11:24p -1.0'
Wed 20 — 5:51a 3.3' / 4:48p 4.1'; 10:51a 1.4' / 12:10a -0.8'
Thu 21 — 6:37a 3.0' / 5:21p 3.9'; 11:23a 1.5' / 12:58a -0.5'
Fri 22 — 7:26a 2.7' / 5:55p 3.7'; 11:55a 1.6' / 1:51a -0.1'
Sat 23 — 8:22a 2.5' / 6:34p 3.3'; 12:34p 1.8'

Sun 24 (◖) — 9:33a 2.3' / 7:28p 2.9'; 2:52a 0.3' / 1:32p 1.9'
Mon 25 — 10:57a 2.4' / 9:27p 2.5'; 4:03a 0.7' / 3:22p 2.0'
Tue 26 — 12:02p 2.6' / 11:54p 2.5'; 5:16a 0.9' / 5:43p 1.7'
Wed 27 — 12:46p 2.8'; 6:17a 1.0' / 7:00p 1.3'
Thu 28 — 1:08p 2.7' / 1:20p 3.0'; 7:03a 1.0' / 7:48p 0.9'
Fri 29 — 1:59p 2.8' / 1:50p 3.2'; 7:40a 1.1' / 8:26p 0.5'
Sat 30 — 2:39a 3.0' / 2:17p 3.4'; 8:12a 1.1' / 9:00p 0.2'

ST. MARKS

	April 1	April 15	April 30
SUNRISE	7:18 a.m.	7:04 a.m.	6:51 a.m.
SUNSET	7:44 p.m.	7:51 p.m.	7:58 p.m.

Florida's Big Bend, plus Naples and the Upper Ten Thousand Islands

Tarpon Train

	High	Low
Pavilion Key	-0:57	-0:43
Chokoloskee	+0:14	+1:07
Everglades City, Barron River	+0:23	+1:18
Indian Key	-1:05	-0:48
Round Key	-1:06	-0:55
Pumpkin Bay	+0:39	+1:00
Coon Key	-0:45	-0:36
Cape Romano	-1:17	-1:03
Marco, Big Marco River	-1:04	-1:08
Naples, (outer coast)	-1:59	-2:04
Indian Rocks Beach, (inside)	-1:29	-1:25
Clearwater	-2:20	-2:07
Dunedin, St Joseph Sound	-2:22	-2:17
Anclote Keys, south end	-2:19	-2:28
TarponSprings, Anclote River	-1:20	-1:13
Indian Bay	-0:46	-0:09
Bayport	-0:59	-0:42
Withlacoochee River entrance	-0:25	+0:23
Cedar Key	-0:29	-0:30
Suwannee River entrance	-0:26	-0:14
Pepperfish Keys	-0:20	-0:08
Steinhatchee R., Ent. Deadman Bay	-0:15	-0:03
Fishermans Rest	-0:14	-0:02
Spring Warrior Creek	-0:09	+0:03
Rock Islands	-0:03	+0:04
Apalachee Bay		
Aucilla River entrance	+0:03	+0:05
St. Marks, St Marks River	+0:36	+1:04
Bald Point, Ochlockonee Bay	+0:20	+0:28
Turkey Point, St James Island	-0:12	-0:18

INSHORE

Big Bend: This is prime time for **tarpon** sight casting in the entire region. Drift fish the outside grassflats for **seatrout**, **mackerel**, **jacks** and **ladyfish**. Watch for **cobia** in that zone, especially around navigational markers. Top bait is a live pinfish under a popping cork, jigs a close second. **Redfish** will cruise and feed over rocky bottom shoreline flats. Sight-casting is best well after sunup if the fish do not tail.

10,000 Islands: **Snook** catch-and-release fishing is a best bet for live-baiters, lure tossers and fly fishers. Overslot specimens stacking in the passes, and around bars and islands on the outside. **Seatrout** and **redfish** are heading to outside flats and bars. Numbers of **tarpon** peaking for sight fishing along the Gulf beaches or back inside dark-water Everglades bays.

OFFSHORE

Top wreck-fishing month. Wrecks as close as 3 miles produce anything from giant **goliath grouper** (all-release) to tasty **lane snappers**. Of course, there are **snapper** and **grouper** in the mix, too. A run of 50 miles or more could reach Loop Current big-game fish. Numerous bait pods hold plenty of **kingfish** and more **Spanish mackerel** than in years past.

ST. MARKS

May Spotlight: TARPON

Tarpon are on the move region-wide. Homosassa flats remain productive for fly fishermen chasing 100-pound-plus fish, exemplified by the 200- and 190-plus-pounder recently caught on fly. Marco and Naples beaches are patrolled by migrating pods of silver kings that eat everything from dead bait to flies. Back bays and rivermouths from Chokoloskee south hold some huge fish that can be dead-baited or sight-fished. Night fishing can be epic.

May 2011

SUNDAY	MONDAY	TUESDAY	WEDNESDAY	THURSDAY	FRIDAY	SATURDAY
1	**2** ●	**3**	**4**	**5**	**6**	**7**
3:16a 2:43p 3.1' 3.6'	3:50a 3:08p 3.2' 3.7'	4:24a 3:33p 3.2' 3.8'	4:59a 3:59p 3.3' 3.9'	5:35a 4:28p 3.3' 3.9'	6:14a 5:00p 3.2' 3.9'	6:58a 5:38p 3.1' 3.8'
8:41a 9:33p 1.1' 0.0'	9:09a 10:05p 1.2' -0.2'	9:38a 10:36p 1.2' -0.3'	10:09a 11:07p 1.2' -0.4'	10:41a 11:41p 1.3' -0.4'	11:17a 12:18a 1.4' -0.4'	11:57a 1.5'
8	**9** ◐	**10**	**11**	**12**	**13**	**14**
7:47a 6:23p 3.0' 3.7'	8:45a 7:21p 3.0' 3.4'	9:48a 8:41p 3.0' 3.1'	10:52a 10:28p 3.1' 2.9'	11:47a 12:09a 3.3' 3.0'	12:36p 1:27a 3.5' 3.2'	1:19p 3.7'
1:00a 12:45p -0.2' 1.6'	12:50a 1:47p -0.1' 1.7'	2:48a 3:08p 0.2' 1.6'	3:55a 4:40p 0.4' 1.4'	5:04a 6:01p 0.7' 0.9'	6:08a 7:08p 0.9' 0.3'	7:04a 8:04p 1.1' -0.2'
15	**16** ○	**17**	**18**	**19**	**20**	**21**
2:30a 2:00p 3.4' 3.9'	3:24a 2:39p 3.5' 4.1'	4:14a 3:18p 3.5' 4.2'	5:00a 3:56p 3.4' 4.2'	5:43a 4:34p 3.3' 4.1'	6:25a 5:11p 3.1' 3.9'	7:06a 5:50p 2.9' 3.7'
7:54a 8:56p 1.3' -0.7'	8:39a 9:44p 1.4' -0.8'	9:20a 10:30p 1.5' -1.0'	8:58a 11:15p 1.6' -0.9'	10:35a 11:59p 1.6' -0.7'	11:13a 12:42a 1.6' -0.3'	11:53a 1.7'
22	**23** ◐	**24**	**25**	**26**	**27**	**28**
7:49a 6:32p 2.8' 3.3'	8:36a 7:25p 2.7' 3.0'	9:29a 8:46p 2.7' 2.6'	10:27a 10:49p 2.8' 2.4'	11:24a 12:27a 2.9' 2.5'	12:13p 1:31a 3.1' 2.6'	12:54p 3.2'
11:24a 12:39p 0.0' 1.7'	2:07a 1:38p 0.4' 1.8'	2:54a 3:00p 0.8' 1.7'	3:47a 4:44p 1.1' 1.6'	4:46a 6:12p 1.4' 1.2'	5:43a 7:13p 1.5' 0.9'	6:35a 8:00p 1.6' 0.5'
29	**30**	**31**	*Cast a bait and enjoy the fun.*			
2:20a 11:30a 2.8' 3.4'	3:02a 2:03p 3.0' 3.5'	3:40a 2:34p 3.1' 3.7'				
7:20a 8:40p 1.6' 0.2'	8:00a 9:16p 1.6' 0.0'	8:38a 9:51p 1.6' -0.2'				

	May 1	May 15	May 30
SUNRISE	6:50 a.m.	6:41 a.m.	6:35 a.m.
SUNSET	7:59 p.m.	8:07 p.m.	8:14 p.m.

St. Marks Station

Florida's Big Bend, plus Naples and the Upper Ten Thousand Islands

Grouper Gang Up

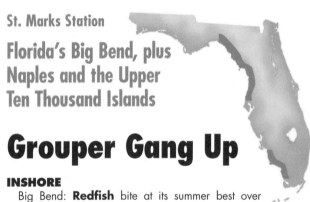

TIDE CORRECTIONS
For St. Marks

	High	Low
Pavilion Key	-0:57	-0:43
Chokoloskee	+0:14	+1:07
Everglades City, Barron River	+0:23	+1:18
Indian Key	-1:05	-0:48
Round Key	-1:06	-0:55
Pumpkin Bay	+0:39	+1:00
Coon Key	-0:45	-0:36
Cape Romano	-1:17	-1:03
Marco, Big Marco River	-1:04	-1:08
Naples, (outer coast)	-1:59	-2:04
Indian Rocks Beach, (inside)	-1:29	-1:25
Clearwater	-2:20	-2:07
Dunedin, St Joseph Sound	-2:22	-2:17
Anclote Keys, south end	-2:19	-2:28
TarponSprings, Anclote River	-1:20	-1:13
Indian Bay	-0:46	-0:09
Bayport	-0:59	-0:42
Withlacoochee River entrance	-0:25	+0:23
Cedar Key	-0:29	-0:30
Suwannee River entrance	-0:26	-0:14
Pepperfish Keys	-0:20	-0:08
Steinhatchee R., Ent. Deadman Bay	-0:15	-0:03
Fishermans Rest	-0:14	-0:02
Spring Warrior Creek	-0:09	+0:03
Rock Islands	-0:03	+0:04
Apalachee Bay		
Aucilla River entrance	+0:03	+0:05
St. Marks, St Marks River	+0:36	+1:04
Bald Point, Ochlockonee Bay	+0:20	+0:28
Turkey Point, St James Island	-0:12	-0:18

INSHORE

Big Bend: **Redfish** bite at its summer best over sand-and-grass bay flats; **seatrout** strong in both numbers and average size. Topwater plugs at first light, and plastic-tail jigs take both species. **Tarpon** run winding down, though fishable numbers exist around Suwannee and other known honeyholes. Catch-and-release **snook** surf fishing excellent around Clearwater and Honeymoon Island.

10,000 Islands: Most **snook** are at the edge of the Gulf now that rainy season is here, but baby **tarpon** relish the fresh water, and bite well in creeks and canals. Spawning snook aggregations should be treated carefully by catch-and-release anglers. Backwater oyster bars should hold **redfish**, and under-cut shorelines and downfalls of middle and outside islands give up large **mangrove snapper** and possibly keeper **gag grouper**.

OFFSHORE

A great time to make that run to distant Gulf hard bottom and wrecks. Out of Clearwater and Tarpon Springs, the Middle Grounds is a much-heralded destination for huge **grouper** and open-season **red snapper**. Boats out of Naples and Marco Island set their sights on the Dry Tortugas, for a surprisingly similar mix of species. **Kingfish**, **barracuda**, **permit**, **cobia** and other resident reef dwellers offer action closer to port.

ST. MARKS

June Spotlight: RED GROUPER

Gags are the headliners for most bottom anglers, but **red grouper** are a good-eating, early summer alternative, though they require long runs offshore. Anglers who carefully study the bottom machine mark the concentrations over hard bottom. Rocky burrows do well with this more indiscriminate feeder that will happily eat any dead bait or jig. Bag limits have been loosened recently, but check for updates before fishing.

June 2011

Twin grins.

St. Marks tide calendar — SUNDAY · MONDAY · TUESDAY · WEDNESDAY · THURSDAY · FRIDAY · SATURDAY

Day	Tide 1	Tide 2	Tide 3	Tide 4
1 (Wed) ●	4:17a 3.2'	3:06p 3.8'	9:14a 1.6'	10:25p -0.3'
2 (Thu)	4:53a 3.3'	3:38p 3.9'	9:50a 1.6'	10:58p -0.5'
3 (Fri)	5:29a 3.3'	5:14p 4.0'	10:28a 1.5'	11:32p -0.5'
4 (Sat)	6:06a 3.4'	4:52p 4.1'	11:08a 1.5'	
5 (Sun)	6:44a 3.4'	5:35p 4.0'	12:07a -0.5'	11:52a 1.5'
6 (Mon)	7:24a 3.3'	6:24p 3.8'	12:45a -0.3'	12:43p 1.4'
7 (Tue)	8:07a 3.3'	7:23p 3.5'	1:26a 0.0'	1:42p 1.3'
8 (Wed) ◑	8:53a 3.3'	8:39p 3.1'	2:13a 0.3'	2:54p 1.2'
9 (Thu)	9:45a 3.4'	10:15p 2.8'	3:05a 0.7'	4:15p 0.9'
10 (Fri)	10:41a 3.5'	11:56p 2.8'	4:05a 1.1'	5:37p 0.5'
11 (Sat)	11:39a 3.6'		5:10a 1.5'	6:50p 0.1'
12 (Sun)	1:20a 2.9'	12:35p 3.8'	6:16a 1.7'	7:52p -0.3'
13 (Mon)	2:26a 3.1'	1:28p 3.9'	7:17a 1.8'	8:47p -0.6'
14 (Tue) ○	3:20a 3.2'	2:17p 4.1'	8:11a 1.8'	9:36p -0.8'
15 (Wed)	4:07a 3.3'	3:04p 4.1'	8:59a 1.8'	10:22p -0.8'
16 (Thu)	4:49a 3.3'	3:47p 4.1'	9:44a 1.7'	11:04p -0.7'
17 (Fri)	5:28a 3.3'	4:28p 4.1'	10:26a 1.6'	11:43p -0.5'
18 (Sat)	6:03a 3.2'	5:07p 3.9'	11:07a 1.5'	
19 (Sun)	6:37a 3.2'	5:46p 3.7'	12:18a -0.2'	11:49a 1.5'
20 (Mon)	7:09a 3.1'	6:27p 3.4'	12:51a 0.1'	12:34p 1.4'
21 (Tue)	7:42a 3.1'	7:13p 3.1'	1:22a 0.5'	1:24p 1.4'
22 (Wed) ◐	8:16a 3.1'	8:12p 2.7'	11:54p 0.8'	2:24p 1.4'
23 (Thu)	8:56a 3.0'	9:38p 2.5'	2:30a 1.2'	3:41p 1.4'
24 (Fri)	9:44a 3.0'	11:27p 2.4'	3:14a 1.5'	5:10p 1.2'
25 (Sat)	10:42a 3.1'		4:11a 1.7'	6:29p 0.9'
26 (Sun)	12:56a 2.5'	11:43a 3.2'	5:18a 1.9'	7:30p 0.6'
27 (Mon)	1:59a 2.7'	12:38p 3.3'	6:24a 1.9'	8:18p 0.3'
28 (Tue)	2:47a 2.9'	1:26p 3.5'	7:22a 1.9'	8:59p 0.0'
29 (Wed)	3:28a 3.1'	2:08p 3.7'	8:11a 1.9'	9:36p -0.2'
30 (Thu)	4:06a 3.2'	2:48p 3.9'	8:56a 1.8'	10:11p -0.4'

ST. MARKS

	June 1	June 15	June 30
SUNRISE	6:35 a.m.	6:35 a.m.	6:38 a.m.
SUNSET	8:15 p.m.	8:21 p.m.	8:23 p.m.

Florida's Big Bend, plus Naples and the Upper Ten Thousand Islands

Shell of a Time

INSHORE

Big Bend: **Scallop** fever has gripped the Big Bend. Dive on clean grassflats off Steinhatchee, Keaton Beach, Homosassa and Crystal River. **Seatrout** fishing in that region is fine early in the day. Schooling **reds** are on rocky ledges and oyster shell. Only time will tell how **snook** fared with the January freeze; last season's bite might be history.

10,000 Islands: Catch-and-release **snook** and **tarpon** fishing is red-hot in rivermouths and passes. Sunrise **trout** is best on outside grassflats from Cape Romano through Pavilion Key. Backcountry baby **tarpon** fishing is great throughout the region. Soak baits for **mangrove snapper** at undercut shorelines.

OFFSHORE

Scout out the markers and flotsam for **cobia** and **tripletail**. Good **kingfish** action can be had where bait is holding, from 20 feet on out to the deep Gulf. Wreck fishing can be a blast for **snapper** with a mix of **kingfish**, **tunas** and others. **Permit** still on wrecks off Marco and Naples, but at this time of summer, thunderstorms dictate early starts and runs in at noon are advised.

TIDE CORRECTIONS For St. Marks	High	Low
Pavilion Key	-0:57	-0:43
Chokoloskee	+0:14	+1:07
Everglades City, Barron River	+0:23	+1:18
Indian Key	-1:05	-0:48
Round Key	-1:06	-0:55
Pumpkin Bay	+0:39	+1:00
Coon Key	-0:45	-0:36
Cape Romano	-1:17	-1:03
Marco, Big Marco River	-1:04	-1:08
Naples, (outer coast)	-1:59	-2:04
Indian Rocks Beach, (inside)	-1:29	-1:25
Clearwater	-2:20	-2:07
Dunedin, St Joseph Sound	-2:22	-2:17
Anclote Keys, south end	-2:19	-2:28
TarponSprings, Anclote River	-1:20	-1:13
Indian Bay	-0:46	-0:09
Bayport	-0:59	-0:42
Withlacoochee River entrance	-0:25	+0:23
Cedar Key	-0:29	-0:30
Suwannee River entrance	-0:26	-0:14
Pepperfish Keys	-0:20	-0:08
Steinhatchee R., Ent. Deadman Bay	-0:15	-0:03
Fishermans Rest	-0:14	-0:02
Spring Warrior Creek	-0:09	+0:03
Rock Islands	-0:03	+0:04
Apalachee Bay		
Aucilla River entrance	+0:03	+0:05
St. Marks, St Marks River	+0:36	+1:04
Bald Point, Ochlockonee Bay	+0:20	+0:28
Turkey Point, St James Island	-0:12	-0:18

July Spotlight: SCALLOPS

Tides may not have much to do with scalloping, but overall currents, in the long run, can affect populations. Some years **scallop** larvae settle farther offshore, or perhaps a bit north or south of past concentrations. Steinhatchee and Homosassa are probably the centers of abundance, but some seasons great catches come out of St. Joseph Bay near Mexico Beach each (westernmost limit of lawful harvest) and Apalachee Bay. Season opens in these areas July 1. No harvest permitted south of Pasco/Hernando county line.

July 2011

SUNDAY	MONDAY	TUESDAY	WEDNESDAY	THURSDAY	FRIDAY	SATURDAY
					1 ● 4:41a 3:28p 3.4' 4.0' / 9:38a 10:45p 1.6' -0.5'	**2** 5:14a 4:09p 3.4' 4.2' / 10:19a 11:17p 1.5' -0.5'
3	**4**	**5**	**6** Nice catch, weather permitting.	**7**	**8** ◐	**9**
5:47a 4:52p 3.5' 4.2' / 11:02a 11:51p 1.3' -0.4'	6:18a 5:37p 3.6' 4.1' / 11:47a 12:24a 1.1' -0.1'	6:51a 6:27p 3.6' 3.8' / 12:36p 1.00a 1.0' 0.2'	7:24a 7:25p 3.6' 3.4' / 1:31p 1:38a 0.8' 0.6'	8:02a 8:34p 3.6' 3.0' / 2:36p 2:20a 0.7' 1.1'	8:45a 10:04p 3.6' 2.7' / 3:53p 3:11a 0.6' 1.5'	9:40a 11:48p 3.6' 2.6' / 5:17p 0.4'
10	**11**	**12**	**13**	**14**	**15** ○	**16**
10:48a 1:18p 3.6' 2.7' / 4:14a 6:37p 1.9' 0.1'	12:04p 2:23a 3.7' 2.9' / 5:31a 7:44p 2.0' -0.2'	1:12p 3:12a 3.8' 3.1' / 6:49a 8:40p 2.1' -0.4'	2:10p 3:53a 4.0' 3.2' / 7:54a 9:27p 1.9' -0.5'	3:00p 4:29a 4.1' 3.3' / 8:49a 10:09p 1.8' -0.5'	3:44p 5:01a 4.1' 3.4' / 9:36a 10:46p 1.6' -0.4'	4:23p 4.0' / 10:18a 11:18p 1.4' -0.2'
17	**18**	**19**	**20**	**21**	**22** ◐	**23**
5:31a 5:00p 3.4' 3.9' / 10:58a 11:47p 1.2' 0.0'	5:58a 5:37p 3.4' 3.7' / 11:36a 12:13a 1.1' 0.3'	6:24a 6:14p 3.4' 3.5' / 12:15p 12:38a 1.1' 0.6'	6:50a 6:55p 3.4' 3.2' / 12:57p 1:05a 1.1' 0.9'	7:16a 7:43p 3.4' 2.9' / 1:44p 1:35a 1.1' 1.2'	7:46a 8:48p 3.3' 2.8' / 2:43p 2:12a 1.2' 1.5'	8:22a 10:24p 3.2' 2.4' / 4:02p 1.2'
24	**25**	**26**	**27**	**28**	**29** ●	**30**
9:11a 12:14a 3.2' 2.5' / 3:02a 5:36p 1.8' 1.0'	10:23a 1:32a 3.2' 2.7' / 4:13a 6:54p 2.0' 0.8'	11:48a 2:25a 3.3' 2.9' / 5:37a 7:50p 2.1' 0.4'	12:56p 3:07a 3.5' 3.1' / 6:52a 8:35p 2.1' 0.1'	1:50p 3:43a 3.7' 3.3' / 7:51a 9:14p 1.9' -0.1'	2:37p 4:15a 4.0' 3.5' / 8:41a 9:50p 1.7' -0.3'	3:22p 4.2' / 9:25a 10:23p 1.4' -0.3'
31 4:45a 4:06p 3.6' 4.3' / 10:08a 10:56p 1.1' -0.3'						

Bird's eye view of the Howard Creek region.

	July 1	July 15	July 30
SUNRISE	6:39 a.m.	6:45 a.m.	6:52 a.m.
SUNSET	8:23 p.m.	8:22 p.m.	8:15 p.m.

ST. MARKS

Florida's Big Bend, plus Naples and the Upper Ten Thousand Islands

Mixed Snapper

INSHORE

Big Bend: **Scallop** season still in full swing, so anglers might consider avoiding weekend crowds to take in some early-morning **seatrout** fishing out of Apalachee Bay and Steinhatchee. **Pompano**, **Spanish mackerel** and **bluefish** are all on outside grassflats. **Gag grouper** gravitate to rock piles.

10,000 Islands: Head for backcountry bays to cast plugs or flies for small **tarpon**. **Snook** are still catch-and-release. **Redfish** active in backcountry oyster bars, mostly Marco Island south. For mixed-bag action, try Rogers and Broad rivers, or Dismal Key Pass. Nearer Marco, Cape Romano and Round Key waters produce everything from **seatrout** to tarpon.

OFFSHORE

King mackerel provide the dependable bite, but trolling deep-diving plugs may also produce **gag grouper**. **Permit**, **mangrove snapper** and **cobia** will rule the reefs and wrecks from Naples south to Chokoloskee. Make a long run, as in 70 miles or more, to where **blackfin tuna**, **dolphin** and other bluewater pelagics are available. Clearwater and Tarpon Springs are closest ports in this tide region.

TIDE CORRECTIONS For St. Marks		
	High	Low
Pavilion Key	-0:57	-0:43
Chokoloskee	+0:14	+1:07
Everglades City, Barron River	+0:23	+1:18
Indian Key	-1:05	-0:48
Round Key	-1:06	-0:55
Pumpkin Bay	+0:39	+1:00
Coon Key	-0:45	-0:36
Cape Romano	-1:17	-1:03
Marco, Big Marco River	-1:04	-1:08
Naples, (outer coast)	-1:59	-2:04
Indian Rocks Beach, (inside)	-1:29	-1:25
Clearwater	-2:20	-2:07
Dunedin, St Joseph Sound	-2:22	-2:17
Anclote Keys, south end	-2:19	-2:28
TarponSprings, Anclote River	-1:20	-1:13
Indian Bay	-0:46	-0:09
Bayport	-0:59	-0:42
Withlacoochee River entrance	-0:25	+0:23
Cedar Key	-0:29	-0:30
Suwannee River entrance	-0:26	-0:14
Pepperfish Keys	-0:20	-0:08
Steinhatchee R., Ent. Deadman Bay	-0:15	-0:03
Fishermans Rest	-0:14	-0:02
Spring Warrior Creek	-0:09	+0:03
Rock Islands	-0:03	+0:04
Apalachee Bay		
Aucilla River entrance	+0:03	+0:05
St. Marks, St Marks River	+0:36	+1:04
Bald Point, Ochlockonee Bay	+0:20	+0:28
Turkey Point, St James Island	-0:12	-0:18

August Spotlight: SNAPPER

The species of **snapper** you'll hook this month depends on the region you fish. The mix will differ in the Naples to Chokoloskee areas compared to the Clearwater and St. Marks stretches. **Yellowtail**, **lane**, and **mutton** snappers are the southern residents. **Red** snapper assume primary role out of St. Marks, where there is a very strong fishery for the species. **Mangrove** snapper are more widespread, ranging throughout the eastern Gulf of Mexico. Expect the mangos (also called **black** snapper) to be in deeper water once you get west of Apalachee Bay.

August 2011

SUNDAY	MONDAY	TUESDAY	WEDNESDAY	THURSDAY	FRIDAY	SATURDAY
	1	**2**	**3**	**4**	**5** ◑	**6**
	5:14a 3.7' / 4:52p 4.3'	5:42a 3.8' / 5:39p 4.1'	6:11a 3.9' / 6:28p 3.8'	6:41a 3.9' / 7:23p 3.4'	7:14a 3.9' / 8:29p 3.0'	7:54a 3.8' / 9:56p 2.6'
	10:51a 0.8' / 11:27p 0.0'	11:36a 0.6' / 11:59p 0.3'	12:23p 0.4'	12:30a 0.7' / 1:16p 0.4'	1:03a 1.1' / 2:18p 0.4'	1:40a 1.5' / 3:33p 0.5'
7	**8**	**9**	**10**	**11**	**12**	**13** ○
8:48a 3.7' / 11:45p 2.5'	10:11a 3.5'	1:16a 2.7' / 11:54a 3.6'	2:12a 2.9' / 1:13p 3.7'	2:53a 3.0' / 2:11p 3.9'	3:27a 3.2' / 2:58p 4.0'	3:57a 3.4' / 3:38p 4.0'
2:24a 1.9' / 5:02p 0.5'	3:29a 2.1' / 6:28p 0.3'	5:05a 2.2' / 7:36p 0.2'	6:42a 2.1' / 8:28p 0.0'	7:51a 1.8' / 9:11p 0.0'	8:43a 1.6' / 9:47p 0.0'	9:26a 1.3' / 10:18p 0.1'
14	**15**	**16**	**17**	**18**	**19**	**20**
4:25a 3.5' / 4:14p 4.0'	4:50a 3.6' / 4:48p 3.9'	5:14a 3.7' / 5:22p 3.8'	5:37a 3.7' / 5:57p 3.6'	6:00a 3.7' / 6:35p 3.4'	6:24a 3.6' / 7:19p 3.1'	6:51a 3.5' / 8:15p 2.8'
10:05a 1.1' / 10:45p 0.3'	10:41a 0.9' / 11:10p 0.4'	11:16a 0.8' / 11:34p 0.6'	11:50a 0.7' / 11:58p 0.8'	12:26p 0.8'	12:25a 1.1' / 1:05p 0.9'	1:55a 1.3' / 1:54p 1.0'
21 ◐	**22**	**23**	**24**	**25**	**26**	**27**
7:25a 3.4' / 9:39p 2.6'	8:11a 3.3' / 11:30p 2.6'	9:23a 3.2'	12:57a 2.8' / 11:07a 3.3'	1:51a 3.0' / 12:33p 3.5'	2:32a 3.3' / 1:35p 3.8'	3:06a 3.5' / 2:28p 4.1'
1:31a 1.6' / 3:02p 1.1'	2:20a 1.9' / 4:38p 1.1'	3:33a 2.1' / 6:08p 0.8'	5:08a 2.2' / 7:13p 0.5'	6:32a 2.1' / 8:01p 0.3'	7:34a 1.8' / 8:42p 0.1'	8:24a 1.4' / 9:20p 0.0'
28	**29** ●	**30**	**31**			
3:37a 3.6' / 3:16p 4.3'	4:06a 3.8' / 4:03p 4.4'	4:33a 3.9' / 4:50p 4.3'	5:01a 4.0' / 5:37p 4.1'			
9:10a 1.0' / 9:54p 0.1'	9:53a 0.6' / 10:27p 0.2'	10:37a 0.3' / 10:59p 0.5'	11:22a 0.0' / 11:30p 0.9'			

Steinhatchee trout.

	August 1	August 15	August 30
SUNRISE	6:53 a.m.	7:00 a.m.	7:07 a.m.
SUNSET	8:14 p.m.	8:03 p.m.	7:48 p.m.

Florida's Big Bend, plus Naples and the Upper Ten Thousand Islands

Snook-tember

TIDE CORRECTIONS
For St. Marks

	High	Low
Pavilion Key	-0:57	-0:43
Chokoloskee	+0:14	+1:07
Everglades City, Barron River	+0:23	+1:18
Indian Key	-1:05	-0:48
Round Key	-1:06	-0:55
Pumpkin Bay	+0:39	+1:00
Coon Key	-0:45	-0:36
Cape Romano	-1:17	-1:03
Marco, Big Marco River	-1:04	-1:08
Naples, (outer coast)	-1:59	-2:04
Indian Rocks Beach, (inside)	-1:29	-1:25
Clearwater	-2:20	-2:07
Dunedin, St Joseph Sound	-2:22	-2:17
Anclote Keys, south end	-2:19	-2:28
TarponSprings, Anclote River	-1:20	-1:13
Indian Bay	-0:46	-0:09
Bayport	-0:59	-0:42
Withlacoochee River entrance	-0:25	+0:03
Cedar Key	-0:29	-0:30
Suwannee River entrance	-0:26	-0:14
Pepperfish Keys	-0:20	-0:08
Steinhatchee R., Ent. Deadman Bay	-0:15	-0:03
Fishermans Rest	-0:14	-0:02
Spring Warrior Creek	-0:09	+0:03
Rock Islands	-0:03	+0:04
Apalachee Bay		
Aucilla River entrance	+0:03	+0:05
St. Marks, St Marks River	+0:36	+1:04
Bald Point, Ochlockonee Bay	+0:20	+0:28
Turkey Point, St James Island	-0:12	-0:18

INSHORE

Big Bend: When shrimp run this month at Apalachicola Bay, **seatrout** come screaming. Elsewhere, trout will feed around rockweed outcrops and over offshore grassbeds. An oyster bar bite might include **redfish**, **black drum** or trout this month. **Spanish mackerel** are on the move, but they will continue south soon. Same goes for **tripletail**, so check the markers to get a good-eating trip in the box.

10,000 Islands: **Snook** are along the beaches, in the passes of Naples, down to mangrove country at Pavilion Key and beyond. **Redfish** will school up for the eventual fall run around outside oyster bars, from Marco Island south. Resident baby **tarpon** on the feed, and southbound migratory fish shadowing increasing bait pods.

OFFSHORE

Along the entire Big Bend and points south, the fall bait run triggers a super **kingfish** and **Spanish mackerel** bite for anglers trolling spoons or plugs. Keep an eye out for southbound **tripletail** and **cobia** on trap buoys and navigational markers. **Red snapper** season is closed, but good wreck and reef fishing is available. Long-rangers with big boats and gas money for 100-mile runs get shots at **dolphin** and **marlin**.

ST. MARKS

September Spotlight: SNOOK

Snook are target number one for anglers in the southern stretch of this tidal region, and the habitat is as wild and desirable as the fish. South of Naples and Marco Island, Florida's Gulf Coast is undeveloped, there's nothing but bonafide snook country—mangrove streams, rivers, oyster bars, and warm, shallow, bait-rich water. Top September snook tactics include working topwater plugs or flyrod poppers and streamers at first light, rolling big jigs along bottom in the passes at night, chucking whitebait in the bushes, and, well, there's not much that won't work for snook this month.

September 2011

SUNDAY	MONDAY	TUESDAY	WEDNESDAY	THURSDAY	FRIDAY	SATURDAY

Calm waters and a bull redfish.

1
5:29a 4.1' | 6:26p 3.8'
12:09p -0.1' | 12:00a 1.2'

2
5:59a 4.1' | 7:20p 3.3'
1:01p 0.0' | 12:31a 1.5'

3
6:33a 4.0' | 8:24p 2.9'
2:01p 0.2' | —

4
7:13a 3.8' | 9:50p 2.6'
1:06a 1.8' | 3:17p 0.5'

5
8:09a 3.6' | 11:38p 2.5'
1:51a 2.1' | 4:48p 0.6'

6
9:56a 3.3' | —
3:08a 2.3' | 6:14p 0.6'

7
12:58a 3.4' | 12:02p 2.7'
5:11a 2.2' | 7:18p 0.5'

8
1:45a 2.9' | 1:17p 3.6'
6:49a 1.9' | 8:06p 0.5'

9
2:19a 3.1' | 2:09p 3.7'
7:49a 1.6' | 8:44p 0.5'

10
2:49a 3.3' | 2:51p 3.8'
8:34a 1.2' | 9:16p 0.6'

11
3:17a 3.5' | 3:27p 3.9'
9:12a 0.9' | 9:43p 0.6'

12
3:42a 3.6' | 4:01p 3.9'
9:47a 0.7' | 10:08p 0.7'

13
4:06a 3.7' | 4:34p 3.8'
10:20a 0.5' | 10:32p 0.8'

14
4:29a 3.8' | 5:07p 3.8'
10:52a 0.5' | 10:56p 1.0'

15
4:51a 3.8' | 5:41p 3.6'
11:24a 0.4' | 11:22p 1.1'

16
5:14a 3.8' | 6:18p 3.5'
11:57a 0.5' | 11:51p 1.3'

17
5:40a 3.7' | 7:00p 3.2'
12:33p 0.6' | —

18
6:09a 3.6' | 7:54p 3.0'
12:24a 1.5' | 12:17p 0.7'

19
6:45a 3.5' | 9:10p 2.8'
12:03a 1.7' | 1:18p 0.9'

20
7:33a 3.4' | 10:47p 2.8'
12:56a 2.0' | 2:43p 0.9'

21
8:49a 3.2' | 12:10a 2.9'
2:15a 2.1' | 4:13p 0.8'

22
10:40a 3.2' | 1:04a 3.1'
3:52a 2.1' | 5:24p 0.6'

23
12:15p 3.5' | 5:14a 1.8'
6:18p 0.5'

24
1:45a 3.4' | 1:22p 3.8'
6:15a 1.4' | 7:03p 0.4'

25
2:19a 3.6' | 2:18p 4.0'
8:05a 0.9' | 8:43p 0.4'

26
2:51a 3.8' | 3:09p 4.2'
8:52a 0.4' | 9:21p 0.6'

27
3:21a 3.9' | 3:58p 4.3'
9:37a -0.1' | 9:56p 0.8'

28
3:51a 4.1' | 4:46p 4.2'
10:22a -0.4' | 10:29p 1.1'

29
4:21a 4.2' | 5:34p 3.9'
11:08a -0.5' | 11:01p 1.4'

30
4:52a 4.2' | 6:23p 3.6'
11:55a -0.4' | 11:33p 1.6'

ST. MARKS

	September 1	September 15	September 30
SUNRISE	7:07 a.m.	7:13 a.m.	7:19 a.m.
SUNSET	7:47 p.m.	7:31 p.m.	7:15 p.m.

Florida's Big Bend, plus Naples and the Upper Ten Thousand Islands

Spots Before Your Eyes

INSHORE

Big Bend: Creeks are tops for **seatrout** and **redfish**. Prime waterways include the creeks at the mouths of the Suwannee, St. Marks and Ochlockonee rivers, due to abundant oyster bars and associated forage. Open-water grassflats produce trout and reds throughout the region. Inshore waters are raided by more **Spanish macks**, and **flounder** gather over mud and shell bottom.

10,000 Islands: **Snook** are still available both on outside points and inside mangrove shorelines as the month progresses. **Redfish** schools increase around oyster beds and shelly points of outside islands of entire region. Chances of hooking **pompano** along sandy beaches or over grassflats increase.

OFFSHORE

Hard bottom off St. Marks and other northern ports attracts **mackerel**, **kingfish** and **gag grouper**. Same can be said for Naples south, where nearshore wrecks also hold **snook**, **permit**, **sharks** and **cobia**, and distant limestone bottom **red grouper** and mixed **snapper**. Northern waters see delicious **sea bass** ganging up on structure in 30 feet or less.

TIDE CORRECTIONS For St. Marks		
	High	Low
Pavilion Key	-0:57	-0:43
Chokoloskee	+0:14	+1:07
Everglades City, Barron River	+0:23	+1:18
Indian Key	-1:05	-0:48
Round Key	-1:06	-0:55
Pumpkin Bay	+0:39	+1:00
Coon Key	-0:45	-0:36
Cape Romano	-1:17	-1:03
Marco, Big Marco River	-1:04	-1:08
Naples, (outer coast)	-1:59	-2:04
Indian Rocks Beach, (inside)	-1:29	-1:25
Clearwater	-2:20	-2:07
Dunedin, St Joseph Sound	-2:22	-2:17
Anclote Keys, south end	-2:19	-2:28
TarponSprings, Anclote River	-1:20	-1:13
Indian Bay	-0:46	-0:09
Bayport	-0:59	-0:42
Withlacoochee River entrance	-0:25	+0:23
Cedar Key	-0:29	-0:30
Suwannee River entrance	-0:26	-0:14
Pepperfish Keys	-0:20	-0:08
Steinhatchee R., Ent. Deadman Bay	-0:15	-0:03
Fishermans Rest	-0:14	-0:02
Spring Warrior Creek	-0:09	+0:03
Rock Islands	-0:03	+0:04
Apalachee Bay		
Aucilla River entrance	+0:03	+0:05
St. Marks, St Marks River	+0:36	+1:04
Bald Point, Ochlockonee Bay	+0:20	+0:28
Turkey Point, St James Island	-0:12	-0:18

October Spotlight: SPOTTED SEATROUT

It's getting more comfortable out, and that calls for all-day fishing for **spotted seatrout**. So you might not need the alarm clock at all. The fish are getting more active with cooling water temps, so put a few on ice before the November-December closure from Pinellas County south. After plugging early, the bite continues for anglers tossing jigs, spoons, streamer flies, or drift-fishing over grass with a frisky shrimp, or a plastic shrimp, under a popping cork. The smaller fish taste best, so consider putting the bigger females back to keep this rebounding fishery strong.

October 2011

SUNDAY	MONDAY	TUESDAY	WEDNESDAY	THURSDAY	FRIDAY	SATURDAY

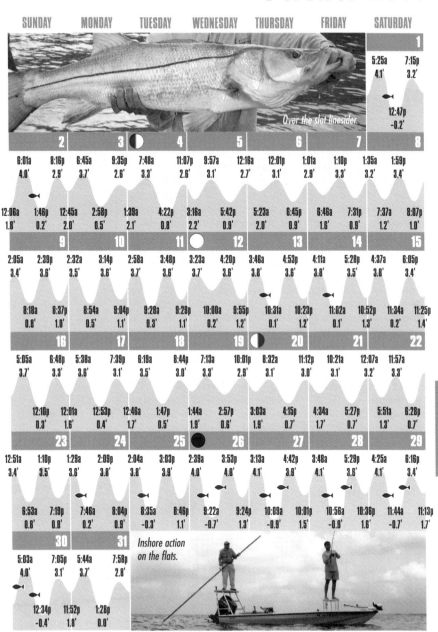

Over the slot linesider.

1
5:25a 4.1' — 7:15p 3.2'
🐟
12:47p -0.2'

2
6:01a 4.0' — 8:16p 2.9'
🐟
12:06a 1.8' — 1:46p 0.2'

3 ◐
6:45a 3.7' — 9:35p 2.6'
12:45a 2.0' — 2:58p 0.5'

4
7:48a 3.3' — 11:07p 2.6'
1:39a 2.1' — 4:22p 0.8'

5
9:57a 3.1'
3:16a 2.2' — 5:42p 0.9'

6
12:16a 2.7' — 12:01p 3.1'
5:23a 2.0' — 6:45p 0.9'

7
1:01a 2.9' — 1:10p 3.3'
6:46a 1.6' — 7:31p 0.9'

8
1:35a 3.2' — 1:59p 3.4'
7:37a 1.2' — 8:07p 1.0'

9
2:05a 3.4' — 2:39p 3.6'
8:18a 0.8' — 8:37p 1.0'

10
2:32a 3.5' — 3:14p 3.6'
8:54a 0.5' — 9:04p 1.1'

11 ○
2:58a 3.7' — 3:48p 3.6'
9:28a 0.3' — 9:29p 1.1'

12
3:23a 3.7' — 4:20p 3.6'
10:00a 0.2' — 9:55p 1.2'

13
3:46a 3.8' — 4:53p 3.6'
🐟
10:31a 0.1' — 10:23p 1.2'

14
4:11a 3.8' — 5:28p 3.5'
🐟
11:02a 0.1' — 10:52p 1.3'

15
4:37a 3.8' — 6:05p 3.4'
11:34a 0.2' — 11:25p 1.4'

16
5:05a 3.7' — 6:48p 3.3'
12:10p 0.3' — 12:01a 1.6'

17
5:38a 3.6' — 7:39p 3.1'
12:53p 0.4' — 12:46a 1.7'

18
6:19a 3.5' — 8:44p 3.0'
1:47p 0.5'

19 ◑
7:13a 3.3' — 10:01p 2.9'
1:44a 1.9' — 2:57p 0.6'

20
8:32a 3.1' — 11:12p 3.0'
3:03a 1.9' — 4:15p 0.7'

21
10:21a 3.1'
4:34a 1.7' — 5:27p 0.7'

22
12:07a 3.2' — 11:57a 3.3'
5:51a 1.3' — 6:28p 0.7'

23
12:51a 3.4' — 1:10p 3.5'
6:53a 0.8' — 7:19p 0.9'

24
1:29a 3.6' — 2:09p 3.8'
7:46a 0.2' — 8:04p 0.9'

25 ●
2:04a 3.8' — 3:03p 3.9'
🐟
8:35a -0.3' — 6:46p 1.1'

26
2:39a 4.0' — 3:53p 4.0'
🐟
9:22a -0.7' — 9:24p 1.3'

27
3:13a 4.1' — 4:42p 3.9'
🐟
10:09a -0.9' — 10:01p 1.5'

28
3:48a 4.1' — 5:29p 3.6'
🐟
10:56a -0.9' — 10:36p 1.6'

29
4:25a 4.1' — 6:16p 3.4'
🐟
11:44a -0.7' — 11:13p 1.7'

30
5:03a 4.0' — 7:05p 3.1'
🐟
12:34p -0.4'

31
5:44a 3.7' — 7:58p 2.8'
11:52p 1.8' — 1:28p 0.0'

Inshore action on the flats.

ST. MARKS

	October 1	October 15	October 30
SUNRISE	7:20 a.m.	7:26 a.m.	7:35 a.m.
SUNSET	7:14 p.m.	6:59 p.m.	6:46 p.m.

FISHING PLANNER 133

St. Marks Station

Florida's Big Bend, plus Naples and the Upper Ten Thousand Islands

Pleasing Pompano

TIDE CORRECTIONS
For St. Marks

	High	Low
Pavilion Key	-0:57	-0:43
Chokoloskee	+0:14	+1:07
Everglades City, Barron River	+0:23	+1:18
Indian Key	-1:05	-0:48
Round Key	-1:06	-0:55
Pumpkin Bay	+0:39	+1:00
Coon Key	-0:45	-0:36
Cape Romano	-1:17	-1:03
Marco, Big Marco River	-1:04	-1:08
Naples, (outer coast)	-1:59	-2:04
Indian Rocks Beach, (inside)	-1:29	-1:25
Clearwater	-2:20	-2:07
Dunedin, St Joseph Sound	-2:22	-2:17
Anclote Keys, south end	-2:19	-2:28
TarponSprings, Anclote River	-1:20	-1:13
Indian Bay	-0:46	-0:09
Bayport	-0:59	-0:42
Withlacoochee River entrance	-0:25	-0:33
Cedar Key	-0:29	-0:30
Suwannee River entrance	-0:26	-0:14
Pepperfish Keys	-0:20	-0:08
Steinhatchee R., Ent. Deadman Bay	-0:15	-0:03
Fishermans Rest	-0:14	-0:02
Spring Warrior Creek	-0:09	+0:03
Rock Islands	-0:03	+0:04
Apalachee Bay		
Aucilla River entrance	+0:03	+0:05
St. Marks, St Marks River	+0:36	+1:04
Bald Point, Ochlockonee Bay	+0:20	+0:28
Turkey Point, St James Island	-0:12	-0:18

INSHORE

Big Bend: With each cold front more **seatrout** high-tail it to the creeks and rivers, so grassflat fishing is good right now. St. Joseph Sound, south of Tarpon Springs, is a trout hotspot, and holds **reds** and, hopefully, **snook** that survived the freeze. Jigging the passes and other deep coastal waterways produces reds, trout, **mangrove snapper**, **sand trout**, **flounder** and more.

10,000 Islands: **Trout** season is closed, so turn your attention to **pompano**, **black** and **red drum**, and **mangrove snapper**. Drift the bays and cast jigs or soak shrimp for a mixed bag. **Snook** are moving inside, so take your shots in "middle" bays where bait hangs over oyster bars. Plugging or jigging mangrove shorelines could produce a few **redfish** as well. Sight-fishing comes on strong on sunny days when backcountry waters cool.

OFFSHORE

Head for hard bottom and rockpiles and drag lipped plugs for **gag grouper**. Many are as shallow as 15 feet of water out of St. Marks, Crystal River and Homosassa. They'll be a bit farther out the farther south you fish. **Kingfish** are numerous region-wide this month. Later, they will move south as water temps plummet. **Pemit** are making their exodus south, so the main wreck-dwellers will be **cobia**.

ST. MARKS

November Spotlight: POMPANO

Once you understand that **pompano** are not just beach bums, you'll catch them more regularly over an array of habitat. Pompano are eating machines, and like most fish follow the food. Sandbars, shell bars, rocky shoals and grassflats with potholes inside Gulf passes begin holding some pomps as water temps dip during winter. Work bucktail or plastic-tail jigs with quick sweeps of the rodtip, and drift where fish have been reported or skip in your boat wake.

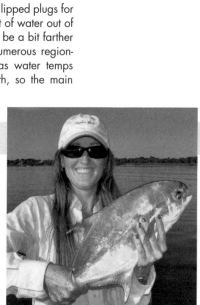

November 2011

ST. MARKS

SUNDAY	MONDAY	TUESDAY	WEDNESDAY	THURSDAY	FRIDAY	SATURDAY
		1 ◐	**2**	**3**	**4**	**5**
		6:32a 3.4' / 8:59p 2.6'	7:39a 3.0' / 10:08p 2.6'	9:39a 2.7' / 11:12p 2.7'	11:40a 2.7'	12:03a 2.9' / 12:53p 2.8'
		12:38a 1.8' / 2:27p 0.4'	1:43a 1.9' / 3:35p 0.8'	3:19a 1.8' / 4:46p 1.1'	5:09a 1.6' / 5:49p 1.2'	6:25a 1.2' / 6:39p 1.3'
6	**7**	**8**	**9** ○	**10**	**11**	**12**
12:43a 3.0' / 11:44a 3.0' / 11:17p 3.2'	12:25p 3.1' / 11:48p 3.4'	1:01p 3.2' / 12:16a 3.5'	1:35p 3.3' / 12:44a 3.5'	2:09p 3.3' / 1:12a 3.6'	2:43p 3.3' / 1:40a 3.6'	3:18p 3.3'
5:17a 0.7' / 5:19p 1.3'	5:58a 0.4' / 5:53p 1.4'	6:35a 0.1' / 6:24p 1.4'	7:10a -0.1' / 6:54p 1.4'	7:43a -0.2' / 7:25p 1.3'	8:15a -0.2' / 7:57p 1.3'	8:47a -0.2' / 8:31p 1.3'
13	**14**	**15**	**16**	**17** ◐	**18**	**19**
2:10a 3.6' / 3:56p 3.3'	2:43a 3.6' / 4:36p 3.2'	3:22a 3.5' / 5:21p 3.1'	4:07a 3.4' / 6:12p 3.0'	5:05a 3.2' / 7:08p 3.0'	6:22a 2.9' / 8:07p 3.0'	8:03a 2.8' / 9:03p 3.1'
9:19a -0.2' / 9:07p 1.4'	9:55a -0.2' / 9:47p 1.4'	10:34a -0.1' / 10:35p 1.5'	11:20a 0.1' / 11:34p 1.5'	12:15p 0.3'	12:48a 1.4' / 1:19p 0.5'	2:09a 1.1' / 2:27p 0.8'
20	**21**	**22**	**23**	**24** ●	**25**	**26**
9:41a 2.9' / 9:53p 3.3'	11:00a 3.1' / 10:39p 3.5'	12:03p 3.3' / 11:22p 3.7'	12:59p 3.5' / 12:05a 3.8'	1:49p 3.5' / 12:47a 3.9'	2:36p 3.4' / 1:29a 3.9'	3:21p 3.3'
3:26a 0.6' / 3:33p 1.0'	4:32a 0.1' / 4:33p 1.1'	5:29a -0.4' / 5:26p 1.3'	6:22a -0.9' / 6:14p 1.4'	7:12a -1.1' / 6:58p 1.5'	8:00a -1.2' / 7:40p 1.5'	8:47a -1.2' / 8:21p 1.5'
27	**28**	**29**	**30**			
2:11a 3.9' / 4:03p 3.1'	2:54a 3.7' / 4:44p 2.9'	3:38a 3.4' / 5:26p 2.8'	4:26a 3.1' / 6:08p 2.7'			
9:33a -0.9' / 9:02p 1.4'	10:17a -0.6' / 9:46p 1.4'	11:01a -0.2' / 10:36p 1.4'	11:45a 0.3' / 11:36p 1.4'			

Cooler temperatures move grouper to shallower water.

	November 1	November 15	November 30
SUNRISE	7:36 a.m.	6:46 a.m.	6:57 a.m.
SUNSET	6:45 p.m.	5:38 p.m.	5:35 p.m.

DST Ends on Nov. 6

Florida's Big Bend, plus Naples and the Upper Ten Thousand Islands

Sheepies for Sure

TIDE CORRECTIONS
For St. Marks

	High	Low
Pavilion Key	-0:57	-0:43
Chokoloskee	+0:14	+1:07
Everglades City, Barron River	+0:23	+1:18
Indian Key	-1:05	-0:48
Round Key	-1:06	-0:55
Pumpkin Bay	+0:39	+1:00
Coon Key	-0:45	-0:36
Cape Romano	-1:17	-1:03
Marco, Big Marco River	-1:04	-1:08
Naples, (outer coast)	-1:59	-2:04
Indian Rocks Beach, (inside)	-1:29	-1:25
Clearwater	-2:20	-2:07
Dunedin, St Joseph Sound	-2:22	-2:17
Anclote Keys, south end	-2:19	-2:28
TarponSprings, Anclote River	-1:20	-1:13
Indian Bay	-0:46	-0:09
Bayport	-0:59	-0:42
Withlacoochee River entrance	-0:25	+0:23
Cedar Key	-0:29	-0:30
Suwannee River entrance	-0:26	-0:14
Pepperfish Keys	-0:20	-0:08
Steinhatchee R., Ent. Deadman Bay	-0:15	-0:03
Fishermans Rest	-0:14	-0:02
Spring Warrior Creek	-0:09	+0:03
Rock Islands	-0:03	+0:04
Apalachee Bay		
Aucilla River entrance	+0:03	+0:05
St. Marks, St Marks River	+0:36	+1:04
Bald Point, Ochlockonee Bay	+0:20	+0:28
Turkey Point, St James Island	-0:12	-0:18

INSHORE

Big Bend: Great **trout** action can be had near bait schools at creekmouths and grass shorelines. Plenty of **redfish** run deep into salty creeks and oyster bays from Steinhatchee to Ochlockonee rivers. **Sheepshead** and **grouper** are active on most nearshore structure.

10,000 Islands: **Snook** catch-and-release action good in backcountry bays. Oversized **redfish** gather on nearshore wrecks from Naples north. **Spanish macks** also gather over wrecks or at rivermouths, often swimming into headwaters. Naples Bay, Keewaydin and back bays of Marco hold **sheepshead**, **snapper** and other panfish.

OFFSHORE

Gag and **red grouper** will bend rods over deep hard bottom. **Kingfish** most plentiful around bait pods from Naples south, but northern waters hold stragglers. Expect to find **Spanish mackerel** and **bonito** where kings are. Wrecks off Sanibel to Marco dependable for **mangrove snapper**, **triggerfish**, **cobia** and some kings. Wreck anglers report 40-pound-plus **red drum** at this time of year.

December Spotlight: SHEEPSHEAD

Sheepshead are a wintertime habit with many anglers. Challenging and delicious is part of the reason. Northern waters of St. Marks and Keaton Beach are famous for producing the biggest sheepshead on reefs in waters 10 to 40 feet deep. In the 10,000 Islands, the barnacle-encrusted mangroves, dock pilings and inland road bridges also hold stout sheepies. But the lion's share are smaller, and all sizes relish shrimp and fiddler crabs. Soak baits near bottom with a sliding sinker, splitshot or jighead.

December 2011

SUNDAY	MONDAY	TUESDAY	WEDNESDAY	THURSDAY	FRIDAY	SATURDAY

Trolling or chumming will get the attention of schoolie kingfish.

				1 ◑	**2**	**3**
				5:27a 2.7' — 6:55p 2.6'	6:55a 2.3' — 7:47p 2.6'	8:52a 2.2' — 8:42p 2.7'
				12:31p 0.7'	12:54a 1.3' — 1:23p 1.0'	2:26a 1.1' — 2:22p 1.3'

4	**5**	**6**	**7**	**8**	**9**	**10** ○
10:23a 2.3' — 9:35p 2.8'	11:25a 2.5' — 10:22p 2.9'	12:11p 2.6' — 11:03p 3.0'	12:50p 2.8' — 11:40p 3.1'	1:26p 2.9' — 12:15a 3.2'	2:01p 3.0' — 12:48a 3.3'	2:35p 3.1'
3:48a 0.8' — 3:23p 1.5'	4:49a 0.4' — 4:19p 1.5'	5:37a 0.1' — 5:07p 1.5'	6:18a -0.1' — 5:49p 1.5'	6:56a -0.3' — 6:27p 1.4'	7:31a -0.5' — 7:04p 1.3'	8:04a -0.6' — 7:40p 1.3'

11	**12**	**13**	**14**	**15**	**16**	**17**
1:22a 3.4' — 3:09p 3.1'	1:57a 3.4' — 3:43p 3.1'	2:34a 3.5' — 4:18p 3.1'	3:16a 3.4' — 4:54p 3.1'	4:04a 3.2' — 5:32p 3.1'	5:01a 3.0' — 6:13p 3.0'	6:14a 2.7' — 7:00p 3.0'
8:36a -0.6' — 8:18p 1.2'	9:07a -0.6' — 8:57p 1.1'	9:40a -0.6' — 9:39p 1.0'	10:15a -0.5' — 10:26p 0.9'	10:53a -0.3' — 11:21p 0.8'	11:37a 0.1'	12:26a 0.7' — 12:27p 0.5'

18 ◑	**19**	**20**	**21**	**22**	**23**	**24** ●
7:47a 2.5' — 7:53p 3.1'	9:28a 2.4' — 8:52p 3.1'	10:55a 2.6' — 9:53p 3.3'	12:02p 2.8' — 10:51p 3.4'	12:56p 3.0' — 11:46p 3.5'	1:44p 3.1'	12:36a 3.6' — 2:26p 3.1'
1:41a 0.4' — 1:27p 0.9'	3:00a 0.0' — 2:35p 1.2'	4:13a -0.4' — 3:46p 1.4'	5:17a -0.8' — 4:52p 1.5'	6:14a -1.1' — 5:51p 1.5'	7:05a -1.3' — 6:42p 1.4'	7:53a -1.4' — 7:29p 1.3'

25	**26**	**27**	**28**	**29**	**30**	**31**
1:24a 3.6' — 3:05p 3.1'	2:09a 3.6' — 3:40p 3.0'	2:51a 3.4' — 4:13p 2.9'	3:34a 3.2' — 4:44p 2.9'	4:17a 2.8' — 5:13p 2.8'	5:06a 2.5' — 5:44p 2.7'	6:09a 2.1' — 6:17p 2.6'
8:36a -1.2' — 8:14p 1.1'	9:16a -1.0' — 8:57p 1.0'	9:53a -0.7' — 9:40p 0.9'	10:26a -0.3' — 10:24p 0.8'	10:57a 0.1' — 11:14p 0.7'	11:27a 0.5'	12:12a 0.7' — 12:00p 0.9'

	December 1	December 15	December 30
SUNRISE	6:57 a.m.	7:07 a.m.	7:14 a.m.
SUNSET	5:35 p.m.	5:38 p.m.	5:46 p.m.

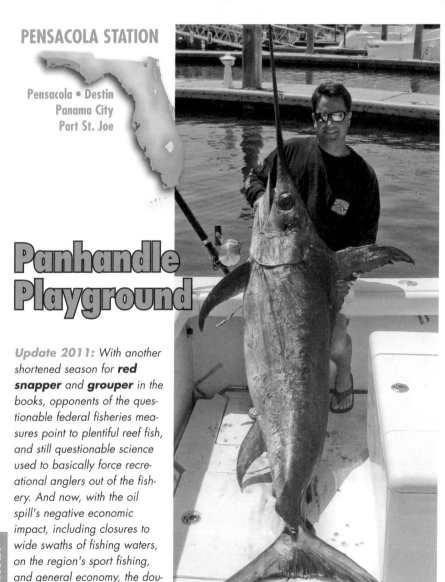

PENSACOLA STATION

Pensacola • Destin
Panama City
Port St. Joe

Panhandle Playground

Update 2011: *With another shortened season for **red snapper** and **grouper** in the books, opponents of the questionable federal fisheries measures point to plentiful reef fish, and still questionable science used to basically force recreational anglers out of the fishery. And now, with the oil spill's negative economic impact, including closures to wide swaths of fishing waters, on the region's sport fishing, and general economy, the double whammy may be tough for charter captains and supportive industries to recover from.*

Swordfish come from deep Panhandle canyons.

Practically eliminating this popular Gulf fishery puts undue pressure on other fisheries. An excellent example is **cobia**, a popular good-eating, easy-to-catch game-fish that makes springtime westbound migrations along Panhandle beaches. Veteran anglers say cobia numbers and average size are declining despite recent tightening of recreational limits to one fish per angler or a maximum of six per boat. Many cobia fishermen are assisting biologists in a tag-and-release effort to better understand how the stocks are faring, and to preserve the fishery.

PENSACOLA

The good news is that regulations for **spotted seatrout**, **redfish**, and both **Spanish** and **king mackerel** appear to be effective due to strong comebacks of these species in Florida Panhandle waters.

Reef fish may get a break from commercial bottom longlines after it was determined that endangered sea turtles are frequent victims of the untended gear. The National Marine Fisheries Service announced emergency rules which would generally force Gulf longliners to operate beyond the 50-fathom line.

Bottom line is, to enjoy what reef fishing is allowed, anglers must stay a step ahead of the constantly changing reef-fish regulations before fishing Gulf of Mexico waters. Rules regarding non-offset, non-stainless steel circle hooks, venting tools and dehookers are likely here to stay.

Florida's Panhandle has long been a favorite destination for anglers throughout the southern states. Each year, thousands make the pilgrimage to Destin, the "World's Luckiest Fishing Village," where charterboats troll for king mackerel, wahoo and dolphin and fish numerous artificial reefs for snapper and grouper. The same enthusiasm surrounds other ports along this coastline. Panama City and Pensacola are important fishing centers, both offering access to offshore and inshore fishing alike.

The climate is different from that of the southern half of the state, as there's a definite change in seasons here. By the latter half of November, most migratory gamefish have headed south, following warm water. This is a time when anglers follow trout and redfish into the many rivers that empty into bays like Choctawhatchee, Escambia and St. Andrew.

April, at the other end of winter, sees the most rapid change of all, when cobia, Spanish mackerel and kingfish begin to arrive, usually in that order. Before you know it, summer's in full swing and everything's biting, it seems.

Tide charts for the Panhandle are based on measurements from Pensacola. Usually, this region has diurnal tides, with one high and one low each day. The reason for this is that the declination of the moon–or the extremes of its ellipse rather than its phase–exerts the strongest influence. When the moon is farthest above or below the earth's equator, the range of the Pensacola tide is greatest. Twice every 29.5 days, the moon crosses the equator and the tides become mixed, usually with two highs and two lows, but the tide range is very small. These are days when very little water flows into and out of bays.

Anglers fish the tides in much the same way as they do elsewhere. Redfish gang up at the mouth of passes on the outgoing tide. Trout respond well to current in bays. All manner of ocean fish frequent the offshore boundary between clear Gulf water and darker river water–the tideline. Also, surf fishermen target the low incoming tide along white-sand beaches, as low water helps reveal washouts in the sandbar, where whiting, pompano and other fish often feed.

The bays of the Panhandle aren't generally as large as some of those farther south, so the corrections aren't as acute as you travel farther inland. Also, be aware that the wider the pass leading into a bay or sound, the faster the tidal change. Where there are wide, deep passes, the corrections more quickly follow the Gulf's tidal range.

PENSACOLA

Average Tidal Range at Pensacola: 1.3 feet

Pensacola to Port St. Joe

TIDE CORRECTIONS
For Pensacola

	High	Low
Port St. Joe, St. Joseph Bay	-0:24	-0:51
St. Andrew Bay		
Channel entrance	-1:31	-2:02
Panama City	-0:43	-0:44
Parker	-0:05	+0:22
Laird Bayou, East Bay	+0:26	+0:40
Farmdale, East Bay	+0:35	+0:55
Wetappo Creek, East Bay	+1:01	+1:40
Lynn Haven, North Bay	-0:06	+0:20
West Bay Creek, West Bay	+0:18	+1:23
Choctawhatchee Bay		
Destin, East Pass	-0:27	+1:20
Harris, The Narrows	+1:37	+2:51
Fishing Bend, Santa Rosa Sound	+0:41	+0:51
Pensacola Bay		
Pensacola Bay entrance	-1:23	-0:34
Warrington, 2 miles south of Pens.	-0:27	-0:30
Lora Point, Escambia Bay	+0:36	+1:03
East Bay	+0:44	+1:17
Bay Point, Blackwater River	+1:23	+1:27
Milton, Blackwater River	+1:40	+1:47

Specks Inside

INSHORE

Anglers target **seatrout** this month under the wire of February's month-long closure. The fish hunker well inshore; try creeks and canals. **Sheepshead** are tight to any structure that holds barnacles and oyster. Hit the water with rods with sensitive tips to feel the wily nibblers, and bait up with fiddler crabs, oysters or shrimp. Big schools of oversize **redfish** are encountered inside Panhandle bays or along the beaches; plugs and jigs take 'em. Troll lipped plugs or soak live baitfish or cutbait for **gag grouper** off Pensacola Bay structure before the Feb. 1 closure.

OFFSHORE

Tuna head for the oil rigs in 1,000-foot depths to find bait concentrations. Make your trip when seas allow, and chum with chunks of Boston mackerel or menhaden. Bury an 8/0 or 10/0 circle hook inside a chunk and let it drift back naturally with the other chum. Metal jigs worked very aggressively can also get a bite. Check rock bottom in 180 feet for big **gag grouper** and **amberjacks**. Near shore, artificial structure will hold spawning flounder; drop down mud minnows or shrimp on fishfinder rigs to nail the big flatties.

January Spotlight: SPOTTED SEATROUT

Spotted seatrout are legal to keep until Feb 1. The fish are tightly schooled in the cold, so head for the deep, protected canals, rivermouths and bayous where the protected water is warmer than that over open, shallow grassflats. Slow down your presentations. Top tactic is slow trolling jigs and plugs. Find the fish and then cast plastic shrimp or jigs into the schools.

PENSACOLA

January 2011

SUNDAY	MONDAY	TUESDAY	WEDNESDAY	THURSDAY	FRIDAY	SATURDAY
						1 8:13p 1.4' 6:42a -0.8'
2 9:05p 1.4' 7:37a -0.8'	**3** ● 9:51p 1.4' 8:25a -0.8'	**4** 10:32p 1.3' 9:04a -0.7'	**5** 11:05p 1.1' 9:32a -0.6'	**6** 11:33p 1.0' 9:48a -0.5'	**7** 11:54p 0.8' 9:52a -0.4'	**8** 9:44a -0.2'
9 12:03a 0.5' 6:12p 0.4' 9:21a -0.1'	**10** 4:59p 0.5' 8:37a 0.0'	**11** ◑ 4:47p 0.6' 7:03a 0.0'	**12** 5:01p 0.8' 4:15a -0.1'	**13** 5:32p 0.9' 4:19a -0.3'	**14** 6:17p 1.0' 4:57a -0.5'	**15** 7:08p 1.2' 5:44a -0.6'
16 8:01p 1.3' 6:33a -0.7'	**17** 8:53p 1.4' 7:20a -0.8'	**18** ○ 9:43p 1.4' 8:02a -0.9'	**19** 10:32p 1.3' 8:41a -0.9'	**20** 11:22p 1.2' 9:14a -0.8'	**21** 12:16a 0.9' 9:39a -0.6'	**22** 9:49a -0.3'
23 1:20a 0.6' 3:50p 0.2' 9:29a 0.0'	**24** 3:00a 0.3' 3:15p 0.5' 9:09p 0.1'	**25** ◑ 3:32p 0.8' 8:05a 0.1'	**26** 4:12p 1.0' 12:23a -0.1'	**27** 5:07p 1.1' 2:21a -0.4'	**28** 6:11p 1.2' 3:43a -0.5'	**29** 7:15p 1.2' 4:52a -0.7' 5:54a -0.7'
30 8:15p 1.2' 6:47a -0.8'	**31** 9:06p 1.2' 7:30a -0.7'					

Blacktip caught from a kayak.

	January 1	January 15	January 30
SUNRISE	6:46 a.m.	6:46 a.m.	6:41 a.m.
SUNSET	4:59 p.m.	5:10 p.m.	5:24 p.m.

Pensacola to Port St. Joe

TIDE CORRECTIONS
For Pensacola

	High	Low
Port St. Joe, St. Joseph Bay	-0:24	-0:51
St. Andrew Bay		
Channel entrance	-1:31	-2:02
Panama City	-0:43	-0:44
Parker	-0:05	+0:22
Laird Bayou, East Bay	+0:26	+0:40
Farmdale, East Bay	+0:35	+0:55
Wetappo Creek, East Bay	+1:01	+1:40
Lynn Haven, North Bay	-0:06	+0:20
West Bay Creek, West Bay	+0:18	+1:23
Choctawhatchee Bay		
Destin, East Pass	-0:27	+1:20
Harris, The Narrows	+1:37	+2:51
Fishing Bend, Santa Rosa Sound	+0:41	+0:51
Pensacola Bay		
Pensacola Bay entrance	-1:23	-0:34
Warrington, 2 miles south of Pens.	-0:27	-0:30
Lora Point, Escambia Bay	+0:36	+1:03
East Bay	+0:44	+1:17
Bay Point, Blackwater River	+1:23	+1:27
Milton, Blackwater River	+1:40	+1:47

Jack Joust

INSHORE

Sheepshead are targeted by anglers looking for fish fry fodder now that **seatrout** are closed in Panhandle waters. Find sheepies on any barnacle-encrusted hard structure. Pier, bridges and dock pilings and similar digs are traditional holes where fiddler crabs, oysters and shrimp get the bite. Most **redfish** encountered now will be over the 27-inch slot and keying on bait schools in the passes, along the beach and in bays. Diving birds show their location. For trout catch-and-release fun, bump jigs on bottom of inland creeks and canals.

OFFSHORE

Tasty **triggerfish** are a passable food fish alternative during the February **snapper-grouper** closure. Heavy-duty sabiki rigs or multi-hook dropper rigs tipped with squid are best on the trigs that congregate on artificial reefs in 75 to 150 feet. Fishing mud minnows or shrimp on sand bottom around shallow wrecks will scare up some **southern flounder**. Anglers running to deep-water oil rigs stand a good chance of tangling with **yellowfin** and **blackfin tuna**. **Amberjack** are thick as flies over artificial wrecks.

February Spotlight: AMBERJACK

If you are hankering for a bent-rod battle, those same artificial wrecks that hold the snapper and grouper that are off-limits this month are lousy with brawny **amberjack**. The AJs are aggressive if not ravenous strikers on live baits, and circle hooks make hookups certain and releases easier. But livies are not a must; lead-head jigs with hair or plastic tails or diamond jigs are deadly. Take care of your back, and keep things fun by wearing a fighting belt. You'll mark and hook most AJs over high-relief artificial wrecks.

PENSACOLA

February 2011

SUNDAY	MONDAY	TUESDAY	WEDNESDAY	THURSDAY	FRIDAY	SATURDAY
		1	**2** ●	**3**	**4**	**5**
		9:48p 1.1'	10:25p 1.0'	10:59p 0.8'	11:34p 0.6'	
		8:02a −0.7'	8:21a −0.5'	8:29a −0.4'	8:24a −0.2'	8:09a −0.1'
6	**7**	**8**	**9**	**10**	**11** ◑	**12**
12:15a 0.4' 2:37p 0.4'	1:11a 0.2' 2:22p 0.5'	2:31p 0.6'	2:58p 0.8'	3:41p 0.9'	4:37p 1.0'	5:40p 1.1'
7:40a 0.0' 8:50p 0.2'	6:51a 0.1' 10:57p 0.1'	12:53a −0.1'	2:23a −0.2'	3:33a −0.4'	4:32a −0.5'	
13	**14**	**15**	**16**	**17** ○	**18**	**19**
6:44p 1.2'	7:45p 1.3'	8:44p 1.3'	9:43p 1.2'	10:46p 1.1'	11:58p 0.8'	1:28p 0.2'
5:24a −0.6'	6:09a −0.7'	6:49a −0.8'	7:26a −0.7'	7:57a −0.5'	8:19a −0.3'	8:20a 0.0' 5:52p 0.1'
20	**21**	**22**	**23** ◑	**24**	**25**	**26**
1:31a 0.6' 12:42p 0.5'	12:52p 0.7'	1:28p 1.0'	2:20p 1.1'	3:23p 1.2'	4:36p 1.2'	5:53p 1.2'
7:37a 0.3' 8:17p −0.1'	10:16p −0.2'	12:12a −0.3'	2:01a −0.5'	3:30a −0.5'	4:40a −0.6'	
27	**28**					
	7:04p 1.2' 8:05p 1.1'					
5:34a −0.5'	6:15a −0.5'					

Pier pilings are a sheepshead castle.

PENSACOLA

	February 1	February 15	February 28
SUNRISE	6:40 a.m.	6:29 a.m.	6:16 a.m.
SUNSET	5:25 p.m.	5:37 p.m.	5:47 p.m.

Pensacola to Port St. Joe

Panhandle Pomps

TIDE CORRECTIONS
For Pensacola

	High	Low
Port St. Joe, St. Joseph Bay	-0:24	-0:51
St. Andrew Bay		
Channel entrance	-1:31	-2:02
Panama City	-0:43	-0:44
Parker	-0:05	+0:22
Laird Bayou, East Bay	+0:26	+0:40
Farmdale, East Bay	+0:35	+0:55
Wetappo Creek, East Bay	+1:01	+1:40
Lynn Haven, North Bay	-0:06	+0:20
West Bay Creek, West Bay	+0:18	+1:23
Choctawhatchee Bay		
Destin, East Pass	-0:27	+1:20
Harris, The Narrows	+1:37	+2:51
Fishing Bend, Santa Rosa Sound	+0:41	+0:51
Pensacola Bay		
Pensacola Bay entrance	-1:23	-0:34
Warrington, 2 miles south of Pens.	-0:27	-0:30
Lora Point, Escambia Bay	+0:36	+1:03
East Bay	+0:44	+1:17
Bay Point, Blackwater River	+1:23	+1:27
Milton, Blackwater River	+1:40	+1:47

INSHORE

Pompano are back on the beach, with **cobia** just a bit farther out. **Spotted seatrout** and **redfish** are leaving wintertime haunts as waters warm up. Fish for them near rivermouths early in the day but then check out grassflats on warmer, sunny afternoons. Still some bull reds around in the surf, particularly near piers, where **jack crevalle** and early cobia also raid the bait schools.

OFFSHORE

Anglers are increasingly focusing on the beachfront **cobia** migration; St. Patrick's Day is considered the real beginning most seasons. Anglers will patrol the beaches in droves (in tower-equipped sportfishers and smaller boats with ladders tied to the deck). There will be far fewer anglers at the deepwater ledges and oil rigs where **wahoo**, **tuna**, **dolphin** and **amberjack** await. A Highly Migratory Species permit is required for billfish and most tuna.

March Spotlight: POMPANO

When the forecast calls for light southeast winds and gentle seas, serious surf anglers hit the beach for delectable **pompano**. Surfcasting gear can be anything from light 8-foot spinning rods to cast jigs when the fish are in close, to 12-foot sticks that launch big sinkers and dropper rig baits a long way to fish parked farther off the sand. Soak sandfleas or fresh-dead shrimp where breaking waves wash back out to sea, sweeping sandfleas and other crustaceans along. Pompano are not only delicious but hard fighting. Kahle hooks held on bottom with pyramid sinkers hook the fish for you, so stick the rod in a spike, and then wind 'em in!

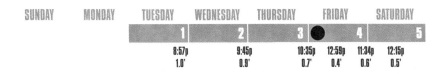

March 2011

SUNDAY	MONDAY	TUESDAY	WEDNESDAY	THURSDAY	FRIDAY	SATURDAY
		1	**2**	**3** ●	**4**	**5**
		8:57p 1.0'	9:45p 0.9'	10:35p 0.7'	12:59p 0.4' / 11:34p 0.6'	12:15p 0.5'
		6:41a -0.4'	6:54a -0.2'	6:53a -0.1'	6:37a 0.1' / 5:07p 0.3'	6:07a 0.2' / 6:48p 0.2'
6	**7**	**8**	**9**	**10**	**11** ◑	**12**
12:52a 0.4' / 12:04p 0.7'	12:10p 0.8'	12:30p 0.9'	1:02p 1.0'	1:47p 1.1'	2:43p 1.2'	3:49p 1.2'
5:19a 0.3' / 7:59p 0.1'	9:03p 0.0'	10:15p -0.1'	11:46p -0.1'	1:28a -0.2'	2:48a -0.3'	
13	**14**	**15**	**16**	**17**	**18** ○	**19**
6:59p 1.3'	8:11p 1.3'	9:24p 1.3'	10:41p 1.2'	12:06a 1.0'	1:50p 0.3' / 1:48a 0.8'	12:45p 0.6'
5:48a -0.4'	6:35a -0.5'	7:16a -0.4'	7:51a -0.3'	8:19a -0.1'	8:32a 0.2' / 6:04p 0.2'	8:12a 0.4' / 8:05p 0.1'
20	**21**	**22**	**23**	**24**	**25** ◑	**26**
12:41p 0.9'	1:06p 1.1'	1:48p 1.3'	2:40p 1.4'	3:41p 1.4'	4:48p 1.4'	6:00p 1.3'
9:36p -0.1'	11:00p -0.3'	12:31a -0.3'	2:10a -0.4'	3:44a -0.4'	4:59a -0.4'	
27	**28**	**29**	**30**	**31**		
7:13p 1.2'	8:25p 1.1'	9:36p 1.0'	10:51p 0.8'	1:15p 0.6'		
5:55a -0.3'	6:32a -0.2'	6:53a 0.0'	6:57a 0.1'	6:42a 0.3' / 6:33p 0.5'		

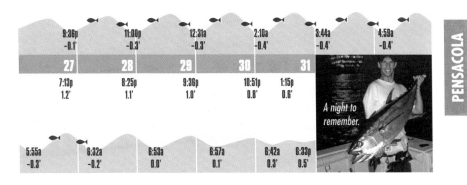

A night to remember.

PENSACOLA

	March 1	March 15	March 30
SUNRISE	6:15 a.m.	6:59 a.m.	6:40 a.m.
SUNSET	5:48 p.m.	6:57 p.m.	7:07 p.m.

DST Starts March 13

Bomber Fever

TIDE CORRECTIONS
For Pensacola

	High	Low
Port St. Joe, St. Joseph Bay	-0:24	-0:51
St. Andrew Bay		
Channel entrance	-1:31	-2:02
Panama City	-0:43	-0:44
Parker	-0:05	+0:22
Laird Bayou, East Bay	+0:26	+0:40
Farmdale, East Bay	+0:35	+0:55
Wetappo Creek, East Bay	+1:01	+1:40
Lynn Haven, North Bay	-0:06	+0:20
West Bay Creek, West Bay	+0:18	+1:23
Choctawhatchee Bay		
Destin, East Pass	-0:27	+1:20
Harris, The Narrows	+1:37	+2:51
Fishing Bend, Santa Rosa Sound	+0:41	+0:51
Pensacola Bay		
Pensacola Bay entrance	-1:23	-0:34
Warrington, 2 miles south of Pens.	-0:27	-0:30
Lora Point, Escambia Bay	+0:36	+1:03
East Bay	+0:44	+1:17
Bay Point, Blackwater River	+1:23	+1:27
Milton, Blackwater River	+1:40	+1:47

INSHORE

Big **spotted seatrout** are no longer an oddity in the Panhandle, and April sees good plugging for gators early in the day, and late afternoon. Deeper water at midday is best for jig-caught schoolies. **Spanish mackerel** are on the beach and in the bays, so break out shiny spoons, jigs or flyrod streamers and work 'em agressively. Piers give up a mixed catch, though all eyes will be peeled for **cobia** by midmonth. Otherwise, mackerel and **sheepshead** will be cranked up to the boards. High-tide beach troughs will be the place for **pompano**. So close at high tide that light tackle and short nylon jigs shine, but surf rods with multi-hook dropper rigs reach pompano farther out.

OFFSHORE

Red snapper would normally be job one come April 15 for reef anglers, but to the dismay of anglers and fishing businesses, both state and federal waters are now closed until June 1. But **grouper** season reopens April 1, so brush up on limit laws before heading for your favorite wreck and reef numbers. When seas behave, it's worthwhile to head for **wahoo**, **amberjack** and **marlin** depths.

April Spotlight: COBIA

The westward **cobia** (a.k.a. ling) migration is a Panhandle event, and has given birth to an entire fishing industry, from tower boats with custom rods and specialized jigs to ladder tie-downs for smaller craft. The brown bombers cruise along well-established troughs off the beach. Anglers who happen upon the hot highway enjoy multiple shots at fish. The drill is to quietly sneak in front of the fish and cast colorful jigs or live bait in their paths. A high perch and polarized glasses are a must for spotting the fish. Fishing pressure and over harvesting has resulted in fewer and smaller fish recently. Dedicated cobia anglers are tagging and releasing more fish for scientific study.

April 2011

SUNDAY	MONDAY	TUESDAY	WEDNESDAY	THURSDAY	FRIDAY	SATURDAY

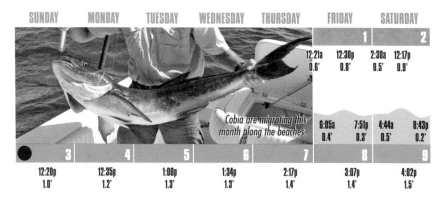

Cobia are migrating this month along the beaches.

1
12:21a 12:30p
0.6' 0.8'
6:05a 7:51p
0.4' 0.3'

2
2:30a 12:17p
0.5' 0.9'
4:44a 8:43p
0.5' 0.2'

3 ●
12:20p
1.0'

4
12:35p
1.2'

5
1:00p
1.3'

6
1:34p
1.3'

7
2:17p
1.4'

8
3:07p
1.4'

9
4:02p
1.5'

10
9:28p
0.1'

11 ◐
10:13p
0.0'

12
11:08p
-0.1'

13
12:17a
-0.1'

14
1:39a
-0.2'

15
2:55a
-0.2'

16
5:02p
1.5'

17
6:08p
1.4'

18 ○
7:27p
1.3'

19
9:09p
1.1'

20
1:25p 11:17p
0.6' 0.9'

21
11:38a
0.7'

22
2:19a 11:10a
0.7' 1.0'

23
3:57a
-0.3'

24
4:45a
-0.3'

25 ◑
5:23a
-0.2'

26
5:54a
0.0'

27
6:11a 4:19p
0.2' 0.6'

28
6:03a 6:34p
0.5' 0.3'

29
4:39a 7:53p
0.7' 0.0'

30
11:20a
1.3'

11:51a
1.5'

12:34p
1.6'

1:24p
1.7'

2:18p
1.7'

3:14p
1.6'

4:09p
1.5'

9:02a
-0.2'

10:11a
-0.3'

11:26a
-0.4'

12:47a
-0.4'

2:06a
-0.3'

3:12a
-0.3'

5:00p
1.3'

5:47p
1.1'

6:34p
0.9'

12:41p 8:41p
0.8' 0.7'

11:23a
0.9'

10:56a
1.0'

10:53a
1.2'

4:01a
-0.2'

4:31a
0.0'

4:42a
0.1'

4:32a 6:34p
0.3' 0.7'

3:55a 7:20p
0.5' 0.5'

7:53p
0.3'

8:25p
0.1'

	April 1	April 15	April 30
SUNRISE	6:38 a.m.	6:22 a.m.	6:06 a.m.
SUNSET	7:08 p.m.	7:17 p.m.	7:26 p.m.

PENSACOLA

Pensacola to Port St. Joe

TIDE CORRECTIONS
For Pensacola

	High	Low
Port St. Joe, St. Joseph Bay	-0:24	-0:51
St. Andrew Bay		
Channel entrance	-1:31	-2:02
Panama City	-0:43	-0:44
Parker	-0:05	+0:22
Laird Bayou, East Bay	+0:26	+0:40
Farmdale, East Bay	+0:35	+0:55
Wetappo Creek, East Bay	+1:01	+1:40
Lynn Haven, North Bay	-0:06	+0:20
West Bay Creek, West Bay	+0:18	+1:23
Choctawhatchee Bay		
Destin, East Pass	-0:27	+1:20
Harris, The Narrows	+1:37	+2:51
Fishing Bend, Santa Rosa Sound	+0:41	+0:51
Pensacola Bay		
Pensacola Bay entrance	-1:23	-0:34
Warrington, 2 miles south of Pens.	-0:27	-0:30
Lora Point, Escambia Bay	+0:36	+1:03
East Bay	+0:44	+1:17
Bay Point, Blackwater River	+1:23	+1:27
Milton, Blackwater River	+1:40	+1:47

Mack City

INSHORE

May brings massive schools of bait from glass minnows to menhaden and mullet to Panhandle waters. Diving birds are the fish-finders which can include **Spanish mackerel**, **seatrout**, **redfish** and more. Look for trout and reds around bait-rich oyster bars and grass-flats. Surf-casters score on **pompano** and **Spanish**. Piers are the place if you seek **cobia**, **sharks** and mackerel. **Sheepshead** still strong around pilings; top baits are fiddler crabs, oysters and shrimp fished with small hooks and light sinkers.

OFFSHORE

Seas are coming down, giving bluewater fans an open door for **marlin**, **tuna**, **wahoo** and **dolphin**. Weedlines form as sea conditions settle down. Troll plastic lures to cover maximum water, or slow-troll live baits over located fish. **Red snapper** are closed until June 1, but **grouper** and **amberjack** fill the void. Search for increasing numbers of **kingfish** anywhere from the beach to deep offshore structure. Smokers can't refuse a big blue runner, Spanish mackerel or rigged ribbonfish. **Cobia** increasingly heading out to deep structure.

May Spotlight: SPANISH MACKEREL

Birds will be your winged compasses to bait schools that attract hordes of ravenous **Spanish mackerel**. The slashing macks push baits to the surface, and diving birds attack from above, creating a wild scene that few anglers can resist. Though the macks are bloodthirsty and sloppy, noisy boat handling can put them down temporarily, so it pays to approach quietly, and make long casts with flashy spoons, jigs or flies. Or, to draw fish in when tougher to find, hang a chumbag, especially when you wish to fly fish. When birds are absent, troll spoons or straw rigs. Keep your lures and flies by tying to a trace of heavy mono or light wire.

May 2011

SUNDAY	MONDAY	TUESDAY	WEDNESDAY	THURSDAY	FRIDAY	SATURDAY
1 11:03a 1.3'	**2** ● 11:24a 1.4'	**3** 11:54a 1.5'	**4** 12:30p 1.6'	**5** 1:12p 1.6'	**6** 1:56p 1.7'	**7** 2:42p 1.7'
9:00p 0.0'	9:41p -0.1'	10:31p -0.2'	11:30p -0.2'	12:32a -0.2'	1:30a -0.3'	
8 3:29p 1.6'	**9** ◐ 4:17p 1.5'	**10** 5:12p 1.2'	**11** 6:42p 1.0'	**12** 11:11a 0.8' 10:09p 0.7'	**13** 10:09a 1.0'	**14** 9:59a 1.3'
2:19a -0.3'	2:59a -0.2'	3:30a -0.1'	3:49a 0.1'	3:48a 0.3' 5:21p 0.6'	2:57a 0.6' 6:36p 0.3'	7:34p 0.0'
15 10:17a 1.5'	**16** 10:51a 1.7'	**17** ○ 11:36a 1.8'	**18** 12:25p 1.9'	**19** 1:16p 1.8'	**20** 2:04p 1.7'	**21** 2:47p 1.6'
8:33p -0.3'	9:35p -0.4'	10:42p -0.5'	11:49p -0.5'	12:51a -0.4'	1:41a -0.3'	
22 3:22p 1.4'	**23** ◑ 3:40p 1.2'	**24** 2:45p 1.0'	**25** 11:07a 0.9'	**26** 9:58a 1.0'	**27** 9:37a 1.2'	**28** 9:39a 1.3'
2:17a -0.2'	2:37a 0.0'	2:37a 0.1'	2:15a 0.3'	1:17a 0.4' 8:21p 0.4'	7:40p 0.2'	7:59p 0.0'
29 9:56a 1.4'	**30** 10:23a 1.5'	**31** 10:58a 1.6'				
8:31p -0.1'	9:13p -0.2'	10:01p -0.3'				

Big gray snapper will make you smile.

	May 1	May 15	May 30
SUNRISE	6:05 a.m.	5:55 a.m.	5:48 a.m.
SUNSET	7:27 p.m.	7:36 p.m.	7:45 p.m.

PENSACOLA

Pensacola to Port St. Joe

TIDE CORRECTIONS
For Pensacola

	High	Low
Port St. Joe, St. Joseph Bay	-0:24	-0:51
St. Andrew Bay		
Channel entrance	-1:31	-2:02
Panama City	-0:43	-0:44
Parker	-0:05	+0:22
Laird Bayou, East Bay	+0:26	+0:40
Farmdale, East Bay	+0:35	+0:55
Wetappo Creek, East Bay	+1:01	+1:40
Lynn Haven, North Bay	-0:06	+0:20
West Bay Creek, West Bay	+0:18	+1:23
Choctawhatchee Bay		
Destin, East Pass	-0:27	+1:20
Harris, The Narrows	+1:37	+2:51
Fishing Bend, Santa Rosa Sound	+0:41	+0:51
Pensacola Bay		
Pensacola Bay entrance	-1:23	-0:34
Warrington, 2 miles south of Pens.	-0:27	-0:30
Lora Point, Escambia Bay	+0:36	+1:03
East Bay	+0:44	+1:11
Bay Point, Blackwater River	+1:23	+1:27
Milton, Blackwater River	+1:40	+1:47

King Me!

INSHORE

Great surf fishing month for **pompano** and **whiting** particularly on early morning incoming tides; set up at deeper troughs and washouts on the flood for best chances. Warming waters have **tripletail** returning to northern Gulf waters, taking up station on the downcurrent side of channel markers, so watch for them at the surface. **Spotted seatrout** and **redfish** are on grassflats targeing bait schools early and late. Bounce a jig or bait up a slip-sinker rig with finger mullet for a shot at **flounder** in Panhandle bays and passes.

OFFSHORE

June 1 is finally here, and you had better get snappin' for **red snapper** while the short season lasts. Reefs and wrecks also produce **grouper**, and **cobia** that have completed their beach run. Brush up on regs that now require non-stainless circle hooks, dehookers and venting tools for all reef fishing. **Kingfish** are making headlines over offshore structure and live bottom. Big-boat anglers take advantage of calm seas to visit the Nipple, Spur and Elbow far to the south for a shot at **wahoo**, **marlin**, **swordfish**, **yellowfin tuna** and **dolphin**.

June Spotlight: KING MACKEREL

Smoker **king mackerel** follow the food, so they will be where the blue runners, bonito and bluefish are—over offshore live bottom. Low-relief structure allows the use of downriggers to slow-troll big live baits or rigged ribbonfish almost on the bottom without fear of hanging up. If the 20-mile run is too adventurous for you, there are plenty of kings feeding on bait schools anywhere from the beach seaward. A smoker's first run is powerful, so choose a soft-tip rod and keep your drag on the loose side to prevent the fish from finding freedom by tearing out the small treble stinger hook that is so important to foil short-striking kings. Rig baits with two feet of light wire and troll a spread to cover the water column.

June 2011

SUNDAY	MONDAY	TUESDAY	WEDNESDAY	THURSDAY	FRIDAY	SATURDAY
			1 ●	**2**	**3**	**4**
			11:38a 1.7'	12:21p 1.8'	1:03p 1.8'	1:45p 1.8'
				10:53p -0.3'	11:42p -0.4'	12:26a -0.4'
5	**6**	**7**	**8** ◑	**9**	**10**	**11**
2:25p 1.7'	3:05p 1.5'	3:44p 1.2'	4:06p 0.9'	9:25a 0.9' 8:15p 0.5'	8:45a 1.1'	8:49a 1.4'
1:03a -0.4'	1:33a -0.3'	1:55a -0.1'	2:01a 0.1'	1:38a 0.4'	5:50p 11:40p 0.5' 0.5'	6:19p 0.2'	7:09p -0.1'
12	**13**	**14**	**15** ○	**16**	**17**	**18**
9:16a 1.6'	9:57a 1.7'	10:46a 1.8'	11:37a 1.9'	12:26p 1.9'	1:10p 1.8'	1:48p 1.6'
8:05p -0.3'	9:05p -0.4'	10:05p -0.5'	11:02p -0.5'	11:51p -0.5'	12:29a -0.4'	
19	**20**	**21**	**22** ◐	**23**	**24**	**25**
2:17p 1.4'	2:34p 1.2'	2:10p 1.0'	9:37a 0.9'	8:27a 1.0'	8:11a 1.1'	8:20a 1.3'
12:53a -0.2'	1:03a 0.0'	12:56a 0.1'	12:30a 0.3'	11:34p 0.4'	9:19p 0.4'	7:10p 0.2' 7:19p 0.1'
26	**27**	**28**	**29**	**30**		
8:45a 1.4'	9:20a 1.5'	10:03a 1.6'	10:48a 1.7'	11:33a 1.8'		
7:53p -0.1'	8:37p -0.2'	9:24p -0.3'	10:09p -0.4'	10:51p -0.4'		

Tis the season to be jolly. For red snapper, that is.

	June 1	June 15	June 30
SUNRISE	5:47 a.m.	5:46 a.m.	5:50 a.m.
SUNSET	7:46 p.m.	7:53 p.m.	7:55 p.m.

Pensacola to Port St. Joe

TIDE CORRECTIONS
For Pensacola

	High	Low
Port St. Joe, St. Joseph Bay	-0:24	-0:51
St. Andrew Bay		
Channel entrance	-1:31	-2:02
Panama City	-0:43	-0:44
Parker	-0:05	+0:22
Laird Bayou, East Bay	+0:26	+0:40
Farmdale, East Bay	+0:35	+0:55
Wetappo Creek, East Bay	+1:01	+1:40
Lynn Haven, North Bay	-0:06	+0:20
West Bay Creek, West Bay	+0:18	+1:23
Choctawhatchee Bay		
Destin, East Pass	-0:27	+1:20
Harris, The Narrows	+1:37	+2:51
Fishing Bend, Santa Rosa Sound	+0:41	+0:51
Pensacola Bay		
Pensacola Bay entrance	-1:23	-0:34
Warrington, 2 miles south of Pens.	-0:27	-0:30
Lora Point, Escambia Bay	+0:36	+1:03
East Bay	+0:44	+1:17
Bay Point, Blackwater River	+1:23	+1:27
Milton, Blackwater River	+1:40	+1:47

Fireworks Galore

INSHORE

The heat is on, so many **spotted seatrout** fans turn to nighttime dock fishing. Check out any lighted dock but approach it quietly and cast small baitfish or shrimp patterns, plastic shrimp or jigs with the current. Trout also feed under flocks of birds at first light. **Redfish** take to shallow grassflats and oyster bars on flood tides. Beach fishermen soak sandfleas and fresh shrimp, or cast tipped jigs for **whiting** or **pompano**. On the piers, **Spanish mackerel**, **bonito**, **bluefish**—even **kingfish**—provide most of the action.

OFFSHORE

July air temps make it paramount to cool off. What better reason to go scalloping? East of Mexico Beach **scallop** season opens July 1, plus **lobster** sport season is July 27-28. Check www.myfwc.com for any new regulations before you gear up. **Tuna**, **dolphin**, **wahoo** and half-ton **blue marlin** come north with Loop Current spinoffs from the Gulf Stream. Combine the bait and debris in these current edges with the famed deepwater structure south of Pensacola, and you have the potential for spectacular catches.

July Spotlight: RED SNAPPER

Next month sees the close of the short Gulf **red snapper** season, so get yours while the getting's good, or shall we say, legal. The tight 2-fish limit has forced veteran anglers to be more creative, such as fishing in the upper half of the water column, often slightly away from structure holding juveniles, to concentrate on 20-plus-pound reds. With such a tight limit, long runs (and big fuel bills) to the 180-foot Edge make a lot less sense than staying closer to home to nab two fish on low-relief concrete rubble and module artificial reefs in 75 to 120 feet of water. Federal law requires that you carry and use venting tools and dehookers, along with non-stainless circle hooks if using cut or live bait.

July 2011

SUNDAY	MONDAY	TUESDAY	WEDNESDAY	THURSDAY	FRIDAY	SATURDAY

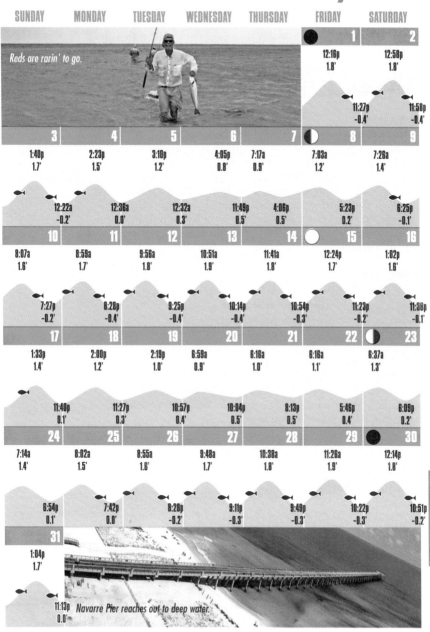

Reds are rarin' to go.

1 ●
12:16p
1.8'
11:27p
-0.4'

2
12:58p
1.8'
11:58p
-0.4'

3
1:40p
1.7'

4
2:23p
1.5'

5
3:10p
1.2'

6
4:05p
0.8'

7
7:17a
0.9'
4:06p
0.5'

8 ◗
7:03a
1.2'
5:23p
0.2'

9
7:26a
1.4'
6:25p
-0.1'

10
8:07a
1.6'
12:22a
-0.2'
7:27p
-0.2'

11
8:59a
1.7'
12:36a
0.0'
8:28p
-0.4'

12
9:56a
1.8'
12:32a
0.3'
9:25p
-0.4'

13
10:51a
1.9'
11:49p
0.5'
10:14p
-0.4'

14 ○
11:41a
1.8'

15
12:24p
1.7'
10:54p
-0.3'

16
1:02p
1.6'
11:23p
-0.2'

17
1:33p
1.4'
11:38p
-0.1'

18
2:00p
1.2'
11:40p
0.1'

19
2:19p
1.0'
11:27p
0.3'

20
6:59a
0.9'
10:57p
0.4'

21
6:16a
1.0'
10:04p
0.5'

22 ◗
6:16a
1.1'
8:13p
0.5'

23
6:37a
1.3'
5:46p
0.4'

24
7:14a
1.4'
6:09p
0.2'

25
8:02a
1.5'
6:54p
0.1'

26
8:55a
1.6'
7:42p
0.0'

27
9:48a
1.7'
8:28p
-0.2'

28
10:38a
1.8'
9:11p
-0.3'

29
11:26a
1.9'
9:49p
-0.3'

30 ●
12:14p
1.8'
10:22p
-0.3'

31
1:04p
1.7'
10:51p
-0.2'
11:13p
0.0'

Navarre Pier reaches out to deep water.

	July 1	July 15	July 30
SUNRISE	5:50 a.m.	5:57 a.m.	6:06 a.m.
SUNSET	7:55 p.m.	7:52 p.m.	7:44 p.m.

PENSACOLA

Pensacola to Port St. Joe

Silver King Fling

INSHORE

Tarpon are on the beach, and can be caught by stealthy anglers who opt for live bait. Sight fishing calls for stealth, too, in crystal clear Choctawhatchee or St. Andrew bays where **redfish** and the biggest **spotted seatrout** in memory forage over sand and grass flats. Try wading for those sharp-eyed gator specks. **Spanish mackerel** are under the bait and birds; troll or cast spoons or jigs to the frenzy. A bag of sandfleas and handful of dropper rigs will keep you busy with **whiting** and **pompano** on the beach.

OFFSHORE

It is time to put the lobsters in the pot! Regular season opens August 6. Look for **spiny** and **bulldozer** (no season on them, and many lobster lovers claim they taste better than spinys) bugs around offshore ledges. Get out pre-dawn to run out and spot **tarpon** rolling in bait schools just off the beach. **Red snapper** season ends August 15, so you have two weeks left. And, you won't have a shot at one until June 1, 2011. Look for big grouper around the 29-fathom Edge. While out there, consider trolling a spread of lures around weedlines and rips for **dolphin**, **wahoo** and **tuna**, and a possible **blue marlin**.

TIDE CORRECTIONS		
For Pensacola		
	High	Low
Port St. Joe, St. Joseph Bay	-0:24	-0:51
St. Andrew Bay		
Channel entrance	-1:31	-2:02
Panama City	-0:43	-0:44
Parker	-0:05	+0:22
Laird Bayou, East Bay	+0:26	+0:40
Farmdale, East Bay	+0:35	+0:55
Wetappo Creek, East Bay	+1:01	+1:40
Lynn Haven, North Bay	-0:06	+0:20
West Bay Creek, West Bay	+0:18	+1:23
Choctawhatchee Bay		
Destin, East Pass	-0:27	+1:20
Harris, The Narrows	+1:37	+2:51
Fishing Bend, Santa Rosa Sound	+0:41	+0:51
Pensacola Bay		
Pensacola Bay entrance	-1:23	-0:34
Warrington, 2 miles south of Pens.	-0:27	-0:30
Lora Point, Escambia Bay	+0:36	+1:03
East Bay	+0:44	+1:17
Bay Point, Blackwater River	+1:23	+1:27
Milton, Blackwater River	+1:40	+1:47

August Spotlight: TARPON

There may be no better inshore sport in the Panhandle than big beach **tarpon**. Pick a flat morning to better spot schools rolling or busting through bait at a distance, preferably in the middle of the week when boat traffic is light. The fish are boat-wise, so get well ahead of the travelers with your outboard, shut it down, and all baitwell pumps, to avoid spooking them, and cast live baits, either under a float or freelined, in their paths. To better stay attached to your head-shaking leaping fish, use a circle hook tied to a 6-foot, 100-pound fluorocarbon leader.

August 2011

SUNDAY	MONDAY	TUESDAY	WEDNESDAY	THURSDAY	FRIDAY	SATURDAY
	1	**2**	**3**	**4**	**5** ◐	**6**
	1:59p 1.4'	3:06p 1.2'	5:04a 0.8' / 4:47p 0.9'	4:37a 1.1'	4:57a 1.3'	5:40a 1.5'
	11:22p 0.3'	11:04p 0.6'	10:26a 0.6' / 9:51p 0.7'	1:18p 0.5'	3:29p 0.2'	5:07p 0.1'
7	**8**	**9**	**10**	**11**	**12** ○	**13**
6:39a 1.7'	7:46a 1.8'	8:54a 1.8'	9:58a 1.8'	10:53a 1.8'	11:40a 1.7'	12:22p 1.5'
6:25p -0.1'	7:32p -0.2'	8:28p -0.2'	9:14p -0.2'	9:48p -0.1'	10:09p 0.1'	10:17p 0.3'
14	**15**	**16**	**17**	**18**	**19**	**20**
1:02p 1.4'	1:45p 1.2'	4:18a 0.9' / 2:38p 1.0'	3:41a 1.0' / 3:56p 0.8'	3:40a 1.2'	3:57a 1.3'	4:29a 1.4'
10:08p 0.4'	9:45p 0.6'	8:35a 0.8' / 9:05p 0.7'	10:44a 0.7' / 7:57p 0.8'	12:27p 0.6'	2:11p 0.5'	3:54p 0.4'
21 ◐	**22**	**23**	**24**	**25**	**26**	**27**
5:16a 1.5'	6:16a 1.6'	7:21a 1.7'	8:25a 1.8'	9:26a 1.8'	10:24a 1.8'	11:23a 1.8'
5:15p 0.3'	6:17p 0.2'	7:08p 0.1'	7:50p 0.0'	8:27p 0.0'	9:00p 0.0'	9:29p 0.2'
28 ●	**29**	**30**	**31**			
12:28p 1.6'	1:43p 1.4'	2:32a 0.8' / 3:21p 1.2'	1:59a 1.1'			
9:49p 0.4'	9:48p 0.7'	7:43a 0.7' / 9:04p 0.9'	9:48a 0.5'			

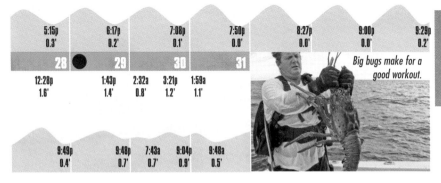

Big bugs make for a good workout.

	August 1	August 15	August 30
SUNRISE	6:07 a.m.	6:16 a.m.	6:24 a.m.
SUNSET	7:43 p.m.	7:31 p.m.	7:14 p.m.

Pensacola Station

Pensacola to Port St. Joe

Red Alert

INSHORE

The tail end of summer means last shots at southbound travelers such as tasty **tripletail**. Check channel markers and crabtrap buoys and toss a live or plastic shrimp, jig or fly from downtide. **Southern flounder** will grab a small finger mullet or mud minnow on a slowly worked jighead, or a fishfinder rig around points and jetties near passes. **Redfish** and **spotted seatrout** go on major feeds as bait schools start migrating south. They will bang a topwater, though jigs and plastic shrimp catch better numbers. **Scallop** season closes Sept. 11, so get in a last dive or two. Beachfront menhaden schools hold bull redfish, **sharks**, **king mackerel** and **tarpon**.

OFFSHORE

Because red snapper are off limits, bottom fishermen turn to **amberjacks** and **gag grouper**. Nothing beats a live bait over deep, high relief structure. Fish conventional gear, or plumb the depths with metal jigs and high-speed, heavy spinning tackle spooled with braided line. Structure also attracts **white marlin** and the occasional **blue**, along with **wahoo**, **tuna** and **dolphin**.

PENSACOLA

September Spotlight: REDFISH

The **redfish** recovery has been monumental, and nowhere has the resurgence of breeder size 20- to 40-pounders been more evident than in the Panhandle, where they once were netted to near extinction. Early fall water temps invigorate them to congregate in huge spawning masses. When schools are at peak numbers in passes, they actually turn surface waters orange. They are eager eaters, so jigs fished deep are candy, but fish pushing bait to the top will crush a topwater plug for unequaled thrills. Fish heavy tackle and de-barb your hook to help facilitate a quick release of that breeder.

September 2011

SUNDAY	MONDAY	TUESDAY	WEDNESDAY	THURSDAY	FRIDAY	SATURDAY

To find schooling reds, watch for diving birds.

1
2:13a 1.4'
11:36a 0.4'

2
2:52a 1.6'
1:27p 0.2'

3
3:46a 1.7'
3:19p 0.1'

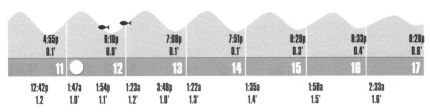

4
4:52a 1.8'
4:55p 0.1'

5
6:08a 1.8'
6:10p 0.0'

6
7:27a 1.8'
7:08p 0.1'

7
8:42a 1.8'
7:51p 0.1'

8
9:48a 1.7'
8:20p 0.3'

9
10:47a 1.6'
8:33p 0.4'

10
11:42a 1.4'
8:28p 0.6'

11
12:42p 1.2
8:03p 0.8'

12
1:47a 1.0'   1:54a 1.1'
7:26a 0.8'   7:19p 0.9'

13
1:23a 1.2'   3:48p 1.0'
8:49a 0.7'   5:53p 1.0'

14
1:22a 1.3'
9:52a 0.6'

15
1:35a 1.4'
10:51a 0.5'

16
1:58a 1.5'
11:58a 0.5'

17
2:33a 1.6'
1:24p 0.4'

18
3:19a 1.6'
3:03p 0.4'

19
4:16a 1.7'
4:23p 0.3'

20
5:20a 1.7'
5:21p 0.2'

21
6:29a 1.8'
6:06p 0.2'

22
7:41a 1.8'
7:43p 0.2'

23
8:55a 1.7'
7:15p 0.3'

24
10:15a 1.6'
7:40p 0.5'

25
11:46a 1.4'
7:49p 0.7'

26
12:57a 0.9'   1:35a 1.3'
6:04p 0.7'   7:25p 1.0'

27
12:07a 1.2'
7:48a 0.5'

28
12:07a 1.4'
9:11a 0.3'

29
12:34a 1.7'
10:32a 0.2'

30
1:17a 1.8'
12:00p 0.1'

PENSACOLA

	September 1	September 15	September 30
SUNRISE	6:25 a.m.	6:33 a.m.	6:42 a.m.
SUNSET	7:12 p.m.	6:54 p.m.	6:35 p.m.

Pensacola to Port St. Joe

Head South

INSHORE

Small **bluefish** and **Spanish mackerel** gather in bays and along beaches, and then begin the south-bound winter migration. This bait train fires up **king-fish**, **tarpon**, **spotted seatrout**, giant **redfish** and **gag grouper**. Pensacola Bay's deepest reaches sees increase in bull reds that surface to feed wherever bait is present. **Tripletail** make a hasty retreat for warmer waters south. **Flounder** pause in passes and oceanfront jetties to feed before midwinter spawning exodus.

OFFSHORE

Marlin, **tuna** and **wahoo** still available far to the south around deep dropoffs and oil rigs. Biggest **gag** and **scamp grouper** on Edge ledges in 180 to 240 feet. Big baitfish best for gags; delicious scamps prefer fresh squid. Bait schools fire up the beach bite for **tarpon** and **king mackerel**—freeline a live menhaden for sure hookups. Smoker kings are taken by anglers slow-trolling live ladyfish, mullet or Spanish mackerel; schoolies come on trolled spoons and cigar minnow-tipped duster rigs.

TIDE CORRECTIONS For Pensacola		
	High	Low
Port St. Joe, St. Joseph Bay	-0:24	-0:51
St. Andrew Bay		
Channel entrance	-1:31	-2:02
Panama City	-0:43	-0:44
Parker	-0:05	+0:22
Laird Bayou, East Bay	+0:26	+0:40
Farmdale, East Bay	+0:35	+0:55
Wetappo Creek, East Bay	+1:01	+1:40
Lynn Haven, North Bay	-0:06	+0:20
West Bay Creek, West Bay	+0:18	+1:23
Choctawhatchee Bay		
Destin, East Pass	-0:27	+1:20
Harris, The Narrows	+1:37	+2:51
Fishing Bend, Santa Rosa Sound	+0:41	+0:51
Pensacola Bay		
Pensacola Bay entrance	-1:23	-0:34
Warrington, 2 miles south of Pens.	-0:27	-0:30
Lora Point, Escambia Bay	+0:36	+1:03
East Bay	+0:44	+1:17
Bay Point, Blackwater River	+1:23	+1:23
Milton, Blackwater River	+1:40	+1:47

October Spotlight: POMPANO

The **pompano** run is on, and these fast-growing, southbound fish have eaten well all summer, so tend to be large. Pick your poison for taking a few: light spinning tackle is adequate for fish concentrated at beach troughs and runouts. Cast short nylon-skirted pompano jigs, tipped with bait or pure. For passive fishing, or when fish are a long cast out, long, beefy surf rods launch 3- to 5-ounce pyramid sinkers and multi-hook dropper rigs baited with sandfleas, shrimp or cut clam. If fishing from a boat, run the beach and watch for pompano skipping out in your wake. Then shut down, and cast jigs in the area.

October 2011

SUNDAY	MONDAY	TUESDAY	WEDNESDAY	THURSDAY	FRIDAY	SATURDAY

Primetime at the Russell-Fields Pier.

1
2:11a 1.9'
1:38p 0.1'

2
3:12a 2.0'
3:12p 0.1'

3
4:20a 1.9'
4:29p 0.1'

4
5:33a 1.8'
5:25p 0.1'

5
6:48a 1.7'
6:04p 0.3'

6
8:04a 1.5'
6:25p 0.4'

7
9:24a 1.3'
6:25p 0.6'

8
2:14a 10:53a 1.0' 1.2'
4:18a 6:00p 1.0' 0.8'

9
12:17a 12:44p 11:46p 1.1' 1.0' 1.2'
6:43a 5:03p 0.8' 0.9'

10
11:42p 1.4'
7:50a 0.6'

11
11:51p 1.5'
8:37a 0.5'

12
12:09a 1.6'
9:20a 0.4'

13
12:36a 1.7'
10:04a 0.3'

14
12:11a 1.7'
10:57a 0.3'

15
12:03p 0.2'

16
1:53a 1.8'
1:20p 0.2'

17
2:40a 1.8'
2:31p 0.1'

18
3:32a 1.8'
3:27p 0.1'

19
4:26a 1.7'
4:10p 0.1'

20
5:27a 1.7'
4:45p 0.2'

21
6:43a 1.5'
5:12p 0.3'

22
8:30a 1.3'
5:26p 0.5'

23
12:30a 10:52a 11:05a 0.9' 1.1' 1.1'
4:36p 5:13p 6:22a 0.9' 0.8' 0.6'

24
10:42p 1.3'
7:33a 0.3'

25
10:53p 1.6'
8:39a 0.0'

26
11:25p 1.8'
9:47a -0.1'

27
12:09a 1.9'
11:03a -0.2'

28
1:00a 2.0'
12:23p -0.2'

29

30
1:56a 2.0'
1:42p -0.2'

31
2:53a 1.9'
2:48p -0.1'

Please, do not attempt.

	October 1	October 15	October 30
SUNRISE	6:42 a.m.	6:51 a.m.	7:02 a.m.
SUNSET	6:34 p.m.	6:18 p.m.	6:03 p.m.

Pensacola to Port St. Joe

Flounder Found!

TIDE CORRECTIONS For Pensacola		
	High	Low
Port St. Joe, St. Joseph Bay	-0:24	-0:51
St. Andrew Bay		
Channel entrance	-1:31	-2:02
Panama City	-0:43	-0:44
Parker	-0:05	+0:22
Laird Bayou, East Bay	+0:26	+0:40
Farmdale, East Bay	+0:35	+0:55
Wetappo Creek, East Bay	+1:01	+1:40
Lynn Haven, North Bay	-0:06	+0:20
West Bay Creek, West Bay	+0:18	+1:23
Choctawhatchee Bay		
Destin, East Pass	-0:27	+1:20
Harris, The Narrows	+1:37	+2:51
Fishing Bend, Santa Rosa Sound	+0:41	+0:51
Pensacola Bay		
Pensacola Bay entrance	-1:23	-0:34
Warrington, 2 miles south of Pens.	-0:27	-0:30
Lora Point, Escambia Bay	+0:36	+1:03
East Bay	+0:44	+1:17
Bay Point, Blackwater River	+1:23	+1:23
Milton, Blackwater River	+1:40	+1:47

INSHORE

Though some inshore species have moved south, **sheepshead** are right at home in the cold, and they chill out around rock jetties and bridge and dock pilings to feast on oysters and barnacles. **Spotted seatrout** and **redfish** are heading into deep, warmer creekmouths and canals in preparation for frigid temperatures. **Flounder** are parked in passes, fattening up for the offshore spawn.

OFFSHORE

Tail end of **king mackerel** season here; they will "fuel up" well before steaming south to Florida Keys winter waters. Top method for a smoker is to slow-troll a live ladyfish, mullet or Spanish mackerel. **Amberjack** are stacked up on high-relief artificial reefs such as the Antares, Angelina B or Hathaway Spans, or give the massive Oriskany wreck a try. Prepare to hook AJs as big as 100 pounds. **Southern flounder** spawning on nearshore wrecks. Fish a big live bait on deep natural structure for **gag grouper**. **Wahoo** and **tuna** make trolling possible when seas cooperate.

November Spotlight: FLOUNDER

PENSACOLA

Southern flounder move out of Panhandle bays, and give their old digs to their smaller cousins, the Gulf flounder. As the water cools, Southern flatties gang up over bottom in the passes until real cold weather triggers them to travel south to Gulf nearshore wrecks to spawn. The same baits and rigs will take them in either locale. Bait up a fishfinder rig with a finger mullet or mud minnow, or lightly bounce bottom with a soft-plastic tail on a jighead. Fish slowly because ambushing flounder are not apt to chase down fast-moving prey. Be alert for the soft take of a flounder; it is akin to snagging a wet rag on bottom.

November 2011

SUNDAY	MONDAY	TUESDAY	WEDNESDAY	THURSDAY	FRIDAY	SATURDAY
		1 ◑	**2**	**3**	**4**	**5**
		3:49a 1.7'	4:40a 1.5'	5:27a 1.3'	6:11a 1.0' / 11:45p 1.0'	9:03a 0.8' / 10:42p 1.1'
		3:37p 0.0'	4:07p 0.1'	4:16p 0.3'	3:59p 0.5'	6:37a 0.8' / 3:02p 0.7'
6	**7**	**8**	**9** ○	**10**	**11**	**12**
8:24p 1.2'	8:26p 1.4'	8:41p 1.5'	9:05p 1.6'	9:36p 1.6'	10:13p 1.7'	10:53p 1.7'
5:13a 0.5'	5:45a 0.3'	6:17a 0.2'	6:52a 0.0'	7:33a 0.0'	8:22a -0.1'	9:18a -0.1'
13	**14**	**15**	**16**	**17** ◐	**18**	**19**
11:35p 1.7'	12:16a 1.7'	12:58a 1.6'	1:40a 1.5'	2:24a 1.2'	3:31a 0.9'	8:39p 0.8'
10:15a -0.2'	11:07a -0.2'	11:51a -0.2'	12:26p -0.2'	12:53p -0.1'	1:09p 0.1'	1:06p 0.4'
20	**21**	**22**	**23**	**24** ●	**25**	**26**
7:29a 0.6' / 7:42p 1.0'	7:33p 1.2'	7:52p 1.5'	8:28p 1.7'	9:14p 1.8'	10:06p 1.8'	10:59p 1.8'
3:19a 0.6' / 12:11p 0.6'	4:17a 0.2'	5:12a -0.1'	6:09a -0.3'	7:12a -0.5'	8:20 a -0.6'	9:28a -0.6'
27	**28**	**29**	**30**			
11:49p 1.7'	12:33a 1.6'	1:10a 1.3'				
10:31a -0.6'	11:22a -0.5'	11:59a -0.3'	12:18p -0.1'			

Pompano in the surf.

	November 1	November 15	November 30
SUNRISE	7:03 a.m.	6:15 a.m.	6:27 a.m.
SUNSET	6:01 p.m.	4:52 p.m.	4:48 p.m.

DST Ends Nov. 6

PENSACOLA

Pensacola to Port St. Joe

Sheep Freeze

TIDE CORRECTIONS
For Pensacola

	High	Low
Port St. Joe, St. Joseph Bay	-0:24	-0:51
St. Andrew Bay		
Channel entrance	-1:31	-2:02
Panama City	-0:43	-0:44
Parker	-0:05	+0:22
Laird Bayou, East Bay	+0:26	+0:40
Farmdale, East Bay	+0:35	+0:55
Wetappo Creek, East Bay	+1:01	+1:40
Lynn Haven, North Bay	-0:06	+0:20
West Bay Creek, West Bay	+0:18	+1:23
Choctawhatchee Bay		
Destin, East Pass	-0:27	+1:20
Harris, The Narrows	+1:37	+2:51
Fishing Bend, Santa Rosa Sound	+0:41	+0:51
Pensacola Bay		
Pensacola Bay entrance	-1:23	-0:34
Warrington, 2 miles south of Pens.	-0:27	-0:30
Lora Point, Escambia Bay	+0:36	+1:03
East Bay	+0:44	+1:17
Bay Point, Blackwater River	+1:23	+1:40
Milton, Blackwater River	+1:40	+1:47

INSHORE

Sheepshead are the main draw for inshore anglers in all of their usual haunts. **Spotted seatrout** and **redfish** are hunkered in winter holes in canals and rivers. Live baits or plastics must be presented slow and deep for hookups. If December has been on the mild side, a few **flounder** may remain in passes where over-slot bull redfish continue to congregate.

OFFSHORE

You'll do well to wait for weather breaks to head for the 29-Fathom Edge for a **gag grouper**. Though big live baitfish are tops, frozen Boston mackerel, sardines or bonito can entice these grouper in cold water. From that point south, big-boaters running to the oil troll for **wahoo** and **tuna**. Closer in, **black sea bass** and **southern flounder** and small grouper are mainstays on the wrecks and reefs in 60 to 90 feet.

December Spotlight: SHEEPSHEAD

Spiny, bait-stealing, wary, but delicious **sheepshead** hang around for the winter credits in the Panhandle. Fish of all sizes congregate around natural and manmade hard-surface structure such as jetty rocks, seawalls, docks and bridge pilings. The key is a good covering of oysters or barnacles. Arm yourself with a sensitive graphite rod, braided line, short leader and a small but strong hook sized right for either a live fiddler crab, oyster meat or shrimp, and lower it down with the lightest weight possible. Some anglers swear by earthworms for bait! Chumming with crushed shellfish brings the fish to you, with their guard a bit down.

December 2011

SUNDAY	MONDAY	TUESDAY	WEDNESDAY	THURSDAY	FRIDAY	SATURDAY

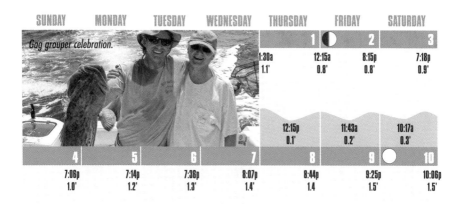

Gag grouper celebration.

1 ◑
1:30a 1.1'
12:15p 0.1'

2
12:15a 0.8'
11:43a 0.2'

3
8:15p 0.8'
10:17a 0.3'

4
7:18p 0.9'
7:06p 1.0'

4	**5**	**6**	**7**	**8**	**9**	**10** ○
7:06p 1.0'	7:14p 1.2'	7:36p 1.3'	8:07p 1.4'	8:44p 1.4	9:25p 1.5'	10:06p 1.5'
5:29a 0.2'	5:23a 0.0'	5:47a -0.2'	6:22a -0.3'	7:04a -0.4'	7:51a -0.4'	8:40a -0.5'
11	**12**	**13**	**14**	**15**	**16**	**17**
10:45p 1.5'	11:23p 1.5'	12:00a 1.4'	12:36a 1.2'	1:11a 0.9'	1:27a 0.6'	6:51p 0.6'
9:24a -0.6'	10:03a -0.6'	10:35a -0.6'	11:01a -0.5'	11:19a -0.3'	11:23a -0.1'	11:00a 0.1'
18 ◐	**19**	**20**	**21**	**22**	**23** ●	**24**
6:12p 0.8'	6:18p 1.0'	6:48p 1.3'	7:32p 1.4'	8:24p 1.5'	9:18p 1.6'	10:10p 1.6'
9:07a 0.2'	3:53a -0.1'	4:42a -0.4'	5:39a -0.6'	6:40a -0.7'	7:42a -0.8'	8:40a -0.9'
25	**26**	**27**	**28**	**29**	**30**	**31**
10:58p 1.5'	11:39p 1.3'	12:12a 1.1'	12:35a 0.8'	12:21a 0.5'	6:23p 0.5'	5:34p 0.6'
9:30a -0.8'	10:09a -0.7'	10:35a -0.5'	10:44a -0.4'	10:32a -0.2'	9:54a 0.0'	8:35a 0.1'

	December 1	December 15	December 30
SUNRISE	6:28 a.m.	6:38 a.m.	6:45 a.m.
SUNSET	4:48 p.m.	4:50 p.m.	4:58 p.m.

PENSACOLA

Special Tips for Fishing Florida's Tides

By Vic Dunaway, Senior Editor
Florida Sportsman Magazine

Nothing affects the movements and feeding habits of inshore fish more than the tide. To be consistently successful an angler must learn where fish are most likely to be under specific conditions of depth and current.

First, be aware that the influence of tides seldom if ever bears any direct relationship to a particular species but only to the manner in which hungry fish respond to changes in their environment—mostly changes in depth and water flow. True, you sometimes hear local experts make such statements as, "Trout should be fished on high water," or "Falling tide is the best time to go after snook." The advice is valid—but only under particular circumstances.

For instance, all over Florida a common approach to fishing for

This angler is scanning the crown of a tidal flat on high water. Opposite, trout taken from a flooded shoreline.

spotted seatrout is to drift over fairly shallow grassflats while casting or trailing natural baits behind the boat. Such fishing is far more likely to produce on higher phases of the tide, from an hour or so past dead low to shortly beyond peak high. As to the falling-tide-for-snook "rule," it is deeply ingrained in the Florida angling conscience simply because so much of our snook fishing is done in coastal streams and in passes, where fast-falling water creates outstanding feeding conditions.

In nearly all circumstances, fish movements are determined by what the tide is doing. Usually, as noted, they like to seek out spots where tidal currents help supply them with food, but sometimes fish are present for no more complicated a reason

Mouths of cuts, canals and creeks are at their best during a falling tide.

than just having enough water to get around in, and to forage.

The mouths of cuts, canals and creeks are almost always at their best during falling tide. They constitute natural feeding stations where hungry but lazy game species need only wait for supper to wash their way.

In mangrove country, another factor joins in to make falling tide the preferred time for fishing streams and other "inside" areas. On high water—especially during spring tides—snook and other fish may be hanging far back under the branches, unreachable by the angler's lures.

Those same falling-tide guidelines apply in large bays. Channels or potholes surrounded by great areas of flats should receive more attention during low tide phases, from late in the ebb to early in the rise. Dropping water chases fish out of the shallows and into the deeper runs, holes and channels.

Shallow flats themselves, obviously, are likely to produce better when the water is higher.

Both bonefish and shallow-feeding redfish are extremely sensitive to tidal movements but in many areas can be found on any tide if you vary your search pattern accordingly. Try looking for them on the outer edges of shallow flats—or even just outside the flats—on late falling or early rising tides. As the water continues to come in, the fish move higher on the flats. At high water they might be anywhere on the flat, but are most likely to be found along the shoreline or in stretches where the flat "humps" and becomes even shallower than the surrounding water.

Wading is the way to go when accessing the skinniest water for spooky gamefish.

But you don't have to be a sight-fisherman to profit by the suggestions in the preceding paragraph. The very same advice holds true for anglers who plug for redfish and snook. Since the ebb is the preferred tide for inside waters, you'd expect the rising tide to be most attractive on the outside, or in large open bays. And indeed it is.

You can start your outside fishing at slack low tide by working along channel edges or the dropoffs of oyster bars. As rising water permits, you work higher onto the bars or adjacent flats.

Anglers casting from a bridge fare best when retrieving lures with the current in a natural manner.

Bridge fishing for predatory fish— snook, tarpon, trout and ladyfish, for instance—always seems to benefit from a strong current, but on many spans it matters little whether the current is flowing in or out. Snook, tarpon and compatriots like to lie just upcurrent of the bridge and wait for a snack. Of course, some bridges do seem to produce more action when the tide is flowing in one direction and not the other, so it always pays to pick up whatever local advice you can.

Inlets (Atlantic Coast) and passes (Gulf Coast) also tend to turn up action of some sort when the tide is running fast, no matter whether it's coming in or going out.

There are some situations, too, in which anglers prefer slack tides.

Along the Atlantic Coast, tidal currents cause rips along reef edges and over wrecks.

Bottom fishermen around bridges and in wide channels like still water because it lets them present their baits easily, especially live baits.

Although some anglers firmly believe that tides have an effect on deepwater fishing too, there is no consensus. Along the Atlantic Coast, tidal currents cause rips along reef edges and over wrecks and artificial reefs. The rips can be beneficial to trollers and drifters. Bottom fishermen, on the other hand, will try to hit times of slower current.

Of course, inshore anglers benefit from the experience they compile over extended periods of fishing their favorite spots at different stages of the tide (and moon).

But even without such experience, and even in strange country, the observant coastal fisherman can always use current tide conditions to help him pick out the most likely places to toss his bait.

Here's How Florida's Tides Work

By Ed Johanson

Ask successful Florida saltwater anglers what's the most important thing working for them and most will say, "Understanding the tides."

Talk to some of the old timers who consistently bring in more fish than everyone else and you'll find that they know *when* to fish, as well as where to fish and how to fish. The *when* to fish depends almost completely on knowing the tides.

The tides are caused by the gravitational attraction of the earth's waters by the moon and the sun. Just like small iron filings are attracted to a magnet, the earth's waters are attracted to the sun and the moon. The complicating factor is that the sun, moon and earth are constantly moving with regard to each other so the tides are constantly changing. However, since the movement of the earth, moon and sun are highly predictable, so too are the tides predictable.

Furthermore, since the movements of the earth, moon and sun only change slightly, from year to year, the annual changes in the tide are very slight. That means, if you make the effort this year to understand the tides, you will be able to use that knowledge every year in the future.

Learning a few tide terms will help to take the mystery out of any material you may read describing the tides.

TIDE STAGE

This is simply a description of what the tide is doing at a particular time. Low tide is the minimum water depth for a particular cycle. At low tide, the water is not moving at all. As it begins to move and depth begins to increase, the tide is rising, flooding or incoming. These three all mean the same thing.

Roughly six hours later, when the water has gotten as deep as it is going to get, high tide occurs. The brief period when there is no discernible

For stealthy presentations, boating anglers without push poles often bail out to wade.

TIDE HEIGHT

This is the vertical distance the water rises, or falls, due to the tide. Tide height in the tide tables that follow is given in feet and tenths of feet. If, for instance, tide height is predicted at 3.2 it means the water depth will be 3.2 feet above the reference plane used to construct the navigation charts used in that area. Most charts were developed using the "mean low water" reference plane, or datum, defined as the average of all low tides. A predicted tide height of 3.2 feet means the water will be 3.2 feet higher than the depth indicated on the chart. However, since the reference plane is an average, some low tides will be lower (or higher) than the reference plane; the actual depth may be somewhat less, or more, than the charted depth.

This dock has been covered by a spring tide high.

water movement is called slack tide. Slack refers to both the high and low tides. Once the tide has topped out and depth begins to decrease, the tide is falling, ebbing or outgoing.

TIDAL RANGE

The range is the difference between a high tide and a low tide. If a low tide is predicted at -0.1 feet and six hours later the high tide is predicted to be 2.2 feet, the tidal range will be 2.3 feet—the difference between -.1 and 2.2. Since fish feeding often is dependent on bait being swept along in the moving water caused by a tide change, the bigger the range the better the fishing—usually. So if you are looking at a tide table, don't just look at when high and low tide occur, look at the two tide heights and determine

the range. This will tell you how much water will be moving during the course of that tide change. If the range is large, a lot of water will move and depths will change rapidly. If the range is small, change in depth may not be nearly as rapid or as evident.

CURRENT

This is the speed of the water as it moves from high to low, or vice versa. In general, maximum current occurs about halfway through both the incoming and the outgoing tides, and for an hour or two on either side of this mid-point, depending on the tide range. Currents diminish toward

Actual tides may not be as predicted due to meteorlogical conditions.

the full high or full low slack periods.

Current doesn't always follow the tide, either. The best example of this is perhaps in the Florida Keys, where often as the tide begins rising on the Atlantic side, the current is moving out of Florida Bay—an incoming tide with an outgoing current. The relationship between current and tide is not always easy to understand. Other times it is clear and simple. It all depends on the area.

SPRING TIDES

In general, when the moon and the sun are in line with the earth, the tides are strong. These are called spring tides, and the term has nothing to do with the season of the year. Florida anglers have spring tides twice a month, when the sun and moon are aligned—during the full moon and the new moon.

NEAP TIDES

When the moon and the sun are at 90 degrees to each other, the tides are weak. These are the neap (pronounced nip) tides. These also occur every two weeks, on the first-quarter and last-quarter moons.

The question of time deserves some consideration as well. While clocks and calendars tell us a day is 24 hours long, a week seven days, and a month 28, 30, or 31 days long, a tidal day is 24 hours and 50 minutes long and the period during which the moon goes through all of its phases is 29.5 days long. Anglers quickly learn to "round off" these changes by assuming that each day the tide is "about an hour later" (actually 50 minutes). Another "round off" is to assume that quarter-moon tides come a week after spring tides. It's actually 7.4 days but a week

is close enough to predict, weekend to weekend, what to expect.

Though tides are primarily affected by the location of the moon and sun, the shape of the basin in which the tide takes place also affects them. It's one thing when the basin is the Atlantic Ocean and quite another when the basin is the relatively small, shallow Gulf of Mexico.

Since Florida coastlines front on both of these basins, it stands to reason that the tides will be different on each coast—and they are indeed! In fact, Florida is perhaps the only state in the nation that has long coastlines enjoying all three tide types—semidiurnal (twice daily), diurnal (daily) and mixed.

Semidiurnal simply means that there are two high and two low tides each 24 hours and 50 minutes (called a tidal day), with both highs about the same height and both lows about the same height. Mixed tides are tides that deliver two highs and two lows in a tidal day, but the two highs and/or the two lows may be at significantly different heights. Finally, diurnal tides have one high and one low during a tidal day.

Particularities of each tidal region are discussed in the introduction to the tide tables for each region.

All of the material discussed thus far relates to the astronomical tides, that is, the tides that are predicted to occur due to the gravitational attraction of the earth's waters by the moon and the sun. The actual tides, however, may be somewhat different from the predicted tides, due to meteorological conditions. Another part of this *Fishing Planner* discusses the effects of barometric pressure on the tides and shows that it is not uncommon to expect six-inch fluctuations in the tide as the barometric pressure changes. The tides are higher when the barometric pressure is low, and vice versa.

A more important factor affecting the tides is the wind. As the wind blows it "pushes" the water in the direction the wind is blowing. The wind affects the rise and fall of the tide by retarding, or increasing, the tidal currents.

The magnitude of the wind's effect on the tide is determined by the direction, strength and the amount of time it blows. A brisk wind of 20-30 knots may not seem to have any effect on the tide for a couple of hours, but let it blow for a half day or more and the tide times will be quite different from those predicted. If you are fishing along the lower Gulf Coast and the wind is blowing from the east (offshore), the effect is to blow water out of the back-country and bays, into the Gulf. This causes extremely low tides and may hold back the incoming high tide, making it smaller and later than predicted.

The opposite effect occurs with an onshore wind. The wind tends to "pile up" water along the shore, making the tide higher than predicted. It also retards the outgoing tidal current to the point where the low tide may not be very low at all. Thus the angler must balance the tide predictions in the tables against the weather—wind and barometer—in order to fine-tune a reasonable set of expectations for the tide on a particular fishing day.

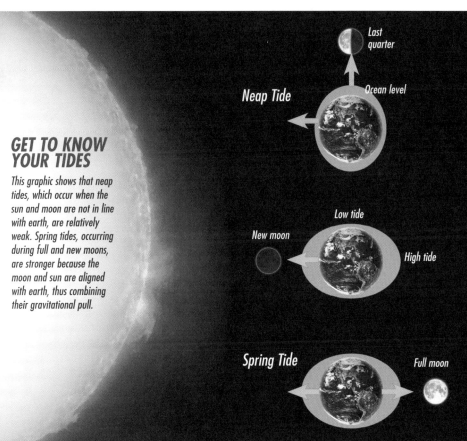

GET TO KNOW YOUR TIDES

This graphic shows that neap tides, which occur when the sun and moon are not in line with earth, are relatively weak. Spring tides, occurring during full and new moons, are stronger because the moon and sun are aligned with earth, thus combining their gravitational pull.

Neap Tide

Last quarter

Ocean level

New moon

Low tide

High tide

Spring Tide

Full moon

Barometric Pressure Affects Your Fishing:

Here's Why

There is little doubt that barometric pressure affects fishing even though facts are few and often difficult to separate from fable.

Barometric pressure is simply the force that the atmosphere exerts on the earth and its waters. Air has weight, and the more it weighs the harder it pushes down on the earth.

Low pressure occurs when the air weighs less, high pressure when it weighs more. Masses of air, varying in weight, pass overhead causing the air pressure to vary. In the winter, weather changes move through Florida approximately every six days and in the summer, about every 13 days. These fronts cause the barometric pressure to change considerably.

Meteorologists don't talk in terms of the average pressure at sea level, they define the normal atmosphere as that capable of supporting a column of mercury 29.91 inches high, at 0 degrees centigrade.

Barometric pressure is measured by the height of a column of mercury in a one-square-inch tube from which all the air has been removed. Typical ranges for barometric pressure in Florida are from 29.9 inches to 30.3 inches of mercury. Extreme pressure changes may accompany summer and winter storms. For instance, in November 1988 "Keith" caused the pressure at Ft. Myers to drop to 29.48 inches: In January 1989 the pressure rose to an extreme of 30.63 inches.

Cold front cometh! Some anglers believe in the "falling barometer" bite. Inset, red sky night, sailor's delight.

Another common method of measuring pressure is the standard atmosphere, or bar, which is of course equal to 1,000 millibars (mb). Thus one atmosphere is equal to 1,013.3 millibars.

Radio, TV and NOAA weather stations all talk about the pressure in inches of mercury. Newspapers, on the other hand, often show a weather map with isobars of pressure, in millibars (these are lines of equal pressure). Typical variances on the charts are 1,015 mb, 1,025 mb, etc.

It's pretty clear when the NOAA weather radio says that the barometer is 29.89 inches and rising, you better run for your boat and get on the water. But if you want to glean the same information from a weather map in the newspaper, you'll need to know how to read and interpret it.

It's not enough to know the barometric pressure is 1,015 millibars. You have to note what direction the weather is moving, and how fast, to know what the change will be like.

If the isobars of pressure only show a small change over a large distance, this means that the air mass is stable and the weather will not be changing much. If the isobars are closely spaced over a short distance, this means the barometric pressure is changing rapidly. When you see large bands of isobars close together, this defines a front, which is the interface between high pressure and low pressure areas.

It's commonly accepted that fish feed best when barometric pressure is changing.

Fronts mean changing weather, or unstable air masses. Fishing just prior to, or just after the passing of a front, usually means a rapidly changing barometer and often can mean windy weather. When reading the weather map, note whether the weather moving toward you contains higher or lower isobars of barometric pressure, in millibars. If higher, the weather is associated with a high pressure area; if lower, a low pressure area. If the lines are far apart, this means the weather will remain the same for a while.

But what does all this have to do with fishing? Pressure changes affect the tides and seem to affect the feeding habits of fish as well.

Since a high tide must lift the air pressing down on the water, and a falling tide is "helped" by the weight of the air pressing down on the water, the tide height is indeed affected by barometric pressure.

Simply stated, high tides are not as high as predicted, and low tides are lower than predicted, when the barometric pressure is high. On the other hand, when the barometric pressure is low, both high and low tides are high-er than predicted. Just remember, the high tide must rise against the weight of the air above it, just as the low tide is pushed down by the air.

The effect of air pressure on tide height can be predicted, based on the height of the mercury in the barometer. Mercury is 13 times as heavy as water, thus the change in height of a column of water would be 13 times greater than the change in the column of mercury in the mercury barometer.

Typical changes in barometric pressure in Florida are from 29.9 inches to 30.3 inches of mercury, or a range of 0.4 inches. The equivalent change in a column of water (like the tide) would be 13 times as great, or about 5.2 inches. In an extreme case like the 30.63 inches of mercury, the tide might be lowered by about nine inches below the predicted tide. When "Keith" dropped the barometric pressure to 29.48 inches of mercury, the tide would have been about 11 inches above normal. Obviously, that can be significant. Thus barometric pressure changes normally might change the predicted tides by about six inches, and the change might reach nine to 12 inches during extreme conditions. Six inches lower might not seem like much, unless you are in the backcountry at low tide and only have six inches of water to start with!

Barometric pressure also seems to affect fish feeding habits. While little actual data is available, it is commonly accepted lore that fish feed well when the barometer is rising and poorly when it is falling. There also seems to be some documentation indicating that the fishing is poor when the barometer is very high or very low.

The late Captain Andy McLean, in his publication, *Fishing Mate*, related the behavior of a snook in a 50-gallon tank during pressure variations. He found that the snook fed best when the pressure was between 29.7 and 30 inches, and rising. The feeding was "good" when the pressure was 30.0 to 30.1 and steady, and "bad" when between 30.0 and 29.7, and falling.

My own experience seems to track Captain Andy's, except that I have caught fish on a falling barometer as well. My best fishing has occurred a day or two after the passing of a low pressure front, when the barometer is rising.

If there is an answer, it seems to be change. Fish seem to feed best when the tide is changing, when a stream comes in and changes the salinity slightly, when the barometer is changing, when dawn or dusk is changing the light intensity. There are no absolute answers to why fish bite, but the when seems closely related to changing environmental conditions.

The Pressure is On

HIGH PRESSURE
Typical Weather: Clear skies
Fishing Trends: Fish slow down, find cover or go to deeper waters

RISING PRESSURE
Typical Weather: Clearing or improving
Fishing Trends: Fish tend to become slightly more active

STABLE PRESSURE
Typical Weather: Fair
Fishing Trends: Normal fishing

FALLING PRESSURE
Typical Weather: Degrading
Fishing Trends: Most active fishing

SLIGHTLY LOWER PRESSURE
Typical Weather: Usually cloudy
Fishing Trends: Fish head away from cover and seek shallower waters.

LOW PRESSURE
Typical Weather: Rainy and stormy
Fishing Trends: Fish will tend to become less active the longer this period remains.

The barometer affects tide height, but effects on deep species aren't clear.

State Size and Bag Limits

The regulations and bag limits at right apply to state waters, out to three miles on the east coast and nine miles on the west coast. While these laws were correct at publication, changes do occur—you are responsible for knowing the current laws. Total-length fish are now required to be measured with tail lobes pinched together. Be alert for changes by reading *Florida Sportsman*. Updates are available from the Florida Fish and Wildlife Conservation Commission, (850) 487-0554, www.myFWC.com. Federal laws may vary, and these are different for Atlantic and Gulf waters. Federal regs are available from the South Atlantic Fishery Management Council, (843) 571-4366, www.safmc.net; Gulf of Mexico Fishery Management Council, (813) 228-2815, www.gulfcouncil.org.

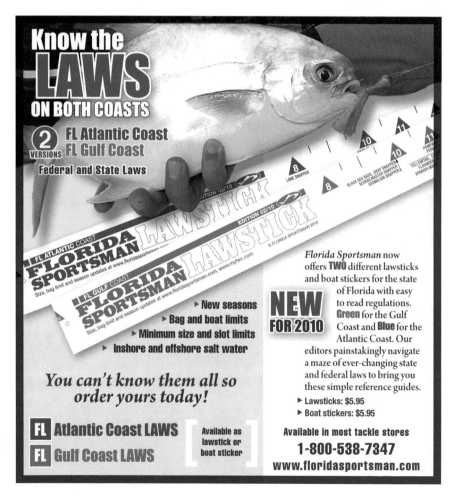

	Min./Max.Size	Fork or Total Length	Bag
Amberjack, Greater	28" Atl./30" Gulf min.	F	1
Amberjack, Lesser & Banded Rudderfish	14"– 22"	F	5 (aggregate)
Bluefish	12" min.	F	10
Bonefish*	18" min.	T	1
Cobia	33" min.	F	1(a)
Dolphin	20" min. Atlantic	F	10/angler, 60/boat (Atl. only)
Drum, Black	14"– 24" (b)	T	5
Flounder	12" min.	T	10
Grouper, Red (C)	20" min.(c)	T	Gulf 2, Atl. 3 (c)
Grouper, Black & Gag*, Atlantic and Monroe County	24" min.	T	1 (c)
Grouper, Black & Gag*, Gulf	22" min.	T	Black 4, Gag 2 (c)
Hogfish	12" min.	F	5
Mackerel, King	24" min.	F	2
Mackerel, Spanish	12" min.	F	15
Mullet	—	—	50/boat
Permit	11"-20" (d)	F	6 (d)
Pompano, African	24" min.	F	2(d)
Pompano, Florida	11"-20" (d)	F	6 (d)
Porgy, Red (Atl. only)	14" min.	T	3
Redfish	18"– 27"	T	1
Sailfish	63" min.	F (e)	1
Sea Bass	12" Atlantic/10" Gulf	T	15 (Atl. only)
Seatrout, Spotted, South Region (f)	15"– 20" (f)	T	4
Seatrout, Spotted, NE & NW Regions (f)	15"– 20" (f)	T	5
Shad	—	—	10
Shark	54"	F	1 (g)
Sheepshead	12" min.	T	15
Snapper: Cubera	12"-30"	T	10 (h)
Snapper: Gray (Mangrove)	10" min.	T	5 (h)
Snapper: Lane	8" min.	T	10 (h)
Snapper: Mutton	16" min.	T	10 (h)
Snapper: Vermilion (h)	12" Atlantic/10" Gulf	T	5 Atl. (h)/20 Gulf
Snapper: Queen, Blackfin, Dog, Mahogany, Silk, Yellowtail	12" min.	T	10 (h)
Snapper: Red (Gulf) (h)*	16" min.	T	2 (h)
Snapper: Red (Atl.) (h)*	20" min.	T	2 (h)*
Snapper: Schoolmaster	10" min.	T	10 (h)
Snook (i)*	28"– 32"(Atl.) 28"– 33"(Gulf, Monroe, ENP)	T	1
Tarpon	—	—	2 (j)
Triggerfish, Gray	12" min.	F	—
Tripletail	15" min.	T	2
Weakfish	12" min.	T	4

(a) No more than 6 per boat.
(b) One in bag may be over max.
(c) For other grouper species, see www.myfwc.com. Most Gulf grouper species closed Feb. through March; federal Atl. closed January through April.
(d) Permit and pompano, 6-fish aggregate, 11"-20". One may be over 20". African pompano, 2 per day per person or vessel, whichever is less.
(e) Lower jaw fork length.
(f) South Region closed Nov. - Dec.; Northwest and Northeast regions closed Feb. Bag may include one over max.
(g) One per person or 2 per boat, whichever is less.
(h) Aggregate limit of snapper is 10 per day. Check www.myfwc.com for closed snapper seasons.
(i) Closed season Dec. 15 - Jan. 31, June - Aug. Atlantic; Dec. - Feb., May - Aug. Gulf, Monroe County, Everglades Nat. Park. Pinch tail lobes when measuring. Snatch hooks and spearing prohibited.
(j) Tag required to kill tarpon.
NO POSSESSION: Goliath grouper, Nassau grouper, sawsharks, sawfish, basking sharks, whale sharks and spotted eagle rays.
Tunas, Marlin, Swordfish: Call 1-800-894-5528. • Anglers must use circle hooks, dehooking devices and venting tools for Gulf reef species.
* Changes pending as of publication.

Prime-Timer Tables for 2011

What about the solar-lunar tables on which our Prime-Timer is based? These tables seem to have originated in the 19th century, as an aid to navigation into coastal ports. Each port had documented the amount of time after the moon passed overhead until the next high tide, as an aid to ships entering ports. Somehow this practice of noting the time of transit of the moon over a specific location (longitude) expanded into a set of tables that purport to document when the fishing (and hunting) will be best. The tables define two major periods and two mi-

Don't plan jack trips around the sun and moon. They seem to eat all the time!

nor periods every 24 hours (actually every 24 hours and 50 minutes since that is the time day-to-day when the moon is directly overhead).

The major periods are the times when the moon is "over" and when the moon is "under" and the minor periods are when the moon is on either horizon. This is an obvious attempt to re-

late fishing and hunting to the astronomical forces that cause the tides, though some anglers still feel that there is some unknown force that the moon exerts on fish, fauna, friend and foe.

At the risk of offending a large number of anglers, there seems to be no correlation between the times in the solar-lunar tables and the feeding habits of saltwater fish. Successful coastal fishing is directly related to the tides, but the tides occur at different times around the peninsula of Florida. The "Moon Over Miami" will be over St. Marks about 16 minutes later, but it takes the high tide four or five hours to get there.

Some solar-lunar advocates think atmospheric tides are important. Atmospheric tides are changes in barometric pressure caused by the sun and the moon's gravitational attraction for the molecules of air, whereas ocean tides are caused by the gravitational attraction of molecules of water in the ocean. The solar-lunar advocates reason that, since fish bite better when the barometric pressure is changing, the atmospheric tides cause the pressure to change and that makes the fish bite. Measurements of the barometric pressure change due to atmospheric tides indicate that they are on the order of 0.003 inches of mercury, which would cause a corresponding change of water height of less than $1/32$ of an inch. Normal pressure fluctuations in the atmosphere are frequently much larger than this, and ripples on the water would cause the fish to feel pressure changes greater than those caused by the atmospheric tides.

Solar-lunar influences on hunting and fishing may be forever debated. But there's no debate about tides.

JANUARY 2011

	Rise	Over	Set	Under
1	4:50 a.m.	10:08 a.m.	3:25 p.m.	10:37 p.m.
2	5:49 a.m.	11:05 a.m.	4:21 p.m.	11:32 p.m.
3	6:42 a.m.	12:01 p.m.	5:19 p.m.	—
● 4	7:30 a.m.	12:54 p.m.	6:18 p.m.	12:25 a.m.
5	8:12 a.m.	1:44 p.m.	7:16 p.m.	1:15 a.m.
6	8:49 a.m.	2:30 p.m.	8:11 p.m.	1:53 a.m.
7	9:23 a.m.	3:14 p.m.	9:05 p.m.	2:47 a.m.
8	9:54 a.m.	3:56 p.m.	9:57 p.m.	3:30 a.m.
9	10:23 a.m.	4:35 p.m.	10:48 p.m.	4:10 a.m.
10	10:53 a.m.	5:46 p.m.	11:40 p.m.	4:51 a.m.
11	11:24 a.m.	6:08 p.m.	—	5:21 a.m.
◑ 12	11:56 a.m.	6:41 p.m.	12:32 a.m.	6:14 a.m.
13	12:32 p.m.	7:27 p.m.	1:26 a.m.	6:59 a.m.
14	1:13 p.m.	8:16 p.m.	2:22 a.m.	7:48 a.m.
15	2:00 p.m.	9:09 p.m.	3:19 a.m.	8:40 a.m.
16	2:53 p.m.	10:04 p.m.	4:18 a.m.	9:36 a.m.
17	3:53 p.m.	11:01 p.m.	5:15 a.m.	10:34 a.m.
18	4:57 p.m.	11:59 p.m.	6:09 a.m.	11:33 a.m.
○ 19	6:04 p.m.	—	7:00 a.m.	12:32 p.m.
20	7:12 p.m.	12:54 a.m.	7:45 a.m.	1:34 p.m.
21	8:19 p.m.	1:50 a.m.	8:27 a.m.	2:23 p.m.
22	9:25 p.m.	2:43 a.m.	9:07 a.m.	3:26 p.m.
23	10:30 p.m.	3:35 a.m.	9:45 a.m.	4:08 p.m.
24	11:34 p.m.	4:26 a.m.	10:23 a.m.	4:59 p.m.
25	—	5:18 a.m.	11:02 a.m.	5:51 p.m.
◐ 26	12:39 a.m.	6:12 a.m.	11:45 a.m.	6:43 p.m.
27	1:42 a.m.	7:07 a.m.	12:31 p.m.	7:38 p.m.
28	2:44 a.m.	8:03 a.m.	1:21 p.m.	8:32 p.m.
29	3:43 a.m.	8:59 a.m.	2:15 p.m.	9:26 p.m.
30	4:37 a.m.	9:55 a.m.	3:12 p.m.	10:19 p.m.
31	5:26 a.m.	10:48 a.m.	4:09 p.m.	11:09 p.m.

FEBRUARY 2011

	Rise	Over	Set	Under
1	6:09 a.m.	11:38 a.m.	5:07 p.m.	11:57 p.m.
2	6:48 a.m.	12:25 p.m.	6:02 p.m.	—
● 3	7:23 a.m.	1:10 p.m.	6:57 p.m.	12:42 a.m.
4	7:54 a.m.	1:52 p.m.	7:49 p.m.	1:26 a.m.
5	8:25 a.m.	2:33 p.m.	8:41 p.m.	2:07 a.m.
6	8:54 a.m.	3:13 p.m.	9:32 p.m.	2:48 a.m.
7	9:25 a.m.	3:54 p.m.	10:24 p.m.	3:28 a.m.
8	9:56 a.m.	4:37 p.m.	11:17 p.m.	4:10 a.m.
9	10:30 a.m.	5:20 p.m.	—	4:54 a.m.
10	11:08 a.m.	6:07 p.m.	12:11 a.m.	5:39 a.m.
◑ 11	11:51 a.m.	6:57 p.m.	1:06 a.m.	6:29 a.m.
12	12:40 p.m.	7:49 p.m.	2:03 a.m.	7:22 a.m.
13	1:35 p.m.	8:45 p.m.	2:59 a.m.	8:17 a.m.
14	2:35 p.m.	9:40 p.m.	3:54 a.m.	9:15 a.m.
15	3:40 p.m.	10:37 p.m.	4:45 a.m.	10:12 a.m.
16	4:48 p.m.	11:33 p.m.	5:33 a.m.	11:11 a.m.
17	5:56 p.m.	—	6:17 a.m.	12:07 p.m.
○ 18	7:04 p.m.	12:28 a.m.	6:59 a.m.	1:02 p.m.
19	8:12 p.m.	1:22 a.m.	7:39 a.m.	1:56 p.m.
20	9:19 p.m.	2:15 a.m.	8:18 a.m.	2:49 p.m.
21	10:26 p.m.	3:09 a.m.	8:59 a.m.	3:34 p.m.
22	11:32 p.m.	4:04 a.m.	9:42 a.m.	4:37 p.m.
23	—	5:00 a.m.	10:28 a.m.	5:33 p.m.
◐ 24	12:37 a.m.	5:58 a.m.	11:18 a.m.	6:28 p.m.
25	1:38 a.m.	6:55 a.m.	12:12 p.m.	7:23 p.m.
26	2:34 a.m.	7:51 a.m.	1:08 p.m.	8:16 p.m.
27	3:24 a.m.	8:45 a.m.	2:05 p.m.	9:07 p.m.
28	4:09 a.m.	9:35 a.m.	3:01 p.m.	9:55 p.m.

MARCH 2011

	Rise	Over	Set	Under
1	4:48 a.m.	10:23 a.m.	3:57 p.m.	10:41 p.m.
2	5:24 a.m.	11:09 a.m.	4:51 p.m.	11:24 p.m.
3	5:56 a.m.	11:50 a.m.	5:44 p.m.	—
● 4	6:27 a.m.	12:32 p.m.	6:36 p.m.	12:06 a.m.
5	6:57 a.m.	1:12 p.m.	7:27 p.m.	12:47 a.m.
6	7:27 a.m.	1:53 p.m.	8:19 p.m.	1:27 a.m.
7	7:58 a.m.	2:35 p.m.	9:11 p.m.	2:09 a.m.
8	8:31 a.m.	3:18 p.m.	10:04 p.m.	2:51 a.m.
9	9:08 a.m.	4:04 p.m.	10:59 p.m.	3:36 a.m.
10	9:48 a.m.	4:51 p.m.	11:54 p.m.	4:23 a.m.
11	10:34 a.m.	5:42 p.m.	—	5:14 a.m.
◑ 12	11:24 a.m.	6:33 p.m.	12:49 a.m.	5:56 a.m.
13	1:21 p.m.	8:27 p.m.	2:42 a.m.	7:57 a.m.
14	2:22 p.m.	9:22 p.m.	3:33 a.m.	8:58 a.m.
15	3:26 p.m.	10:16 p.m.	4:21 a.m.	9:54 a.m.
16	4:32 p.m.	11:10 p.m.	5:06 a.m.	10:49 a.m.
17	5:39 p.m.	—	5:48 a.m.	11:44 a.m.
18	6:47 p.m.	12:05 a.m.	6:29 a.m.	12:38 p.m.
○ 19	7:55 p.m.	12:58 a.m.	7:09 a.m.	1:32 p.m.
20	9:04 p.m.	1:52 a.m.	7:50 a.m.	2:27 p.m.
21	10:13 p.m.	2:49 a.m.	8:33 a.m.	3:23 p.m.
22	11:21 p.m.	3:46 a.m.	9:19 a.m.	4:20 p.m.
23	—	4:45 a.m.	10:10 a.m.	5:18 p.m.
24	12:26 a.m.	5:45 a.m.	11:04 a.m.	6:15 p.m.
25	1:26 a.m.	6:39 a.m.	12:01 p.m.	7:10 p.m.
◐ 26	2:19 a.m.	7:39 a.m.	12:59 p.m.	8:03 p.m.
27	3:07 a.m.	8:32 a.m.	1:57 p.m.	8:53 p.m.
28	3:48 a.m.	9:21 a.m.	2:53 p.m.	9:39 p.m.
29	4:25 a.m.	10:06 a.m.	3:47 p.m.	10:23 p.m.
30	4:58 a.m.	10:49 a.m.	4:40 p.m.	11:05 p.m.
31	5:30 a.m.	11:31 a.m.	5:32 p.m.	11:46 p.m.

APRIL 2011

	Rise	Over	Set	Under
1	6:00 a.m.	12:12 p.m.	6:23 p.m.	—
2	6:30 a.m.	12:52 p.m.	7:14 p.m.	12:27 a.m.
● 3	7:01 a.m.	1:34 p.m.	8:06 p.m.	1:08 a.m.
4	7:33 a.m.	2:16 p.m.	8:59 p.m.	1:49 a.m.
5	8:09 a.m.	3:01 p.m.	9:54 p.m.	2:34 a.m.
6	8:48 a.m.	3:49 p.m.	10:49 p.m.	3:21 a.m.
7	9:32 a.m.	4:38 p.m.	11:43 p.m.	4:11 a.m.
8	10:21 a.m.	5:29 p.m.	—	5:02 a.m.
9	11:14 a.m.	6:21 p.m.	12:37 a.m.	5:56 a.m.
10	12:12 p.m.	7:14 p.m.	1:27 a.m.	6:49 a.m.
◑ 11	1:13 p.m.	8:06 p.m.	2:15 a.m.	7:44 a.m.
12	2:15 p.m.	8:58 p.m.	2:59 a.m.	8:52 a.m.
13	3:19 p.m.	9:50 p.m.	3:41 a.m.	9:30 a.m.
14	4:25 p.m.	10:43 p.m.	4:21 a.m.	10:23 a.m.
15	5:31 p.m.	11:35 p.m.	5:00 a.m.	11:16 a.m.
16	6:39 p.m.	—	5:39 a.m.	12:09 p.m.
○ 17	7:48 p.m.	12:30 a.m.	6:21 a.m.	1:05 p.m.
18	8:57 p.m.	1:27 a.m.	7:06 a.m.	2:02 p.m.
19	10:06 p.m.	2:27 a.m.	7:56 a.m.	3:01 p.m.
20	11:10 p.m.	3:28 a.m.	8:50 a.m.	4:00 p.m.
21	—	4:29 a.m.	9:47 a.m.	4:57 p.m.
22	12:08 a.m.	5:28 a.m.	10:47 a.m.	5:54 p.m.
23	1:00 a.m.	6:24 a.m.	11:47 a.m.	6:46 p.m.
24	1:45 a.m.	7:15 a.m.	12:45 p.m.	7:35 p.m.
◐ 25	2:24 a.m.	8:03 a.m.	1:41 p.m.	8:20 p.m.
26	2:59 a.m.	8:47 a.m.	2:35 p.m.	9:03 p.m.
27	3:31 a.m.	9:29 a.m.	3:27 p.m.	9:45 p.m.
28	4:02 a.m.	10:10 a.m.	4:18 p.m.	10:25 p.m.
29	4:32 a.m.	10:51 a.m.	5:09 p.m.	11:05 p.m.
30	5:02 a.m.	11:32 a.m.	6:01 p.m.	11:47 p.m.

● First Quarter   ○ Full Moon   ◐ Last Quarter   ● New Moon

MAY 2011

	Rise	Over	Set	Under
1	11:33 p.m.	3:51 a.m.	9:05 a.m.	4:19 p.m.
2	—	4:47 a.m.	10:01 a.m.	5:11 p.m.
3	12:21 a.m.	5:40 a.m.	10:58 a.m.	6:01 p.m.
4	1:04 a.m.	6:29 a.m.	11:54 a.m.	6:48 p.m.
5	1:42 a.m.	7:15 a.m.	12:48 p.m.	7:32 p.m.
6	2:16 a.m.	7:59 a.m.	1:42 p.m.	8:15 p.m.
7	2:47 a.m.	8:41 a.m.	2:34 p.m.	8:55 p.m.
8	3:16 a.m.	9:21 a.m.	3:26 p.m.	9:36 p.m.
9	3:46 a.m.	10:02 a.m.	4:18 p.m.	10:17 p.m.
10	4:16 a.m.	10:45 a.m.	5:13 p.m.	11:01 p.m.
11	4:48 a.m.	11:28 a.m.	6:09 p.m.	11:47 p.m.
12	5:24 a.m.	12:16 p.m.	7:08 p.m.	—
13	6:05 a.m.	1:07 p.m.	8:09 p.m.	12:36 a.m.
14	6:51 a.m.	2:01 p.m.	9:12 p.m.	1:30 a.m.
15	7:45 a.m.	2:59 p.m.	10:12 p.m.	2:29 a.m.
16	8:45 a.m.	3:57 p.m.	11:09 p.m.	3:29 a.m.
17	9:49 a.m.	4:55 p.m.	—	4:29 a.m.
18	10:55 a.m.	5:50 p.m.	12:01 a.m.	5:28 a.m.
19	12:00 a.m.	6:43 p.m.	12:46 a.m.	6:23 a.m.
20	1:05 p.m.	7:35 p.m.	1:26 a.m.	7:16 a.m.
21	2:08 p.m.	8:24 p.m.	2:04 a.m.	8:06 a.m.
22	3:11 p.m.	9:13 p.m.	2:40 a.m.	8:50 a.m.
23	4:13 p.m.	9:58 p.m.	3:15 a.m.	9:44 a.m.
24	5:16 p.m.	10:54 p.m.	3:42 a.m.	10:29 a.m.
25	6:20 p.m.	11:47 p.m.	4:31 a.m.	11:26 a.m.
26	7:23 p.m.	—	5:14 a.m.	12:19 p.m.
27	8:24 p.m.	12:43 a.m.	6:02 a.m.	1:16 p.m.
28	9:21 p.m.	1:39 a.m.	6:54 a.m.	2:08 p.m.
29	10:13 p.m.	2:35 a.m.	7:49 a.m.	3:01 p.m.
30	10:58 p.m.	3:30 a.m.	8:46 a.m.	3:52 p.m.
31	11:38 p.m.	4:21 a.m.	9:43 a.m.	4:40 p.m.

JUNE 2011

	Rise	Over	Set	Under
1	—	5:08 a.m.	10:38 a.m.	5:26 p.m.
2	12:14 a.m.	5:53 a.m.	11:32 a.m.	6:09 p.m.
3	12:46 a.m.	6:35 a.m.	12:25 a.m.	6:51 p.m.
4	1:16 a.m.	7:17 a.m.	1:17 a.m.	7:31 p.m.
5	1:45 a.m.	7:57 a.m.	2:08 p.m.	8:12 p.m.
6	2:15 a.m.	8:38 a.m.	3:01 p.m.	8:54 p.m.
7	2:46 a.m.	9:21 a.m.	3:56 p.m.	9:38 p.m.
8	3:19 a.m.	10:06 a.m.	4:53 p.m.	10:26 p.m.
9	3:58 a.m.	10:56 a.m.	5:54 p.m.	11:18 p.m.
10	4:42 a.m.	11:49 a.m.	6:56 p.m.	—
11	5:33 a.m.	12:46 p.m.	7:58 p.m.	12:15 a.m.
12	6:31 a.m.	1:45 p.m.	8:58 p.m.	1:14 a.m.
13	7:35 a.m.	2:46 p.m.	9:53 p.m.	2:17 a.m.
14	8:42 a.m.	3:42 p.m.	10:42 p.m.	3:18 a.m.
15	9:50 a.m.	4:38 p.m.	11:25 p.m.	4:16 a.m.
16	10:57 a.m.	5:31 p.m.	—	5:11 a.m.
17	12:02 p.m.	6:22 p.m.	12:05 a.m.	6:03 a.m.
18	1:05 p.m.	7:11 p.m.	12:41 a.m.	6:53 a.m.
19	2:07 p.m.	8:00 p.m.	1:17 a.m.	7:42 a.m.
20	3:09 p.m.	8:50 p.m.	1:53 a.m.	8:31 a.m.
21	4:12 p.m.	9:42 p.m.	2:31 a.m.	9:21 a.m.
22	5:14 p.m.	10:36 p.m.	3:12 a.m.	10:13 a.m.
23	6:15 p.m.	11:31 p.m.	3:57 a.m.	11:06 a.m.
24	7:12 p.m.	—	4:46 a.m.	11:59 a.m.
25	8:05 p.m.	12:26 a.m.	5:39 a.m.	12:52 p.m.
26	8:53 p.m.	1:21 a.m.	6:36 a.m.	1:45 p.m.
27	9:35 p.m.	2:13 a.m.	7:32 a.m.	2:34 p.m.
28	10:12 p.m.	3:02 a.m.	8:29 a.m.	3:20 p.m.
29	10:46 p.m.	3:48 a.m.	9:24 a.m.	4:05 p.m.
30	11:16 p.m.	4:32 a.m.	10:17 a.m.	4:47 p.m.

JULY 2011

	Rise	Over	Set	Under
1	11:46 p.m.	5:12 a.m.	11:09 a.m.	5:29 p.m.
2	—	5:53 a.m.	12:00 p.m.	6:00 p.m.
3	12:15 a.m.	6:29 a.m.	12:52 p.m.	6:48 p.m.
4	12:44 a.m.	7:15 a.m.	1:45 p.m.	7:31 p.m.
5	1:16 a.m.	7:50 a.m.	2:40 p.m.	8:16 p.m.
6	1:52 a.m.	8:45 a.m.	3:38 p.m.	9:05 p.m.
7	2:32 a.m.	9:36 a.m.	4:39 p.m.	9:59 p.m.
8	3:19 a.m.	10:29 a.m.	5:40 p.m.	10:58 p.m.
9	4:14 a.m.	11:28 a.m.	6:42 p.m.	11:59 p.m.
10	5:15 a.m.	12:27 p.m.	7:39 p.m.	—
11	6:22 a.m.	1:27 p.m.	8:32 p.m.	1:01 a.m.
12	7:32 a.m.	2:26 p.m.	9:19 p.m.	2:02 a.m.
13	8:41 a.m.	3:21 p.m.	10:01 p.m.	3:00 a.m.
14	9:49 a.m.	4:14 p.m.	10:40 p.m.	3:55 a.m.
15	10:55 a.m.	5:06 p.m.	11:17 p.m.	4:48 a.m.
16	11:59 a.m.	5:57 p.m.	11:54 p.m.	5:38 a.m.
17	1:03 p.m.	6:47 p.m.	—	6:29 a.m.
18	2:06 p.m.	7:39 p.m.	12:31 a.m.	7:19 a.m.
19	3:08 p.m.	8:32 p.m.	1:11 a.m.	8:09 a.m.
20	4:09 p.m.	9:26 p.m.	1:55 a.m.	9:02 a.m.
21	5:07 p.m.	10:19 p.m.	2:43 a.m.	9:55 a.m.
22	6:01 p.m.	11:15 p.m.	3:32 a.m.	10:47 a.m.
23	6:50 p.m.	—	4:29 a.m.	11:39 a.m.
24	7:33 p.m.	12:08 a.m.	5:25 a.m.	12:29 p.m.
25	8:12 p.m.	12:57 a.m.	6:21 a.m.	1:16 p.m.
26	8:46 p.m.	1:46 a.m.	7:16 a.m.	2:01 p.m.
27	9:18 p.m.	2:28 a.m.	8:10 a.m.	2:44 p.m.
28	9:48 p.m.	3:11 a.m.	9:03 a.m.	3:26 p.m.
29	10:17 p.m.	3:51 a.m.	9:54 a.m.	4:06 p.m.
30	10:46 p.m.	4:31 a.m.	10:45 a.m.	4:46 p.m.
31	11:17 p.m.	5:12 a.m.	11:38 a.m.	5:28 p.m.

AUGUST 2011

	Rise	Over	Set	Under
1	11:50 p.m.	5:54 a.m.	12:31 p.m.	6:21 p.m.
2	—	6:39 a.m.	1:27 p.m.	6:57 p.m.
3	12:27 a.m.	7:26 a.m.	2:25 p.m.	7:48 p.m.
4	1:10 a.m.	8:17 a.m.	3:24 p.m.	8:42 p.m.
5	1:59 a.m.	9:12 a.m.	4:24 p.m.	9:40 p.m.
6	2:56 a.m.	10:10 a.m.	5:23 p.m.	10:42 p.m.
7	4:00 a.m.	11:09 a.m.	6:17 p.m.	11:43 p.m.
8	5:08 a.m.	12:07 p.m.	7:07 p.m.	—
9	6:18 a.m.	1:06 p.m.	7:53 p.m.	12:43 a.m.
10	7:28 a.m.	2:01 p.m.	8:34 p.m.	1:41 a.m.
11	8:36 a.m.	2:55 p.m.	9:13 p.m.	2:35 a.m.
12	9:44 a.m.	3:48 p.m.	9:51 p.m.	3:29 a.m.
13	10:50 a.m.	4:40 p.m.	10:29 p.m.	4:20 a.m.
14	11:55 a.m.	5:33 p.m.	11:10 p.m.	5:12 a.m.
15	12:59 p.m.	6:26 p.m.	11:53 p.m.	6:05 a.m.
16	2:02 p.m.	7:21 p.m.	—	6:58 a.m.
17	3:02 p.m.	8:17 p.m.	12:40 a.m.	7:51 a.m.
18	3:57 p.m.	9:11 p.m.	1:31 a.m.	8:44 a.m.
19	4:48 p.m.	10:04 p.m.	2:25 a.m.	9:37 a.m.
20	5:33 p.m.	10:55 p.m.	3:20 a.m.	10:26 a.m.
21	6:12 p.m.	11:41 p.m.	4:16 a.m.	11:14 a.m.
22	6:48 p.m.	—	5:11 a.m.	12:00 p.m.
23	7:20 p.m.	12:27 a.m.	6:05 a.m.	12:43 p.m.
24	7:51 p.m.	1:09 a.m.	6:58 a.m.	1:25 p.m.
25	8:20 p.m.	1:50 a.m.	7:50 a.m.	2:05 p.m.
26	8:49 p.m.	2:30 a.m.	8:41 a.m.	2:45 p.m.
27	9:19 p.m.	3:11 a.m.	9:33 a.m.	3:26 p.m.
28	9:51 p.m.	3:52 a.m.	10:25 a.m.	4:08 p.m.
29	10:27 p.m.	4:36 a.m.	11:20 a.m.	4:54 p.m.
30	11:07 p.m.	5:17 a.m.	12:16 p.m.	5:42 p.m.
31	11:52 p.m.	6:11 a.m.	1:14 p.m.	6:33 p.m.

SEPTEMBER 2011

	Rise	Over	Set	Under
1	—	7:02 a.m.	2:12 p.m.	7:19 p.m.
2	12:45 a.m.	7:57 a.m.	3:09 p.m.	8:26 p.m.
3	1:43 a.m.	8:53 a.m.	4:04 p.m.	9:26 p.m.
4	2:47 a.m.	9:51 a.m.	4:55 p.m.	10:24 p.m.
5	3:54 a.m.	10:48 a.m.	5:41 p.m.	11:22 p.m.
6	5:03 a.m.	11:43 a.m.	6:24 p.m.	—
7	6:12 a.m.	12:38 p.m.	7:04 p.m.	12:18 a.m.
8	7:21 a.m.	1:33 p.m.	7:44 p.m.	1:13 a.m.
9	8:29 a.m.	2:26 p.m.	8:23 p.m.	2:07 a.m.
10	9:36 a.m.	3:20 p.m.	9:04 p.m.	3:00 a.m.
11	10:43 a.m.	4:15 p.m.	9:47 p.m.	3:54 a.m.
12	11:49 a.m.	5:13 p.m.	10:34 p.m.	4:48 a.m.
13	12:52 p.m.	6:09 p.m.	11:25 p.m.	5:43 a.m.
14	1:50 p.m.	7:05 p.m.	—	6:38 a.m.
15	2:43 p.m.	7:59 p.m.	12:19 a.m.	7:31 a.m.
16	3:30 p.m.	8:51 p.m.	1:15 a.m.	8:23 a.m.
17	4:12 p.m.	9:39 p.m.	2:11 a.m.	9:12 a.m.
18	4:49 p.m.	10:25 p.m.	3:06 a.m.	9:58 a.m.
19	5:22 p.m.	11:08 p.m.	4:01 a.m.	10:32 a.m.
20	5:53 p.m.	11:49 p.m.	4:53 a.m.	11:23 a.m.
21	6:23 p.m.	—	5:45 a.m.	12:04 p.m.
22	6:52 p.m.	12:30 a.m.	6:37 a.m.	12:45 p.m.
23	7:22 p.m.	1:10 a.m.	7:28 a.m.	1:26 p.m.
24	7:54 p.m.	1:51 a.m.	8:21 a.m.	2:08 p.m.
25	8:29 p.m.	2:34 a.m.	9:15 a.m.	2:52 p.m.
26	9:07 p.m.	3:20 a.m.	10:11 a.m.	3:39 p.m.
27	9:51 p.m.	4:07 a.m.	11:08 a.m.	4:30 p.m.
28	10:40 p.m.	4:58 a.m.	12:05 p.m.	5:23 p.m.
29	11:35 p.m.	5:51 a.m.	1:02 p.m.	6:19 p.m.
30	—	6:56 a.m.	1:56 p.m.	7:16 p.m.

OCTOBER 2011

	Rise	Over	Set	Under
1	12:35 a.m.	7:41 a.m.	2:47 p.m.	8:13 p.m.
2	1:39 a.m.	8:36 a.m.	3:33 p.m.	9:09 p.m.
3	2:44 a.m.	9:30 a.m.	4:16 p.m.	10:04 p.m.
4	3:51 a.m.	10:24 a.m.	4:56 p.m.	10:57 p.m.
5	4:58 a.m.	11:17 a.m.	5:35 p.m.	11:50 p.m.
6	6:05 a.m.	12:10 p.m.	6:14 p.m.	—
7	7:12 a.m.	1:03 p.m.	6:54 p.m.	12:43 a.m.
8	8:20 a.m.	1:59 p.m.	7:37 p.m.	1:37 a.m.
9	9:28 a.m.	2:56 p.m.	8:24 p.m.	2:33 a.m.
10	10:34 a.m.	3:54 p.m.	9:14 p.m.	3:29 a.m.
11	11:37 a.m.	4:53 p.m.	10:09 p.m.	4:26 a.m.
12	12:34 p.m.	5:50 p.m.	11:05 p.m.	5:21 a.m.
13	1:25 p.m.	6:44 p.m.	—	6:15 a.m.
14	2:09 p.m.	7:34 p.m.	12:03 a.m.	7:06 a.m.
15	2:48 p.m.	8:21 p.m.	12:59 a.m.	7:53 a.m.
16	3:23 p.m.	9:06 p.m.	1:54 a.m.	8:39 a.m.
17	3:55 p.m.	9:49 p.m.	2:48 a.m.	9:22 a.m.
18	4:25 p.m.	10:28 p.m.	3:40 a.m.	10:03 a.m.
19	4:54 p.m.	11:09 p.m.	4:31 a.m.	10:43 a.m.
20	5:24 p.m.	11:50 p.m.	5:23 a.m.	11:23 a.m.
21	5:55 p.m.	—	6:15 a.m.	12:05 p.m.
22	6:29 p.m.	12:32 a.m.	7:09 a.m.	12:49 p.m.
23	7:07 p.m.	1:17 a.m.	8:05 a.m.	1:36 p.m.
24	7:50 p.m.	2:05 a.m.	9:02 a.m.	2:26 p.m.
25	8:38 p.m.	2:55 a.m.	10:00 a.m.	3:19 p.m.
26	9:31 p.m.	3:48 a.m.	10:57 a.m.	4:14 p.m.
27	10:29 p.m.	4:41 a.m.	11:52 a.m.	5:11 p.m.
28	11:31 p.m.	5:41 a.m.	12:43 p.m.	6:07 p.m.
29	—	6:30 a.m.	1:30 p.m.	7:03 p.m.
30	12:35 a.m.	7:24 a.m.	2:13 p.m.	7:56 p.m.
31	1:39 a.m.	8:16 a.m.	2:52 p.m.	8:48 p.m.

NOVEMBER 2011

	Rise	Over	Set	Under
1	2:43 a.m.	9:02 a.m.	3:30 p.m.	9:39 p.m.
2	3:47 a.m.	9:57 a.m.	4:08 p.m.	10:30 p.m.
3	4:52 a.m.	10:49 a.m.	4:46 p.m.	11:22 p.m.
4	5:58 a.m.	11:43 a.m.	5:27 p.m.	—
5	7:06 a.m.	12:39 p.m.	6:11 p.m.	12:17 a.m.
6	8:13 a.m.	1:37 p.m.	7:00 p.m.	1:12 a.m.
7	9:18 a.m.	2:36 p.m.	7:54 p.m.	2:09 a.m.
8	9:19 a.m.	2:35 p.m.	7:51 p.m.	2:20 a.m.
9	10:13 a.m.	3:31 p.m.	8:49 p.m.	3:12 a.m.
10	11:02 a.m.	4:25 p.m.	9:48 p.m.	3:56 a.m.
11	11:44 a.m.	5:14 p.m.	10:44 p.m.	4:46 a.m.
12	12:21 p.m.	6:00 p.m.	11:39 p.m.	5:33 a.m.
13	12:54 p.m.	6:43 p.m.	—	6:17 a.m.
14	1:25 p.m.	7:36 p.m.	12:32 a.m.	6:59 a.m.
15	1:54 p.m.	8:04 p.m.	1:24 a.m.	7:39 a.m.
16	2:24 p.m.	8:46 p.m.	2:15 a.m.	8:20 a.m.
17	2:55 p.m.	9:28 p.m.	3:07 a.m.	9:01 a.m.
18	3:28 p.m.	10:12 p.m.	4:00 a.m.	9:44 a.m.
19	4:04 p.m.	10:58 p.m.	4:55 a.m.	10:30 a.m.
20	4:45 p.m.	11:48 p.m.	5:52 a.m.	11:19 a.m.
21	5:32 p.m.	—	6:51 a.m.	12:12 p.m.
22	6:25 p.m.	12:41 a.m.	7:50 a.m.	1:08 p.m.
23	7:23 p.m.	1:36 a.m.	8:47 a.m.	2:05 p.m.
24	8:25 p.m.	2:32 a.m.	9:40 a.m.	3:03 p.m.
25	9:29 p.m.	3:27 a.m.	10:28 a.m.	3:59 p.m.
26	10:32 p.m.	4:21 a.m.	11:12 a.m.	4:52 p.m.
27	11:36 p.m.	5:13 a.m.	11:53 a.m.	5:45 p.m.
28	—	6:03 a.m.	12:30 p.m.	6:35 p.m.
29	12:39 a.m.	6:53 a.m.	1:07 p.m.	7:24 p.m.
30	1:41 a.m.	7:42 a.m.	1:43 p.m.	8:14 p.m.

DECEMBER 2011

	Rise	Over	Set	Under
1	2:45 a.m.	8:34 a.m.	2:22 p.m.	9:06 p.m.
2	3:49 a.m.	9:26 a.m.	3:03 p.m.	9:59 p.m.
3	4:55 a.m.	10:22 a.m.	3:49 p.m.	10:55 p.m.
4	6:00 a.m.	11:20 a.m.	4:40 p.m.	11:51 p.m.
5	7:02 a.m.	12:19 p.m.	5:35 p.m.	—
6	8:00 a.m.	1:17 p.m.	6:34 p.m.	12:48 a.m.
7	8:51 a.m.	2:12 p.m.	7:33 p.m.	1:43 a.m.
8	9:37 a.m.	3:04 p.m.	8:31 p.m.	2:35 a.m.
9	10:16 a.m.	3:52 p.m.	9:28 p.m.	3:23 a.m.
10	10:52 a.m.	4:37 p.m.	10:22 p.m.	4:10 a.m.
11	11:24 a.m.	5:19 p.m.	11:14 p.m.	4:53 a.m.
12	11:54 a.m.	6:00 p.m.	—	5:34 a.m.
13	12:23 p.m.	6:40 p.m.	12:06 a.m.	6:15 a.m.
14	12:53 p.m.	7:21 p.m.	12:57 a.m.	6:55 a.m.
15	1:25 p.m.	8:04 p.m.	1:49 a.m.	7:37 a.m.
16	2:00 p.m.	8:50 p.m.	2:43 a.m.	8:22 a.m.
17	2:38 p.m.	9:38 p.m.	3:39 a.m.	9:09 a.m.
18	3:23 p.m.	10:30 p.m.	4:37 a.m.	10:00 a.m.
19	4:13 p.m.	11:23 p.m.	5:36 a.m.	10:55 a.m.
20	5:10 p.m.	—	6:34 a.m.	11:52 a.m.
21	6:12 p.m.	12:21 a.m.	7:31 a.m.	12:52 p.m.
22	7:17 p.m.	1:17 a.m.	8:22 a.m.	1:49 p.m.
23	8:23 p.m.	2:13 a.m.	9:09 a.m.	2:46 p.m.
24	9:28 p.m.	3:08 a.m.	9:52 a.m.	3:40 p.m.
25	10:32 p.m.	4:00 a.m.	10:31 a.m.	4:32 p.m.
26	11:35 p.m.	4:50 a.m.	11:08 a.m.	5:22 p.m.
27	—	5:40 a.m.	11:45 a.m.	6:12 p.m.
28	12:38 a.m.	6:30 a.m.	12:22 p.m.	7:02 p.m.
29	1:41 a.m.	7:21 a.m.	1:02 p.m.	7:54 p.m.
30	2:45 a.m.	8:15 a.m.	1:45 p.m.	8:47 p.m.
31	3:49 a.m.	9:11 a.m.	2:33 p.m.	9:37 p.m.

YOUR COMPLETE FISHING MAGAZINE

Offshore

Inshore

Fly Fishing

Fresh Water

▶ More full feature how-to than any other magazine.

▶ Every issue will help you catch more fish, thus helping you enjoy your time on the water.

▶ Every month the Tropical Sportsman section covers The Bahamas, Caribbean and the American Tropics.

▶ The Action Spotter section splits Florida into 11 regions and Sportsman's regional experts guide you to the hotspots in your area.

Don't miss out on the world's hottest fishing
SUBSCRIBE BY MAIL, PHONE OR ONLINE

What's Your Fish's Weight?

I f you don't have a flexible tape measure, you can figure girth with a piece of string or fishing line. Just wrap it around the thickest part of the fish, and measure against a ruler.

For skinny fish, like barracuda, dividing by 900 may give a more accurate figure; likewise, rotund fish, such as lunker largemouth bass, are sometimes figured with 1,200. Also, veterans sometimes add 10 percent to the weight of very big tarpon, such as those caught at Homosassa.

For record purposes, you'll need to weigh fish on a certified scale that's on solid ground (not a boat), but you can feel secure in knowing that many anglers rely on the formula to guesstimate weights.

If you'd prefer not to take a calculator fishing, take this chart. Find the number closest to your fish's length (in inches) on the horizontal axis, then look on the vertical to find its girth. Where the two intersect, you'll find that fish's weight in pounds.

A handy way to estimate how much your fish weighs is to multiply its Length by its Girth squared and divide by 800.

$$\frac{L \times G^2}{800}$$

Length (inches)

Girth (inches)	16	18	20	22	24	26	28	30	35	40	45	50	55	60	65	70	75	80
10	2	2.3	2.5	2.8	3	3.3	3.5	3.8										
12	3	3.3	3.6	4	4.3	4.6	5	6	7									
14	4	4.5	5	5.5	6	6.5	7	7.5	8.5	10								
16	5	6	6.5	7	7.5	8	9	10	11	13	14.5							
18		7	8	9	10	11	11.5	12	14	16	18	20						
20			10	11	12	13	14	15	17	20	23	25	30					
22				13	15	16	17	18	21	24	27	30	33	36				
24				17	19	20	22	25	29	32	36	40	43	47				
26					22	24	25	30	34	38	42	46	51	55	60			
28						27	30	34	39	44	49	54	59	64	69	74		
30							34	40	45	51	56	62	68	73	79	85	90	
32								45	51	58	64	70	77	83	90	96	102	
34									59	65	72	79	87	94	101	108	116	
36										73	81	89	97	105	113	122	130	
38											90	100	108	117	126	135	144	
40												110	120	130	140	150	160	
42													132	143	154	165	176	
44														157	169	182	194	

Water Temperatures For Saltwater Gamefish

Hardy redfish have a fairly wide temperature tolerance range.

The exclusive *Fishing Planner* chart on the next page lists the typical range of water temperatures in which you're likely to encounter Florida's favorite inshore and offshore sportfish.

For migratory species like mackerels, water temperature can cue you into when the run will show up off your part of the coastline. Monthly predictions, such as those found in this book, are only useful if you're willing to keep watch over the actual conditions.

Remember that surface temperature often differs greatly from that of deeper water. Consequently, you'll often find bottom fish like snapper and grouper living in water that might seem too hot or too cold.

Similarly, you might catch a cobia off a north Florida wreck when it's freezing cold outside.

Inshore, the flats angler may decide to move to another spot if it's too warm or cold—that is if he doesn't find the fish he's looking for. In the Keys, for example, midsummer is a time to look for water below 85 degrees for bonefish. Often that means a light-colored sea bottom with good current early in the morning.

These figures should be used judiciously—they are meant to serve only as baselines. The best approach is to keep a logbook of your catches, and fine-tune these predictions with figures that you find appropriate for your waters.

Preferred Water Temperatures

Degrees Fahrenheit

Species	55°	60°	65°	70°	75°	80°	85°	90°
Amberjack			■	■				
Barracuda					■	■	■	
Black Drum		■	■					
Blackfin Tuna				■	■			
Bluefish		■	■	■	■			
Blue Marlin					■	■	■	
Bonefish					■	■		
Cero Mackerel				■	■	■		
Cobia			■	■	■	■		
Dolphin					■	■	■	
Flounder	■	■	■	■				
Jack Crevalle			■	■	■	■		
Kingfish				■	■	■		
Mangrove Snapper			■	■	■	■	■	
Permit					■	■	■	
Pompano				■	■			
Redfish			■	■	■	■		
Red Grouper			■	■				
Red Snapper	■	■						
Sailfish					■	■		
Sheepshead				■	■			
Snook				■	■	■		
Spanish Mackerel			■	■	■	■		
Tarpon					■	■	■	
Trout		■	■	■	■			
Wahoo					■	■		
White Marlin				■	■	■		
Yellowfin Tuna			■	■				

FISHING
FLORIDA SPORTSMAN
& BOAT SHOW

FLORIDA'S BIGGEST & BEST FISHING EXPO

GOIN' FISH'N

Tune in — when you need to know where to go

There are two ways to know where to fish this weekend. The first is to have fished all week and then spend your evenings calling around to find out what other people have caught. The second is to tune in to *Florida Sportsman Magazine Live* and let the area's best fishermen tell you what and where they're biting. In just one hour you'll know where to plan your next fishing trip. Get up-to-the-minute fishing conditions from a team of local and regional experts.

Rainfall
Normal Monthly PRECIPITATION, in inches, for selected Florida locations—based on 30-year average.

	Jacksonville	Miami	Key West	St. Petersburg	Tallahassee	Pensacola
JANUARY	3.07	2.08	1.74	2.44	4.66	4.47
FEBRUARY	3.48	2.05	1.92	3.13	5.00	4.90
MARCH	3.72	1.89	1.31	3.69	5.60	5.66
APRIL	3.32	3.07	1.49	2.28	6.13	4.45
MAY	4.91	6.53	3.22	3.32	6.16	5.87
JUNE	5.37	9.15	5.04	6.12	6.55	5.75
JULY	6.54	5.98	3.68	8.06	8.75	7.18
AUGUST	7.15	7.02	4.80	8.73	7.30	7.04
SEPTEMBER	7.26	8.07	6.50	7.60	6.45	4.75
OCTOBER	3.41	7.14	4.76	3.08	3.10	3.52
NOVEMBER	1.94	2.71	3.32	2.10	3.31	3.42
DECEMBER	2.59	1.86	1.73	2.55	4.58	4.15

Temperatures Mean Maximum and Minimum
TEMPERATURES for selected Florida locations—based on 30-year average.

	Jacksonville	Miami	Key West	St. Petersburg	Tallahassee	Pensacola
JANUARY	65	75	72	70	63	61
	42	59	66	54	40	43
FEBRUARY	67	76	75	71	66	64
	43	60	65	55	41	45
MARCH	73	79	79	76	73	69
	49	64	70	60	48	51
APRIL	80	82	82	82	80	77
	56	68	73	65	54	59
MAY	85	85	85	87	86	84
	63	72	76	70	62	66
JUNE	89	87	89	89	90	89
	69	75	80	75	69	72
JULY	91	89	89	90	91	90
	72	76	80	76	72	74
AUGUST	90	89	89	90	91	90
	72	77	79	76	72	74
SEPTEMBER	87	88	87	89	88	87
	69	76	76	75	69	71
OCTOBER	80	84	84	83	80	79
	59	72	76	69	56	60
NOVEMBER	72	80	80	77	72	69
	49	66	71	61	46	50
DECEMBER	66	76	75	71	65	63
	43	61	67	55	41	44

State and World Records

Josh Anyzeski holds a new IGFA smallfry line class record after catching this 22-pound, 8-ounce tripletail off Jupiter in 2010.

Here's an abbreviated list of state and world all-tackle records. As testimony to Florida's incredible angling potential, note that 10 of the world records were set in our waters.

There are certain guidelines you'll need to follow if you wish to enter a fish for record consideration.

For information, contact the International Game Fish Association, 300 Gulfstream Way, Dania Beach, FL 33004; (954) 927-2628; www.igfa.org; or the Florida Fish and Wildlife Conservation Commission, 620 S. Meridian St., Tallahassee, FL 32399-1600; (850) 488-4676; www.state.fl.us/fwc.

Species	Florida lbs./oz.	World lbs./oz.
African Pompano	50/8	50/8
Amberjack	142	155/12
Barracuda	67	85
Black Drum	96	113/1
Bluefish	22/2	31/12
Bonefish	16/3	19
Cobia	130/1	135/9
Dolphin	81	87
Flounder, Southern	20/9	20/9
Grouper, Black	113/6	124
Gag	80/6	80/6
Red	42/4	42/4
Warsaw	436/12	436/12
Jack Crevalle	57	58/6
Ladyfish	6/4	8
Mackerel, Cero	17/2	17/2
King	90	93
Spanish	12	13
Marlin, Blue	1,046	1,402/2
White	161	181/14
Permit	56/2	60
Pompano	8/4	8/4
Redfish	52/5	94/2
Sailfish, Atlantic	126	141/1

Species	Florida lbs./oz.	World lbs./oz.
Shark, Blacktip	152	270/9
Bull	517	697/12
Hammerhead	1,060	1,280
Lemon	397	405
Spinner	190	197/12
Tiger	1,065	1,785/11
Sheepshead	15/2	21/4
Snapper, Cubera	116	124/12
Gray	17	17
Lane	6/6	8/3
Mutton	30/4	30/4
Red	46/8	50/4
Yellowtail	8/9	11
Snook, Common	44/3	53/10
Spotted Seatrout	17/7	17/7
Swordfish	612/12	1,182
Tarpon	243	286/9
Tripletail	40/13	42/5
Tuna, Blackfin	45/8	49/6
Yellowfin	240	388/12
Little Tunny	27	36
Wahoo	139	184
Weakfish	10	19/2

2011

January 2011
S	M	T	W	T	F	S
						1
2	3	4	5	6	7	8
9	10	11	12	13	14	15
16	17	18	19	20	21	22
23	24	25	26	27	28	29
30	31					

February 2011
S	M	T	W	T	F	S
		1	2	3	4	5
6	7	8	9	10	11	12
13	14	15	16	17	18	19
20	21	22	23	24	25	26
27	28					

March 2011
S	M	T	W	T	F	S
		1	2	3	4	5
6	7	8	9	10	11	12
13	14	15	16	17	18	19
20	21	22	23	24	25	26
27	28	29	30	31		

April 2011
S	M	T	W	T	F	S
					1	2
3	4	5	6	7	8	9
10	11	12	13	14	15	16
17	18	19	20	21	22	23
24	25	26	27	28	29	30

May 2011
S	M	T	W	T	F	S
1	2	3	4	5	6	7
8	9	10	11	12	13	14
15	16	17	18	19	20	21
22	23	24	25	26	27	28
29	30	31				

June 2011
S	M	T	W	T	F	S
			1	2	3	4
5	6	7	8	9	10	11
12	13	14	15	16	17	18
19	20	21	22	23	24	25
26	27	28	29	30		

July 2011
S	M	T	W	T	F	S
					1	2
3	4	5	6	7	8	9
10	11	12	13	14	15	16
17	18	19	20	21	22	23
24	25	26	27	28	29	30
31						

August 2011
S	M	T	W	T	F	S
	1	2	3	4	5	6
7	8	9	10	11	12	13
14	15	16	17	18	19	20
21	22	23	24	25	26	27
28	29	30	31			

September 2011
S	M	T	W	T	F	S
				1	2	3
4	5	6	7	8	9	10
11	12	13	14	15	16	17
18	19	20	21	22	23	24
25	26	27	28	29	30	

October 2011
S	M	T	W	T	F	S
						1
2	3	4	5	6	7	8
9	10	11	12	13	14	15
16	17	18	19	20	21	22
23	24	25	26	27	28	29
30	31					

November 2011
S	M	T	W	T	F	S
		1	2	3	4	5
6	7	8	9	10	11	12
13	14	15	16	17	18	19
20	21	22	23	24	25	26
27	28	29	30			

December 2011
S	M	T	W	T	F	S
				1	2	3
4	5	6	7	8	9	10
11	12	13	14	15	16	17
18	19	20	21	22	23	24
25	26	27	28	29	30	31

2012

January 2012
S	M	T	W	T	F	S
1	2	3	4	5	6	7
8	9	10	11	12	13	14
15	16	17	18	19	20	21
22	23	24	25	26	27	28
29	30	31				

February 2012
S	M	T	W	T	F	S
			1	2	3	4
5	6	7	8	9	10	11
12	13	14	15	16	17	18
19	20	21	22	23	24	25
26	27	28	29			

March 2012
S	M	T	W	T	F	S
				1	2	3
4	5	6	7	8	9	10
11	12	13	14	15	16	17
18	19	20	21	22	23	24
25	26	27	28	29	30	31

April 2012
S	M	T	W	T	F	S
1	2	3	4	5	6	7
8	9	10	11	12	13	14
15	16	17	18	19	20	21
22	23	24	25	26	27	28
29	30					

May 2012
S	M	T	W	T	F	S
		1	2	3	4	5
6	7	8	9	10	11	12
13	14	15	16	17	18	19
20	21	22	23	24	25	26
27	28	29	30	31		

June 2012
S	M	T	W	T	F	S
					1	2
3	4	5	6	7	8	9
10	11	12	13	14	15	16
17	18	19	20	21	22	23
24	25	26	27	28	29	30

July 2012
S	M	T	W	T	F	S
1	2	3	4	5	6	7
8	9	10	11	12	13	14
15	16	17	18	19	20	21
22	23	24	25	26	27	28
29	30	31				

August 2012
S	M	T	W	T	F	S
			1	2	3	4
5	6	7	8	9	10	11
12	13	14	15	16	17	18
19	20	21	22	23	24	25
26	27	28	29	30	31	

September 2012
S	M	T	W	T	F	S
						1
2	3	4	5	6	7	8
9	10	11	12	13	14	15
16	17	18	19	20	21	22
23	24	25	26	27	28	29
30						

October 2012
S	M	T	W	T	F	S
	1	2	3	4	5	6
7	8	9	10	11	12	13
14	15	16	17	18	19	20
21	22	23	24	25	26	27
28	29	30	31			

November 2012
S	M	T	W	T	F	S
				1	2	3
4	5	6	7	8	9	10
11	12	13	14	15	16	17
18	19	20	21	22	23	24
25	26	27	28	29	30	

December 2012
S	M	T	W	T	F	S
						1
2	3	4	5	6	7	8
9	10	11	12	13	14	15
16	17	18	19	20	21	22
23	24	25	26	27	28	29
30	31